OBJECT-ORIENTED PHILOSOPHY

OBJECT-ORIENTED PHILOSOPHY
The Noumenon's New Clothes

PETER WOLFENDALE

URBANOMIC

First published in 2014 by
URBANOMIC MEDIA LTD,
THE OLD LEMONADE FACTORY,
WINDSOR QUARRY,
FALMOUTH TR11 3EX,
UNITED KINGDOM

Reprinted with corrections 2019

BRITISH LIBRARY CATALOGUING-IN-PUBLICATION DATA

A full catalogue record of this book is available
from the British Library

ISBN 978-0-9575295-9-5

Distributed by the MIT Press,
Cambridge, Massachusetts and London, England

Type by Norm, Zurich
Printed and bound in the UK by
TJ International, Padstow

www.urbanomic.com

CONTENTS

Preface   vii

Introduction   1

1. The Lava that Dare not Speak its Name   9
   1.1. Withdrawal   13
   1.2. The Fourfold   17
   1.3. Vicarious Causation   23

2. The Withdrawal of Arguments   27
   2.1. Tools, Knowledge, and Distinctness   39
   2.2. Heidegger, Husserl, and Kripke   79
   2.3. Occasionalism, Independence,
       and Supplementation   97

3. Objection-Oriented Philosophy   107
   3.1. Sense and Sensuality   113
   3.2. Qualities and Qualia   135
   3.3. What are Relations Anyway?   163
   3.4. What are Objects Anyway?:
       On Ontological Liberalism   209
   3.5. What is Metaphysics Anyway?   299
   3.6. What Does it all Mean?   327

4. Speculative Dystopia   337
   4.1. The Spectre of the Past   341
   4.2. The Sins of the Present   359
   4.3. The Horrors of the Future   391

5. Specious Realism   399

Postscript: Speculative Autopsy *by Ray Brassier*   407

Index of Names   423

Index of Subjects   433

PREFACE

I have been haunted by a single question for the last two years or so: 'Why are you *still* writing this, Pete?' Echoed by friends, family, and my own conscience, it has been a constant refrain. It seems that I am finally in a position to provide an answer— to retrospectively justify the amount of time and effort that has gone into writing this rather *unusual* book, and to provide some context for those wondering why they should devote their own time and effort to reading it. The fact that this is my first book only exacerbates its eccentricities: it addresses a contemporary and perhaps fleeting philosophical moment, yet it does so by delving deep into the discipline's past; it speaks of recent developments in the world of 'Continental' philosophy, yet it often draws upon 'analytic' ideas that are uncomfortably alien to that world; and above all, it undertakes a long and detailed discussion of a single philosopher's work, and yet it aims to show that his work does not warrant such serious attention. Why read, let alone write, such an odd book? A brief explanation of its origins might shed some light on the matter.

In August 2009, I began a philosophy blog[1] as a way to work through ideas outside the scope of my PhD thesis, which had begun as an exploration of Deleuze's metaphysics and undergone a gradual methodological regression towards Heidegger's question of Being. In doing so, I became involved in a thriving forum for philosophical discussion, in which a number of other graduate students and fellow travellers dis-satisfied with the stagnant state of Continental philosophy were experimenting with ways of changing things. It is perhaps unsurprising that this loose network of blogs had crystallised around 'Speculative Realism' (SR)—a new and exciting trend

---

1.   <http://deontologistics.wordpress.com>.

which had emerged onto the scene two years earlier. It is hard to convey precisely what it was like to be involved in this online community—if nothing else, it was permeated by a certain enthusiasm, ambition, and intensity that offline academia seemed to lack. Although I never identified as a 'Speculative Realist', I am certain that the extensive online discussion and correspondence that SR inspired was formative for my philosophical development. It is in this context that I first seriously encountered Graham Harman's Object-Oriented Philosophy (OOP), initially in discussion and then through his own blog;[2] and it is as part of this community that I witnessed the genesis and dissemination of Object-Oriented Ontology (OOO). For our purposes, the most important encounters were a short debate with Harman himself and a series of debates with Levi Bryant,[3] who had begun to develop his own metaphysics under Harman's influence.[4]

It is important to emphasise how much I gained from these debates. It is all too easy in contemporary philosophical discourse to use the mere fact that one seriously disagrees with another's ideas as a reason not to explore the nature of the disagreement any further. But it is worth remembering that doing so can improve our understanding of the relevant issues and stimulate the evolution of our own ideas. This is certainly what I got out of exploring my disagreements with OOP/OOO. However—and this is where things took an unusual turn— these theoretical gains did not come from uncovering useful philosophical insights or novel dialectical distinctions lingering

---

2.   <http://doctorzamalek2.wordpress.com>.

3.   <http://larvalsubjects.wordpress.com>.

4.   These debates are catalogued on my blog: <http://deontologistics.word-press.com/commentary/>.

beneath the surface. Quite the reverse: whenever I began to address seemingly simple ideas that struck me as problematic, their flaws would turn out to run much deeper than was initially apparent. Time and again, I discovered that I couldn't pull on a single loose thread without unravelling the whole fabric. This implied a profound asymmetry between the amount of effort required to articulate the relevant ideas and that required to effectively criticise them. If nothing else, this asymmetry was productive: it forced me to sharpen my understanding of foundational concepts (e.g., existence, relation, causation, etc.) and to address the methodological issues underlying metaphysical debates involving them (e.g., what it means to talk about 'reality'); but it also consumed time and resources that could perhaps have been better spent elsewhere. Why then, did I persist? If I am honest, it is largely because I find it difficult to turn down a challenge.

After our blog exchange had become somewhat one-sided, Harman made me an offer: either (a) summarise my objections in a single blog post that he could address more easily; or, better yet, (b) summarise my objections in an article in a formal publication (e.g., in *Speculations*, a journal specialising in the nascent ideas of SR). At the time I replied that, despite having expended considerable effort addressing our differences online, I could not commit to writing an article for publication, which I considered would take far longer and would demand far higher standards of thoroughness. At the time, I had not read all of Harman's published books. Thus, without ruling out a more extensive engagement in print, I demurred from making any promises for the near future.[5]

---

5.   Private correspondence with Harman (June, 2010).

Harman's response to this was to withdraw offer (a), on the basis that he had less to gain (and more to lose) from a blog exchange than I did. Admittedly, this irked me a little, not least given Harman's enthusiastic advocacy of the blogosphere as an appropriate venue for philosophical debate;[6] but no one is obliged to respond to anyone else on the Internet. That's just how it goes. I resolved to write an article when I had the time to do it properly. However, a short time later Levi Bryant referenced this exchange between Harman and myself in public, in a less than flattering way:

> At the risk of breaching blog etiquette, Pete was recently asked if he wouldn't care to carry out this debate in a formal setting. He responded by claiming that he holds his published writing to a higher standard than his blog writing and that we just don't have enough in common to have a debate. This raises the question of why Pete has obsessively and endlessly written lengthy posts on OOO, striving to undermine our positions, while withdrawing from any sort of serious debate with us. Perhaps Pete should take the time to determine what our arguments are, rather than treating us as fodder or matter to run through the machine of his Brandomian-Habermasian mill from afar.[7]

Now, it is almost certainly the case that his misrepresentation of my response to Harman was down to a miscommunication between Harman and Bryant, but this did little to assuage my irritation. As far as I was concerned, this transformed the

---

6.   Cf. The introduction to G. Harman, L. Bryant, and N. Srnicek (eds), *The Speculative Turn: Continental Materialism and Realism* (Melbourne: re.press, 2011).

7.   <http://larvalsubjects.wordpress.com/2010/06/22/knowledge-representation-and-construction-a-response-to-pete-part-2/>.

offer to engage in a formal setting into a *challenge* to do so. I resolved not merely to write the article, but to be as 'serious' as possible. In short order, I bought the rest of Harman's books and began to sketch an outline of the essay.

Of course, nothing ever quite goes to plan. I set out to expand the outline by presenting Harman's system and the arguments for it as clearly and thoroughly as possible, before moving on to a discussion of its deeper significance. This proved to be much more difficult than I had anticipated: I spent an exasperating six months reading through all of Harman's published books and as many papers as seemed relevant, only to realise that there was no core argument, but rather a patchwork of argumentative fragments, rhetorical devices, and literary allusions. It gradually became apparent that a thorough engagement was going to require a great deal more reconstruction than I had originally thought. When it finally appeared in *Speculations* the next year, the article clocked in at seventy-six pages and did not get any further than reconstructing and criticising Harman's arguments.[8] I promised that a second half would be published in the next issue, but this too turned out to be overly optimistic. It took another two years of exegetical tangents and ramifying chapter headings before the original outline was completely filled in, and along the way the project expanded beyond the scope of an article and became a full-length book. If nothing else, it is by far the most exhaustive engagement with Harman's work to date.

---

8.   P. Wolfendale, 'The Noumenon's New Clothes (Part I)' in *Speculations* IV (2012), 290–366. This forms the basis of chapters 1 and 2 of the present book. It is worth noting that it has yet to receive a response, though I believe that Harman plans to address it alongside other criticisms in a forthcoming book.

So, why didn't I stop at the article? I could simply have abandoned the project at this stage, and moved on to other things —there are plenty of other unfinished essays in my drafts folder that would have kept it company. There were a number of reasons—not least my own stubbornness—but the most obvious was OOP's increasing popularity: not only were Harman's books now being read and referenced throughout the humanities, but the phrase 'object-oriented' began to appear in calls for papers both in and outside of philosophy, while 'objects' became a new and supposedly exciting theme for art exhibitions. This ascendancy demanded thorough examination and criticism: a philosophy that attracts followers on the basis of grandiose promises, theoretical or otherwise, should have its ability to deliver on those promises carefully scrutinised. Moreover, as OOP's popularity increased, it began to dominate online discussion, gradually narrowing discursive parameters and alienating many who had been actively involved in the online SR community. The SR *trend* slowly transmuted into the SR/OOO *brand* as Harman asserted himself as its spokesman, and the community's unique dynamic dissolved as a result. This gradual collapse demanded a proper explanation and remonstration: a philosophy that prospers by hijacking discussion and stifling dissenting viewpoints, more or less deliberately, deserves to have its approach analysed and its strategies exposed. It thus seemed obvious that someone should address OOP and its influence directly, but the amount of effort required to do so properly remained highly asymmetric and thus highly prohibitive. Ultimately, the amount of time I had already devoted to understanding OOP put me in the best position to do what needed to be done.

As such, this book is essential reading for anyone already familiar with OOP/OOO—whether they're tempted by its tenets or suspicious of its spread—but why should anyone else read it? The two remaining reasons I persisted in writing this critique provide the best motivations for reading it: (a) that, though more difficult, a deeper exploration of OOP's flaws yielded deeper theoretical insights that can be applied elsewhere; and (b) that, though seemingly idiosyncratic, a more synoptic analysis of OOP revealed that it condenses and exemplifies a number of important conceptual and sociological dynamics distinctive of contemporary anglophone Continental philosophy, giving us a unique opportunity to address the latter's problems in microcosm. Taken together, these transform the book from a simple exercise in philosophical critique into a more rounded pedagogical project.

This pedagogical bent is reflected in the overall trajectory traced by the various chapters: I begin by bracketing as many of my own substantial philosophical commitments as possible so as to focus on reconstructing Harman's metaphysics and its justification (chapters 1 and 2), but this bracketing gradually recedes as I turn to the underlying conceptual themes motivating Harman's position (chapter 3). However, rather than imposing a complete alternative metaphysics, my aim is to allow a series of constraints on any adequate alternative to emerge naturally—I exploit OOP's flaws to clarify the concepts of *representation* (3.1), *quality* (3.2), and *relation* (3.3), and progressively elaborate some substantive claims about *objects* (3.4), *metaphysics* (3.5), and *meaning* (3.6). The section on objects (3.4) provides the best demonstration of the above-mentioned asymmetry between articulation and criticism, being by far the largest and most technically demanding part of the book. In it I locate OOP at the centre of a wider contemporary trend towards *ontological liberalism*, a proper examination of which requires detailed discussion of both the history of ontology and the logic of quantification. Overall, the purpose of these clarifications, elaborations, and examinations is to enable the reader to learn from the various substantial and methodological mistakes instructively united in Harman's system.

After this, the book turns to the historical and sociological significance of OOP (chapter 4): I integrate the insights uncovered earlier into a synoptic picture of the rise of *correlationism* after Kant (4.1), in order to describe the genesis of OOP/OOO in the present (4.2), and then provide a 'hyperbolic reading' of a future in which its influence is unopposed (4.3). This is the culmination of a historical story that slowly develops over the second half of the book (3.4, 3.5, and 4.1), and which encompasses the overarching dialectic of metaphysics, its split and parallel development in the analytic and Continental traditions, and the evolution of the Kantian *noumenon* within the latter tradition. This story forms the background for a sociological account of the development of the Continental tradition from the middle of the twentieth century to the present day (4.1), which explains the influence of correlationism, its imbrication with the project of *critique*, and the emergence of an opposing *constructive* orientation. Taken together, these analyses do more than let us understand where OOP/OOO has come from and where it is going—they give us a chance to take stock of where we are as a discipline, and what must be done if we want to divest ourselves of the pathological dynamics typified by Harman's work. The conclusion (chapter 5) connects this overall trajectory with my concerns regarding SR and its sublimation into SR/OOO, and attempts to distil a moral from the book as a whole. This is perfectly complemented by Ray Brassier's generous and insightful postscript ('Speculative Autopsy'), which as far as I am concerned presents the last word on Speculative Realism. To summarise, this book *is* a critique of Object-Oriented Philosophy and what it stands for, but it is also far more than *just* a critique.

During its long gestation, this book has benefited immeasurably from my discussions with Ray Brassier, Damian Veal, Jon Cogburn, Daniel Sacilotto, Dustin McWherter, Nick Srnicek, Alex Williams, Benedict Singleton, and Reza Negarestani, some of whom were gracious enough to provide comments on early drafts of the material that has come to compose it. It has also benefited from the comments of numerous more or less anonymous individuals who have read and responded to the informal engagements already mentioned. My parents, Chris and Dave Wolfendale, deserve a special mention for supporting me both emotionally and financially throughout the writing process, with only my word that it has been worthwhile, as does my partner Tanya Osborne, without whom I might never have finished. Finally, I owe an immense debt to Fabio Gironi (editor of the original *Speculations* article) and Robin Mackay (editor of the completed book), without whose incredible patience and careful encouragement it never would have appeared.

INTRODUCTION

A spectre is haunting Continental philosophy—the spectre of **Object-Oriented Ontology** (OOO). All the disciplines and groupings that have traditionally allied themselves with Continental theory in the anglophone world are poised to greet its manifestation: aesthetic theory and artistic practice, political philosophy and heterodox geography, Francophile post-post-structuralists and Germanist neoromantics. Who among them has not heard the siren song of OOO's litanies of inhuman objects (menageries of stock markets and stock cubes, quarks and clerks, etc.)? Who among them has not begun to shrug off the oppressive, anthropocentric legacy of post-Kantian philosophy, bravely railing against the tyrannical correlationists of the Continental academy, the dreary technicians of the analytic mainstream, and even the scientistic fury of its neo-Kantian heirs?

Excuse the bombast, but there is a certain grandeur to the pronouncements regarding the emergence of OOO as a philosophical movement that invites parody. Nevertheless I have every intention of taking these pronouncements as seriously as possible—perhaps even more seriously than they are intended. Graham Harman, the erstwhile leader of this most vocal faction of what was once, fleetingly, called **Speculative Realism** (SR), has often expressed a preference for what he calls **hyperbolic readings** of philosophies.[9] The idea here is to imagine the relevant philosophy in a position of nigh-unassailable strength, so as to reflect upon what would be missing from a world in which it had become dominant. To imagine a given philosophical tendency actually winning the discursive battles in which it is

9. 'Delanda's Ontology: Assemblage and Realism', in *Continental Philosophy Review* 41:3 (2008), 367–83; *Prince of Networks: Bruno Latour and Metaphysics* (Melbourne: re.Press, 2009), 121–2; *Quentin Meillassoux: Philosophy in the Making* (Edinburgh: Edinburgh University Press, 2011), 152–8.

engaged is to treat it with the utmost seriousness—to treat it as a genuine contender for truth, whose claims to truth are *sincere* enough to be taken at face value. This is the kind of respect with which any serious philosophical position should be treated, especially nascent philosophical movements that claim to have wide-ranging implications and applications alike. The aim of this book is to take OOO seriously, and to treat it with at least this level of respect.

However, the hyperbolic method is surprisingly difficult to apply to OOO itself, given both the diversity and tentativeness of the commitments of its principal practitioners (canonically: Graham Harman, Levi Bryant, Ian Bogost, and Tim Morton). There is most definitely a common rhetoric binding these figures together: an insistence upon ontological egalitarianism, a rehabilitation of the concept of substance, and a pervasive metaphorics of withdrawal. But a deeper examination of each of these themes raises serious questions regarding the content of the shared commitments they stand for. There are disagreements regarding just *how* egalitarian we must be (e.g., what it is to say that *everything* is an object), just *what it means* to return to a metaphysics of substance (e.g., whether it is permissible to conceive it in *processual* terms), and precisely *what it is* to say that objects are withdrawn, and how that limits what we can *know* about them. These ideas obviously address a certain number of common problems, but it is not clear that they represent *genera* of common solutions that could be neatly broken up into variant *species*. It is quite possible that this problem will be alleviated by time, but for now, at least, we must pursue another strategy.[10]

---

10. Some may think that this is a hasty conclusion. I would direct them to my more informal (but nonetheless extensive) attempts to engage with and understand the differences between Harman's and Bryant's variants of OOO, in the commentary section of my blog <http://deontologistics.wordpress.com>.

The aim of this book is to lay the groundwork for a proper engagement with OOO by focusing on the philosophical system of its progenitor: Graham Harman's own Object-Oriented Philosophy (OOP). As the oldest and most well-defined variant of OOO, this provides us with the best starting point for any wider engagement with the movement. However, to treat OOP with proper respect means to deal with it in its specificity—that is, outside the context of the overarching rhetoric that binds together the different strands of OOO. This is particularly important insofar as, while it is sometimes clear what the proponents of OOO think, it is often far less clear *why* they think it, which only exacerbates the problem of the divergences between them.

The first step of my approach (chapter 1) will thus be to present as complete and concise a summary of the 'what' of OOP as I can, breaking down the metaphysical system into three distinct aspects: withdrawal (1.1), the fourfold (1.2), and vicarious causation (1.3). The second step (chapter 2) will then be to present as charitable an interpretation of the 'why' of OOP as I can, teasing out and reconstructing the possible arguments for each of these three aspects in as much detail as is feasible, before assessing them on their merits. The third step (chapter 3) will be to make a number of overarching criticisms of the project of OOP on the basis of this assessment, pinpointing several key problems that run throughout it. The final step (chapter 4) will then be to present the hyperbolic projection of OOP initially promised, and to draw some conclusions about precisely what OOP (and perhaps OOO) has to offer on these grounds.

Like the other variants of so-called 'Speculative Realism' (those of Iain Hamilton Grant, Ray Brassier, and

Quentin Meillassoux), OOP claims to offer a response to the **correlationism** that has dominated philosophy since Kant.[11] Although he is willing to admit that his philosophy amounts to a radicalisation of a certain kind of correlationism (the weak form), in similar fashion to Meillassoux's philosophy (in relation to the strong form), Harman nevertheless presents his work as both a trenchant critique of, and an important step beyond, the menace of correlationism in contemporary philosophy. I do not intend to dispute the idea that there is such a correlationist menace (though I do take it to be more complicated than it is sometimes thought to be); but I do take issue with Harman's presentation of his own relationship to it. In fact, I shall argue that, properly understood, Harman's work should be seen not as a critique of correlationism, but as a consolidation of its central tenets. Harman essentially attempts to overcome the inconsistencies inherent within correlation-ism by sacrificing one of its core features—the prohibition on metaphysics—in order to construct a metaphysical prop whose purpose is nothing less than to bolster the rest of the calamitous edifice. He revives and transforms Kant's noumenal realm in order to preserve the most disastrous prejudices of the correlationist tradition he claims to break with. Far from being a truly 'weird' realism, OOP is no more than the eccentric uncle of the correlationist family. The metaphysical spoils it claims to have liberated from the Kantian stronghold are so

---

11. For the canonical text on Speculative Realism see R. Mackay (ed.), *Collapse* vol. 3 (Falmouth: Urbanomic, 2007); for a definition of Correlationism see Q. Meillassoux, *After Finitude: An Essay on the Necessity of Contingency*, tr. R. Brassier (New York and London: Continuum, 2008); for Harman's discussion of his relationship to correlationism see his *Philosophy in the Making*; for my own detailed discussion of these see chapter 3.3 subsection IV, chapter 3.4 subsection I, chapter 3.5 subsection III, and chapter 4.1.

much ashes and rust. After all is said and done, it returns to us naked, claiming to be wreathed in the finest vestments. The only proper gesture of respect, in such circumstances, is to point out its immodesty.[12]

---

12.   As this indicates, this book is indeed a polemic of sorts. I will not preempt this polemic by endeavouring to outline its scope in advance, but I will attempt to preempt the objection that I violate my own principle of respect simply by adopting a polemical *tone*. Harman's own words on this topic are eminently suited for this purpose: 'Polemical writing in philosophy no longer enjoys its previous level of acceptance, and is now often dismissed as the product of incivility, aggression, even jealousy. Against this attitude, we should appreciate the clarifying tendencies of polemic—always the favoured genre of authors frustrated by the continued clouding of an important decision, whether through fashionable cliché or dubious conceptual maneuvers'. (*Guerrilla Metaphysics* [La Salle, IL: Open Court, 2005], 11).

1

THE LAVA
THAT DARE NOT
SPEAK
ITS NAME

Before performing exploratory surgery on the beating heart of OOP, it is first necessary to present the customary compliments regarding the overall shape and style of its vascular architecture. Whatever else may be said about Harman's presentation of OOP, it is certainly compelling. On the one hand, it attempts to reveal the inherent *oddness* of the world in which we live, depicting a reality in which everything is radically individual, cut off from everything else in almost every respect, connected only by fleeting glimmers of phenomenal appearance. On the other, it attempts to *humble* humanity by seeing humans as just one more disparate association of objects within the universal diaspora, and the intentional terms through which they relate to one another as merely an expression of a more fundamental sensual connectivity in which everything may partake. Such willingness to countenance counterintuitive metaphysical conclusions and to embrace ontological humility is to be applauded.

Moving on, the central axis around which Harman's metaphysical system turns is the distinction between the **real** and the **sensual**. He is fond of describing this by appealing to a volcanic metaphor: the reality of things consists in their 'molten cores', the liquid specificities of which withdraw behind a 'sensual crust' of visible features. On this view, the substantial *magma* at the heart of every entity is forever trapped beneath a rocky outer surface whose stillness is only occasionally interrupted by the tectonic forces it unleashes. However, these occasional eruptions always catch us unawares. We never glimpse the molten essence as it leaks through the faultlines in its phenomenal facade, but only catch it as it cools, already crystallising into new sensual continents. The lava itself is nowhere to be found. To twist this metaphorical register for the purposes of summary: Harman's is a world of disconnected volcanic island nations floating in a cool sensual sea—a world in which you can travel as much as you like, but you'll always be a tourist. No matter how hard you try, you'll never see the *real* island, only beaches full of foreign holidaymakers and chintzy gift shops. You might get the occasional *taste* of it—a whiff of the exotic food the real islanders eat as you pass by, or a stolen glimpse of the real lives of the inhabitants over a whitewashed wall—but that's all you'll ever get.

In order to provide an adequate exposition of Harman's noumenal cosmology, I shall divide my discussion of the split between the real and the sensual into three parts. I will first tackle the relation between the real and the sensual under the heading of **withdrawal**, which is the most famous aspect of Harman's position. I will then show how this is complicated by the introduction of a second axis—the distinction between **objects** and **qualities**—under the heading of the **fourfold**, which is the name of the structure Harman derives from their intersection. Finally, I will address the most prominent metaphysical problem that emerges from Harman's system, and his solution to it, which goes by the name of **vicarious causation**.

1. WITHDRAWAL

It is all too easy to say that Harman's world is divided into two: a celestial plane of intentional facades masking a hellish realm of machinic forces, an open space of sensual contact concealing the endlessly churning reality that makes it possible. The truth is that these two sides of his cosmos are folded into one another at every opportunity: there is no straight line from one sensual point to another that does not pass through a real one, and vice versa. What we have here is a pluriverse of infernal engines that present themselves to one another only so as to hide their internal machinations. Like the many hells of Buddhist lore, each of these engines is a realm unto itself, composed of further layers of tortuous machinery; each part of which is available to its fellows only in outline, containing its own inexplicable depths, concealing further strange and sulphurous landscapes, ever more intricate and malicious economies of action yet to be explored. This is the world of **real objects**. It is a world to which we ourselves belong, along with everything that has any real *effect* upon us—or indeed, upon anything at all. This is the site of everything that really *happens* in the world.

It is important to distinguish between two kinds of happening, though: **execution** and **causation**. For Harman, a real object just *is* its execution, which is to say its *being-whatever-it-is*, or rather, *doing-whatever-it-does*. This is to say that each real object is defined by some inscrutable end for which it is the corresponding act. The relation between every real thing taken as a whole and the parts that compose it is to be understood in terms of **functional relations**, like the relation between a machine and its components. The real object consists in the unitary action of its parts deployed towards the given end: it *is* its execution insofar as it is a *function in action*. There is more that could be said about this, but for now it is important to recognise that although this action is certainly a happening of sorts, it is the occurrence of sameness, or simple **persistence**. The various machinic arrangements of parts and wholes that compose the real are essentially *synchronic*. For Harman, causation is the occurrence of difference, or **change**, and it emerges from *diachronic* relations of interaction between real objects. The paradox with which he closes his first book, *Tool-Being*,[13] is that his characterisation of such objects as persisting unities seems to preclude the possibility that they could effect change in one another—implying an essentially static cosmic order, in opposition to the seeming reality of change that constantly assails our senses.

The reason for this is that the reality of persistence *qua* execution implies that real objects **withdraw** from one another, unable to affect one another at all. This withdrawal has two facets: the **excess** of everything over its presentations, and the **independence** of everything from everything else. Excess follows from the inscrutability of the end governing each object, which occludes the object's *internal economy* of action (execution) and thereby the *external capacities* for action (causation) that emerge from it. Execution is a pure act of persistence underlying every actual interaction, and a pure actuality underlying every possible interaction. This means that it *transcends* both interaction and possibility. We can never *know* the sheer execution of the thing that lies behind every possible encounter. Insofar as **ontological humility** demands that we treat the way we grasp the capabilities of objects—through

---

13. LaSalle, IL: Open Court, 2002, §25–6.

either *theoretical* or *practical* engagement with them—as

just one more instance of an encounter between any two real objects, we must conclude that our inability to grasp an object's veiled execution through any particular possible inter- action is a deeper fact about the metaphysics of encounters. This is the fact that the world also contains **sensual objects**. Our own experience of the world is *phenomenologically* con- stituted by intentional relations directed at *unitary objects*, and this implies that objects' experience of one another is *metaphysically* constituted by something similar. If objects encounter one another as unities, and yet fail to encounter one another *directly*, then encounters must be mediated by unitary intentional facades or caricatures entirely *distinct* from the executant realities that project them. Independence follows from this, insofar as every real object is protected from every other by an honour guard of distinct sensual objects, forever precluding access to it, at least by default.

Finally, it must be emphasised that withdrawal does not merely occur *between* isolated real objects, like a non-aggres- sion pact between the many hells; it also occurs *within* them, in the form of **mereological isolation**. It is easy to see how this involves the mutual withdrawal of the parts of an object from one another, insofar as they are real objects in their own right; but it also consists in the withdrawal of parts from the wholes they *compose*, and wholes from the parts they *contain*. Of course, the whole is dependent upon its parts, insofar as it cannot subsist without them, but at the same time it is inde- pendent of them, in two senses: (a) it is entirely possible for its parts to be replaced without significantly altering its internal economy; and (b) this economy produces capacities which exceed the capacities of the parts taken in isolation. Similarly, although the parts may be reciprocally dependent upon one another to some extent (insofar as they require certain conditions in which to function), they are equally independent of their context in two senses: (a) it is entirely possible for them to be transplanted into a different whole without dissolving their own distinct unity; and (b) new contexts may reveal hitherto unexpressed capacities that were previously suppressed. A real object considered as a whole is a specific arrangement of parts that both transcends and fails to exhaust their specificity. Despite the fact that the real object consists in transcending this excess of specificity, it nevertheless plays an additional role, insofar as the whole draws upon it in generating the sensual objects it hides behind. The various inessential features of a real object's parts become resources for producing the phenomenal **accidents** that cloak its executant reality.

2. THE FOURFOLD

Once we begin to talk about the features and capacities of objects as distinct from the objects themselves, we stumble upon the second fundamental axis around which Harman's system turns: the distinction between *objects* and their *qualities*. Things are not just torn between their subterranean execution and its phenomenal effects, but also between their persistent **unity** and its constituent **plurality**. This does not concern how a singular whole is *composed* of multiple parts (e.g., the composition of an ice cube out of molecules), although this is a related issue, but how a single entity is *determined* in various ways (e.g., the coldness, hardness, or translucency of the ice cube). The mutual withdrawal between parts and whole noted above consists in wholes having qualities their parts lack (e.g., the molecules are neither translucent nor hard), and parts having qualities their wholes ignore (e.g., the unique chemical properties of the trace amount of minerals in the water is usually entirely irrelevant to the ice cube). Qualities are not objects, even if the qualities a thing possesses somehow bubble up from the objects that compose it.[14]

These two distinctions—real/sensual and object/quality—are not merely parallel, but cut across one another. This produces a fourfold of terms: in addition to the distinction between sensual objects (SO) and real objects (RO), there is a distinction between **sensual qualities** (SQ) and **real qualities** (RQ). The objects that appear in our phenomenal experience are 'encrusted' with sensible features that may vary

---

14. We will complicate this claim to some extent in chapter 2.1, subsection III and chapter 2.2, subsection I.

from moment to moment, but the latter are entirely distinct from the real features 'submerged' in the silent execution they conceal. Here we begin to see how the four poles interact with one another to form Harman's ten categories. The relation between a sensual object and its sensual qualities (SO–SQ) is the condition of the variation of its encrusted accidents, or **time** itself, whereas the relation between a sensual object and its real qualities (SO–RQ) is the submerged anchor around which this variation is fixed, or what Edmund Husserl calls **eidos**. These two categories are the first of what Harman calls the 'tensions' between object and quality. The emergence of sensual objects in our experience is dependent upon the sensible features the corresponding real objects allow them to present from perspective to perspective; and the distinctness of these underlying real objects is in turn dependent upon differences between the features they can never present. This gives us the remaining two tensions. The relation between a real object and its sensual qualities (RO–SQ) is the condition under which it can relate to another object through a sensuous facade, or **space**, whereas the relation between a real object and its real qualities (RO–RQ) is its principle of uniqueness, or what Xavier Zubiri calls **essence**. Taken together, these four tensions provide the schema of *sameness* and *difference* between objects, both real and apparent, along with their *constancy* and *variation*.

Harman calls the changes that emerge within this schema 'fissions' and 'fusions'. This is because two of the tensions (time and eidos) involve a persistent state of connection between object and quality—so that any change would entail fission of this connection—and the other two (space and essence) involve a persistent state of separation—so that any change would entail fusion of that which is separated.

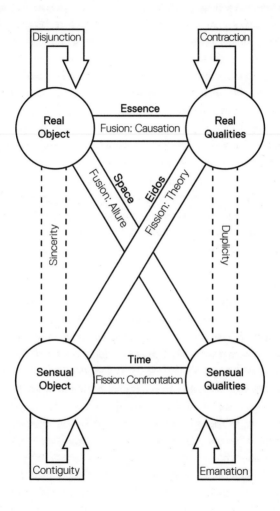

Fissions. It is important to recognise that the fissions take place within the sensual realm, insofar as they involve breaks in the connections between the sensual objects we experience and their qualities. In **confrontation**, a sensual object is split from its sensual qualities (time), so that its accidental features are somehow revealed *as* accidental. This occurs when we recognise something *as* something (e.g., a tree *as* a gallows), thereby separating those qualities that are relevant to this characterisation (e.g., height, branch structure, etc.) from those that are not (e.g., colour, foliage, etc.). In **theory**, the sensual object is split from its real qualities (eidos), so that its eidetic features are somehow contrasted with its accidental ones. This occurs when we strive to grasp the constants that underlie the shifting surface variations to which all things are subject (e.g., when we analyse the tree's morphology, or its genetic structure).

Fusions. By contrast, only one of the fusions marks the emergence of real objects within the phenomenal sphere, so as to redraw its boundaries from within; whereas the other fusion is entirely withdrawn, and therefore is only apparent in the ways it redraws these boundaries from without. The first fusion is **allure**, where a real object interacts with the features of the sensible facades it projects (space), such that there is an apparent juxtaposition between its accidental elements and its eidetic core. This occurs in various aesthetically significant experiences (e.g., cuteness, beauty, humour, embarrassment, humility, disappointment, loyalty),[15] but is most prominently manifest in the use of metaphor (e.g., when we frame our experience of the tree by describing it as 'a flame'). The second fusion is **causation**, where the real object interacts with its own real features (essence) so as to unlock its capacities to affect

---

15. *Guerrilla Metaphysics*, 212–13.

the withdrawn core of other things. As already indicated, the possibility of causation is called into question by withdrawal, and this in turn necessitates the theory of vicarious causation, which will turn upon the real object's relation with allure.

Before getting into this though, we must examine the remaining six categories, which are divided into 'radiations' between qualities and qualities, and 'junctions' between objects and objects. Much as there was a rift between one of the tensions and the other three with regard to their role in experience, there is a crucial difference between the roles that radiations and junctions play therein. On the one hand, the radiations cover the way that qualities are related *within* experience by the sensual objects that populate it: the relation between two sensual qualities (SQ–SQ) is their **emanation** through the same object of experience, the relation between two real qualities (RQ–RQ) is their **contraction** behind this same object, and the relation between the sensual qualities and the real qualities (SQ–RQ) is their **duplicity** in the way they differ from one another. On the other hand, the junctions cover the way that relations between objects constitute experience in relation to ourselves *qua* real objects: the relation between two sensual objects (SO–SO) can only take place as **contiguity** within our experience, the relation between two real objects (RO–RO) is the **withdrawal** of the corresponding real objects behind our experience, and the relation between a real object and a sensual object (RO–SO) is the **sincerity** that constitutes this experience itself. Together, the three radiations and three conjunctions provide the framework in which the three experiential tensions can unfold. They give us an abstract map of the phenomenal realms that lie between infernal kingdoms of execution—the borderlands through which they smuggle causal contraband, or the embassies through which they communicate.

3. VICARIOUS CAUSATION

We can now turn to the problem of _how_ this communication occurs. The independence of real objects from one another demands such an explanation: How can mutually withdrawn objects possibly interact, so as to produce **real changes** in one another? The latter are quite distinct from the mere phenomenal variations that sensual objects undergo in experience, because they can reconfigure the very intentional space within which experience occurs. Yet it is only within these intentional spaces that a real object can encounter the variable facades projected by other real objects, and only through these sensual vicars that any sort of contact can be established between them. The fact that all causal contact arises out of an **intentional relation** between an _experiencing_ real object and an _experienced_ sensual object that mediates between it and its real counterpart implies that the causal relation is not just vicarious, but also **asymmetrical** and **buffered**. It is asymmetrical because the relation has direction, proceeding from the object the vicar conceals to the object the vicar appears to. This means that causation can occur one-way between real objects, without reciprocation (e.g., when a bee is hit by an oncoming car, the bee may be destroyed while the car is entirely unscathed). And it is buffered because there are many _contiguous_ sensual objects present in the same experience, and this does not result in interactions between the real objects they hide (e.g., the bee may be drawn into the path of the truck by an enticing flower, but the truck and the flower may be entirely unrelated). This means that a real object's _sincerity_ in encountering a sensual object is the condition of that object's receptivity.

However, we are not causally affected by every object we experience. The phenomenal realms that real objects find themselves immersed in are filled to the brim with myriad sensual unities, many of which have no impact upon them at all. This means that intentional relations are not necessarily causal relations. So what more is there to causal contact than mere sincerity? Harman responds by invoking the link between *causation* and *allure* mentioned above. Genuine change is *internal* to a real object, insofar as it only occurs when a real object becomes connected to its qualities in regenerating its *essence*; but this nevertheless requires an *external* trigger, which can only take the form of some variation within the intentional space in which it is immersed. Harman proposes that the *confrontations* usually precipitated by such variation are insufficient to trigger causal contact, because the qualities encountered therein are still tied to the facade that hides the *triggering* object from the *triggered* object. It is only in *allusion* that these ties are broken, and the qualities allowed to orbit the real object underlying them (e.g., when the metaphorical comparison of the tree with a flame highlights the relevant qualities in a way that makes them alien to the tree with which we are familiar). Allure lets reality obliquely slide into appearance, striking the object that experiences it in a way that surpasses the sensual flux it is accustomed to, so that the accidental features of the *affecting* object catalyse the reshuffling of essential features within the *affected* object.

Nevertheless, the affected object does not strictly *see* the affecting object, even if it *feels* it in some specific aesthetic mode (e.g., as humorous) and to some specific degree of aesthetic intensity (e.g., as only *mildly* humorous). The brief suspension of causal independence that occurs in causal connection never really overcomes the corresponding epistemic excess.

Allure may play an important role in enabling us to reconfigure the ways we think about entities, but it never amounts to knowledge of them. This is why Harman grants aesthetics a special philosophical privilege. According to him, examining the varieties of allure and their relationships gives us an insight into the metaphysical structure of reality, an insight that forever escapes the stale practice of epistemology. With the tenfold categorical schema derived from the fourfold, Harman has provided a *general* theory of objects—which he calls **ontography**—capable of application to the various *specific* domains of objects that compose the cosmos. Yet it is only through an extending of the sorts of aesthetic analysis indicated by his theory of allure that these domains can be fleshed out. Ultimately, Harman proposes an alliance of aesthetics and metaphysics that promises to lay bare the various regions of the cosmos to renewed philosophical inquiry. It now falls to us to assess this proposal, and its worth.

2

THE WITHDRAWAL
OF ARGUMENTS

Having looked into the 'what' of OOP, it is time to concern ourselves with the 'why'. This means locating the various arguments that Harman presents for each of the different aspects of his metaphysical system distinguished above. As I hinted in the introduction, this is by no means an easy task. Although Harman's work is peppered with phrases such as 'I will show...', 'I have already argued...', or 'As argued repeatedly...', these often do not refer to specific arguments so much as to the overarching dramatisation of a given idea that takes place throughout the work.[16] There are a few notable exceptions to this, as we shall see, but what arguments there are in Harman's work tend to be blended together in ways that make them hard to tease apart—a task which is vital if they are to be properly assessed. To draw on Harman's own preferred metaphors once more, the arguments often seem to *withdraw* into themselves, leaving textual vicars that tantalise one's cognitive faculties by *alluding* to their real logical depths. Our current task is thus to draw them out of hiding and expose them to the light of reason.[17]

---

16.   These examples are all taken from *Tool-Being* (19, 61, and 70), but one can find many similar phrases in all his works. It is very rare to find such a phrase that is tied in any way to a specific chain of inferences (for instance by referencing the pages upon which the supposed argument takes place).

17.   Harman himself looks down on this sort of critical engagement with the arguments underlying a philosophical position for various reasons (cf. *Guerrilla Metaphysics*, §12A), some of which are curiously intertwined with elements of his own position. Instead of systematically critiquing a position on the basis of flaws in its argumentation, he would rather that we strove to present counternarratives that construct *suggestive* alternatives to it. Even while Harman admits that 'such debunking may be necessary work at times', he nevertheless maintains that 'we should not forget that it is mainly the work of dogs (*cynics*, to say it in Greek)' (ibid.). Even if we grant this, it cannot get in the way of the work that *respect* demands. Mere preference cannot dictate when the dogs should be released. Woof.

Of course, Harman also has his own (fairly derogatory) opinions about the role of reason and argument within philosophy, as a part of his wider concern with the importance of philosophical 'style', a concern that must be taken into account.[18] We shall address these later on (chapter 4.2). For now, our aim is to *delineate* and perhaps even *repair* as much as is feasible of the justificatory tissue holding together the skeletal structure of Harman's corpus that was revealed in chapter 1. This is a delicate operation that requires exegetical care, logical skill, and no small amount of discursive charity. We are about to move from exploratory to reconstructive surgery. In order to facilitate this, I shall highlight three different ways in which Harman frames his ideas with an eye to their justification: **historical narrative**, **phenomenological description**, and **metaphysical argument**.

Historical narratives introduce an idea by reconstructing its genesis within a particular historical dialectic, usually constituted by a series of different thinkers each of whom makes some important contribution to the problematic in which the idea gestates, only to emerge fully formed in Harman's own work. These rational reconstructions are an important philosophical tool deployed by many of the great figures in the history of philosophy.[19] The philosophies of Hegel, Heidegger, and Deleuze would not be as compelling or even as accessible without the thematic vectors they trace through their forebears in the direction of their own work. Harman is thus

---

18. Cf. *Prince of Networks*, 169–75.

19. For an account of the logic of this process of reconstruction, see Robert Brandom's work on the historical dimension of rationality in the introduction to *Tales of the Mighty Dead* (Cambridge, MA: Harvard University Press, 2002) and his own reconstruction of Hegel in *Reason in Philosophy* (Cambridge, MA: Harvard University Press, 2009), chapter 3.

to be commended for wielding this method of exposition with some skill. However, the danger associated with this method is that it can easily slip from licit *exposition* to illicit *justification* in the form of arguments from authority. Such arguments can be useful as shorthand forms of justification (equivalent to saying 'you need to go read Aristotle/Hegel/Heidegger/ etc. before we can talk seriously about this'); but they wither under more sustained forms of philosophical scrutiny. The issue is exacerbated where the readings of the figures in question are particularly controversial, as is Harman's reading of Heidegger, which forms a crucial part of his own object-oriented history.[20] As such, in separating out these narratives from the other forms of exposition and argument in Harman's work, my primary goal will be to ensure that they play no such illicit justificatory role.

Phenomenological descriptions play an important part in Harman's work, insofar as his metaphysics is thoroughly influenced by an appropriation of the ideas of Husserl and Heidegger. His is a metaphysics of intentional relation, and his account of intentionality is fundamentally culled from the phenomenological tradition and its methodology of immanent description. However, the methodological questions regarding the *nature* and *status* of phenomenological description that were of such concern to Husserl and Heidegger receive little attention in Harman's work. He is often all too eager to delve directly into

---

20. This is an area in which I can speak with at least enough authority to be taken seriously, given the fact that my PhD thesis (*The Question of Being: Heidegger and Beyond*, Warwick University 2012, <http://deontologistics. wordpress.com/thesis/>) presents a synoptic reading of Heidegger's work which, while diverging from both the standard analytic and Continental readings, much as Harman's does, comes to conclusions radically different (and, I would argue, far more nuanced) than Harman's.

phenomenological analysis without clarifying precisely *what it means to do so*. Whereas Husserl devotes a enormous amount of time and effort to elaborating the various aspects of the phenomenological reduction, and Heidegger devotes a serious (if not necessarily comparable) effort to modifying this within his own existential-hermeneutic framework, Harman gives us little in the way of phenomenological methodology. This not only makes the precise content of many of his phenomenological claims unclear, but more worryingly brings into question the *metaphysical* conclusions that are leveraged on the basis of these claims. It is thus of the utmost importance to identify precisely which of Harman's claims are motivated by phenomenological analysis, and how they are deployed in the attempt to justify his more contentious metaphysical claims.

This brings us to the third form of exposition: *metaphysical argument* itself. Specifically, it raises the question of what qualifies either a philosophical claim or its justification as 'metaphysical'. In other words: Just *what is* metaphysics anyway? (chapter 3.5 will address this explicitly.) This question should weigh heavily on the shoulders of anyone intending to engage in renewed metaphysical speculation regardless of their preferred method, but this weight becomes particularly acute when one intends to derive metaphysical *conclusions* from phenomenological *premises*. Although it is possible to find his account wanting, it could hardly be said that Heidegger merely identifies phenomenology and ontology without addressing and attempting to justify this quite radical divergence from the metaphysical tradition.[21] Heidegger's detailed historical and methodological work on the problem of metaphysics and the question of Being garners almost no attention in Harman's work, nor is it supplemented

---

21.   For details, consult my *The Question of Being*.

by any detailed alternative schema. Indeed, the most sustained engagement with the question I have been able to locate dismisses the possibility of even addressing the methodological task of clarifying the question of Being prior to answering it: 'the question of [B]eing cannot be elucidated until the meaning of [B]eing itself has already somehow been clarified, prior to any special description of Dasein.'[22] This sidelining of methodological issues is rather worrying given Harman's unapologetic calls to return to the problems of precritical metaphysics.[23]

All of this indicates just how important it is to separate out the roles these different forms of exposition play in the more or less *explicit* arguments within Harman's work, and the way overlaps between them further complicate many of the *implicit* assumptions undergirding the latter. However, the critical purchase upon Harman's work this would provide requires an exhaustive approach that presents its own particular problems. Firstly, the ideal of exhaustiveness places exegetical demands upon a commentator (and critic) that are often unrealistic, and this can easily lead to accusations of impropriety. I have gone

---

22. *Tool-Being*, 40.

23. It is also helpful to note that despite using the term 'being' quite extensively throughout *Tool-Being*, Harman never provides any generic definition or analysis of the term that goes beyond his own metaphysical account of it. If pushed to provide a quick analysis of his usage of the term, I would say that he uses it in one of two senses: (a) in the *particular* sense to refer to the being of a given object (cf. *Tool-Being* 85), or (b) in the *singular* sense to refer to the totality of objects (cf. Ibid., 294). This almost entirely elides the *general* sense referring to the Being of objects *as such* with which Heidegger himself is principally concerned (as the subject of the question of Being). In addition, in accordance with his own metaphysical proclivities, the senses in which Harman does use the term are almost universally deployed in opposition to *seeming* (cf. 26), which is only one of the major oppositions that Heidegger outlines (and indeed, questions) in the course of his career (cf. *Introduction to Metaphysics*, tr. G. Fried and R. Polt [New Haven, CT: Yale University Press, 2000], 103–22).

out of my way to read as much of Harman's extant work as I can, in order to forestall such accusations, but I expect them nonetheless.[24] Secondly, it places hermeneutic demands on those who would read (and perhaps respond to) the commentary—demands that are substantial if not unreasonable. Not only must readers be willing to cover the same exegetical ground as the commentator; they must also keep track of multiple different arguments and their intersections. I have endeavoured to organise this book in as accessible a manner as possible, but this can only ameliorate these problems rather than obviate them entirely. Thirdly, the exhaustive approach often has profoundly counterproductive psychological effects. It is an unfortunate fact that it is often easier to convince someone of the falsity of a theory or the wrongness of a policy by focusing upon a single objection to it, rather than aiming to present several, equally serious objections. We all have a finite amount of attention, and thus a limited ability to cope with barrages of arguments; and these unavoidable limitations can often lead to our dismissing arguments that overload our attentional capacities. This phenomenon is a serious problem in many mainstream political debates, where certain multifariously flawed ideas often survive precisely because no unitary line of attack upon them is obvious. I enjoin the reader to recognise this phenomenon, and not to take the lack of a singular knockdown criticism as a point in favour of the position criticised.

---

24.   The footnotes throughout this book will reveal the full extent of this reading. I have consulted all published books and essay collections, but I have not read all of Harman's published papers, nor any unpublished material that may be circulating. I have also followed the writings on his blog (<http://doctorzamalek2.wordpress.com>) rather extensively, though I have refrained from referencing them in justifying any of the substantial points in this paper, for obvious reasons. I consider this to be an eminently reasonable level of work to justify the present book, even if I cannot completely rule out the possibility that I have missed something crucial in the writings I have not read.

This brings me to the last substantive point in this prolegomena, which regards the nature of philosophical disagreement and its presentation. In previous, more informal debates, Harman has complained that I fail to follow the proper procedure for engaging with a discursive opponent: firstly outlining the areas in which one agrees with one's interlocutor, and then proceeding to outline the relevant disagreements.[25] My response is that, sometimes, there simply are not enough points of agreement to make this anything more than an empty gesture. My own commitments, which I have endeavoured to keep out of this book wherever possible,[26] are quite radically different from Harman's, and this leaves little ground for praise on my part. Nevertheless, I will mention six areas in which there is something resembling agreement between us: (i) we both think that *correlationism* is problematic; (ii) we both hold that *individuality* is an important metaphysical topic; (iii) we agree that there is more to *panpsychism* than is often thought; (iv) we each take it that *aesthetics* is an important philosophical field with wider ramifications than commonly accepted; (v) we are jointly committed to both the possibility and necessity of *metaphysics* in some form; and (vi) we strongly agree that *realism* is essential if this metaphysics is to be pursued properly.

The problem is that, once we begin to define what is meant by the core terms in each case (correlationism, individuality, panpsychism, aesthetics, metaphysics, and realism), the

---

25.   Private correspondence.

26.   For an unpolished overview of my own position, I recommend reading the available draft of my *Essay on Transcendental Realism* (<http://deontologistics.wordpress.com/2010/05/essay-on-transcendental-realism.pdf>). This is a rough draft that has yet to be revised and expanded for publication, but it does a reasonable job of outlining the central themes of my work.

agreements turn out to have been fairly superficial: (i) I agree with Quentin Meillassoux[27] that the essence of correlation-ism is epistemological rather than metaphysical, and that it must be challenged on this terrain rather than dismissed as ontologically arrogant; (ii) I think that there can be no study of the metaphysics of individuality that does not begin with its logic (e.g., identification, quantification, existential commitment, etc.) rather than leaping headlong into intui-tive speculation; (iii) the history of panpsychism I am con-cerned with (e.g., Spinoza, Leibniz, Nietzsche, Whitehead, and Deleuze) is characterised by its generalisation of non-intentional features of thought (i.e., conation and sensation); (iv) I am convinced that aesthetics, as the study of a certain kind of value, has less to do with the sensations and feelings that signal its presence than with the actions this demands of us; (v) I predict that a return to metaphysical speculation without the methodological awareness accompanying an answer to the question 'What is metaphysics?' is doomed to failure; and (vi) I think that there can be no viable 'realism' without a *definition* of 'real' more subtle than 'that which is always other than our knowledge of it'.

This is all I shall say about these disagreements for now. The criticisms upon which they turn will be revealed as we look at Harman's arguments themselves. I shall group these arguments on the basis of the aspect of his system that they underpin (withdrawal, the fourfold, and vicarious causation, respectively), so that the order of the following subsections corresponds directly to the order of those in the previous section. Each section will deal with a number of different

---

27. 'Speculative Realism', in *Collapse* vol. 3, 445–6, in conversation with Peter Hallward.

arguments of varying strength and complexity, with varying degrees of reconstruction on my part. Each is shorter than the last, as the relevant arguments build upon one another. I will do my best to indicate exegetical concerns surrounding my reconstructions, but my aim is to present the strongest possible forms of each argument, so as to make the corresponding criticisms as strong as possible.

Harman has several arguments for his account of withdrawal. By far the most famous is the reading of Heidegger's tool-analysis presented in his first book, *Tool-Being*. However, despite the fact that the tool-analysis is referred to and summarised to different degrees throughout Harman's work, it remains fairly opaque in its logical structure.[28] This is principally because, although it is referred to as if it were a single argument, Harman's version is really a blend of a number of distinct arguments, mixing all three forms of exposition discussed above: historical, phenomenological, and metaphysical. Disentangling these expository and justificatory strands is difficult enough when focusing on one text, but its manifold presentation confronts us with some serious choices about how to proceed. I have decided to focus upon two presentations of the analysis: the original and most detailed presentation of it in *Tool-Being*, and a more recent and concise presentation of it in Harman's book on Meillassoux, *Philosophy in the Making*.[29] I highly recommend reading the relevant sections of these texts alongside my reconstruction of the tool-analysis, so as to confirm the fidelity of my reconstruction. These preliminaries aside, I shall break down the tool-analysis into two separate parts. I call these the argument from **execution** and the argument from **excess**. This will be followed by an examination of

---

28. To give a representative example, in the collection *Towards Speculative Realism* (Winchester: Zero Books, 2010), 8 out of 11 essays contain truncated summaries of the tool-analysis.

29. *Philosophy in the Making*, 135–6.

an additional argument that often accompanies them, and which I call the argument from **identity**.

I. HARMAN'S HEIDEGGER

Before delving into the details of the tool-analysis, we must address the exegetical elephant in the room. I have already announced my disagreement with Harman's reading of Heidegger. Harman is very clear that his version of the tool-analysis is not one that Heidegger would himself endorse, and that as such it must be assessed on its own merits. This is precisely what I intend to do. However, in line with my earlier remarks about the role of historical narrative, it will be helpful to present the crucial errors of Harman's reading of Heidegger as I see them. On the one hand, this inoculates against any illicit slip from exposition to justification, and, on the other, it helps to situate within their correct historical context many of the issues Harman is dealing with.

There are five principal aspects of Harman's reading with which I disagree: (i) he reads Heidegger's critique of presence as championing a complementary notion of execution; (ii) he takes the distinction between the ontological and the ontic to be equivalent to the distinction between the ready-to-hand and the present-at-hand; (iii) he claims that the 'world' should not be understood as a phenomenological horizon; (iv) he holds that Dasein is not central to Heidegger's ontology; and (v) he identifies the encounter with the broken tool with the as-structure. I shall tackle these disagreements by addressing several characteristic criticisms that Harman deploys liberally against other interpreters of Heidegger. (If understanding these exegetical points is of little interest to you, you may wish to skip the rest of this subsection, though I do not recommend it.)

To begin with, Harman repeatedly criticises other interpreters for mistaking the significance of the distinction between readiness-to-hand (*Zuhandenheit*) and presence-at-hand (*Vorhandenheit*) for a distinction between *types* of entity. He zealously reminds his readers that ready-to-hand entities are not those specific things that happen to be used as tools by humans, but rather that any extant entity may be taken as ready-to-hand or present-at-hand.[30] This point is certainly misunderstood by a number of interpreters. However, even combined with his reading of Heidegger's use of the word 'mere' (*Bloß*) to denigrate the status of *presence* (*Anweisenheit*),[31] this does not show that Heidegger is championing a complementary notion of *execution* (*Vollzug*) as the real meaning of 'Being' that the metaphysical tradition overlooked. On the contrary, it is possible to view this as a distinction between different *modes* of Being (*Seinsarten/Seinsweisen*) without reducing it to a distinction between mutually exclusive *types* of beings. This is precisely how Heidegger describes the distinction.[32] Moreover, the fact that Harman will develop this notion of execution into a new conception of *substance* (*ousia*), bemoaning the inability of Heidegger commentators to see the connection between *Zuhandenheit* and *ousia*,[33] indicates that he has diverged from Heidegger somewhere upstream of this point.[34]

---

30. Cf. *Tool-Being*, 38.

31. Ibid., 48–9.

32. Cf. *Basic Problems of Phenomenology*, tr. A. Hofstadter (Bloomington, IN: Indiana University Press, 1988), 305; *Metaphysical Foundations of Logic*, tr. M. Heim (Bloomington, IN: Indiana University Press, 1984), 151–2.

33. *Tool-Being*, 270.

34. Heidegger's criticism of presence is inexorably tied up with his critique of substance, at least in his most systematic presentations of it (cf. *Introduction to Metaphysics*).

Secondly, Harman claims that Heidegger's insights cannot be truly *ontological* ones if they are understood in terms of the *intelligibility* of entities to Dasein. The argument for this essentially boils down to the idea that intelligibility to Dasein is *seeming* for Dasein, and Harman defines 'Being' in opposition to seeming.[35] For Harman, ontology is the study of beings as they are in themselves, as distinct from their appearances. This is almost the opposite move made by most orthodox Heidegger scholars, who define 'Being' as the intelligibility of beings as distinct from any 'metaphysical' conception of the underlying *grounds* of this intelligibility. For them, ontology is the study of appearances freed from the mistaken metaphysical search for the substantial basis of these appearances. In fact, both of these readings are seriously misguided, since Heidegger does not *define* 'Being' in either of these ways. However, each has an element of truth to it. In line with the orthodox interpretation, Heidegger does indeed try to argue, against the metaphysical tradition, that Being is to be understood in terms of intelligibility (unconcealing). And in line with Harman's interpretation, he also thinks that something must be said about that which resists or escapes intelligibility (concealing). His later work in particular attempts to show that the revelation of each entity to our understanding is tempered by its being situated within a broader field of meaning (world) which is always in tension with reality in itself (earth). Every entity thus appears as a local modification of this global struggle (strife/truth).

Thirdly, this brings us to Harman's criticism that, in interpreting Heidegger's use of 'world' as a phenomenological horizon within which entities appear to each given Dasein, Heidegger scholars have stumbled into a disastrous regress towards

---

35. See p. 33 n. 23 above.

ever deeper unitary grounds (e.g., *Zeitlichkeit*, *Temporalität*, *Ereignis*, etc.).[36] Again, as much as this is a legitimate lampooning of the stylistic and exegetical excesses of much Heidegger scholarship, it does not amount to a proof that there is no well-defined regress of unitary grounds in Heidegger. Even if there is a certain overworn argumentative trope in Heidegger, this does not excuse us from examining the specificities of its instances. It is thus entirely possible (and desirable) to determine that there are only a specific number of steps in Heidegger's analyses, and that they actually have an end point in some more or less well-delimited unitary structure (e.g., *Temporalität* in the early work, or *Ereignis* in the later work). Harman's alternative is to read 'world' as a complete totality of entities rather than a phenomenological horizon within which entities appear. This is a disastrous misreading, one that is explicitly counselled against by Heidegger.[37]

Fourthly, this sets the stage for Harman's attack on anthropocentric readings of Heidegger. Although Harman recognises that Heidegger himself grants Dasein ontological privilege, he takes this to be entirely unnecessary, insofar as every entity can be interpreted as a *for-the-sake-of-which* engaging with other things in terms of projective understanding.[38] Harman explicitly claims that although Heidegger uses the term 'understanding' (*Verstand*) here, this can be interpreted non-anthropocentrically as covering all interactions between things. This is indicative of a really pernicious misunderstanding of Heidegger's project that underlies the other points addressed so far.

---

36. He even parodies this regress by way of a children's sleepover game (*Tool-Being*, 27).

37. Cf. *Fundamental Concepts of Metaphysics*, §67.

38. *Tool-Being*, 41–2.

Let us briefly summarise Heidegger's account of understanding: he thinks that Dasein relates to the things it encounters in terms of the possibilities for action that they provide it, and that what characterises Dasein *qua* Dasein (*Existenz*) is that set of conditions (*Existentiale*) without which Dasein could not count as freely choosing, and thus acting in any real sense. Harman is fond of ridiculing Heidegger's analysis of the mode of Being of *animality* as distinct from Dasein's mode of *existence*, precisely because he fails to see that Heidegger is describing entities which have similar behavioural capacities to Dasein (drives) but which nevertheless lack the specific conditions of organisation that enable choice (as opposed to mere disinhibition).[39]

This brings us back to our preceding point: Harman cannot see what it would be to be world-poor precisely insofar as he does not see what it means for something to have a 'world' in Heidegger's sense: an internally articulated space of possible action (i.e., the projection of what is possible), involving a grasp of both generality and particularity (e.g., the possibilities of pens *as such* vs. the possibilities of *this* particular pen), in isolation and situation (e.g., the possibilities of this pen in relation to paper *as such* vs. the possibilities of *this* pen in relation to *that* piece of paper), organised in terms of a hierarchy of ends (e.g., the end of writing a letter, itself a means to maintaining a friendship, itself a means to... etc.) united by the fundamental goal of becoming oneself (i.e., Dasein as its own *for-the-sake-of-which*). Entities appear in the world for Heidegger insofar as they modify this space of possibility: their actuality consists in the way they open up certain specific possibilities for action while closing down others. This explains an

---

39. Cf. *Fundamental Concepts of Metaphysics*, part 2, chapters 3–6.

even earlier criticism: Harman cannot see that differences in modes of Being (e.g., *Zuhandenheit*, *Vorhandenheit*, *Existenz*, etc.) are not simple differences between types of beings, because he does not see the different ways they are supposed to be individuated as actualities within the world *qua* space of possibility. So, it is true that all spatio-temporally located particulars are *both* ready-to-hand and present-at-hand in some sense (even if the *space* and *time* in question are not straightforwardly identical); but this is a matter of the difference between our grasp of possibilities as tied to the everyday forms of activity we inherit from the culture we are *thrown* into (e.g., pens *qua* writing implements), and our grasp of possibilities as *abstracted* from these activities (e.g., pens *qua* ink-filled molded plastic).

Finally, this brings us to Harman's persistent criticisms of pragmatist readings of Heidegger in general, and of the tool-analysis more specifically. These are inextricably bound up with the other criticisms already presented, but there is an important additional dimension here: Harman's claim that Heidegger's concern with the use of equipment has nothing to do with use as we normally understand it, but should be understood as a matter of reliance upon equipment.[40] It is the fact that reliance is an essentially *causal* notion that underpins Harman's claim that all interactions between entities can be described as entities 'understanding' one another 'as' something, and the development of this into the further claim that all such interactions are analogous to the encounter with the broken tool. We shall return to the independent methodological problems with this claim, but for now it suffices to point out the sheer extent to which it misunderstands Heidegger's account

---

40.   *Tool-Being*, 18–21.

of the as-structure and its relation to the broken tool encounter. The crucial point is that Heidegger distinguishes between the hermeneutic 'as' and the apophantic 'as', and associates these with the ready-to-hand and the present-at-hand, respectively. The relationship between the former circumscribes the relationship between the latter: this is essentially a matter of the relation between the *implicit* and the *explicit*.

It is important to understand that the 'as' is indicative of generality. We grasp something 'as' something insofar as we grasp a particular as an instance of a general type. The idea behind the split in the as-structure is that our understanding of this generality can be articulated in two distinct ways, even if these forms of articulation are fundamentally inseparable and always combined to different degrees. We grasp the entities around us principally through the hermeneutic 'as' insofar as the specific possibilities we are immediately presented with by them (e.g., writing a letter) are articulated by an implicit grasp of the general types of equipment they instantiate (e.g., pens and paper *qua* equipment for writing). This implicit grasp is the condition of interpretation, which is the process through which we reconsider these immediate possibilities, taking them apart and bringing forth the generalities that articulate them. However, this process of interpretation is not yet linguistic: it is the move to making assertions about entities that transforms the hermeneutic 'as' into the apophantic 'as'. The latter involves the use of special linguistic equipment to isolate and then rearticulate the general possibilities that constitute these types, thus enabling a process of progressive abstraction which extricates the **causal capacities** of entities from the **normative functions** through which our everyday understanding grasps them. The present-at-hand is nothing but the correlate of the limit-case of this process of abstraction. It is not constituted by *pure presence*, or actuality devoid of possibility, but rather by *pure capacity*, or possibility devoid of function. The exemplars of the present-at-hand are those entities posited by science independently of any role they could have in everyday practices (e.g., electrons, black holes, mitochondria, etc.). Science is thus hardly the domain of pure presence in this vacuous sense, but rather the forefront of our attempt to work out what is *really* possible, over and above the expectations implicit in our parochial forms of life.

The encounter with the broken tool must be understood in terms of this complex interplay between causal capacity and normative function. The important thing to realise is that the tool cannot break unless it behaves in a way it is not *supposed* to: there is no malfunction without proper function. It is the fact that we grasp equipment (e.g., pen and paper) in terms of a set of normatively articulated everyday activities (e.g., letter writing, drawing, doodling, etc.) that enables it to surprise us by *failing* to behave as it should in the context of those activities (e.g., the pen leaking ink all over the paper). This means that we must already encounter the equipment *as* equipment: without a prior hermeneutic 'as', nothing can break. This prior 'as' forms the basis of the response to the encounter, insofar as the surprise malfunction incites us to reinterpret our grasp of the tool's possibilities. This interpretation can then either stay at the hermeneutic level, or be developed apophantically by using assertions to draw out the causal capacities the tool possesses independently of its functional role; or rather, independently of its status *as a tool*. It is in this sense that the encounter with the broken tool amounts to a *transition* between the tool as ready-to-hand and the tool as present-at-hand: it is an invitation to a different form of understanding.

What all of this reveals is that Harman's reading cannot be an interpretation of the substance of Heidegger's ideas—even one that Heidegger himself would disagree with. It is possible to read thinkers against themselves, but this requires that there is some essential element present in their work that the work itself fails to live up to.[41] But the element that Harman tries to unearth in Heidegger's tool-analysis is not even there.[42] The only reason he can propose to extend the intentional relation between Dasein and its tools to cover all interactions between entities is that he has stripped this relation of everything that makes it recognisably Heideggerian. He has excised the structure of projective understanding wholesale, and thereby completely abandoned the semantic and epistemological framework within which the encounter with the tool is described. This becomes clear once we ask a question such as: Just what would it be for a screen door to encounter a knife *as* a knife?[43] Harman has an answer—that it would

---

41.   This is a hermeneutic strategy that Brandom calls *de re* interpretation, as opposed to *de dicto* interpretation: the attempt to be faithful to the subject matter, rather than the words used to express it (Brandom, *Tales of the Mighty Dead*, chapter 1).

42.   Another point to make here about Harman's reading *qua* reading is that even if there were some evidence that Heidegger did see the tool-analysis in something resembling this way, then it would still be far-fetched, given the extent of the other aspects of Heidegger's work it invalidates: theory, mood, space, time, etc. (cf. *Tool-Being*, §§4–7). Harman gives us a long list of features of his thought about which Heidegger can say nothing specific, despite his sincere and extensive attempts to do so. The sheer amount of Heidegger's work that Harman's reading disqualifies thus constitutes a pretty good *reductio ad absurdum* of it as a reading of Heidegger, even if we ignore the misunderstandings just discussed.

43.   This is Harman's own example (*Tool-Being*, 30–32).

consist in the door's being affected by the knife in a way that is common to all knives—yet this does not warrant his using the word 'encounter' in an intentional sense. The screen door has nothing that could qualify it as having anything like an **awareness** of generality. There is no hermeneutic 'as' circumscribing its engagements with things. This leaves us saying that what it is for a screen door to interact with a knife *qua* knife is for it to be affected in the way that knives affect screen doors—an empty tautology unworthy of metaphysical scrutiny.[44]

II. THE ARGUMENT FROM EXECUTION

The principal argument derived from the tool-analysis in *Tool-Being* is what I have called the argument from execution. This argument aims to establish that the reality of entities consists in their execution (or tool-being), and on this basis to demonstrate that they withdraw from all *epistemic* and *causal* contact. Insofar as it is supposed to reconstruct Heidegger's own phenomenological analysis, the argument is presented as a phenomenological description.[45] Its aim is to reveal the **absolute invisibility** of objects *qua* execution, by presenting three interrelated characterisations of execution: as **causal capacity** (or 'effect'), as **pure action** (or 'impact'), and as **functional role** (or 'reference'). However, as already noted, Harman provides no clarification regarding the nature of his phenomenological method, nor how it might be expected to yield metaphysical results. This is complicated by the fact that many of Harman's claims are patently more metaphysical than phenomenological. This raises the possibility

44.   For a further example of Harman's attempt to universalise the as-structure in this way, see his discussion of tectonic plates towards the end of *Tool-Being* (221–2).

45.   *Tool-Being*, 18.

that in some cases he has simply imported metaphysical assumptions instead of collecting phenomenological evidence. We will thus have to be very careful to keep all the elements of his analyses separate in reconstructing their logical form.

Harman's take on Heidegger's phenomenological analysis opens by specifying its object: our ubiquitous encounters with the entities that we 'use' in the course of living. His break with Heidegger's analysis occurs already in this first paragraph:

> Heidegger demonstrates that our primary interaction with beings comes through 'using' them, through simply *counting on them* in an unthematic way. For the most part, objects are implements taken for granted, a vast environmental backdrop supporting the thin and volatile layer of our explicit activities. All human action finds itself lodged amidst countless items of supporting equipment: the most nuanced debates in a laboratory stand at the mercy of a silent bedrock of floorboards, bolts, ventilators, gravity, and atmospheric oxygen.[46]

This break is subtle, and does not become completely apparent until a few pages later, when Harman explicitly substitutes the word 'rely' for 'use'.[47] The examples that Harman focuses on are indicative of this shift. Gone is the emphasis upon equipment *actively deployed* toward a goal (e.g., hammers, cars, signals, etc.), to be replaced with a focus upon 'equipment' necessary to *passively sustain* a given state (e.g., ventilators, gravity, oxygen, etc.). It is not that Heidegger is not concerned with some examples of this kind—sustaining a state is as eligible a goal as achieving one—but rather that Harman

Handwritten margin notes: THE MOVEMENT OF AN OBJECT / THING IS EXHAUSTED / IT MOVES FROM HORIZONTAL / GOAL ORIENTATED TO VERTICAL ↓ FOCUS

"LOOK DOWN"

---

46. Ibid., 18.
47. Ibid., 20.

Handwritten: THE UNI. FORM. SUIT SHIFTZ.

narrows the scope of the analysis by collapsing active use into passive reliance, while simultaneously expanding its scope to include cases of dependence that lack anything that could be construed as *awareness* of the thing depended upon. This move enables execution to take on the role of *persistence* we saw earlier, and at the same time facilitates the *universalisation* of intentionality to encompass all objects, not to mention the flaying of Heidegger's account of intentionality that accompanies it.

We can already see the pretense of phenomenology slipping here. Harman has subtly shifted the focus of his analysis from our practical comportment toward things to our causal dependence upon them. We are invited to conclude that phenomenological description is as apt to describe my relation to my internal organs, the geological strata that I stand upon, or the delicate balance of environmental factors necessary for life on earth as it is to describe my relation to the various socially delineated props I passively engage in carrying out everyday tasks. This shift hinges upon a delicate ambiguity with regard to the sense in which encounters with things can be 'unconscious' or 'unthematic'.[48] It consists in misunderstanding what Heidegger calls *circumspection* (*Umsicht*). Heidegger's intention in introducing this sort of 'unthematic' understanding was to provide a phenomenological analysis of comportments that lacked a *specific kind* of awareness, rather than lacking awareness as such. He would not consider my relation to my internal organs to be an intentional relation unless it consisted in some *implicit grasp* of general ways in which they are involved in carrying out practical activities, either as obstacles (e.g. an

---

48. It is also helped by an ambiguity in the sense of 'reliance', which can be read either as an intentional relation involving an *expectation* regarding whatever is relied upon, or as a matter of brute causal dependence.

awareness of my fickle digestive system) or resources (e.g., the metabolic control achieved by certain yogic masters), or some *explicit grasp* of their general modal features (e.g., the theoretical understanding of a biologist or surgeon). For Heidegger's concern with the 'unconscious' encounter as *awareness without attention*, Harman substitutes a concern with it as *dependence without awareness*.

Bearing all of this in mind, we can turn to the first step in Harman's analysis. This is his claim that *what* we encounter in relying upon equipment is its *causal capacity* to produce the specific effect that we rely upon. This is his first characterisation of the execution that constitutes the reality of the tool, and he vehemently opposes it to the idea that the tool consists in the ways humans expect to use it:

> Equipment is not effective 'because people use it'; on the contrary, it can only be used because it is *capable of an effect*, of inflicting some kind of blow on reality. In short, the tool isn't 'used'—it *is*.[49]

On the face of it, this is a perfectly good inference—successful reliance upon a thing demands that it possess the causal capacity to produce the effect relied upon—but the way in which it is introduced and used by Harman is questionable precisely insofar as it is metaphysical rather than phenomenological. Harman is already straying into metaphysics in describing the thing as *consisting* in this capacity, rather than simply *possessing* it, and he will stray further when he fleshes out his characterisation of this capacity *qua* execution. He does not linger in this register though. He rapidly returns to phenomenology when he insists

---

49. *Tool-Being*, 20.

upon the invisibility of this capacity.[50] But invisibility is apparent only when we focus upon precisely those un-Heideggerian cases that Harman has smuggled in (e.g., the invisibility of my organs). This paradoxical *revelation of invisibility* essentially consists in our discovery that we *really* have no awareness of those things upon which we depend without being aware of it—at least, that is, until we turn our phenomenological gaze upon them. This has no force whatsoever, because there is no correlation between dependence and awareness either way. Prima facie, it is entirely possible for me to be aware or not aware of the things I depend on, to varying degrees.[51] Becoming aware of the myriad environmental factors that make our lives possible does not in and of itself alter our dependence upon them.

Let us move deeper into the nature of execution and its purported invisibility, then. The second characterisation of execution is its status as *pure action*, and this has two aspects: Firstly, the equipment is never what it is simply because it is *capable* of an effect, but must also *enact* this effect at every moment: 'Equipment is forever *in action*, constructing each moment the sustaining habitat where our explicit awareness is on the move.'[52] Secondly, this perpetual action is *unitary:* its effect cannot be broken down into subsidiary actions that might be held in reserve. It must be 'an agent thoroughly deployed in reality, as an *impact* irreducible to any list of

---

50.   Ibid., 21.

51.   No doubt some will claim that although there may indeed be *degrees* of awareness, this never amounts to *complete* awareness, and that this is sufficient to underwrite the putatively 'absolute' character of invisibility. This is a entirely separate argument, which I will deal with in the next subsection as the *argument from excess*.

52.   *Tool-Being*, 18.

properties that might be tabulated by an observer'.[53] There are at least two distinct tensions inherent in this characterisation: a modal tension between *possibility* and *actuality*, and a temporal tension between *dynamism* and *stasis*. The former comes from the contrast between this and the first characterisation of execution in terms of capacity, insofar as it flattens whatever possible effects a thing might have into its current actual effects. The latter comes from the characterisation of the thing as *always already* in action, an act whose occurrence is such that we only encounter it in a state of silent repose, or diachronic transition so pure it is the very essence of synchronic persistence. These tensions are seemingly constitutive for the invisibility of equipment. Try as we might to understand any specific capacity, we never reach the unitary effect that silently whirs behind it:

> Whatever is visible of the table in any given instant can *never* be its tool-being, *never* its readiness-to-hand. However deeply we meditate on the table's act of supporting solid weights, however tenaciously we monitor its presence, any insight that is yielded will always be something quite distinct from *this act itself*.[54]

Try as we might to understand the way an occurrence unfolds, the things it involves are events already past yet ongoing:

> A tool exists in the manner of enacting itself; only derivatively can it be discussed or otherwise mulled over. Try as hard as we

---

53. Ibid., 21.

54. Ibid.

might to capture the hidden execution of equipment, we will always lag behind.[55]

Harman provokes us like a zen master wielding a koan: a pure act rests behind all superficial acts, a pure actuality grounds all potential actualities. One hand claps slowly.[56]

It now seems we may have gone too deep after all. What should we make of these tensions within the account of execution from the perspective of the split between phenomenology and metaphysics? At best, they constitute a brute phenomenological description of dubious plausibility. Despite the *general paradox* of the accessibility of inaccessibility, and the more *specific paradoxes* of modality and temporality it poses, we might simply have to throw up our arms and admit: 'Well, things do *seem* this way, just like he says!' Even so, we should have to be receptive to any analysis that could dissolve these seeming paradoxes, as opposed to using them for effect. At worst, they constitute a series of strange and strained metaphysical assumptions extending the reification of capacity carried out by the first characterisation, assumptions we are given *anything but* good reason to endorse. Just what is really going on here?

Harman seems to have transposed the phenomenological analysis of tools as deployed *in* actions—which he otherwise ignored in favour of *passive dependence*—into a metaphysics of tools *as* actions. This has a peculiar effect that can best be described as 'performative phenomenology'. The revelation of invisibility is merely an artefact of the way in which execution is introduced. The general paradox is underwritten by the

---

55. Ibid., 22.

56. Before withdrawing into itself, and disappearing in a puff of *metaphysics*.

specific ones. We encounter the invisibility of equipment as an *ineffability* engendered by the impossible tensions contained in the ways in which it is described. The supposed demonstration of epistemic inaccessibility is actually an elaborate numbing of our epistemic faculties, performed by multiplying the incompatible aspects of the mysterious withdrawn tool. Single hands don't clap after all.[57]

We now turn to the third and final characterisation of execution: as *functional role*. This builds upon the previous two characterisations by articulating the *effect* which the capacity produces in its pure action as a *means* to an *end* of some sort. This is how Harman cashes out Heidegger's account of *reference* (*Verweis*): he takes every entity to *refer* to those things whose persistence depends upon its own. The reference of a thing's execution is another thing whose execution it *sustains*. Reference and dependence are thus unified into a single relation of functional dependence. This is responsible for Harman's machinic descriptions of entities, insofar as it underwrites his discussion of dependence relations in mereological terms, not merely as between part and whole, but as between component and system. What happens here is that the *causal capacities* actualised in composition are transformed into *normative functions* through being normatively underwritten by the whole they *actually* compose. The various girders, nuts, and bolts that compose a bridge are simultaneously depended upon by the bridge and captured in executing their functional role in sustaining the bridge as a systematic effect upon which further things depend.[58] It is this interpretation of reference relations that collapses Heidegger's account of world into a simple totality, insofar as it takes them

---

57. It turns out to have been a puff of *logic*.

58. *Tool-Being*, 22–25.

to hold exclusively between individuals, understood in terms of their actual states, rather than (as Heidegger intends) within a complex horizon that involves relations between both types and instances, understood in terms of their possible states. According to Harman, this characterisation implies the second fundamental aspect of Heidegger's tool-analysis: what he calls the tool's **totality** as opposed to its invisibility. To understand this, it is important to see that Harman takes functional dependence to extend beyond intuitive forms of *mereological* dependence (e.g., my dependence upon my *internal* organs), to include things like *environmental* dependence (e.g., my dependence upon *external factors* such as gravity and oxygen), and even goes so far as to incorporate *negative* dependence relations (e.g., my dependence upon a meteorite *not* falling from space into me). Moreover, although both dependence and reference are *asymmetric* relations, they go in opposite directions: if *x* depends on *y* then *y* refers to *x*, and each relation is *transitive*, meaning that if *x* depends on *y* and *y* depends on *z*, then *x* depends on *z*, and therefore *z* also refers to *x*. The world becomes a network of functional dependence relations in which each specific entity is individuated through its location relative to everything else. The bridge is what it is in virtue of depending upon precisely what it actually depends upon, and supporting precisely what it actually supports; and the same is true for every nut, bolt, girder, and environmental condition upon which it depends, not to mention everything upon which they depend, ad infinitum; the same is true also for every passing traveller, supply chain, or local business the bridge exists in aid of, and everything they in turn support, ad infinitum. This converts the world from a simple totality of disparate individuals into a unified individual in its own right: the plurality of local systems of execution becomes an integrated network of components in a single global system or 'world-machine'.[59] The numerous ends at which execution aims are subsumed within a single system of ends, the ultimate purpose of which can only be to sustain the system itself.

This produces a relational tension alongside the modal and temporal tensions we have already uncovered. This one is more complicated since it arises from a conflict between the relational holism Harman attributes to Heidegger and the radical individualism that he aims to derive from the principles upon which it is founded. The tension consists in Harman's attempt to convert holism into individualism by transforming execution from something *individuated through* the functional dependence relations it is bound up in, to something *prior to* these relations which makes them possible. This makes the bridge's execution a condition of its relations to the economy of actions it supports, rather than something that consists in those relations. The tension becomes manifest in the way Harman connects totality and invisibility through the characterisation of execution as functional role. His attempt to derive invisibility from functionality is far more reminiscent of Heidegger than the other arguments for invisibility we have discussed: 'The function or reference of the tool is effective not as an explicit sign or symbol, but as something that *vanishes into* the work to which it is assigned.'[60] For Heidegger, our *attention* is inevitably drawn towards the immediate ends of our activity, rather than the various subordinate tasks and the means they involve. We focus upon what we are doing with

---

59. *Tool-Being*, 33.

60. Ibid., 25, my emphasis.

the hammer—putting up shelves—rather than the mechanics of the hammer and our use of it. Nevertheless, this phenomenological insight is not meant to preclude the possibility of our turning our attention to any of these easily overlooked details. Our *awareness* of the task as an articulated whole enables us to shift our attention back to any aspect of it. We shift focus to our grip upon the hammer, thereby adjusting it to optimise the force we can achieve at the odd angle the space allows us. Harman's reading warps this insight: the *activity* becomes the *thing*, and the *focus* of our attention *upon* the end of the activity becomes the *vanishing* of our awareness of the thing *into* whatever it sustains. This mutates further when exposed to Harman's totalising logic of reference: all awareness vanishes into the world-machine, as the unitary activity within which everything plays its sustaining role.[61]

So far, then, Harman appears to have derived the invisibility of everything except the world as a whole from his functional account of individuation. But perhaps the strangest move is yet to come, because he converts this claim about invisibility back into a claim about individuation:

> Every being is entirely absorbed into this world-system, assigned to further possibilities in such a way that there could never be any singular end-point within the contexture of reference. *In the strict sense, the world has no parts.*[62]

It is not merely the *visibility* of the parts but their *distinctness* that collapses into the whole—*vanishing* becomes *absorption*. This is highly problematic, because it uses an account of the

61.   *Tool-Being*, 32–3.

62.   Ibid., 43.

articulation of systems into distinct components to deny that there is any such articulation at all. It presupposes the fact that there are distinct entities with differentiated capacities that can be combined and configured in a variety of ways, only to interpret this combination and configuration in such a way as to deny the distinctness that it is predicated upon.

We would be forgiven for insisting upon a *reductio ad absurdum* of some, if not most, of Harman's premises at this point. He does indeed intend to perform a *reductio* of sorts, but it is not the one we might expect—and indeed, should insist upon.[63] He ignores the inconsistency at the heart of his account of functionality and instead focuses upon the fact that his account of invisibility contradicts the 'existence of [distinct] objects as a glaring experiential fact'.[64] He combines this with a further contradiction he takes to be implied by the account: 'If [this] were the case, physical causation could never occur, since there would be no individual objects, but only a single system, with no explanations for why this system should ever alter'.[65] Harman treats the apparent existence of diachronic causal interaction (as opposed to synchronic causal dependence) and a multiplicity of distinct objects (as opposed to a singular world-machine) as two sides of the same problem.

What is Harman's *reductio* then? What is it that converts Heidegger's purported holism into the radical individualism of OOP? It is the introduction of the break between the *real* and the *sensual*—which is to say, the core of the account of withdrawal. This emerges in Harman's interpretation of the

63. Ibid.

64. Ibid.

65. Ibid., 34.

as-structure and the way he identifies it with the broken-tool encounter.[66] The principal motivation for this theoretical supplement is its ability to diffuse the live contradictions hovering in the background. However, it will only be warranted if it can integrate the three facets of the account of execution into the individualist account of substance, at least in outline, and thereby dissolve the relational tension between this account and its functional foundations. How this is supposed to work, and whether it can also dissolve the accompanying modal and temporal tensions, is now our principal concern. We shall tackle it one contradiction at a time.

On the one hand, Harman aims to resolve the contradiction between functional totality and apparent individuality by reconceiving the very notion of appearance itself. Harman's concern with invisibility up until this point has turned upon an *implicit* conception of awareness, which, as we have seen, has not yet been made *explicit* through the provision of a phenomenological methodology. Nevertheless, the invisibility of things has been 'shown' through purportedly phenomenological analyses of the scope of this awareness. What now changes is that the phenomenal aspect of this implicit conception is explicitly severed from the epistemic aspect: awareness is split in two, so that multiple individuals may *phenomenally appear*, even while the singular whole from which they appear *epistemically withdraws*. We can *see* the hammer, but we can never *know* the intricate system that harbours its hidden essence. This rift constitutes the difference between the hammer as *presence* and the hammer as *execution*, the hammer *as* hammer and the hammer *in itself*, and the *malfunctioning* hammer and the *functioning* hammer,

---

66. Ibid., §4.

respectively. It permits the conversion from invisible to visible in the encounter with the broken tool precisely because the underlying execution of the tool is not *really* made visible. The malfunction throws off an epistemically irrelevant husk that can at best hint at the silent reality of proper functioning.

On the other hand, Harman aims to resolve the contradiction between functional fixity and apparent change by uniting the question of causal interaction and the question of phenomenal presence. Although this is often hinted at, it only becomes completely explicit towards the end of *Tool-Being* itself:

> [T]he time has come to admit to the reader that I have been guilty
> of a deliberate over-simplification [...] In fact, it is impermissible
> to replace the tool/broken tool distinction with the difference
> between causality and visibility. For it turns out that *even brute
> causation already belongs to the realm of presence-at-hand.*[67]

If we accept Harman's identification of presence with malfunction, then the above makes a certain amount of sense: If the world is taken to have a fixed order because it is constituted by a network of functional dependence relations, then any change to this order must amount to a break with these relations, and thus to a malfunction of some sort. This would make the question of interaction/presence a matter of explaining how components rebel against the systems in which they are seemingly subsumed, so as to generate the abundance of individuality in our phenomenal experience. This is not a question Harman takes the tool-analysis to answer. He simply takes it to have posed the problem in the correct terms. Nevertheless, he insists that the analysis implies that any solution must

---

67. *Tool-Being*, 221.

move beyond the *appearance* of individuality to the *reality* of individuality, because entities can break with the functional order in which they are enmeshed only if they hold something in reserve that is not determined by this order.[68] This is where the relational tension becomes most acute: Just how is the account of execution that implies holism to be modified so as to permit the individualism it seemingly demands?

The tension is more serious than might initially be apparent. This is because Harman extends the identification of presence with causality beyond diachronic interaction to include the cases of synchronic dependence upon which his initial characterisations of execution were built. This can be seen in his example of a bulky metal appliance sitting upon a frozen lake: 'When the lake supports the appliance, this act of supporting unfolds entirely within the as-structure, not within the kingdom of tool-being.'[69] It is this move that enables Harman to convert the distinction between execution and presence into the distinction between **substance** and **relation**, insofar as it enables him to treat all causal relations in the same way. Whatever is held in reserve in order to change the relations of functional (and thus causal) dependence that entities are bound up in, withdraws from all current relations, as the substance that underlies them. However, as Harman continues: 'This raises the following question: If the fact that the frozen lake supports an object is *not* its tool-being, then *what is*?'[70] As he puts it slightly earlier:

In short, tool-being is not at all what we have thought it was

---

68.   Ibid., 229–30.

69.   Ibid., 223.

70.   Ibid.

up till now. It must lie at a still deeper level than that of force or relation. It is no longer an effect as opposed to an appearance, but rather an executant *being* that is neither of these.[71]

We are once more told what execution *is not*, but we are still none the wiser about just what it *is*.

Here is where we stand then: The relational tension consists in the fact that Harman's individualist conception of execution as *substance* is incompatible with the holistic conception of execution as *functional role* from which it is derived; but he does not make clear which aspects of the latter conception are abandoned, and thus precisely how the former differs from it, apart from its purported individualism. He does not stop characterising execution in terms of function.[72] He continues to think of objects in terms of systematic unity.[73] When he needs to talk about the substantial reserve that necessitates individuality, he simply turns to his earlier characterisations of execution: it stands independent of all relations as an actuality 'richer than all possibility'[74] and prior to all effects as a 'real execution, silently resting in its vacuum-sealed actuality'.[75] Far from dissolving the modal and temporal tensions discussed above, he intensifies them, and he nowhere provides an account of how the functional character of execution is to be curtailed, let alone how it is to be integrated with its status as capacity and act. When they are acknowledged, the three tensions we have located (modal,

---

71.   Ibid., 222.

72.   Cf. Ibid., 285.

73.   Cf. Ibid., 288.

74.   Ibid., 229.

75.   Ibid., 283.

temporal, and relational) are presented as paradoxical intuitions that open up room for further metaphysical speculation, but, at best, they are an argument left hanging.[76] Harman has not yet succeeded in discharging the contradictions that arise from his assumptions. He has failed to provide us with a good reason to adopt his partial reconstruction of what he takes to be Heidegger's inconsistent system, rather than simply rejecting its core presuppositions.

How does this reflect upon the relation between phenomenology and metaphysics? Let's take one last look. I think the core methodological issues emerge from the attempt to provide an account of modality. Here it is useful to contrast Harman's approach with the brief summary of Heidegger we provided earlier. Heidegger provides us with an intricate modal epistemology. He builds a phenomenological framework within which he analyses both our understanding of the entities we encounter in terms of the *normative features* they acquire through the practices we are socialised into, the unthematic understanding of the *causal features* of these entities that is implicit in this, and the various levels of thematic understanding that can be developed out of it. His analysis of the encounter with the broken tool is a subtle demonstration of the interface between these levels of modal understanding.

By contrast, Harman's approach can only be described as **modal mysterianism**. It begins with *phenomenological descriptions* of our experience of things, from which it derives a pseudo-Heideggerian functional vocabulary, but almost immediately converts this into a *metaphysical inquiry* into our causal relations with things, in the process hypostatizing this

---

76.   Harman explicitly presents two unresolved paradoxes at the end of *Tool-Being* (287–8), but they are not the tensions I have outlined here, which emerge more sporadically throughout the work.

functional vocabulary into a **metaphysical teleology**. It is important to emphasise how contentious this move is. There are deep and divisive arguments about the reality of functions running from Plato and Aristotle, through Leibniz and Spinoza, Kant and Hegel, all the way to contemporary debates regarding the correct interpretation of Darwin. Harman makes this move not by providing a compelling reason for it, but by simply ignoring an important methodological distinction. As we have seen, the other claims he makes about the metaphysical basis of causal capacities are equally methodologically suspect. Where Heidegger does his best to delineate the modal relations between normative functions and causal capacities, showing both how they differ and how they are related, Harman systematically conflates them under the single heading of execution, which he then fails to sufficiently integrate. Thus his purported justification for epistemic inaccessibility on the basis of these modal features (excess) is stuck halfway between a questionable attempt to *phenomenologically delimit* phenomenal access (the revelation of invisibility), and a dubious *metaphysical reinterpretation* of phenomenal access itself that simultaneously undercuts his phenomenological pretensions (the split in awareness) and fails to provide a coherent account of the inaccessible (the unresolved tensions). The philosophical framework he builds in *Tool-Being* leaves us with no grasp of what tool-being *is*—and simply to decree that 'that's the point!' is to lapse into mysterianism.

III. THE ARGUMENT FROM EXCESS

The other argument that Harman associates with the tool-analysis, which I have called the argument from excess, can be found intermingled with elements of the argument from execution at several points in *Tool-Being* and elsewhere,[77] but it becomes the dominant strain of argument by the time of his presentation of the tool-analysis in *Philosophy in the Making*.[78] It is fairly brief, and its conclusion is more often simply asserted than properly derived from its premises, but it is possible to reconstruct a reasonably concise version of it on the basis of these examples. I will first quote the relevant sections from the Meillassoux book, to provide a basis for reconstruction:

> In Heideggerian terms it is true that phenomena in consciousness fail to do justice to the full depths of things, to their inscrutable being withdrawn from all presence. Yet it is *also* the case that the practical handling of entities fails to do them justice as well [...] [H]uman theory and human praxis are both translations or distortions of the subterranean reality of [tool-being], which is no more exhausted by sentient action than by sentient thought.[79]

Here Harman opens with an outright assertion of the thesis of withdrawal, but he frames it in two important ways. He articulates it as a matter of the **inexhaustibility** of tool-being, and he identifies theoretical understanding and practical use in terms of their inability to exhaust it. The framing of withdrawal in terms of inexhaustibility will form the centrepiece of the argument, whereas the identification of theory and praxis paves the way for the more controversial identification

---

77. Cf. *Tool-Being*, 96, 98, 223; 'A Fresh Look at Zuhandenheit', in *Towards Speculative Realism*, 54–5; 'The Revival of Metaphysics in Continental Philosophy', in *Towards Speculative Realism*, 116–17.

78. *Philosophy in the Making*, 135–6.

79. Ibid., 135.

of knowledge and causation. This is followed by a sort of retroactive argument for withdrawal that works from within this frame:

> All of these activities could possibly be linked under the term 'intentionality', but whereas the intentionality of Brentano and Husserl is a matter of *immanent* objectivity, we are now concerned with a transcendent kind of object. It is true that the hammer takes on a specific configuration both for the construction worker and for the scientific specialist on hammers (assuming the latter person exists). But what is most relevant here is the *transcendent* hammer that startles us with surprises, shattering in our hands or rotting and rusting more quickly than expected. The present-at-hand hammer cannot explain these sudden surprises, and hence by subtraction we arrive at the notion of a withdrawn, subterranean tool that enters into relation with me and other animate and inanimate entities as well.[80]

What we have here is an argument that aims to proceed from the *obvious fact* that the causal capacities of an object can exceed our understanding of them (and thereby 'surprise' us) to the *contentious claim* that we cannot encounter the real objects in which this excess consists, but only the distinct sensual objects that they withdraw behind.

What follows is my best attempt to reconstruct the transition between the two. I shall begin by splitting the obvious fact into two fairly uncontentious claims:

> (i) Our knowledge of things does not exhaust all of their features. There is more to them than we actually know.

---

80.   Ibid., 136.

(ii) Our causal interactions with things do not exhaust all their capacities. There is more to them than we actualise.

Harman obviously adopts the example of the hammer's causal capacities exceeding our grasp from the analysis of the broken tool; but its real import comes from the manner in which it straddles the divide between (i) and (ii). Although his various presentations will emphasise one or the other, the justification of the thesis of withdrawal depends upon equivocating between these two claims in some fashion, be it by leaning upon aspects of the argument from execution (e.g., interpreting praxis as reliance) or by simply treating the identity of intentional and causal relations as a given. This equivocation exemplifies the collapse of phenomenology and metaphysics into one another discussed earlier. What is important is that the combination of (i) and (ii) gets interpreted in a somewhat more contentious way than either of them:

(iii) Our knowledge/interactions can *never* exhaust all the features/capacities of things. There is more to them than we could *possibly* encounter.

This move converts a *factual excess* of features/capacities into an *essential excess*. The move is strictly illicit, but, although it leads to a stronger claim than either (i) or (ii), it is still not all that contentious. There are many who would agree with (iii) for independent reasons, or simply because it is reasonably intuitive. The really contentious claims are those that are subsequently inferred from (iii):

(iv) Our knowledge/interactions can never exhaust all the

features of a thing, because there is some feature of every thing *qua* thing that we can never encounter.

This move aims to explain the necessity of excess by locating it in a feature *common* to all things, as opposed to something which *varies* from thing to thing. It holds that excess is essential because there is an essential feature of entities that is excessive. This makes sense if one demands an *intrinsic* explanation of excess which locates the reason for the excess in the encountered object, as opposed to an *extrinsic* one which locates it in the encountering object. When the latter is understood as a *knowing subject*, the extrinsic explanation of excess has traditionally taken the name of *finitude*. This posits an internal limit upon the cognitive abilities of the subject that precludes it from knowing objects in full. This limit need not be interpreted in terms of some common *qualitative excess*, but could be seen as a disparate *quantitative excess*. It could simply be the case that the subject can only grasp a finite number of the infinity of features belonging to each thing, but that there is no *particular* feature that is in principle ungraspable.

Harman insists upon an intrinsic explanation, as can be seen in the above quote, but it is important to recognise that this is underwritten by the equivocation between knowledge and causation: 'I am convinced that objects far exceed their interactions with other objects, and the question is both *what* this excess is, and *where* it is.'[81] In other words, he takes the issue of essential excess to be equivalent to the issue of *substantial reserve* discussed in the argument from execution.[82]

---

81. 'The Revival of Metaphysics in Continental Philosophy', in *Towards Speculative Realism*, 117.

82. This is precisely how the arguments intertwine in *Tool-Being* (223).

The localisation of epistemic excess is thus predicated upon the localisation of causal excess. This sets the stage for the final (and most contentious) inference:

> (v) Our knowledge/interactions can never exhaust a thing, because we can never encounter the *essence* of the thing. We only encounter the (*sensual*) *appearance* of the thing, never its (*real*) *being*.

This move converts the essential excess into an *excessive essence*. Harman takes the common essential feature of all things that cannot be encountered to be *what things are in themselves*, or essence *as such*. This is supposed to warrant the absolute distinction between the real and the sensual, insofar as it implies that whatever epistemic/causal contact there is with a thing must be contact with something *other* than what it really is. It thereby moves from localisation to isolation. However, this exploits the same equivocation as (iv), albeit in reverse, insofar as it makes sense of causal isolation in terms of epistemic isolation. While it is easy to understand withdrawal as the impossibility of *direct epistemic access*, it is much less clear how we are to understand independence as the impossibility of *direct causal contact*. There is a clear quantitative line from *some* access to *no* access, because we can intuitively grasp what it would be to completely fail to know anything about a thing despite seeming to; but there is no such clear line from *some* contact to *no* contact, because we cannot intuitively grasp what it would be to completely fail to activate any of a thing's capacities, despite seeming to.

Of course, this is not how Harman conceives of independence. He bypasses the quantitative considerations involved in (i) to (iv) by treating that which underlies causal interaction as a unitary execution as opposed to a multiplicity of distinct capacities. The actualisation of capacities through causal contact is then treated as something qualitatively distinct from the *independent substance* which underlies them, much as the appearance of features through phenomenal access is treated as qualitatively distinct from the *withdrawn essence* which underlies them. This qualitative break is what divides execution and causation into distinct forms of actuality (modal tension) and activity (temporal tension). The equivocation between knowledge and causation thus disguises an illicit leap from quantitative to qualitative excess, along with the mysterian tensions it invokes.

The overall shape of this argument is thus another *reductio ad absurdum* of sorts. It begins by assuming that there is partial contact between objects, only to try to demonstrate that its essentially partial character implies the impossibility of any contact at all. It slides easily from quantity to quality on the back of Harman's characteristic universalisation of inten-tional relation, but as with the argument from execution, this conceals problems that warrant rejecting the terms in which it is framed. However, there is a further aspect of the move from quantity to quality worth considering:

> But the following objection to this theory often arises: why exag-gerate and say that things cannot touch at all? Does it not seem instead that things *partly* make contact with each other? [...] The problem is that objects cannot be touched 'in part,' because there is a sense in which objects have no parts.[83]

---

83.   *The Quadruple Object* (Winchester: Zero Books, 2010), 73.

Harman is very insistent that withdrawal is complete. Our knowledge of things is not merely limited, but entirely inadequate. Objects are foreclosed to us. But here he presents the mereological missing link in his reasoning from quantitative excess to qualitative excess. It seems that he takes the idea that a whole is *more* than its parts to imply that the whole is *entirely distinct* from its parts, such that to know the parts is not to know the whole—not even partially, as it were. This is somewhat questionable, but it is not the whole story, since it only works if we treat the features and/or capacities of objects as if they are parts. This provides a path between (iv) and (v), but it is a highly dubious one.

IV. THE ARGUMENT FROM IDENTITY

The final argument, which I call the argument from identity, will require even more reconstruction than the argument from excess. This is because, although it is frequently invoked, it is usually presented without a detailed analysis of how it is supposed to work. Though it does appear in the context of the tool-analysis,[84] usually in conjunction with some form of the argument from excess, it also appears independently,[85] as the snappiest and most condensed statement of the case for withdrawal. The most explicit presentation it has so far received is in Harman's criticism of James Ladyman and Don Ross's *Every Thing Must Go*, which I will quote at length:

> Let's imagine that we were able to gain exhaustive knowledge of
> all properties of a tree (which I hold to be impossible, but never

---

84. Cf. *Tool-Being*, 224; *Philosophy in the Making*, 136.

85. Cf. *Guerrilla Metaphysics*, 83, 103; *Prince of Networks*, 132; *The Quadruple Object*, 28, 73.

mind that for the moment). It should go without saying that even such knowledge would not itself be a tree. Our knowledge would not grow roots or bear fruit or shed leaves, at least not in a literal sense. Even in the case of God, the exhaustive knowledge of a tree and creation of a tree would have to be two separate acts. Now, it has sometimes been objected to this point that it is a straw man. After all, who confuses knowledge of a tree with an actual tree? The answer, of course, is that no one does, since no one could openly identify a thing with knowledge of it and still keep a straight face. Yet the point is not that people defend this view openly, which they do not. Rather, the point is that many people uphold a model of the real that *entails* that knowledge of a tree and a real tree would be one and the same, and hence their views are refuted by reductio ad absurdum. Namely, if someone holds that there is an isomorphic relationship between knowledge and reality, such that reality can be fully mathematized, then it also follows that a perfect mathematical model of a thing should be able to step into the world and do the labor of that thing. But this is absurd.[86]

The essence of this argument is the attempt to derive the impossibility of *complete knowledge* of a thing from the *onto-logical distinction* between a thing and our knowledge of it. Although it sometimes appears that this invocation of non-identity is an argument for withdrawal proper, it is really an argument for the epistemic component of premise (iii) of the argument from excess. The rejection of *complete* knowledge must then be leveraged into a rejection of *partial* knowledge, as is clear from the article just quoted, in which the above

---

86. 'I am also of the opinion that materialism must be destroyed', in *Society and Space*, vol. 28 (2010), 788–9.

section finishes with a short appeal to the mereological component of the argument from excess discussed above.[87]

The inference from ontological distinction to the impossibility of complete knowledge once more takes the form of a *reductio ad absurdum*. The principle that underlies it is the claim that complete knowledge of a thing would somehow have to be identical to the thing, thereby contradicting ontological distinction. It is this principle which is nowhere given a detailed analysis, and which therefore we must reconstruct. The major problem we face here is that Harman's use of the term 'knowledge' is never really backed up by an *epistemology* that could answer questions about the distinction between completeness and incompleteness, how this relates to the distinction between correctness and incorrectness, and whether knowledge of an object is composed of distinct representations. I have thus endeavoured to reconstruct the argument on the basis of reasonable assumptions about what Harman means by knowledge, the most important of which is that although Harman tends to simply talk about knowledge of an object as a unitary phenomenon (e.g., knowing a tree), the notion of completeness/incompleteness implies that this must be composed out of correct representations of distinct features of the object (e.g., its species, size, shape, colouration, location, etc.). I shall thus begin with some premises that codify this implicit epistemology:

> (i) For any representation of an object to be *correct*, the object must in some sense be *the same* as it is represented as being: I know the tree is an elm only if I represent it as being an elm *and*

---

87.   Ibid., 789.

the tree is actually an elm, or if the *tree-for-me* and the *tree-in-itself* are the same in the relevant respect.

(ii) For a *composite* representation of an object to be correct, every distinct *piece* of it must be correct: my representation of the tree will not amount to knowing the tree if I misrepresent its structure, despite correctly representing its species, or if there is a *difference* between the *tree-for-me* and the *tree-in-itself*.

(iii) For a composite representation of an object to be *complete*, it must be both *correct* and *exhaustive*: I know the tree completely only if there is no feature of the tree that is not accurately represented by some component of my representation of it as a whole.

From these premises it is then possible to infer the following claim:

(iv) For any knowledge of an object to be complete, the *object-for-us* and the *object-in-itself* must be *the same in every respect*.

We now only require Leibniz's principle of the identity of indiscernibles to reach the principle from which our contradiction is derived:

(v) For any knowledge of an object to be complete, the *object-for-us* and the *object-in-itself* must be *identical*.

This means that, as long as we have good reason to think that the object-for-us and the object-in-itself must be ontologically distinct, the *reductio* will work. Harman's argument depends upon the self-evidence of this fact.

However, if we dig into this self-evidence, we will find that all is not as straightforward as it might initially seem. I take the intuitive basis for ontological distinction to be the conjunction of two ideas: what I'll call the **possibility of error** and the **necessity of identity**. The former is the idea that for any representation to *be* a representation there must be a possibility of its being incorrect, because correctness makes no sense without the possibility of incorrectness. The latter is the generally accepted principle that if two things are identical it is not possible that they could have been distinct. If we add these to (v), we can derive ontological distinction by *reductio ad absurdum*. This is because, if the object-for-us and the object-in-itself were identical, then our knowledge of the object would be necessarily complete, and therefore its component representations would have to be infallible, thereby violating the possibility of error. However, the fact that this demonstration includes (v) should give us pause for thought. It indicates that there is something fishy about the connection between (v) and ontological distinction, something that should be pursued further. What it indicates is that (v) already has some onto-logical content. Some potentially questionable metaphysical assumptions have been snuck in via the back door.[88]

---

88. It should be noted that to reject these questionable assumptions and the hasty proof of ontological distinction given above is not necessarily to reject the brute fact of ontological distinction. Another way of looking at the issue is to say that our knowledge (or its *representational content*) and its object are distinct by *default*, insofar as, *pace* Harman, the question of their iden-tity simply cannot arise. To give a parallel example, Julius Caesar is distinct from the number 9 because, although we have procedures for determining whether numbers are identical, and whether people are identical, we have no procedures that cross the number/person divide. Similarly, we have ways of

There is an illicit assumption concealed in (i) that only becomes explicit with the invocation of the identity of indiscernibles in inferring (v) from (iv). It all comes down to how the notion of *sameness* is interpreted. In order for the inference from (iv) to (v) to work—that is, in order for us to conclude that the object-for-us and the object-in-itself are identical from the fact that they must be the same in every respect— the uncontroversial idea that a correct representation must somehow *represent* the object as being the same as it actually is, must be converted into the much more controversial idea that a correct representation must somehow *be* the same as the object is. This means that correctly representing some feature of an object is interpreted as standing in some relation to *another* object that also possesses that feature. Knowing that the tree-in-itself is an elm involves standing in some curious relation to a tree-for-me that is an elm *in precisely the same sense* as the tree-in-itself. For the principle of the identity of indiscernibles to work, the object-for-us and the object-in-itself must not only be able to have the same features, they must also possess these features in the same sense. What this shows is that the argument from identity can contribute to the proof of withdrawal only if Harman is allowed to base his epistemology upon a metaphysical distinction (object-for-us/object-in-itself) closely resembling the distinction between the sensual object and the real object it is intended to demonstrate. The *fact* of a distinction between types of object is already given, even if

---

determining whether representational contents are identical (e.g., whether you and I are saying *the same* thing in speaking the same sentence), and these are not necessarily compatible with our procedures for identifying the objects they represent.

2. HEIDEGGER, HUSSERL, AND KRIPKE

Moving on to the second aspect of Harman's system, the *fourfold* obviously emerges from the combination of the real/sensual distinction provided by the arguments for withdrawal with the object/quality distinction. There are a number of different ways in which Harman introduces the latter distinction and thereby facilitates this emergence. However, the fourfold lacks any obvious counterpart to withdrawal's tool-analysis: there is no single argument which stands out above all others. Rather, there is a mix of the three forms of exposition, which, although it can be broken down into two core arguments—the argument from **eidos** (taken from Husserl) and the argument from **essence** (taken from Leibniz, Zubiri, and Kripke)—is principally organised by Harman's interpretation of Heidegger's famous fourfold (*das Geviert*) of earth (*Erde*), sky (*Himmel*), gods (*Göttlichen*) and mortals (*Sterblingen*). As such, we must once more preface our examination of Harman's own arguments with a brief analysis of his reading of Heidegger.

I. HARMAN'S HEIDEGGER REVISITED

Harman's reading of the fourfold is to be praised for refusing either to sideline it as an unimportant feature of Heidegger's work, or to deny the numerical specificity of the categories constituting it. Moreover, it is to be commended for interpreting these categories as the result of the intersection of two distinctions that it basically gets right: cleared/concealed, and multiple/unitary. It is in the interpretation of these distinctions that everything goes wrong. The most serious problem is that Harman conflates the more well-known fourfold discussed above with another fourfold schema found earlier in Heidegger's works—namely, in his lecture course during the Freiburg Emergency War Semester of 1919. This is the intersection of a distinction between the *pre-theoretical* (*vortheoretische*) and the *theoretical* (*theoretische*) and a distinction between the generic and the specific, producing these four categories: the *preworldly something* (*vorweltliche Etwas*), the *world-laden something* (*welthaftes Etwas*), the *formal-logical objective something* (*formallogisches gegenständliches Etwas*), and the *object-type something* (*objektartiges Etwas*).[90] This is complicated by the fact that Harman also misreads the 1919 schema, reading its concern with the 'something' as a matter of singularity as opposed to universality, of beings as opposed to Being.

It is understandable that Harman takes the pre-theoretical/ theoretical distinction to correspond to his own real/sensual distinction, but, as we have already seen, this is a misreading of Heidegger's concern with the difference between the ready-to-hand and the present-at-hand. The latter is not a distinction between that which is understood (the sensual) and that which exceeds understanding (the real), but a distinction between theoretical (apophantic) and pre-theoretical (hermeneutic) modes of understanding. The more serious error is that he confuses the distinction between beings considered *generically* (beings *qua* beings) and beings considered *specifically* (e.g., this pen, that piece of paper, etc.) with the distinction between the *unitary* bearer of qualities (e.g., this pen, *qua this*) and the *multiplicity* of its qualities (e.g., this pen *qua* pen, *qua* plastic, *qua* blue, etc.). Although in considering something as

---

90. T. Kisiel, *The Genesis of Heidegger's Being and Time* (Oakland, CA: University of California Press, 1992), 21–5.

a generic something we are indeed abstracting away from its specific determinations, we are not thereby moving from multiplicity to unity: the object-type something is already unitary; it is simply a unit of a specific type (e.g., a pen) with many other specific features (e.g., it is made of plastic, it is blue, etc.). The point is not to investigate the *singularity* of each being as distinct from the *plurality* of its qualities, but to investigate the *universality* of its Being as distinct from the *particularity* of its type and its other features. In essence, the 1919 schema is an early articulation of the connection between projective understanding and the question of Being: it circumscribes the relationship between the general structure of our theoretical understanding of beings (formal-logical objective something) and the primordial source of our understanding (pre-worldly something). This is just what Heidegger will later characterise as the relationship between Being and time.[91]

The later fourfold most famously appears in an essay entitled 'The Thing' (1950), in Heidegger's analysis of the conditions under which a humble jug appears to us. But hints of the themes that compose it appear at least as early as his masterful 'On the Origin of the Work of Art' (1935) and run rampant across the jumble of musings that compose *Contributions to Philosophy* (1936–8). Harman overlooks these for the most part, in favour of his attempt to read a continuity with the 1919 schema. It is ironic, then, that his interpretation of the twin distinctions that constitute the fourfold gains more traction upon these works.

---

91. Of course, Heidegger never provided a complete account of his analysis of Being in terms of time. The third division of part one of *Being and Time* which was supposed to contain this analysis was never published, although we have fragments of the ideas that would have made it up in the form of *Basic Problems of Phenomenology*, which provides the most extensive version of the analysis, along with the best account the projection of Being upon the primordial source of temporal understanding (*Temporalität*).

This is because what they present is essentially a modification and extension of the account of the strife between earth and world briefly discussed earlier. The important differences are that: (a) world *qua* projected space of possibility is renamed *sky*; (b) Dasein's role in the projection of this space is made explicit in the form of *mortals*; and (c) the enigmatic *gods* are added as a counterpart to mortals. This leaves us with a split between a unitary *horizon* of appearance (sky), multiple agents who *clear* this horizon (mortals), a unitary locus of *resistance* to this clearing (earth), and multiple foci where this resistance is *hinted* at within the horizon itself (gods). The mirror play between these four is then nothing but an extended account of *strife*: the process through which we attempt to negotiate a coherent and comprehensive grasp of reality by wrestling with that reality itself.

Harman underplays Heidegger's version of the cleared/concealed and multiple/unitary axes in order to draw a continuity with his own fourfold.[92] The crucial difference between them is that Heidegger interprets the multiple/unitary axis as a distinction between beings *as such* (the plurality of beings) and beings *as a whole* (the totality of beings), whereas Harman interprets it as the distinction between the multiplicity of a being's *qualities* and its singularity as *bearer* of these qualities. This reflects their differing interpretation of the other axis, insofar as the later Heidegger understands concealing principally in terms of the whole (earth), of which particular concealings (gods) are derivative, whereas Harman takes particular concealings to be, not only the primary, but the only real form of

---

92. I say 'underplays' here because there are points at which he seems to recognise that Heidegger's later schema simply does not fit his own. This is somewhat implicit in *Tool-Being* (266), but it is explicit by the time of *The Quadruple Object* (87–8).

concealing (withdrawal). Harman does not so much think that the whole conceals itself, as that it doesn't exist. It is nothing but the mutual withdrawal of every being from every other.[93] This raises the issue of the relation between the multiple/unitary distinction and the part/whole distinction. Harman's rejection of the whole turns on interpreting it not merely as the totality of beings, but as a single being composed out of all other beings. As we have seen, this is precisely how he interprets Heidegger's account of totality. This makes Heidegger's position into a variant of what he would call onto-theology, insofar as it comprehends Being in terms of a single privileged being. This misinterpretation reveals a deeper issue though, insofar as Harman seems to blend these two distinctions in explaining his own schema. Specifically, the multiplicity of a thing's real qualities and its unity as bearer of these qualities is often exchanged for the distinction between the thing's real parts and its unity as the whole these parts compose.[94] This conflation sometimes comes out into the open, only to disappear once more.[95] We must be careful not to let it pass without notice.

---

93. *Tool-Being*, 294–6.

94. This is most explicit in the section of *Tool-Being* where he explains the distinction between real objects and real qualities by way of Zubiri's account of essence: 'The object lives with a dual tension in its breast. On the one hand it fluctuates between the vacuum of its tool-being and the power of its impact on neighbouring beings. *On the other hand it is itself a systematic empire swarming with interior parts*'. (266, my emphasis).

95. The sheer extent of this is dramatised across *Guerrilla Metaphysics*, in which the distinction between parts and qualities finally becomes evident, as if suddenly discovered, only to metamorphose through a number of different forms (cf. §7B, §10, §11) before finally settling upon a rejection of the plurality of qualities in favour of the plurality of parts (228–9). A detailed commentary upon these convoluted transitions is beyond the scope of this book (although see chapter 3.2, subsection II); but the need for one is ameliorated by the subsequent fading of this bold position in the formulation of the object/quality distinction presented in *The Quadruple Object* (cf. 88).

III. THE ARGUMENT FROM EIDOS

It is clear that any argument Harman presents for his fourfold schema and the categorical structures he derives from it will inevitably depend upon the arguments for withdrawal we have already presented. Beyond this, Harman does not really need to argue for the distinction between objects and qualities, at least insofar as it is a correlate of the intuitive distinction between subjects and predicates. Rather, what must be argued for is his interpretation of the way this distinction intersects with the distinction between the real and the sensual, to create a divide between two kinds of quality. The first such argument we will consider, from *The Quadruple Object*, attempts to reverse-engineer this distinction by independently deriving one of the categories that emerges out of it. It aims to demonstrate the divide between kinds of quality from within experience itself by appropriating Husserl's phenomenological analysis of *eidos*. Harman is fond of remarking that despite the avowedly idealist character of Husserlian phenomenology, it nevertheless has a distinctly realist flavour.[96] He finds this flavour concentrated in the analysis of eidos, where he attempts to separate it out from the bitter overtones of Husserl's idealism.

Harman begins by introducing Husserl's theory of **adumbration** (*Abschattung*).[97] The basic idea underlying this phenomenological concept is that in ordinary perception we encounter things from different perspectives, and that the way the thing is presented may vary between them, highlighting some features and concealing others, despite the object remaining the same. We can stand outside a house and view

96.   E.g. *The Quadruple Object*, 20.

97.   Ibid., §1B.

it from various angles, and even walk within it, touching its walls and smelling its scents, but we are always encountering the same house, even if the encounters themselves are distinct. From this, Harman draws the phenomenological insight that the object is distinct from the qualities that it presents in these adumbrations, not because it is *more* than them, but because there is some sense in which it is *less* than them. This is because it is possible to *subtract* them from the object without its ceasing to be the same object. However, there is a limit upon subtraction, because if we could subtract *all* of a sensual object's qualities there would be nothing to distinguish it from other such objects.[98] There are some *essential* features without which the sensual object cannot be what it is, and it is possible to compare different adumbrations of the same object and strip away the *inessential* features they present, in order to leave these behind. Husserl calls this process **eidetic variation**, and its result, *eidos*.

Harman then claims that, according to Husserl, eidetic qualities are never revealed in perceptual adumbrations in the way that accidental ones are, but only through the process of eidetic variation, or the categorial intuition that arises from it. Harman then criticises Husserl, and amends his account in the following way:

> Husserl is wrong to distinguish between the sensual and the intellectual here; both sensual and categorial intuition are forms of intuition, and to intuit something *is not the same as to be it*. Hence the eidetic features of any object can never be made present even through the intellect, but can only be

---

98. Ibid., §1C.

approached indirectly by way of allusion, whether in the arts or in the sciences.[99]

The argument from identity thus makes a reappearance here to invoke the split between the real and the sensual. But what is more important is the way this is configured in relation to the analysis of eidetic variation. Harman draws a distinction between sensual and intellectual modes of engagement with a thing's eidetic features, only to collapse it by insisting that these features must lie beyond both. He thus converts the distinction between accidental and eidetic features into his distinction between sensual and real qualities: 'For the qualities of its eidos are also withdrawn from all access, and "real" is the only possible name for such a feature.'[100] Here we once again encounter the strange interface between metaphysics and phenomenology in Harman's work. Just what is eidetic variation if the features it was supposed to reveal can never actually be revealed?

The truth of the matter is that Harman had parted ways with Husserl long before this move was made. Husserl's concept of eidos is an account of general essence, as opposed to the account of individual essence that Harman is attempting to develop. Husserl principally talks about eidetic hierarchies of *genus* and *species* (e.g., the eidetic features of trees as opposed to those of elms) which eidetic variation and its corresponding modes of intuition allow us to traverse on the basis of our intuitions of individuals.[101] He insists that all eidetic features

99. Ibid., 28, my emphasis.

100. Ibid.

101. E. Husserl, *Ideas Pertaining to a Pure Phenomenology and to a Phenomenological Philosophy, I,* tr. F. Kersten (Dordrecht: Kluwer, 1982), 8–15.

'*belonging to the essence of the individuum another individuum can have too*',[102] in contrast to the idea that eidos could be *unique* to a given sensual object. However, this claim is not just in conflict with Harman's take on essence, but also with his take on the qualities that compose it: 'qualities as described in this book are always individualised by the object to which they belong.'[103] Harman not only thinks that the process of eidetic variation aims at what makes a sensual object the unique individual that it is; he thinks that it does so by considering qualities that are unique to it *qua* individual. This dearth of generality means that there is no basis for the process of comparison, insofar as there are no qualities that could possibly be shared.[104] This makes the basis of the process of subtraction entirely mysterious, as there are no criteria for sorting accidents from eidos.[105]

In essence, what Harman does here is capitalise upon this mystery, in a manner similar to that we have seen in

---

102. Ibid., 8.

103. *The Quadruple Object*, 30.

104. We have already seen this dearth of generality in Harman's interpretation of Heidegger's phenomenology (cf. *Tool-Being*, 84–5), but it is equally present in his reading of Husserl's. For instance, the example of the phenomenological reduction he presents in *Guerrilla Metaphysics* (§10B) never moves beyond the level of the individual, but simply decomposes sensual wholes into sensual parts and explores the relations between them. We will discuss this further in chapter 3.2, subsection II.

105. Going further than this, in 'On Vicarious Causation' (in R. Mackay [ed.], *Collapse* vol. 2 [Falmouth: Urbanomic, 2007], 171–205), Harman claims that Husserl's method is superficial, because it cannot analyse eidetic qualities without turning them into 'something like accidents' (214). He even goes so far as to claim that, not only are qualities individualised, but there is really only one quality—the singular eidos. He thus sees eidetic variation as a sort of frantic scrabbling to unwrap a present in which we never reach the gift itself, only ever more layers of wrapping paper.

the arguments from execution and excess. He converts the absence of criteria for *differentiating* between essential and inessential qualities in any given case into an *absolute difference* between essential and inessential qualities in all cases. That there are no conceivable features that could be the end point of the process of determining eidos so described is used as a reason to treat eidetic features as inconceivable. Ultimately, the paucity of Harman's account of eidetic variation is actually best indicated by the way he appeals to *allusion* to fill it in. Not only does this bear no resemblance to the Husserlian phenomenological method on which the argument is supposedly founded, but it raises difficult questions about the categorical schema derived from the fourfold, insofar as it seemingly conflates *allure* (space-fusion) with *theory* (time-fission).

III. THE ARGUMENT FROM ESSENCE

The second argument for the distinction between sensual qualities and real qualities is less localised. It must be reconstructed out of two components that are liberally spread throughout Harman's work, one associated with Kripke's work on *rigid designators*,[106] and one associated with Leibniz and Zubiri's work on individuation and essence.[107] When taken together, these components allow for a reverse-engineering of the distinction similar to that of the argument from eidos, by deriving the corresponding category of *essence*. Also like the argument from eidos, it depends upon the distinction between sensual and real established by the arguments for withdrawal.

---

106. Cf. *Tool-Being*, 124, 213–15; *Guerrilla Metaphysics*, 28–9, 108–10, 197–8; *Prince of Networks*, 175; *The Quadruple Object*, 67.

107. Cf. *Tool-Being*, §§23–24; *Guerrilla Metaphysics*, 82–3, 147, 162, 192; *The Quadruple Object*, 48–9.

This is because it needs to conceive the relation between the sensual object and the real object in terms of *reference*. This does not mean that it must be described in terms of Heideggerian functional relations between *things* and *things* (*Verweis*), but rather that it must be described in terms amenable to the debates regarding how *words* relate to *things* inaugurated by Frege's theory of sense (*Sinn*) and reference (*Bedeutung*). This is facilitated by the fact that the Husserlian terms in which Harman couches his theory of sensual objects were developed in dialogue with Frege. It is this concern with the *intentional basis* of reference that connects his work with the issues that Kripke raises for the theory of names.[108]

Harman draws on Husserl's concept of *nominal acts* to explain the relationship between the sensual object and its real counterpart.[109] He interprets Husserl's claim that all other intentional acts are founded upon nominal acts as saying that in any intentional relation we are *acquainted* with an immediate 'this' (sensual object) that in turn *refers* to a shadowy 'this' (real object). Names are attached to the former as if they are the *senses* that determine their references. This means that *distinct* sensual objects can refer to the *same* real object insofar as one thing can have many names. The crucial point is that, although Harman thinks that we can become acquainted with a sensual object by means of a *description* of the object that would draw our attention to it, and thus that we can learn how to use names through using descriptions (e.g., '"Pete" refers to the person who wrote the book you are currently reading'), he does not think that this is necessary for acquaintance. As he explains in his reading of Ortega y Gasset, our acquaintance

108.   S. Kripke, *Naming and Necessity* (Oxford: Blackwell, 1981).

109.   *Guerrilla Metaphysics*, 28–9.

with the sensual object is a sort of *feeling*, and the object a sort of *feeling-thing*, which any particular description can never completely capture.[110]

However, this inability of descriptions to capture the *feel* of sensual objects is not yet the inability to capture the *meaning* of names that Kripke reveals. Harman takes the latter inability to consist in the relation between the name and its reference rather than the name and its sense: 'For Kripke, names are "rigid designators" that point to (or stipulate) realities beyond all possible descriptions of them.'[111] Whereas the immediate 'this' is something *more* than the *particular descriptions* that give us purchase upon it, the shadowy 'this' is something *other* than every *possible description*. It's helpful to quote Harman at some length on this point:

> Kripke's 'rigid designator' is meant to serve as a proper name pointing to something that remains identical even when all known features of the thing are altered, so that the moon remains the moon even if we turn out at some future point to have been catastrophically wrong about all its properties [...] However, the question for us is whether the inviolate 'this' beneath all apparent properties is something lying within perception, or is instead a real object lying somewhere beneath it.[112]

Obviously, Harman answers this question in the affirmative; but it is important to see that he does so for *epistemo-logical* reasons. He thinks that because we can use names to talk about the same thing regardless of any *possible*

---

110. *Guerrilla Metaphysics*, 108–10.

111. *The Quadruple Object*, 67.

112. *Guerrilla Metaphysics*, 197–8.

disagreements about how we should describe it, every name must therefore refer to a mysterious 'inaccessible "X" lying behind any descriptions that might be given of it'.[113] What this means is that, because Kripke shows that the *reference* of names is somehow independent of our beliefs about their qualities, the *individuation* of the objects they refer to cannot have anything to do with these beliefs. This is the first component of the argument.

The second component is much simpler. It amounts to a rather straightforward claim about the nature of individuation, which enables us to draw consequences regarding how the individuation of real objects *does* work from the above claim about how it *doesn't*. Harman discusses this in relation to Zubiri's work, but his simplest statements of it are invariably his remarks on Leibniz:

> [Leibniz] observes that even though each monad must be one monad, each also needs a multitude of qualities to be what it is, to differ from other monads rather than being interchangeable with them.[114]

For real objects to be distinct from one another, they must possess some qualities that distinguish them. There can be no individuation without qualities. This claim interacts with the Kripkean component in the following way:

> The basic point is that we can no longer simply distinguish between a sensual world of properties and a deeper hidden core of the essential 'this.' [...] The 'this' may be separable from all

---

113.   *Tool-Being*, 213.

114.   *The Quadruple Object*, 49.

sorts of specific and falsifiable features, but it is never separable from a specific essence, and is therefore no 'bare particular.' [115]

Real objects must have *individual essences* that distinguish them from all other things, even if these cannot be adequately described in terms of any sensual qualities whatsoever. Therefore, if sensual qualities are unable to compose these essences, there must be an entirely distinct type of quality capable of doing so. The need for essence thus demonstrates the need for a distinction between real qualities and sensual qualities.

The issue with this argument is that, much as we saw with Husserl in the argument from eidos, Harman's attempt to integrate Kripke's insights into his metaphysical framework ends up seriously warping them. We could focus on the fact that Kripke would not endorse the account of indirect reference that Harman's division between sensual and real objects implies, but this is a tortuous point, given the intricacies of neo-Fregean attempts to account for names as rigid designators.[116] A more salient point is that although Kripke also develops a conception of individual essence out of his account of rigid designation, it is remarkably different from Harman's. Kripke does not take his account of rigid designation to imply that the essential properties of things must be of a completely different kind to their inessential ones.[117] For him, it is entirely possible for one thing to possess a property *essentially* (e.g., a living cell's

---

115. *Guerrilla Metaphysics*, 197–8.

116. I have in mind the work of Gareth Evans, John McDowell and Robert Brandom. I personally endorse Brandom's own anaphoric approach to integrating the Fregean sense/reference distinction and rigid designation, which he calls 'tactile Fregeanism' (R. Brandom, *Making It Explicit* [Cambridge, MA: Harvard University Press, 1994], chapters 7–8).

117. Cf. Kripke, *Naming and Necessity*, 39–53, 110–15.

salinity, which must remain within a narrow range in order for it to function) and for another to possess the same property *accidentally* (e.g., a cooked piece of pasta's salinity, which can vary well outside of this range without dissolution). Of course, he might simply have failed to recognise the implications of his own theory, but it should give us pause for thought. As such, we should take a look at his argument against descriptivism.

Kripke claims that the meaning of a name such as 'Aristotle' cannot be composed out of descriptions such as 'the most famous student of Plato', 'the tutor of Alexander the great', or 'a Greek philosopher with an impressive beard', even if these descriptions *uniquely* pick out the relevant object, either individually or in conjunction. Put in its simplest form, the argument for this claim is that we would otherwise be unable to make sense of statements such as 'Aristotle *might not* have been the greatest student of Plato', 'Aristotle *could* have died before Alexander was born', or 'It was possible for Aristotle to shave off his beard and abandon philosophy'. For any descriptive feature that is supposed to belong to the meaning of a name, we can construct a seemingly reasonable *counterfactual* statement involving that name in which the object lacks it, thereby producing a contradiction. The important contrast to draw with Harman's presentation of the argument is that this is straightforwardly *modal* rather than *epistemic*: it involves differences between the way the world *actually* is and ways it *could* have been, rather than differences between the way the world *really* is and ways we *take it* to be. What Kripke means when he says that names are rigid designators is simply that they pick out the same thing in all counterfactual scenarios. Moreover, he does not think that the name successfully refers to an object in every proposed scenario. He holds that some counterfactual statements (e.g., 'Aristotle could have been a pig') are false precisely because there are some essential features (e.g., humanity) that could not be absent from a scenario without the object being absent. He thus does not think that grasping the *essence* of a thing is impossible, but simply that it is distinct from grasping the *meaning* of a name that refers to it. There may be independent reasons not to endorse Kripke's essentialism, but they are not necessarily reasons to endorse Harman's alternative.

Harman's account of rigid designation has thus mutated into *stubborn designation*, insofar as names not only refer to the same thing throughout counterfactual variations, but across *all* possible appearances. For Kripke and those who attempt to incorporate his insights, there is still at least some role for descriptions of the features and history of the objects our names refer to, in determining whether two different names refer to the same thing: There can be entirely separate causal histories (or anaphoric chains) determining the reference of different names (e.g., 'morning star' and 'evening star') and yet facts about these can help determine whether they have been referring to the same thing all along (e.g., 'the morning star is the evening star', since both are names for Venus). For Harman, we can at best use descriptions to determine whether the sensual objects our names are attached to are the same, but never whether distinct sensual objects might refer to the same real object. This makes the boundaries between real objects as mysterious as their qualities.[118] The sensual chair I am sitting on and the sensual tree I am staring at are *sensually distinct*, but they might not be *really distinct*. The sun, the sea, and the strudel I had for breakfast may *really* have been the same thing all along. The messy business of working out just

---

118.   I owe this point to Daniel Sacilotto.

what it is we're talking *about* can only be given over to allure in the same fashion that the *theorisation* of eidos seems to have been. It therefore seems as if the whole issue of reference from which the argument began has gone out of the window.

Even more worryingly perhaps, we are left wondering why we must affirm the reality of discreteness at all, rather than some singular *Apeiron* underlying a plurality of discrete appearances. Harman's own analysis of appearance cannot but dissolve the 'glaringly obvious fact' of discreteness that he himself held up against Heidegger's purported holism. His radical dissociation of the individuation of sensual objects from the individuation of real objects precludes any appeal to apparent discreteness in order to prove real discreteness, and thereby undermines his seemingly radical individualism. If we cannot know anything about the criteria of individuation of real objects, then we are left with the real possibility that there might only be one.

3. OCCASIONALISM, INDEPENDENCE, AND SUPPLEMENTATION

In considering the arguments for the final aspect of Harman's system, namely *vicarious causation*, we are again put in a difficult position. Though Harman devotes a considerable amount of space to elaborating his account of allure,[119] and presents some additional reasons why we should want such an account of causation, the principal motivation for the account is provided by the arguments we have already considered and rejected. Harman issues the following challenge to those who would assess his account of causation in *Guerrilla Metaphysics*:

> Once it was conceded that the world is made up of withdrawn objects, utterly sealed in private vacuums but also unleashing forces upon one another, all the other problems follow in quick succession. Let anyone who does not agree with the strategies of guerrilla metaphysics specify clearly which of its initial steps is invalid.[120]

This is precisely what I have done. None of these initial steps has proved valid, let alone all of them. This seems to rule out vicarious causation by default. Still, there are some more probative reasons that Harman presents for his account of causation. He provides a further historical narrative regarding the tradition of **occasionalist** accounts of causation, which is meant to suggest that the problem his theory responds

---

119. Cf. *Guerrilla Metaphysics* §§8–12; 'On Vicarious Causation'.

120. *Guerrilla Metaphysics*, 97.

to emerges from a broader range of concerns than his own. He also suggests that the scientific account of causation demands **supplementation** by a metaphysical theory of causation of precisely the kind he provides. I will now address both of these claims, but in between them I will try to reconstruct the core of Harman's argument for vicarity on the basis of the **independence** of objects from one another. This will provide a proper contrast with the motivations of the occasionalists, as well as contextualize the demand for supplementation.

I. HARMAN'S OCCASIONALIST TRADITION

According to Harman, the problem of how distinct things can causally interact has a long lineage.[121] On the one hand, he sees it being raised in explicitly metaphysical terms in the Islamic occasionalism of the Ash'arite school, the modern occasionalism of Descartes, Malebranche, and Leibniz, and in the more contemporary occasionalism of Whitehead. All of these thinkers invoke God as a mediator capable of overcoming what they see as the causal gap between entities, whether as the source of all causal power (the Ash'arites), the source of the connection between different kinds of substance (Descartes), or the medium through which entities are able to encounter one another (Malebranche, Leibniz, and Whitehead). On the other, he sees it being raised implicitly in the epistemological scepticism/critique of Hume and Kant. He reads these thinkers as invoking the mind as a mediator which provides the causal connections between appearances, whether through mere habit (Hume) or through transcendental necessity (Kant). Harman criticises both of these trends for advocating a 'global occasionalism', insofar as they require all causal

---

121. Cf. 'On Vicarious Causation', 188, 202, 218–19; *Prince of Networks*, §5C.

relations to be mediated by the same thing—God in the former, the mind in the latter—and proposes, along with Latour, a 'local occasionalism' in which causal relations between entities are mediated by further entities.

Now, although this strikes me as presenting a somewhat perverse reading of Kant and Hume, insofar as it reads their epistemological concerns in metaphysical terms they would abjure, there are definite continuities here. There are overlapping themes that seem to motivate a similar account of causation, insofar as they all demand some form of *causal mediation*. However, this demand does not arise from a single *problem* held in common by the various sub-traditions that make up this narrative. For instance, not only did Islamic occasionalism provide a *theological solution*, it was motivated by a *theological problem* about the power of God. This is remarkably different from Descartes's problem concerning the split between thought and extension, Leibniz's problem concerning compossibility, and is light years from the concerns with the nature of explanation that motivate Latour's occasionalism. If we do not share any of these diverse concerns, then this problem has no hold on us. Harman hardly takes the theological concerns of the Ash'arites to be pressing, so he cannot lean upon them to motivate his own theory of causation. In short, we still need some good reasons, above and beyond this narrative, to accept the problematic status of unmediated causal relations.

II. THE ARGUMENT FROM INDEPENDENCE

Harman's own reasons for taking unmediated causal relations to be impossible all stem from his claims about the independence of objects from their relations to one another. These turn up at various different points in the three arguments for withdrawal we have considered, but they are never motivated independently of claims about the excess of objects over our grasp of them, whether they are explicitly connected or implicitly conflated. This should be unsurprising given the dominance of phenomenological themes throughout these arguments, even when they are illicitly intertwined with metaphysical ones. My aim now is to make this tangle of claims about epistemic access and causal interaction a bit clearer, not by reconstructing a further argument, but by unearthing a non sequitur underlying the other arguments. This amounts to a final attempt at cutting the Gordian knot of methodological issues underlying Harman's project, prior to considering his ideas about the relationship between philosophy and science.

I think the key here is Harman's offhand remark that 'despite its various degrees of efficacy, [physical causation] must ultimately either work or fail to work'.[122] This remark is made in the context of an exposition of the parallels between causation and allure, which he similarly takes to either succeed or fail in this binary fashion. This adds an extra layer of depth to the picture of vicarious causation presented above: not only is sincerity insufficient for causal interaction, allure is sometimes insufficient too. Successful causation requires successful allure. But what is really interesting is the claim that causal interaction should be understood in terms of success *at all*. If the problem of how one object can *affect* another is actually the problem of how one object can *successfully* affect another, then this tells us something more about the implicit motivations of the problem. Knowledge can be understood in terms of representational success. If one conflates representation and causation by treating causation in intentional terms, then one

---

122. *Guerrilla Metaphysics*, 176.

can seemingly infer the impossibility of successful causation (causal independence) from the impossibility of knowledge (epistemic excess). This conflation can only be held together by the sort of functional language that Harman refuses to abandon at the end of the argument from execution, as it lets us treat things as *striving* for ends. We can say that things *try* to affect one another, even if they always *fail*.

Of course, there still must be some way in which causation can succeed. The absolute ban upon causal contact is thus qualified using the notion of directness: all *direct* access fails, therefore all *direct* causation fails. The hope of an *indirect* form of access (if no longer strictly epistemic in character) thus holds open the hope of an *indirect* form of causation. This hope is answered in both cases by allure. The latter provides a supposedly non-representational way for us to *access* the real, and in doing so provides a way for the real to *affect* us. However, the fact that these relations proceed in *opposite* directions should give us pause for thought. The object that tries to affect is the object hiding behind the sensual object, whereas the object that tries to access is the object encountering this facade. What is going on here?

The crucial question may be put as follows: In precisely what way can allure be said to *succeed* where representation *fails*? It is the equivocation between the standards of representational success and causal success that allows us to convert epistemic excess into causal independence. If there is no sense in which allure is held to the former standard, or to some deeper standard that it shares with representation, then there is no good sense in which it can overcome causal independence. The problem is that the only concrete standards of success that Harman ever deploys in his discussions of allure concern how the allure *affects* the one who experiences it.[123] Does the joke make me laugh? Does my mistake embarrass me? Does the metaphor make me think? The fact that these are the questions that determine the success of allure indicates why successful allure is a model for successful causation. These allusions can only succeed or fail insofar as there is some *effect* they are *supposed* to produce upon us. They are thus more like access to *narcotics* than access to *information*. It doesn't *seem* to matter that there is no substantive comparison with representational success, only because allure is *already* understood in causal terms. The non sequitur is hidden by blatant circularity. Harman's aesthetics is an introspective theory of emotional affection.

III. THE ARGUMENT FROM SUPPLEMENTATION

Finally, we come to Harman's defence of the importance of his theory of vicarious causation by way of his thoughts on the relationship between philosophy and science. Let's jump straight in at the deep end:

> For several centuries, philosophy has been on the defensive against the natural sciences, and now occupies a point of lower social prestige and, surprisingly, narrower subject matter. A brief glance at history shows that this was not always the case. To resume the offensive, we need only reverse the long-standing trends of renouncing all speculation on objects and volunteering for curfew in an ever-tinier ghetto of solely human realities: language, texts, political power. Vicarious causation frees us from such imprisonment by returning us to the heart of the inanimate world, whether natural or artificial. The uniqueness of philosophy

---

123. Cf. *Guerrilla Metaphysics*, §§8–9, 211–13.

is secured, not by walling off a zone of precious human reality that science cannot touch, but by dealing with the same world as the various sciences but in a different manner.[124]

Harman thus sees his metaphysical system as an attempt to return philosophy to its rightful subject matter. He defends philosophy's right to tackle the same topics as the sciences by claiming that it can approach them through other means. Given the difficulties we have encountered in determining Harman's methodology thus far, we are entitled to some curiosity regarding just what these means are, and how they are supposed to differ from those of the sciences. This is where the theory of vicarious causation is supposed to shine, by providing us with an exemplar of the divergence between the scientific and philosophical approaches:

> From the naturalistic standpoint, ignoring for now whatever complications one might wish to infer from the quantum theory, causation is essentially a physical problem of two material masses slamming into each other or mutually affected through fields. One object becomes directly present to the other, whether through physical contact or some other form of intimacy. But there is also a *metaphysical* problem of causation.[125]

The initial problem with this is that all of the contrasts Harman makes between the supposed scientific understanding of causality and his own metaphysical one present an incredibly crude version of the sciences.[126] Although he pays lip service

---

124. 'On Vicarious Causation', 190.

125. *Guerrilla Metaphysics*, 18.

126. Cf. *Tool-Being*, 19, 209; *Guerrilla Metaphysics*, 79.

to the implications of quantum mechanics, he entirely ignores the advanced mathematical techniques (e.g., phase space modelling, statistical analysis, information theory, etc.) that the sciences have developed to model phenomena since Hume talked about billiard-ball dynamics, along with the intricate theoretical questions regarding the nature of causation that these have spawned, both in the sciences and the philosophy of science (e.g., emergent capacities, statistical causality, information transmission, etc.).[127] However, on second thought, the real problem is that Harman's approach precludes him from paying any attention to these things anyway. As far as he is concerned, the sciences don't tell us anything about *reality*. They only talk about it as it *seems*, whereas philosophy can talk about it as it *is*. This isn't to say science is useless, but simply that the truth is entirely inaccessible to it. Maybe this truth will be relevant to the sciences, maybe it won't, but there's no real debate to be had here, even if there might be mutual inspiration.

There is a tremendous irony in this: the strange methodological hybrid of phenomenological description and metaphysical argument that Harman adopts amounts to the practice of **introspective metaphysics**. It is important to understand that this is different from what is often called 'armchair metaphysics' insofar as it has nothing to do with the a priori as traditionally understood. It is not a matter of retreating from observation to contemplate and reason about the fundamental concepts that underpin observation, but a matter of seeking out a special kind of intuition unknown to the sciences. Harman claims to get

---

127. This is evident in the way he approaches the work of Ladyman and Ross in 'I am also of the opinion that materialism must be destroyed', 772–90, where he all but explicitly refuses to consider the scientific issues that motivate many of their crucial metaphysical choices.

at the reality that the sciences can never describe by closely describing the structure of seeming. Far from challenging the retreat of philosophers from the world into the bastion of consciousness, he has simply extended the domain of consciousness into the world. On this basis, he provides us with an introspective theory of causation modelled upon emotional intensity. This theory is independent of the sciences insofar as it is based on a form of evidence entirely alien to them, but it strikes me as equally alien to the proper practice of philosophy. The phenomenological trappings in which Harman's metaphysical introspection are clothed are at best a bad disguise, as if an unusually pensive crook were to don a rubber Husserl mask to preserve his anonymity during a hold-up. What they hide is a series of questionable assumptions and sometimes outright misunderstandings regarding important epistemological and metaphysical issues. Our next task must be to peel back this mask and bring these assumptions into the open, in order to better understand why one might be tempted to endorse OOP despite the convoluted and deeply flawed arguments presented for it.

3

OBJECTION-ORIENTED PHILOSOPHY

Now that I have followed the various threads of argument that run through Harman's work and uncovered some *specific* problems with them, it's time to consider the pattern that these threads weave as a whole, and draw some *general* conclusions about Harman's philosophical system. The surface flaws we have encountered in the argumentative patchwork that serves to justify OOP point back to a number of much deeper conceptual tangles responsible for their proliferation. These knots of questionable assumptions often serve to lend Harman's system a certain stability in the face of the fickle winds of casual criticism, but a more thorough and sustained approach can untie them, and thereby reveal both their problematic character and the vital lessons they teach us about how *not* to construct our own philosophical tapestries.

The crucial problem lying at the heart of OOP is its attitude toward *explanation*, which is confused (if well-intentioned) at best, and careless (bordering on downright pernicious) at worst. This brings us back to a question that has cropped up at least twice already: What *is* metaphysics? And more specifically, what does it *do*? Just what, if anything, does metaphysics *explain*? As already noted, this isn't something of which Harman has a particularly detailed account. Regardless, if we elaborate upon the traditional idea that metaphysics is *first philosophy*, then we can set the stage for revealing some crucial features of Harman's philosophical practice.

The principal characteristic of metaphysics practised as first philosophy is that it is the discourse within which one formulates and defends one's most fundamental assumptions.[128]

---

128. This holds for many philosophers who use the term 'metaphysics' without having any opinion on its description as 'first philosophy', such as David Lewis (see chapter 3.5, subsection II). This is a *practical* feature of how metaphysical discourse is used, rather than a *theoretical* issue of how it is understood by those who use it.

This includes both narrow *ontological assumptions* about the kinds of entities one can appeal to in non-metaphysical explanations, and more broadly *categorial assumptions* about the various features of these entities (e.g., properties, relations, essences, etc.) that can be involved in such explanations along with the relevant constraints upon their involvement. This makes metaphysics the default site for dispute over the *explanatory primitives* out of which one can build explanatory frameworks in other domains (or, to put it another way, the dumping ground for such primitives). As a general rule, the ability to explain more phenomena with fewer primitives is a prized feature of such frameworks. This means that a framework that treats as primitive things which another framework can treat as *explanatory derivatives* without having to make any additional assumptions is to be preferred by default. The less you have to assume to get the same explanatory result, the better. My principal contentions are that OOP is confused insofar as it acts as if it is explaining a bunch of phenomena that it is actually treating as metaphysically primitive (it is *explanatorily impotent*), and it is careless insofar as it actively undermines our ability to provide useful explanations of a number of important phenomena in the process (it is *explanatorily regressive*). The first two parts of this chapter will justify these claims by analysing Harman's take on the semantic phenomenon of **reference** and the metaphysical phenomenon of **property possession**, respectively.

The secondary characteristic of metaphysics practised as first philosophy (which Heidegger names *the forgetting of Being*) is a lack of methodological self-consciousness regarding precisely what it is doing in setting up the explanatory resources available to other domains of discourse. It undertakes ontological commitments to the fundamental types of entities there are without understanding what ontological commitment (i.e., genuine *existence*) is; and discriminates between the other metaphysically permissible features that these entities may possess, without having an adequate grasp of the fundamental concepts in terms of which these discriminations are articulated (e.g., *property*, *relation*, *essence*, etc.). This leads to a number of characteristic errors (some of which Heidegger groups under the heading of *onto-theology*) which doom speculative metaphysics as an explanatory project. My secondary contentions are that OOP's pervasive evasion of methodological questions leaves it dependent upon an intuitive grasp of certain fundamental notions (e.g., *object*, *quality*, *relation*, *space/time*, etc.) that results in a number of disastrous ambiguities and conflations that doom the project from the start—and that this portends similar fates for the other variants of OOO which take them up. The third and fourth parts of the chapter will justify these contentions by analysing Harman's use of the concepts of **relation** and **object**, respectively. The remainder of the chapter will attempt to provide an answer to the question of what metaphysics is, and to explain why Harman goes awry in his approach to it, by addressing the relations between logic, metaphysics, and meaning.

1. SENSE AND SENSUALITY

It is all too easy to label Harman's metaphysics as *anti-representational*, given his emphasis on the impossibility of correctly representing things as they are in themselves. However, there is a more nuanced story to be told about representation that complicates matters a great deal. To tell this story it is important to make two distinctions. Firstly, we must distinguish between the *predicative* and *referential* dimensions of representation.[129] Respectively, these are the aspect of a representation that governs *how* it represents a thing as being (e.g., representing a man as a philanderer), and the aspect that governs *which* thing it represents as being this way (e.g., Bill Clinton). Secondly, we must distinguish between representational *purport* and representational *success*. This distinguishes the manner in which each of these aspects attempt to represent the world (e.g., representing Bill Clinton as a philanderer) from the extent to which this attempt is successful (e.g., whether there is in fact someone called 'Bill Clinton' and whether he is indeed a philanderer). The intersection of these distinctions provides the scope of what must be explained by any theory of representation: how a representation attempts to pick out an object; how it represents it as having certain properties (or standing in certain relations);

---

129.   It is important to note that this distinction is neither exclusive to discursive (or linguistic) forms of representation, nor does it project the structure of such forms of representation onto representation more generally. It is simply meant to distinguish the manner in which a representation stores *qualitative* information about something from the manner in which it *corresponds* to it. This is as applicable to a map as it is to a sentence with subject-predicate syntax.

how it can succeed or fail to pick out an object; and how it can represent its properties (and relations) correctly or incorrectly.

We can now distinguish *weak* and *strong* forms of anti-representationalism. The former refuses to appeal to any or all of these representational notions (predication/reference, purport/success) as explanatory primitives in other domains (e.g., metaphysics, aesthetics, or psychology) without first providing an independent explanation of them. The latter refuses to appeal to them entirely, along with the demand to provide such an independent explanation, by denying that there is anything to be explained. Weak anti-representationalism merely denies the primacy of representation, whereas the strong form denies its very existence. The manifold structure of representation allows for numerous possible permutations of these positions, but what we are interested in is the specific form that Harman's anti-representationalism takes. Obviously, with regard to the predicative dimension of representation, his approach involves a kind of strong anti-representationalism, insofar as it denies that there is anything like predicative success to be accounted for. However, with regard to the referential dimension of representation, it is anti-representationalist in neither sense.

Harman's account of predicative failure in terms of withdrawal depends upon a form of referential success, insofar as it claims that one real object is *intentionally* related to another real object that withdraws from it. The first object fails to grasp the second, but it nevertheless fails in its *attempt* to grasp *that specific object*. This shows that Harman does not eliminate either predicative purport, referential purport, or referential success. Moreover, it should be clear that Harman licenses broad use of these notions in explanation insofar as the intentional relation forms the basis of his account of causation. If we pull on this thread a bit more, we will see that Harman not only licenses their role in explanation, but in essence transforms them into explanatory primitives which are not themselves accounted for, thereby revealing a pernicious representationalism underlying the anti-representationalism that was initially apparent. In order to see this clearly, it will be useful to examine some other theories of reference whose explanatory problems parallel Harman's own: Meinong's theory of **subsistence** and Frege's theory of **sense**.

I. SUBSISTENCE AND SENSE

The essence of Meinong's theory of reference is that every thought has a referent, even if this referent does not actually exist (e.g., a golden mountain) or never could exist (e.g., a round square). Such objects, although nonexistent, nevertheless possess a metaphysical status, which Meinong calls subsistence. Subsistent object are like existent objects in every respect other than existence. This means that they share what Meinong calls *Sosein* (or being-so). A golden mountain exhibits goldenness and mountainhood in precisely the fashion that my parents' wedding rings and Everest do. Even a round square is genuinely both round and square, although the conjunction of these properties precludes the possibility of existence. The problem with this theory is that although it might at first glance seem to explain the difference between successful and failed reference, it means that all purported reference is now in some sense successful reference. It thus dodges the explanatory demand by transferring the issue from the representation to the thing represented. Brandom describes the problem best:

> The trouble with taking it that there is something that is successfully represented by every purported representing is not just

that it involves commitment to a luxuriant ontology; *ontological self-indulgence is a comparatively harmless vice. But it can be symptomatic of a failure to shoulder an explanatory burden.* In this case it evidently (and ultimately unhelpfully) transforms the demand for an account of the relation between correct and incorrect, unfulfilled or merely purported and actually successful representing, into a demand for an account of the relation between the statuses of what is represented in the two cases: between mere subsistence and robust existence.[130]

We might disagree with Brandom about the harmlessness of ontological self-indulgence, but his diagnosis is otherwise perfect: in Meinong's theory, the difference between successful and failed reference is *hypostatized* into a primitive metaphysical distinction between existent and subsistent objects. This both fails to explain the relevant features of representation and simultaneously derives the metaphysical structure of the world from them.

Frege's theory of reference is more explanatorily satisfactory than Meinong's, insofar as it sets out to solve the problem of how there can be informative identity claims. This is the question of how a claim like 'Hesperus is Phosphorus' can provide new information if both Hesperus and Phosphorus name the same object (namely, the planet Venus). The question is essentially as follows: What makes the informative claim 'Hesperus is Phosphorus' different from the trivial claim 'Hesperus is Hesperus'? Frege's answer is his famous distinction between sense and reference. He distinguishes the aspect of a representational content that purports to refer (*sense*) from the object it refers to (*reference*). This means that the names 'Hesperus'

---

130. Brandom, *Making It Explicit*, 71, my emphasis.

and 'Phosphorus' can have different senses even if they share the same referent, and that the identity claim ('Hesperus is Phosphorus') is indeed informative, since someone may grasp the two *senses* without it being epistemically transparent that they refer to the same object. Frege's approach also avoids the trap Meinong falls into, insofar as it allows reference to fail—there can be senses without referents (e.g., 'the largest prime number', 'Santa Claus', etc.). But the problem with Frege's theory emerges in his account of what senses are. His basic idea is that senses are *modes of presentation* of objects, such that the same object (e.g., Venus) can be presented in many different ways (e.g., as the morning star and the evening star). However, he is very clear that such modes of presentation are not subjective states of any kind. This would lead to some form of *psychologism*. In opposition to this, Frege claims that senses must be objective in order to ensure that the thoughts of different individuals can share the same representational content. A claim such as 'Hesperus is a planet' has to mean the same thing upon my tongue as it does upon yours, even if we have different subjective experiences of Hesperus, and even if we disagree about whether it is in fact Venus. The problem is that Frege achieves this objectivity by positing senses as abstract Platonic entities like mathematical objects. This hypostatizes referential purport in much the same way that Meinong hypostatizes referential success and failure, thereby precluding a sufficient explanation of referential purport, including both how senses are individuated and how they are grasped by thinkers.

Returning to Harman's own theory, we are now in a position to examine the picture of representation contained in the implicit epistemology underlying its argument from identity.[131]

---

131. See chapter 2.1, subsection 3.

What is interesting about this picture is that it combines aspects of both Fregean and Meinongian approaches—although it is clear that whatever Fregean elements it has are inherited from Husserl, whose account is similar.[132] The core of the picture is a distinction between the *object-for-us* and the *object-in-itself*, which correspond loosely to sense and reference. However, unlike Frege's sense and like Meinong's subsistent objects, the object-for-us is treated as genuinely *possessing* the properties we ascribe to the object-in-itself in the predicative part of representation. To put it another way, Harman's *senses* have *Sosein*. We've already noted that this is a pretty idiosyncratic conception of representation, and that it essentially prefigures Harman's full-blooded distinction between sensual and real objects. The task now is to show how this loose hybrid of Fregean/Husserlian and Meinongian ideas develops into that distinction, so as to unearth some of the more tenebrous ideas motivating it. This means digging a little deeper into the theory of reference.

II. REFERENCE AND RIGIDITY

We must first distinguish between referring *de dicto* and referring *de re*. This is the difference between those types of referring in which the choice of words composing the referring expression play an important role, and those in which there is an independent relationship between the words and the thing referred to that is important. Referring using *definite descriptions* is the paradigm case of the former (e.g., 'the 41st president of the United States') and referring using *proper*

---

132. Cf. P. Simmons, 'Meaning and Language', in B. Smith and D.W. Smith (eds), *The Cambridge Companion to Husserl* (Cambridge: Cambridge University Press, 1995), 112.

names is the paradigm case of the latter (e.g., 'Bill Clinton'). Other important cases of *de re* reference include *demonstratives* (e.g., 'this' and 'that') and *indexicals* (e.g., 'here' and 'now'), but we will ignore these for the moment.

The important thinkers to introduce here are Russell and Kripke. Russell's famous theory of descriptions was designed to undermine Meinong's argument that we must posit subsistent objects (e.g., the golden mountain) insofar as they have *Sosein* (e.g., being golden and a mountain) by analysing claims using definite descriptions (e.g., 'the golden mountain is awesome') into three parts (i.e., 'there is something that is a golden mountain' [existence], 'there is only one of these' [uniqueness], and 'it is awesome' [predication]). The salient point here is that Russell breaks down reference into two parts: *existence* and *uniqueness*, enabling him to give an analysis of the role that the descriptive content (the *dictum*) plays in determining reference. After this, Fregean senses, including those of proper names, tended to be understood as descriptive in the Russellian manner (or as *de dicto* senses). This isn't really Frege's own view, but it is this supposed Frege/Russell axis that became the target of Kripke's arguments against descriptivist views of proper names. As we saw earlier, these show that definite descriptions cannot account for the fact that proper names *rigidly designate* the same object across counterfactual scenarios. These arguments do indeed torpedo descriptivist approaches to proper names, but there is a whole school of neo-Fregeans (e.g., Evans, McDowell, and Brandom) who overcome Kripke's arguments by providing an account of *de re* senses. We won't explore the intricacies of these debates any further, but will instead focus on Kripke's influence on Harman.

We have already examined Harman's explicit appeals to Kripke in our discussion of the argument from essence,[133] but we are now in a position to uncover a more subterranean influence, or at the very least a confluence of themes. It is first important to see that the representational notion of *descriptive content* corresponds to the metaphysical notion of *Sosein*. We can see this clearly from the role it plays in Russell's attempt to defuse Meinong's argument for the necessity of subsistence. This means that, if one looks at Kripke from a principally metaphysical direction (as it seems Harman does), it might seem as if he has shown not only that there is more to the *representational content* of proper names than descriptions, but that there is more to the *metaphysical constitution* of objects than *Sosein*. This is perhaps encouraged by the fact that Kripke was quick to draw metaphysical conclusions from his own results, using them to motivate a neo-Aristotelian account of individual and general essences. It certainly paral-lels Harman's distinction between *objects* and their *qualities*, even if it is probably not the origin of it. Nonetheless, it is important to pay attention to the way this idea is manifest in Harman's account of representation.

As we've seen, because Harman is a Husserlian, he demands something like the sense/reference distinction which Kripke abjures. This means demanding something like the *de re* senses with which the neo-Fregeans are concerned. However, Harman is still more of a Meinongian, insofar as he takes these senses to be *objects* in their own right, rather than *mere representations* of objects. Just as we *purport* to represent an object with certain qualities only insofar as we *succeed* in representing a special kind of object that possesses those

---

133.　See chapter 2.2, subsection III.

qualities, so we purport to represent a *unified* object that is *more* than these qualities only if we succeed in representing a special kind of object that is *itself* more than them. The Kripkean claim that *names* must be more than sets of descriptions is thus transmuted into the Husserlo-Meinongian claim that *sensual objects* (which provide their senses) must be more than 'bundles of qualities'. Sensual objects pick out the *real objects* they correspond to directly, rather than picking them out indirectly through qualitative similarity. This leads to a situation in which reference *as such* is collapsed into the metaphysical relation between sensual objects and their corresponding real objects.[134] According to Harman, even if we grasp a *sensual* object by means of a definite description, this does not amount to grasping the *real* object by means of that description. However we may grasp the sensual object, its relation to the real object is a metaphysical black box, and the question whether we successfully represent something real at all cannot be answered since this box can never be levered open.

Harman's representationalism is now in full view: he combines the Fregean and Meinongian explanatory dodges in such a way that he precludes explaining either referential purport or referential success. For Meinong it could at least be said that when we successfully refer to an existent object *de dicto*, we do so in virtue of a connection between the descriptive dictum and the object's *Sosein*. This cannot be said for Harman. The connection between the predicative and referential

---

134. It should be noted that this connection is not the same as Harman's category of *sincerity*, which is the relation between an experiencing real object and the sensual facade of another object it encounters, rather than between a real object and its own sensual counterpart.

dimensions of representation is thereby severed entirely. As such, his account of representation not only fails to explain it, but deliberately flaunts the demand for explanation. Everything is collapsed into a primitive metaphysical relation between sensual and real objects whose provenance remains as mysterious as it is ubiquitous. This reconstruction of Harman's account of the referential dimension of representation does not necessarily imply his account of the predicative dimension, namely, the *withdrawal* thesis that all such representation fails. That requires the additional arguments we have already addressed. However, it is important to see just *how* this account makes room for withdrawal: it does so by completely eliminating any role that description might play in picking out real objects. Harman makes it possible to occupy a position in which no properties we could possibly use to describe such objects correctly describe them. One can even see the sense in moving to such a position on this basis: if all genuine descriptive thought about entities in themselves is *referentially redundant*, it may as well be redundant more generally.

III. SENSUALITY AND HAECCEITY

So much for the underlying representational logic of Harman's metaphysics, but there is still something more to be said about the manner in which sensual objects function as senses. In particular, it is worthwhile examining the manner in which Harman adapts the ideas of Ortega y Gasset in elaborating his account.[135] Ortega holds that the unity things possess in our encounters with them consists in a unique *feeling* that is distinct from any of the particular qualities they exhibit. Harman adapts this claim into the idea that sensual objects

---

135. *Guerrilla Metaphysics*, chapter 8.

are **feeling-things**, whose independence from their sensual qualities consists in the dissonance between this *immediate* feeling and any *mediated* purchase we might gain through consideration of these qualities. He deploys this idea in interpreting Kripke's theory as follows:

> [A] Kripkean theory of reference [uses] proper names to point to some unknown X called "gold" or "Richard Nixon," names that remain distinct from any known properties of these objects. What we have with proper names as rigid designators are the feeling-units "gold" or "Nixon," not gold and Nixon *in themselves*, since these consist only in executing their own reality and can never be reduced to names or thoughts any more than to definite descriptions. A proper name simply is not the thing itself, even if it points more closely to that thing than does an adjective.[136]

This diverges from Kripke's own interpretation of his theory in two important ways. Firstly, as we have already noted, Kripke does not endorse anything like a sense/reference distinction, but adopts a Millian theory of names wherein the content of the name simply *is* the object referred to. On this view, the content of the names 'Hesperus' and 'Phosphorus' is the same, even if this is not transparent to us, and the identity claim 'Hesperus is Phosphorus' is a *necessary* truth, even if it is an a posteriori one. Secondly, and more importantly, Kripke tells a story about how names come to have the referents they do in virtue of the *causal history* of their usage. The details of this story are much disputed, but the basic idea is that there is some sort of initial naming event to which all subsequent uses

---

136. Ibid., 109.

of the word are causally connected, such that the referent of 'Hesperus' can be traced back to the first time someone pointed at Venus in the night sky and uttered the word. What is important about this theory (and its successors)[137] is that it aims to provide an explanation of how names purport to pick out unique objects that transcends introspective analysis, be it a strictly causal theory or an account of the normative pragmatics governing the way language users track dependence relations between one another's uses of linguistic tokens.[138]

The salient point here is that, without this additional referential apparatus, there is little to distinguish proper names from demonstratives. This means that to talk of 'Hesperus' or 'Bill Clinton' is tantamount to talking about 'this' or 'that', in such a way that the use of a name is little better than a gesture we simply have to 'get'—something that points or orients us toward a unique and simple feeling. This semantic synthesis of Kripkean *rigid designation* and Husserlean *nominal acts*[139] produces something resembling Russellian *acquaintance*: names function through a primitive act of reference, independent of any semantic framework that could make sense of it. This might be mediated insofar as there is a sensual sense standing between the subject and their real referent, but this means little when both the subject-sense relation and the sense-reference relation are themselves immediate. When converted back into a metaphysical register, this produces a pervasive **haecceity**: everything is principally characterised by its 'thisness', in such a way that the very *feeling* of thisness is a thing in its own right.

---

137. Cf. Brandom's theory of anaphoric chains: *Making It Explicit*, chapters 5 and 7.

138. Ibid.

139. Cf. 'Physical Nature and the Paradox of Qualities', in *Towards Speculative Realism*, 128, 137.

The problem with this axis of *semantic* acquaintance and *metaphysical* haecceity is that it rests upon a *phenomenological* fulcrum. Insofar as the sensual object *qua* sense is phenomenologically defined in terms of a feeling of uniqueness, it is destined to be imprisoned within the intentional relation that this feeling characterises. This is a point which Harman acknowledges to some extent:

> Sensual objects would not even exist if they did not exist for me, or for some other agent that expends its energy in taking them seriously.[140]

However he is careful to qualify this so as to downplay any *psychological* interpretation:

> [T]he location of sensual objects cannot be inside the mind, since both the mind *and* its sensual objects are located on the interior of a more encompassing object. If I perceive a tree, this sensual object and I do not meet up inside my mind, and for a simple reason: my mind and its object are two equal partners in the intention, and the unifying term must contain both.[141]

As far as Harman is concerned, sensual objects only exist insofar as they are contained within intentional relations between real objects; but even though these are modelled upon our own psychologically analysable encounters with things, their metaphysical provenance is more fundamental. Although this may distance Harman's account of sense from *psychology*, it still leaves it open to Frege's argument against *psychologism*:

---

140.   *The Quadruple Object*, 74.

141.   Ibid., 115–16.

as long as the sensual object through which I encounter Venus only exists on the inside of an intentional relation between myself and Venus, it cannot function as a sense that is common to the thoughts of different subjects. This means that the representational content of 'Hesperus' must be different in my mouth than it is in yours.

Obviously, this problem with containment reveals a crucial inadequacy in Harman's approach to representation, but it equally causes problems for his metaphysics, insofar as it undermines his treatment of unreal objects (e.g., Popeye, El Dorado, phlogiston, etc.). Harman has previously put forward the ability of his account of sensual objects to explain such things as *fictional entities* as one of its most compelling features.[142] He has presented those who would deny ontological status to fictions and similar things as metaphysical party-poopers, who would deny artists and others the menagerie of objects with which they intuitively grapple. By contrast, and in line with Meinong's theory of subsistence, he aims to allow such entities a sort of metaphysical status even if he denies them reality in the full-blooded sense.[143] This is meant to open up the possibility of appealing to Popeye *qua* sensual object in explaining the role that fictions play in the domains of art and social theory. However, the containment of sensual objects within intentional relations in fact closes off this possibility. This is because no sensual object can be *the* Popeye. Instead, we have a plurality of Popeye objects spread across the various

---

142. 'The Road to Objects', in *Continent* 3.1 (2011), 171–9.

143. During a *Transcendental Ontology* summer school at the University of Bonn, Harman suggested that he was reconsidering his views on this point, and was open to the idea that fictional objects are in fact real objects in some sense. This would of course blunt the current objection, but only by abandoning the supposed advantage of the sensual/real distinction it argues against.

intentional relations entered into by Popeye lovers everywhere. The old man chuckling at a Popeye comic, the child fixated on a Popeye cartoon, and the woman idly speculating about her friend's resemblance to the eponymous sailor are all focused upon a distinct feeling-thing unique to their own experience. These are distinct sensual objects that pop in and out of existence along with the relevant intentions, and thus cannot be deployed in explaining common features of such encounters. Ironically, this means that despite incorporating aspects of both Fregean and Meinongian approaches to representation, the resulting doctrine of containment vitiates the advantages of both.

IV. METAPHOR AND MEANING

We have now more or less completely circumscribed Harman's account of representation, but we must still address his account of **metaphor**.[144] There are two reasons for this: On the one hand, Harman holds that the semantic (or 'cognitive') content of metaphor is of a different type than that of ordinary representation (paradigmatically, literal language). On the other, he cashes this out in terms of the idea that we encounter sensual objects as unities that exceed any of their particular qualities. He makes both points clearly in his criticism of Donald Davidson's theory of metaphor:

> Davidson's central prejudice is his notion that there is only one kind of cognitive content: that of plain, literal prose. In fact, there are exactly *two* kinds of cognitive content. There is the kind concerned with attributes, and the kind concerned with a thing as a total infrastructure that unifies those attributes. [...]

---

144. *Guerrilla Metaphysics*, chapter 8.

The reason we cannot decide the literal content of a metaphor is because it has a meaning that can never be paraphrased.[145]

Harman defends this idea by considering two examples: 'the cypress is a flame' (taken from Ortega y Gasset) and 'man is a wolf' (taken from Max Black). In each case he claims that what is at stake is something other than a straightforward comparison of the properties of each term. There may be some superficial resemblance between the two that triggers the metaphoric connection (e.g., the similar shape of the cypress tree and a flickering flame), but this only serves to call our attention to more indirect resonances between the *systems* of properties the two exhibit.

For Harman, the metaphorical connection between wolf and man does not consist in 'discovering that both humans and wolves have backbones and two eyes, inhabit portions of Alaska, and live in violent hierarchical packs', but in the transposition of a way of thinking about the former onto our way of thinking about the latter, so that we come to view man through the lens of wolfhood.[146] To take the quote from Black that Harman himself uses:

A suitable hearer will be led by the wolf-system of implications to construct a corresponding system of implications about
the principal subject [i.e., 'Man'] [...] Any human traits that can
without undue strain be talked about in 'wolf-language' will be
rendered prominent, and any that cannot will be pushed into

---

145. Ibid., 122–3.

146. Ibid., 119.

the background. The wolf-metaphor suppresses some det.. emphasizes others—in short, *organizes* our view of man.[147]

This seems to me a fairly apposite description of how metaphor functions, but I am far less sanguine about the way Harman interprets this within his metaphysical framework. This is because he slides directly from the idea that metaphors involve a correspondence between systems *of properties* to the idea that they involve a correspondence between unitary systems that are somehow *in excess* of their properties, i.e., a correspondence between sensual objects. To interject another quote from the critique of Davidson:

> This is already quite visible in the ambivalence of the very phrase 'wolf-system', since any system is both singular and plural simultaneously: a *system* of features, and a system *of features*.[148]

There is of course some unity involved in the systems of implication that are transposed here, but it is not clear that this unity has the character that Harman imputes to it. He thinks that the terms of the metaphor pick out distinct sensual objects (e.g., cypress-feeling and flame-feeling), and that the metaphorical connection between the two creates a third such object ('cypress-flame-feeling-thing') which consists in the perpetually unresolved tension between their features.[149] It is such *fused-objects* that supposedly constitute the semantic content proper to metaphor. However, it is not

---

147. M. Black, 'Metaphor', in *Models and Metaphors* (Ithaca, NY: Cornell University Press, 1962), 41.

148. *Guerrilla Metaphysics*, 122.

149. Ibid., 109.

obvious that the transposition between systems of implication moves beyond the features of the things considered, even if it does move beyond simple comparison of them—let alone that it constitutes a *fused-sense* distinct from those the metaphor relates.

The problem becomes more apparent if we consider the wolf-metaphor in more detail. Whereas the cypress example deals with *individuals* ('*the* cypress'), the wolf example deals with *general kinds* ('man', rather than '*a* man'). Harman elides this difference when he elucidates the metaphor:

> On the one hand, what we have are two simple *unities*, human and wolf, whatever they may be: no one in the world can give an exhaustive description of the features of these entities. The words point us vaguely towards recognizable stock characters of the cosmos without specifying any of their traits in particular. On the other hand, human and wolf are not just units, but *determinate* units. Although none of us can sum up everything there is to know about these two very dangerous animals, we can all give a fairly rough description of them.[150]

These general kinds—human and wolf—may be legitimately thought of as *unities* of a sort, insofar as they unify sets of features that are common to the groups of individuals (humans and wolves) that instantiate them; but this does not necessarily make them *units*. Harman has certainly not put forward any platonic theory of universals that would enable him to treat them as objects in their own right (though neither has he ruled such a thing out).

---

150. Ibid., 118–19.

In the absence of such a theory, one might argue that we are dealing with *arbitrary individuals* (e.g., 'a man' and 'a wolf' that are nevertheless not identical with any given man or wolf), wherein the features of the individual considered are restricted purely to those held in common by instances of their kind. One could even make a case for *generic individuals* (e.g., 'the generic man' and 'the generic wolf'), wherein the features the individual possesses are only those held in common by instances of their kind. In each case the individual would be a sensual object that would not even need to have a real counterpart. Nevertheless, in either case the unity in question—that of a set of features common to a kind of individual—is not the unity of the arbitrary or generic individual, but a prior unity that they presuppose insofar as they are defined as an arbitrary or generic instance of *this* kind. This is made more problematic by the fact that we can construct examples of metaphors relating unities that are neither individuals nor general kinds: 'to be powerful is to be poisoned', 'the taste of chocolate is the taste of tears', or 'love is nought but gravitation'. These metaphors connect non-sortal[151] properties and relations, and, as such, the unity of features they involve has nothing to do with the unity of the individuals that might exhibit them.

What this shows is that the unity in question is not the unity of senses *qua objects*, but the unity of objects *qua senses*. Metaphors can establish connections between objects, properties (sortal and non-sortal), relations, and whatnot, even when they are not defined (or even definable) through an exhaustive set of features. They do so by connecting the more

---

151.   See p. 256–7 below for an explanation of the difference between sortal and non-sortal properties.

or less unified 'systems of implications' that the corresponding words are bound up in.[152] This is just to say that metaphors are concerned with **meanings** whose unity persists despite lacking an explicit definition, rather than objects whose unity exceeds any possible definition. This is adequately demonstrated by the fact that we can use *family resemblance terms* in crafting metaphors. The classic example of such a term—'game'—we owe to the later Wittgenstein.[153] This term is meant to pick out a variety of different practices that share overlapping chains of similarities (e.g., competition, scores, stakes, etc.) which nevertheless fail to amount to a core of common features, or a set of necessary and sufficient conditions for being a game (i.e., for any of the relevant features an example can be found that lacks it). It is possible to construct metaphors which not only function *despite* but even thrive *upon* this incipient plurivocity. Take the suggestive phrase: 'Capitalism is the game of accumulation.' This invites us to think about capitalism in terms of the rules, aims, and associated behaviours of games, but it does not restrict us to any core group of these features. We might conjure up the image of capitalism as a game one plays against oneself (e.g., solitaire), the aim of which is only one's own personal wealth; but we might equally conceive it as a competition in which personal wealth becomes a score through which to compare oneself to others. There are numerous other points of contact: team behaviour, chance and risk, interacting play strategies, playfulness, enjoyment, and

---

152. I do not wish this point to be dependent upon my own commitment to semantic inferentialism, but it is worthwhile pointing out that for this approach the meaning of a word consists precisely in such a 'system of implications', insofar as semantic content consists in inferential role.

153. L. Wittgenstein, *Philosophical Investigations*, (Oxford: Blackwell, 2001), §§65–69.

the other overlapping semantic threads that are woven into the meaning of 'game'. The way these are connected in the meaning of a single word provides us with a veritable buffet of possible implications.[154]

A lot more could be said on this topic, but for now, the above considerations suggest that metaphorical language and descriptive language do not bear distinct types of semantic content. If metaphors are not translatable into plain descriptions, this is not because they deploy a different kind of content, but because they deploy the same kind of content in a different fashion. Of course, metaphor plays many different roles in our linguistic lives (both *aesthetic* and *expressive*), and I do not aim to offer anything like a comprehensive alternative theory here. However, I will suggest that the transposition of systems of implication so appositely described by Black is adequately explained in terms of **semantic grafting**. The wolf-metaphor organises our view of man by offering us the opportunity to take whatever bits of semantic structure we like from the concept of wolf and *experimentally* transplant them onto the concept of man. This is not only to transpose properties from one kind to the other (e.g., predatoriness, pack-mentality, etc.), but to transpose more or less complex patterns of reasoning about relationships (e.g., 'man is to *x*, as wolf is to *y*', 'the history of the domestication of wolves into breeds of dog, as a

---

154. Family resemblance terms are only one example of this sort of complex and underlying semantic structure. At least as far back as Aristotle's discussion of the term 'health', we have been aware of words with multiple meanings that are related through a primary meaning (so-called *core-dependent homonyms*). More recently, Mark Wilson has provided an exceptionally in-depth analysis of these sorts of complex semantic structure in terms of what he calls *theory facades* (M. Wilson, *Wandering Significance* [Oxford: Oxford University Press, 2006]).

model for the history of the cultural development of divisions of labour', etc.).[155] This is a creative process in which both the extent and ultimate results of the semantic graft are not immediately apparent. The metaphor merely functions as an invitation to such semantic experimentation. On the one hand, this shows that disparate terms such as 'game' merely provide us with a greater range of samples to graft from. On the other, it reveals the development of metaphors into **analogies** as the formalisation of these experiments, in which the specific correspondences and their precise scope are gradually made explicit. This reinforces the earlier point that, despite its difference from *description*, metaphor is not for all that opposed to *definition*. It may often and profitably deal with words that are without definition, but equally, it lays the foundations of the process of defining them, by allowing us to borrow content from some terms to improve our grasp of others.

---

155. I cannot be more precise than this without returning to the topic of inferentialism (see footnote 152 on p. 132, above). The loose idea would be that metaphor enables us to abstract inference schemas implicit in the content of some concept and modify them in such a way that they can be incorporated into another concept, however tentatively.

I have already said much about the problematic intersection of phenomenological and metaphysical themes in Harman's work, but it is worth discussing what I consider the most egregious result of this methodological car crash in more detail. I refer to the conceptual disaster that is Harman's theory of qualities. There are three related criticisms to be made of this theory: (i) that in taking *sensible qualities* (e.g., colour, texture, weight, etc.) as its model it provides an impoverished account of *empirical properties* more generally (e.g., chemical composition, electrical conductivity, mass, etc.); (ii) that in focusing upon qualities as *tropes* it precludes any account of qualities as *universals*; and (iii) that in insisting on the non-relational actuality of real qualities it undermines the possibility of any positive account of *modality*. Taken together these criticisms show that the pervasive metaphysics of haecceity identified in the last section straddles the object/quality distinction, leaving us lost amidst a swarming mass of *thises* that appear to us *thusly*, with nothing to tell between them but more *thisness*.

I. SENSIBLE QUALITIES AND EMPIRICAL PROPERTIES

The first criticism stems from the observation that the examples of sensual qualities provided by Harman throughout his work are almost exclusively *sensible*: e.g., 'an apple is not the sum total of its red, slippery, cold, hard, and sweet features'.[156] This is to say that they are the sorts of features one would

---

156. *The Quadruple Object*, 25.

pick out if one were asked to describe the features of an object available to one's senses, or to describe the object as it appears to them. This is unsurprising given the phenomenological origins of Harman's metaphysics in this sort of introspection.[157] However, the domain of sensual qualities is supposed to extend beyond the reach of the senses to include those features that lie only within the reach of the intellect: e.g., the electrical conductivity of a piece of copper, the rate of inflation in a national economy, or the charge and spin of subatomic particles. Though the identification and study of these features is *empirical* insofar as it depends upon perceptual observation, this study is mediated by experimental apparatuses, scientific procedures, and theoretical edifices in a way that the immediate deliverances of our senses are not. There is thus a legitimate question as to whether the model of sensual qualities Harman draws from the sensible can be extended to the more broadly empirical.

It must be admitted that the intuitive contrasts between sense/intellect and immediate/mediated access which motivate this question are deliberately not very precise. This is because the ways in which Harman registers these contrasts are so tangled as to discourage premature precision. We can see the two main ways he does this in the following paragraph:

> In Husserl's philosophy, not all qualities are transient accidents floating along the surface of things and shifting with the flow of time. Some qualities are the essential ones, without which the thing would not be what it is for us, and these are the ones to

---

157. An extended example of this sort of introspective analysis of sensual qualities can be found in Harman's discussion of the imaginary battle of centaurs in *Guerrilla Metaphysics* (§10B).

be found through the so called "eidetic reduction." That is why I often use the name *eidos* for this tension between accessible sensual objects and the inaccessible qualities that are of structural importance for them. In Lovecraft this happens as a result of scientific failure, with the unstated implication that scientific success would have given us the real qualities. And Husserl generally seems to agree, holding that complete knowledge of the qualities is possible. Yet he also admits that they can never be *sensual*, but can be known only through the mind, and in this way he at least concedes that they are not of the same order as sensual qualities.[158]

What we have here are two different ways of introducing the distinction between real (essential) and sensual (accidental) qualities. The first is the argument from eidos discussed earlier.[159] As we have seen, this argument aims to derive the distinction through a reading of Husserl's method of eidetic variation. The peculiarity of this derivation consists in how it hinges upon a difference between the sensual and the intellectual which it subsequently collapses. The second is contained in Harman's interpretation of the work of H.P. Lovecraft, in which he claims that Lovecraft manages to allude to the existence of real qualities by describing the inability of empirical science to classify the alien artifacts discovered by his protagonists. This hinges upon a difference between mere sense perception and thoroughgoing empirical investigation that Harman again collapses. In each case, Harman appeals to an intellectual process that is supposed to move beyond the qualities that are immediately perceived to gain intuitive

---

158. *Weird Realism: Lovecraft and Philosophy* (Winchester: Zero Books, 2012).

159. See chapter 2.2, subsection II.

purchase upon a deeper order of qualities, only to then deny that the process can actually achieve access to this order.

What this means is that, in order to establish the distinction between real and sensual qualities, Harman appeals to something like the intuitive contrasts underlying the distinction between the empirical and the sensible—only to then subdue those contrasts by subsuming the empirical within the sensual. This manoeuvre is highly suspect, but what should concern us for the moment is how the appeals to eidetic variation and empirical investigation encourage us to think about sensual qualities, and to what extent they provide different intuitive purchase upon the notion. To this end, we must focus upon the way in which they incline us to characterise the *immediacy* of sense perception, insofar as it is the attempt to intellectually transcend this immediacy that constitutes their striving for real qualities, rather than any positive conception of what they are striving toward. As such, the failure to achieve knowledge of real qualities is to be understood as a failure to overcome the immediate in some sense, and the empirical belongs to the sensual insofar as it partakes in this intractable immediacy.[160]

The appeal to eidetic variation encourages us to characterise the immediacy of sense perception in terms of *perspective*. This can be seen from the way that Harman associates the accidents presented by sense perception with perceptual profiles or adumbrations of objects seen from different perspectives, be they merely spatio-temporal or involving other variations in observational conditions. He does this either by contrasting them with essential qualities, or by means of examples:

---

160. Harman identifies this immediacy as the crucial feature of the sensual realm (or 'ether') in *Guerrilla Metaphysics* (153).

We cannot construct a mailbox by piling up essential qualities any more than by piling up outward profiles. The object is one; its qualities are many, whether they be accidental or eidetic.[161]

[W]hen I approach a tower and see it by means of slightly different qualities at each moment, I ignore these variations as unimportant, as if they were the mere jewellery of the princess rather than the Royal Highness herself. In general, perception is the zone of accidents of a thing as distinct from the thing itself.[162]

Eidetic variation is thus an exercise of the *imagination* that aims to compare, contrast, and explore such varying perspectives on an object and the accidental features they display in order to uncover the invariant essence that supports them. This suggests that the distinction between sensual and real qualities is that between those that are somehow *perspective-dependent* and those that are *perspective-independent*. This means that eidetic variation fails because perspective is somehow ineliminable. This is consistent with Harman's claim that no number of different perspectives on an object is sufficient to grasp it—even every possible perspective.[163]

The appeal to empirical investigation encourages us to characterise the immediacy of sense perception in terms of *givenness*. This point requires a good deal of reconstruction on our part, since Harman does not elaborate on the example he draws from Lovecraft in any detail. We can perhaps supplement this example with a passage from *The Quadruple Object*:

---

161. *The Quadruple Object*, 27.

162. *Guerrilla Metaphysics*, 187.

163. Ibid., 17.

> The necessary qualities of a sensual object are sunk beneath its surface like the hull of a Venetian galley, invisible to the observer who is dazzled by the flags and emblems covering the ship, or the music played on its deck by captive singers and drummers. Though the hull is submerged, it remains vital for the seaworthiness of the ship. By analogy, the real qualities of the sensual object can only be inferred indirectly rather than witnessed.[164]

This passage suggests that the distinction between sensual and real qualities can be understood in terms of the difference between those properties that are directly *given* to our senses and those whose presence must be indirectly *inferred* from this information. For example, one might distinguish the colour, malleability, and even perhaps the peculiar tangy taste of a piece of copper wire from its electrical conductivity, its melting point, and from a litany of its more interesting chemical and physical properties. If we understand empirical investigation as the exercise of *reason* in drawing inferences about the *unobservable* on the basis of the *observable*, then this seems to capture the relevant intuitive contrast. Nevertheless, this is insufficient if it treats givenness in purely negative terms—as opposed to inferential mediation—insofar as it leaves us with no sense of what scientific reasoning is failing to transcend through inference.

I think the positive conception of givenness implicitly guiding Harman's picture here is inextricably bound up with some conception of **qualia**—the intrinsic character of the sensations corresponding to sensible qualities, 'what it is like' to experience them, or *how* they are given. The view I have in mind is that sensible qualities are dependent upon their *mode*

---

164. *The Quadruple Object*, 29.

of givenness, insofar as our grasp of them consists in a sort of immediate acquaintance with their qualia in introspection. For example, one might hold that it is possible for a colour blind scientist to know everything about colour perception in normal human visual systems, and to know *that* an object is red, either by testimony or inference, without thereby knowing *what it is* for it to be red, insofar as she has never experienced the sensation of redness.[165] I have to be careful in attributing this view to Harman. On the one hand, the sort of introspection in terms of which qualia are defined cannot be understood as access to anything like raw 'sense data', such as isolated colour patches that have yet to be unified into objects, as he very clearly rejects this idea.[166] On the other, if this introspection is simply understood as access to the sensual realm of objects and qualities, then it would seem as if we have merely gone in a circle. What suggests this interpretation regardless is the way it interacts with a further distinction between types of qualities that seems to be lurking in the background.

I refer to the traditional distinction between those properties that things possess *independently* of observation, and those properties that can only be understood in terms of their *relation* to observers. For example, one could distinguish the shape, motion, and solidity of the piece of copper wire from its colour, taste, and smell. This is the distinction between *primary* and *secondary qualities*.[167] Although he explicitly claims that

---

165. This example is obviously borrowed from Frank Jackson's infamous knowledge argument (F. Jackson, 'Epiphenomenal Qualia', in *Philosophical Quarterly* 32 [1984], 127–36).

166. *Guerrilla Metaphysics*, 156–9.

167. Meillassoux has famously called for the resurrection of this distinction by characterising primary qualities as those that are independent of observation insofar as they are inherently mathematisable (*After Finitude*, chapter 1).

'[o]bject-oriented philosophy makes no distinction between primary and secondary qualities',[168] what Harman appears to be denying is that there is any such distinction internal to either the domain of sensual qualities or that of real qualities. We have already seen that Harman constructs his distinction between sensual and real qualities out of that between accidental and essential qualities, by harnessing the intuitive contrasts we have been outlining; but we can see the influence of the contrast between secondary and primary qualities here too, in his description of real/essential qualities as those of 'structural importance', or, by way of Zubiri's conception of 'the physical', as those 'pertaining to all that belongs intrinsically to any object'.[169] This emphasis on the *structural* and the *intrinsic* is traditionally associated with discussion of primary qualities.

The interaction between these ideas consists in the fact that it is precisely the sort of dependence on the mode of givenness characteristic of sensible qualities that is usually taken to distinguish secondary from primary qualities. It is insofar as a mode of givenness is not merely dependent upon the observed object, but also upon the sensory capacities of the observer, that a quality dependent upon it cannot be thought of as intrinsic to the object. Put more concretely, insofar as 'what it is like' to sense the redness of an apple is thought to be inherently subjective, it cannot be said to present an objective feature of the apple. We can see that these ideas are at play in Harman's thinking during one of his discussions of Ortega y Gasset:

---

168. *Guerrilla Metaphysics*, 84.

169. *Guerrilla Metaphysics*, 98; cf. *Tool-Being*, §22.

Ortega's traditional breakthrough, already a half-step further than Heidegger ever went, consists in his noticing that there is also an executant inner reality stirring behind the facades of buckets, candles, supermarkets, clay-pits, bank robberies, helicopter accidents, and trees. He cites the example of a red leather box lying before him, and notes that the redness and smoothness of the box are mere perceptions in his mind, while the box *itself* is actually embedded in the fate of being red and smooth—unlike Ortega himself. In one of the most radical sentences of twentieth-century philosophy, he tells us that "just as there is an I-John Doe, there is also an I-red, an I-water, and an I-star ... Everything, from the point of view within itself, is an I."[170]

Here the intrinsic character of the redness and smoothness of Ortega's perceptions of the box are taken to be distinct from the intrinsic character of the box's *being-red* and *being-smooth*. Put differently, what it is like *to experience* redness and smoothness is distinguished from what it is like *to be* red and smooth. This is the archetypal form of the distinction between sensual and real qualities. What is interesting about it is that it frames the inaccessibility of real qualities as the inaccessibility of the 'inwardness of things'[171] or a thing's 'point of view within itself'. This is to say that it treats the inaccessibility of a thing's real qualities as analogous to the inaccessibility of someone else's qualia. This indicates that there is a sense in which Harman uses sensible qualities as a model not just for sensual qualities, but for qualities *per se*. We will return to this point later.

---

170.   *Guerrilla Metaphysics*, 104.

171.   Ibid., 105.

For now, it is important to recognise that, despite what has just been said, Harman is not committed to the idea that there is a one-to-one mapping between sensual and real qualities, as if every sensual quality (e.g., sensual red) simply *represented* a corresponding real quality (e.g., real red). His appeal to empirical investigation is meant to suggest that the way sensual qualities are individuated should not reveal the way real qualities are individuated, much as the sensation of weight does not reveal the intricate relationship between intrinsic mass and extrinsic gravitational fields. However, insofar as mass is supposed to be as much a sensual quality as weight, Harman wants to say that they must both somehow consist in entirely distinct real qualities, even though their relationship to these qualities cannot be explanatorily circumscribed in the same way as that between mass and weight themselves. This is why Harman categorises the relation between sensual and real qualities as a matter of 'duplicity'.

Nevertheless, it is enlightening to consider how all of this connects to the implicit account of representation we examined earlier. What we established there was that Harman understands representing an *object-in-itself* as possessing a certain quality (e.g., *believing that* an apple is red) as standing in a certain relation to an *object-for-us* that actually possesses this quality. What we can now see is that this does not so much explain the representational content of sense perception (e.g., *seeing that* an apple is red) as employ sense perception as a model for all representational content. On this model, the relation to the object-for-us in which representation consists is analogous to sensation, and understanding the content of one's representations is analogous to introspecting the deliverances of one's senses.[172] This is to say that the object-for-us (the dimension of *referential purport*) is treated as a sensory appearance, and its qualities (the dimension of *predicative purport*) as its corresponding qualia. It is the fact that Harman's sensual realm is derived from this model of representational purport that makes sensual qualities essentially perspectival and immediately given.

Thus the interesting question is why the relation between sensual and real qualities is essentially duplicitous, given that it seems to be implicitly derived from representation. The answer is that this derivation proceeds by ignoring the distinction between the *vehicle* of a representation and its *content*. This distinction is important because it is possible for distinct representations to have the same content (e.g., for there to be different copies of the same novel, different maps of the same terrain, or utterances in different languages that say the same thing). In these cases we have distinct vehicles whose properties may diverge even though they express the same content (e.g., books of different sizes and formats, maps with different colours and scales, or utterances with different phonology and grammar). Although Harman has nothing concrete to say about the nature of sensation as a vehicle of representation (e.g., the causal-functional structure of our particular sensory systems), the disconnect between sensual and real qualities he proposes is predicated upon treating the former as the properties of sensation *qua* representational vehicle. If we take representation to consist in the object-for-us *sharing* the qualities of the object-in-itself while simultaneously

---

172. I think it likely that this is a derivative of Husserl's account of intuitive fulfilment (*Logical Investigations*, vol. 2, tr. J. M. Findlay [New York and London: Routledge, 2001], Investigation VI).

treating the object-for-us as a sensory appearance, then it becomes impossible to represent qualities that cannot be possessed by such appearances. One then only has to think that the relevant qualities of these appearances are *unique* to them in order to make correct representation of any sort impossible. This is precisely the significance of treating them as qualia that are inextricably tied to their mode of givenness within introspection.

Returning to our initial question then, the failure of Harman's account of sensual qualities to do justice to empirical properties is indexed by the extent to which the model of representation from which it is derived fails to do justice to the representations of the world produced by the sciences. Although the account seems intuitively plausible in the case of beliefs that can be observationally acquired (or confirmed), insofar as we can always imagine their objects (as if we were observing them), it becomes rapidly less plausible the further we move into the realm of the unobservable. For instance, though it is certainly possible that physicists picture the interactions between quarks in their mind's eye, it would seem absurd to claim that their understanding of the flavours of these quarks (e.g., up, down, strange, charm, etc.) consisted in their acquaintance with the intrinsic character of these pictures, rather than their mastery of the mathematical intricacies of the standard model. Moreover, beyond the applicability of some notion of perceptual adumbration or visual profile, it becomes equally strange to talk about their 'perspective' upon the quarks in anything other than a metaphorical sense (e.g., 'historical perspective'). However, although this disanalogy between sensory experience and scientific theory demonstrates the inadequacy of sensual qualities in relation to the empirical properties the latter represents, the full scope of this inadequacy will only become apparent once we address the remaining two criticisms.

II. QUALITY AND HAECCEITY

The second criticism of Harman's theory of qualities was prefigured in my earlier comments on his appropriation of Heidegger's account of the *as-structure*[173] and Husserl's account of *eidos*,[174] which entirely ignore both philosophers' concerns with generality, and in my discussion of his account of metaphor, which tends to elide the distinction between individuals and general kinds. This implicit rejection of generality becomes explicitly codified in Harman's theory of qualities:

> Husserl speaks of real qualities in generic terms, such that a certain shade of green can be embodied in many different particular objects; the same holds for the "eternal objects" of Whitehead, and for most other thinkers who have dealt with the topic of essence. By contrast, qualities as described in this book are always individualized by the object to which they belong. To put it in the terms of analytic philosophy, they are "tropes".[175]

> [Qualities] are not changeable from one object to the next, since we have seen that they belong entirely to the object from which they emerge.[176]

What this means is that the qualities possessed by an object are always *unique*: an apple is not generically red in a manner

---

173. See chapter 2.1, subsection I.

174. See chapter 2.2, subsection II.

175. *The Quadruple Object*, 30.

176. *Guerrilla Metaphysics*, 232.

that could be shared with other apples, but displays a pattern and shade of redness whose infinite detail is such that, in principle, it could not be shared with anything else. It is worth considering the origins of this surfeit of specificity. The above quotes present it as a feature of both real and sensual qualities that derives from their relation to the object that possesses them, but this is not the only way in which Harman presents it.

In *Guerrilla Metaphysics*, Harman borrows the term 'element' from Levinas to distinguish the completely specific qualities of sensual objects from the impossible 'free floating' qualities that he equates with 'raw sense data'.[177] Taking the most detailed example he provides:

> *An element is a sensual object incarnated in highly specific form.* If the sensual object is the monkey that seems identical to us through all variations in our perceptions of it, the element is always the monkey at twilight or dawn, viewed from a specific angle or in a determinate mood, and currently eating, climbing, fighting, or screeching with accidents, like a car glistening with ice after an overnight storm [...] An element is always one specific, ruthlessly sincere incarnation of a sensual object. An element is not just the monkey in its pure perceptual monkey-hood, enduring over time, but rather the monkey down to every last trivial detail of its actions and physical posture.[178]

---

177. *Guerrilla Metaphysics*, 159–67. It is quite difficult to follow the discussion of elements in *GM*. For example, we are at one point told that: 'In this respect, we can say that the *elements are the notes of sensual objects*' (171) only to be informed later that: 'We now determine, somewhat paradoxically, that *the elements of the world are nothing other than sensual objects*'. (178). The following interpretation is the most consistent I have been able to piece together in spite of such apparent contradictions.

178. *Guerrilla Metaphysics*, 194–5.

What this means is that, in effect, elements are just the perceptual profiles of sensual objects. The uniqueness of these profiles is not directly derived from the individuality of their objects, but consists in the way in which their various details are *enmeshed* with one another. This is another aspect of sensual qualities that Harman draws from sense perception. Specifically, it is drawn from the inevitable excess of sensory details over our ability to describe what we see. It seems that the sheer immediacy of this excess is supposed to prevent us from separating out these details without distorting them. However, insofar as these details are themselves qualities, this suggests that qualities derive their uniqueness from their relations to one another. The problem with this is that it collapses an object's plurality of qualities into a single unitary quality. And indeed this is precisely the position that Harman is forced into: 'The oneness of a sensual flame is no different from the particularity of that flame, because its [qualities] (or rather, the single flame-[quality]) exist only within that union.'[179] Once this line is crossed, there is nothing to prevent this singular quality from dissolving into the unitary object that possesses it: 'All objects are both unified and completely specific in the same stroke, not by way of two separate dimensions, not even if these dimensions are termed "inseparable"'.[180]

Harman pulls back from this position after *Guerrilla Metaphysics* and abandons talk of elements entirely. As far as I can tell, this is because it undermines the object/quality axis of the fourfold schema, the preservation of which is essential for the system of categories developed in *The Quadruple Object*. Harman continues to discuss the uniqueness of sensual qualities

179. Ibid., 228.

180. Ibid.

in a manner reminiscent of sensory excess, but he grounds it in the relation between these qualities and the objects they belong to rather than any relations between the qualities themselves (now categorically circumscribed as *radiations*). Qualities cannot be shared by multiple objects because they essentially belong to specific individuals. This creates a serious problem for Harman's account of real qualities. A crucial feature of the argument from essence was the Leibnizian contention that the individuation of real objects requires that they possess a multiplicity of qualities. This means that they are never *simply* distinct from one another, but are always distinct *in virtue* of some qualities that they do not share. However, if objects can *never* share any qualities because qualities are always unique to their objects, then objects are distinct from one another in virtue of the fact that they are distinct from one another, or rather, they *are* simply distinct. Furthermore, even if we took the uniqueness of qualities to be primitive rather than derived, this would still undermine the requirement that an object possess many qualities, as a single quality would be sufficient to individuate them. The integrity of the fourfold structure is thus threatened either way.

These problems suggest that there is an alternative logic underpinning the object/quality axis of the fourfold schema. The clue to this logic lies in the way Harman attempts to reinforce the distinction between the singularity of the object and the multiplicity of its qualities. In *Guerrilla Metaphysics*, he attempts to soften his conclusion that there *really* aren't many distinct qualities by explaining why there nevertheless *appear* to be:

> I hold that the individual thing is simply one, and that any plural-
> ity it might have actually comes from its parts, not from its

[qualities]. The thing actually has only one [quality], not many—it seems to have many only because it remains linked to its parts, which line it like handles or portholes.[181]

Although, as we have seen, he subsequently rejects the idea that the plurality of a thing's qualities is *merely* apparent, he retains the idea that it is to be explained by appeal to the plurality of its parts:

[W]hy are we dealing with multiplicities here at all? Why is it that a sensual tree has numerous different sensual qualities, and a real dog has numerous different real qualities? The answer, I propose, comes from the fact that any real or sensual object is made up of multiple pieces. When these pieces join together to form the object in question, the excessive properties of the parts that are not needed by the interaction are left over, as a sort of gas or aroma of qualities surrounding the object—an industrial byproduct of the process through which it was fabricated. The same holds in a different way for the relation between real objects and real qualities as well: for even if a real object is not attached to its multiple qualities in the same way as a sensual object is, those qualities need to be filtered through some real object to be available for possible use later on.[182]

This explanation is evidently circular, insofar as it attempts to explain the fact that whole objects have many qualities by differentiating between the contributions of the many qualities of their component objects. Ignoring this circularity though, the persistence of the part/quality connection suggests that

---

181. *Guerrilla Metaphysics*, 229.

182. *The Quadruple Object*, 133.

Harman's object/quality distinction is actually a sublimated form of the whole/part distinction. On the one hand, this accounts for the dubious mereological component of the argument from excess.[183] On the other, it suggests that the divergence between the sensual and real domains is at least partially accounted for by transposing the distinction between subject and predicate onto different mereological models: the relation between a *phenomenal unity* and its various *profiles*,[184] and that between a *functional unity* and its various *components*.[185] It is this logical juxtaposition that enables Harman to seem as if he is providing an analysis of property possession, or the relation between universal and individual, without having to address anything but relations between individuals, or even having to account for their individuation. This is more than simple agnosticism about the existence of universals.[186] It is a deeper failure to acknowledge the metaphysical problems that theories of universals are attempting to solve.

III. MODAL MYSTERIANISM

The third and final criticism of Harman's theory of qualities emerges from my earlier charge that the argument from execution results in modal mysterianism.[187] It is important to remember that this mysterianism doesn't consist in an evasion of the issue of modality, as we saw in the case of generality.

---

183. Chapter 2.1, subsection II.

184. This is apparent in the above discussion of elements, but it also seems to inform the lines of thought regarding partial and complete knowledge running through the arguments from excess and identity.

185. See p. 83 n. 94.

186. Cf. *Guerrilla Metaphysics*, 153.

187. Chapter 2.1, subsection I.

We have already seen that Harman quite explicitly addresses the topic of modality, at least insofar as the argument from execution aims to locate the ground of a thing's causal capacities in its withdrawn tool-being. The mysterianism lies in the fact that the argument merely emulates explanation, by providing a paradoxical characterisation of tool-being that performatively invokes some ineffable hidden essence, as opposed to anything like a concrete analysis of causal capacity. However, the modal tension between possibility and actuality at the heart of this characterisation evolves into a crucial feature of Harman's theory of qualities. Though it begins as the stipulated equivalence between execution as a capacity *to act* and as a capacity *in action*, wherein the various possible relations that are thereby *actualised* are nevertheless somehow extrinsic to the substances these capacities constitute, it develops into an insistence that substance must have a distinct form of *actuality* that underpins the actualisation of these relations. To quote the relevant passage from *Tool-Being*:

> If an entity always holds something in reserve beyond any of its relations, and if this reserve also cannot be located in any of these relations, then it must exist somewhere else. And since this reserve is what it is, quite apart from whatever might stumble into it, it is actual rather than potential. But it is not present-at-hand, because I have shown that presence-at-hand turns out to be *relational*, against what is usually believed.[188]

Harman appropriates the negative term 'vacuous actuality' from Whitehead to name this non-relational actuality of the

188.   *Tool-Being*, 230.

real/withdrawn in contrast to the relational actuality of the sensual/present, reinterpreting 'vacuous' as *in vacuo,* or 'apart from any accidental collision with other objects'.[189]

In order to see the problem with the notion of vacuous actuality, we have to consider the antipathy to *potentiality* that motivates it in more detail. Harman unpacks his argument further elsewhere:

> [T]he concept of 'potential' should be avoided wherever possible. To say that an acorn is a potential oak tree is clearly true, but the real question is this: what *actual* aspect of the acorn allows it to be potentially an oak tree? To talk about an object in terms of potential is really to view it from the outside, in terms of some future relations it might have, and this enables one to dodge the question of what the actuality of unexpressed qualities might be, here and now.[190]

In parsing this argument we must be wary of the way that Harman maps the distinction between substance and relation onto that between the real and the sensual. Sensual qualities are distinguished from the real qualities that withdraw behind them by their relations to the objects that encounter them. As such, it might sound as if the 'future relations' referred to in this passage are of the same kind, and thus that Harman's insistence that real qualities are not potential is simply a consequence of the claim that they are not sensual. However, the difference between the acorn and the oak tree cannot be reduced to the novel relations to its environment that the latter has acquired through gestation. It is thus not a matter of

---

189. Ibid., 228.

190. *Towards Speculative Realism*, 117.

whether real qualities should be characterised in terms of the possible relations between *objects* they enable (e.g., between the future oak tree and the soil it is planted in), but whether they should be characterised by relations to possible *states of affairs* (e.g., between the present acorn and its possible future as an oak tree), including but not limited to *relational* states of affairs (e.g., between the present acorn and the range of possible interactions between the future oak and its environment). This suggests that the argument rests on a familiar worry about the circularity of causal explanations that appeal to dispositional properties—namely, that if properties are defined purely in terms of their effects, then they cannot informatively explain the causal relations between the things which possess them and the effects they produce. This is exemplified by Molière's philosopher, who explains that opium puts people to sleep because it possesses a 'dormative virtue'.

Although this convincingly suggests that we should not entertain such brute dispositional properties (i.e., 'a propensity to...'), it is not clear that this is the only possible link between quality and potentiality. This can be made apparent by way of another historical parallel: the debate between Hume and Kant regarding causal necessity. Hume's challenge is an *epistemological* one. He argues that causal inferences about the future are strictly unjustified, even if they are habitually unavoidable, because causal relations between actual states of affairs cannot be found in our experience in the same way as the states themselves. Kant's response to this argument is *semantic*. Rather than claim that causal connections are actually present in experience in a way Hume had missed, he argues that Hume's challenge relies upon a demarcation between our understanding of the way things *actually are* and the way things *could be* that cannot be maintained. Brandom articulates this point very precisely:

> Kant was struck by the fact that the essence of the Newtonian concept of mass is of something that, by law, *force* is both necessary and sufficient to *accelerate*. And he saw that all empirical concepts are like their refined descendants in the mathematized natural sciences in this respect: their application implicitly involves counterfactual-supporting dispositional commitments to what *would* happen *if*. Kant's claim, put in more contemporary terms, is that an integral part of what one is committed to in applying any determinate concept in empirical circumstances is drawing a distinction between counterfactual differences in circumstances that *would* and those that *would not* affect the truth of the judgment one is making. One has not grasped the concept cat unless one knows that it would still be possible for the cat to be on the mat if the lighting had been slightly different, but not if all life on earth had been extinguished by an asteroid-strike.[191]

The significance of Kant's claim that causation is a categorial feature of the structure of experience is that to recognise objects *as* the particular objects they are (e.g., as cats, acorns, copper wires, etc.) involves having some grasp of their particular causal capacities (e.g., mobility, growth, conductivity, etc.). This is what it means to understand the *content* of the relevant general concepts, or the *essence* of the corresponding properties. This does not mean that causal capacities and relations are entirely transparent. Our beliefs about them can be as incorrect or incomplete as any of our other beliefs

---

191.   Brandom, *Between Saying and Doing*, 97.

about objects. It is simply that we must have *some* beliefs about these capacities in order to have *any* beliefs about objects at all. Put differently, one cannot even incorrectly believe *that* something is a cat without having some idea of *what it is* for something to be a cat; and this means having at least some appreciation of what *can, can't,* and *must* be the case if this is so. We have already seen how Heidegger extends this Kantian insight, by showing how our theoretical understanding of such causal capacities is grounded in our practical understanding of the functional roles they play in possible action—what *may, may not,* and *should* be done with them.[192]

The problem with Hume's argument is that it depends upon the assumption that there is a primitive layer of experience that can be made intelligible without appeal to these sorts of modal notions. This is the *foundationalism* inherent in traditional empiricism—the idea that there is a level of description prior to all explanation, upon which all explanations are ultimately founded. Crucially, the empiricists were tempted into this position by focusing upon sensible qualities (e.g., redness, smoothness, solidity, etc.) as the exemplars of empirical properties, much as Harman does in his account of sensual qualities. As we have already seen, the problem with this narrow focus is that it encourages the view that we can understand *what it is* to be red simply through immediate acquaintance with the sensation of redness. This supposed immediacy underwrites the assumption that seeing *that* something is red is to see something *purely* actual—i.e., devoid of all relation to possibility and necessity—by obviating the need for modal relations to constitute the content of the seeing.

192. Chapter 2.1, subsection I.

However, as Hegel impresses upon us in the 'Perception' section of the *Phenomenology of Spirit*, even these seemingly simple qualities are thoroughly mediated: understanding that an object is red involves understanding that it is *impossible* for it to also be green, transparent, or without spatial extension. The modal relations of *incompatibility* between these properties are constitutive features of what they are.[193]

Empiricism is only able to ignore this point by exploiting a systematic ambiguity regarding whether the sensible qualities it focuses on belong to our sensations of objects (as qualia) or the objects themselves (as genuine properties). Harman has rightly complained that empiricism tends to treat qualities as given prior to objects, and that this makes objects into mere bundles of qualities that are subsequently unified theoretically.[194] In doing so, it treats these qualities as primarily features of sensation, and only derivatively as features of objects. This model of experience engenders modal scepticism by requiring that causal relations between objects be inferred from regularities in patterns of sensation that can be described without reference to these objects. If we are to reject this model, as Harman recommends, then we have to treat sensible qualities as essentially belonging to objects, but this means recognising the way our grasp of them is mediated by modal relations of incompatibility. This is because objects are essentially *loci* of such incompatibilities.[195] What is precluded by the incompatibility of two qualities is their possession *by the same object* (e.g., *a* can be red and *b* can be green, but neither *a* nor *b* can

---

193. Brandom, *Tales of the Mighty Dead*, chapter 7.

194. *The Quadruple Object*, 23; *Weird Realism*, 29.

195. This point derives from a refinement of Hegel's ideas that Brandom develops at length in *Between Saying and Doing*, chapter 6.

be *both* red and green). The distinctness of two objects entails that, all else being equal, the qualities one actually possesses do not constrain which qualities the other could possess in this way; but this makes no difference unless they are not distinct from themselves, which is to say, unless incompatibilities between qualities do constrain which qualities they can possess. This means that a quality cannot belong to a *specific* object unless that object is thereby precluded from possessing some other qualities, because the object's *specificity* consists in its inability to possess incompatible qualities (i.e., it wouldn't be *a*'s redness unless it precluded *a* from being green). As such, we cannot treat qualities as genuinely belonging to objects unless we treat them as having at least some incompatibility relations and thus as having a minimal modal content.

Returning to the notion of vacuous actuality and the argument against potentiality that motivates it, we can now see that we are no better off explaining causation by means of qualities that are entirely non-relational than we are explaining it by means of qualities that are defined purely in relation to their effects. Let us consider the example of the acorn once more. It is clear that defining the quality which enables it to grow into an oak as a potentiality to do so is circular; but it is equally clear that describing it as an actuality that *just is what it is* (or a certain *je ne sais quoi*) is entirely empty—quite literally vacuous. A genuine explanation of this capacity would describe the intervening stages of the process of germination and growth, and the differing roles that the acorn's component parts play within it: by means of capacities for cellular division and differentiation, which would themselves have to be explained by means of capacities for DNA replication and modified gene expression, and so on. These capacities inhere in and constitute the relevant properties of the acorn and its components, from the distribution of and internal structure of its cells, to the specific molecular sequence of their DNA.

It might be claimed that although such an explanation is neither circular nor vacuous, it is nevertheless regressive, because it always leaves us seeking a further explanation for those capacities appealed to in the former explanation. However, this regress is entirely virtuous: understanding is gained at each stage, and this is not mitigated by the fact that there is yet more to understand. To answer the question 'why won't this gas react with anything?' by saying 'because it is helium' is not the same as saying 'because it won't react with anything'; but neither is it an answer for which further explanation cannot be demanded. To understand that helium atoms *cannot* form molecular bonds is to understand something about *what it is* for them to be helium; but to understand *why* this is so involves looking into the *what* of electron shells and nuclei, for which there will inevitably be further *whys*. Our ability to describe objects as possessing certain qualities is inseparable from our ability to use these descriptions in the ongoing process of explanation through which our understanding of these qualities is developed and refined.

We can now see that, although he rejects the empiricist account of objects, Harman inadvertently perpetuates the problems of the empiricist account of qualities. Though Harman's metaphysical approach to causation and Hume's scepticism are undoubtedly at odds, their shared focus on sensible qualities at the expense of empirical properties more generally leads them both to treat qualities as pure actualities that simply *are what they are*. Harman's approach is largely congruent with Hume's at the level of sensual qualities, in that it takes the causal capacities underlying the configurations of apparent qualities to be absent from experience. However, although he diverges from Hume by locating these capacities in a deeper level of real qualities that can never be experienced, this turns out to be little more than a projection of the sensual level. As we saw in Harman's discussion of Ortega y Gasset, he treats real qualities almost as if they were sensual qualities that are merely inaccessible to us in principle, as qualia that reside in the private inner worlds of the things themselves rather than in the sensoria of whatever encounters them. Both kinds of qualities are inscrutable haecceities that are simply individuated in themselves, without either modal relations with other qualities or coinstantiation relations with other objects. The difference between them consists in the fact that sensual qualities have an *immediacy* that the latter lack—we can assure ourselves that we see *this* shade, smell *this* scent, and taste *this* flavour, rather than *that* one. Real qualities are unknowable because we cannot hold them before our mind's eye in this way, but they remain as simple and primitive as their sensual kin. We are left with a cosmos populated with absolutely distinct yet entirely indistinguishable singularities—singular things with singular qualities—some that we can point to (and internally scream '*this* is like *this!*'), and some that we cannot (because presumably, '*that* is like *that*').

In the end, it is as if Harman thinks that objects are *unitary*, seamless refrigerators (real objects), filled with a *multiplicity* of wonderful and potentially delicious flavours of ice cream that we can never taste (real qualities). We can spy their sheer variety behind the frosty glass, but not only can we never open the door, there is no door we could possibly open (withdrawal). We are condemned to choose between the flavours on display (sensual qualities) behind the snack counters (sensual objects) that litter the foyer of the great cinema of life (the glittering surface world), even while a further, mysterious selection stands idling forever out of reach of the assorted pubescent attendants (the molten subterranean world). The only saving grace of this situation is that we can always hop the counter, force the attendant to one side, and press our tongues to the glass, hoping against hope to detect a faint trace of the afferent miasma emanating from the delights trapped within (allure). Harman's picture reduces us to *reality junkies*, permanently debasing ourselves for one more tantalising *lick* of the real.[196] In the end, OOP collapses into a kind of bizarre **gastronomic mysticism**.

---

196. The situation is not dissimilar to the predicament Russell describes in relation to Bergson: 'the reader is like the child who expects a sweet because it has been told to open its mouth and shut its eyes. Logic, mathematics, physics disappear in this philosophy, because they are too "static"; what is real is an impulse and movement towards a goal which, like the rainbow, recedes as we advance, and makes every place different when we reach it from what it appeared to be at a distance' (B. Russell, *Our Knowledge of the External World* [London: Routledge Classics, 2009], 11).

3. WHAT ARE RELATIONS ANYWAY?

Perhaps the most noticeable effect that OOP has had upon contemporary metaphysical debates has been to bring renewed attention to the status of relations between entities.[197] According to Harman, the battle lines dividing up this conceptual terrain pit a contemporary **relationist** orthodoxy—which dissolves objects into their relations with one another—against his own **substantialist** heresy—which defends the independence of objects from all such relations. For Harman, correlationism is implicitly responsible for this orthodoxy to some extent by invariably making objects dependent upon some *vertical* relations to subjects. He also identifies more explicitly metaphysical champions of relationism—split roughly between those he draws influence from (Whitehead, Latour, and DeLanda) and those he merely opposes (Deleuze, Badiou, and Ladyman and Ross)—who make objects dependent upon some *horizontal* relations to one another. However, as we have already seen, the genesis of Harman's substantialism occurs in his opposition to Heidegger, both as a reaction against Heidegger's identification of substance (*ousia*) with presence (*Anwesenheit*), and as a corrective to the putatively relational ontology of readiness-to-hand (*Zuhandenheit*) that Harman finds in his work.[198] Indeed, the two halves of Harman's notion of withdrawn substance can both be traced back to his appropriation of Heidegger's work on relations: the epistemic excess of objects over their presence is obtained

---

197.   Cf. S. Shaviro 'The Actual Volcano', in Bryant, Srnicek, and Harman (eds), *The Speculative Turn*, and Harman's 'Response to Shaviro' in the same volume.

198.   Chapter 2.1, subsection II.

by means of a *general model* drawn from the account of intentional relations; and this excess is converted into their causal independence from one another by means of *specific cases* (synchronic dependence and diachronic affection) drawn from the account of functional relations. Although we have already examined this genesis and its flaws in detail, further consideration will reveal deeper problems with the manner in which Harman frames the overarching question regarding the metaphysics of relations.

To begin with, it is important to understand that Heidegger does not present us with anything like a general theory of relations. He does provide an account of intentionality as a system of vertical relations between subjects (or Dasein) and objects, and an account of functionality as a system of horizontal relations between objects, locations, and functional roles; but neither of these is intended as an account of relations *qua* relations—they are *species* of relation, rather than the *genus*—nor is one meant to be analysed in terms of the other—functional relations are not a *subspecies* of intentional relation (or vice versa). Of course, Harman is aware of this, and explicitly acknowledges that Heidegger would not countenance his universalisation of intentionality. Nevertheless, this does raise the question of why one might think intentionality is an adequate model not just for functional relations, but for relations *per se*. Moving beyond Harman's appropriation of Heidegger, the core motivation for this idea can be found in the way he positions himself in relation to Kant:

> We might summarize the philosophical position of Kant by saying that he makes two basic claims: 1) Human knowledge is finite, since the things-in-themselves can be thought but never known;

2) The human-world relation (mediated by space, time, and the categories) is philosophically privileged over every other sort of relation; philosophy is primarily about human access to the world, or at least must take this access as its starting point.

Object-oriented philosophy agrees with the first Kantian point and disagrees with the second, while for speculative materialism it is precisely the reverse. For object-oriented philosophy, the things-in-themselves remain forever beyond our grasp, but not because of a specifically *human* failure to reach them. Instead, relations *in general* fail to gasp their relata, and in this sense the ghostly things-in-themselves haunt inanimate causal relations no less than the human-world relation, which no longer stands at the center of philosophy.[199]

What this shows is that Harman's universalisation of intentionality is motivated by a radical form of *ontological humility*. He takes it that to grant any sort of special metaphysical status to the human would be hubristic, and that to restrict the provenance of intentional relations of knowing to humans is to do just this, regardless of whether they can be successful or not. It is a correspondingly radical form of *epistemological humility* that then denies the possibility of genuine knowledge of things, and thus, in collusion with its ontological counterpart, implies that all relations must be modelled as failed attempts to understand an object.

Now, we might wonder precisely why the restriction of knowledge relations constitutes an illegitimate metaphysical privilege when the restriction of other types of relation does not (e.g., not all objects are able to 'consume', 'magnetize', or even perhaps 'marry' something else). However, pursuing this

---

199. 'The Road to Objects', 171.

question would mean probing the methodological relationship between epistemology and metaphysics in far greater depth than we have so far, and perhaps even asking why we should treat epistemic relations as having any metaphysical status at all. This is a bigger can of worms than I care to open here. Nevertheless, there is more to be said about why Harman thinks knowledge (or intentionality more generally) is capable of providing an adequate model for other relations.

According to modern logic, relations are a type of *predicate*. Predicates are loosely defined as *mathematical functions* that take objects as arguments (e.g., **Fx**) and return truth or falsity as values (e.g., **Fa** returns true iff **a** is **F** and false otherwise),[200] or as *open sentences* that require the addition of singular terms or quantified noun phrases in order to form complete sentences (e.g., '…is red', '…is out of tune', '…knows a good place to park his car', etc.). The examples just given are *monadic* predicates, which only have one argument place. These are usually taken to denote properties or qualities. However, predicates can easily have a different *addicity*, or number of argument places (e.g., **Fxy**, '…is larger than…'). It is these *n-ary* predicates that correspond to relations. This means we can have three-place relations such as '…is between … and…', which is true of something if it is located between two other things, and even eleven-place relations such as '…compose a

---

200. In some interpretations (e.g., possible world semantics) predicates do not directly return truth values, but return propositions which are themselves understood as functions from contexts (e.g., possible worlds) to truth values. This is to account for the fact that non-mathematical propositions such as that expressed by 'the earth is the third planet from the sun' are true when evaluated in ordinary contexts (e.g., in talking about the actual world), but might be false if evaluated in a different context (e.g., in a hypothetical discussion of a possible world in which the solar system formed differently).

soccer team', which is true of some group of eleven people if they are in fact members of the same soccer team. Moreover, two-place relations are usually characterised by their *algebraic properties*: as potentially *reflexive* (e.g., if **x** is near to **y**, then **x** is near to **x**), *transitive* (e.g., if **x** is larger than **y**, and **y** is larger than **z**, then **x** is larger than **z**), and *symmetric* (e.g., if **x** is married to **y** then **y** is married to **x**). Given that knowing is a two-place relation that is neither reflexive, transitive, nor symmetric, how is it supposed to provide a model for relations with different addicities or algebraic properties?

The answer to this question is that Harman never really intended knowledge (or intentionality) to provide a model for these cases, because he uses the term 'relation' in an idiomatic fashion that doesn't include them. The scope of Harman's usage is made clear in the following passage:

> [E]lements are the basis of *all* relations, not just sentient ones. For not only is sentient perception object-oriented, bonded to fugitive objects in the night—but also *interaction in general* is saddled with this fate, and elements are the vehicle through which this destiny is enacted.[201]

The crucial point to take away from this passage is that Harman treats 'all relations' and 'interaction in general' as synonyms. The scope of this idiomatic usage becomes more explicit later in the same book:

> We have said repeatedly that every relation immediately forms a new object, since every relation has a full inner life not exhaustible by any outer perception of it. But this might be cause for

---

201. *Guerrilla Metaphysics*, 169, my emphasis.

confusion, since the word "relation" is generally used to describe the relation between two things that *do not* fuse together into a new object. The numerous keys and toothpicks lying before me can obviously be said to relate to each other in a certain sense, but we have been employing the term "relation" for a closer kind of fusion between parts that give birth to a new thing [...] Instead of saying that the various side-by-side elements of perception are related, we will say instead that they are *contiguous* or *adjacent*.[202]

That contiguity, which eventually becomes a full-blown category (SO–SO) in Harman's ontography, is not a 'relation' in his sense of the word should make it clear that anything like *locative relations* (e.g., **x** is to the left of **y**, **x** is earlier than **y**, etc.) and perhaps even *comparative relations* (e.g., **x** is larger than **y**, **x** is less important than **y**, etc.) are not 'relations' either, because they do not describe interactions between objects that can themselves be viewed as further objects.[203] As already noted, the only relations that Harman deals with (as 'relations') are the specific cases he develops out of Heidegger's account of functionality: *synchronic dependence* (execution) and *diachronic affection* (causation), or the interactions through which entities *persist* and *change*, respectively. The reason these are at least *prima facie* susceptible to analysis in intentional terms is that they share (or can be made out to share) the asymmetrical two-place structure

---

202. *Guerrilla Metaphysics*, 195.

203. Harman once suggested, during the *Real Objects or Material Subjects* conference at Dundee (2010), that comparative relations might be viewed as exclusively constituting sensual objects, but this was an off the cuff remark.

of intentional relations.[204] One might be forgiven for thinking that this is nothing but an issue of terminology. However, not only does Harman's peculiar sense of relation distort his presentation of the metaphysical debate between relationism and substantialism; it also generates blind spots in his thinking that warp his treatment of certain fundamental topics.

The distortions engendered by Harman's terminology are often masked by his choice of interlocutors. Latour's metaphysics of **networks** is principally concerned with precisely the sorts of synchronic dependence relations that Harman begins with, in virtue of its origin as an extension of his sociological methodology (**Actor Network Theory [ANT]**) for describing how certain relatively stable social systems function; but it does not distinguish between these and other types of relations (e.g., spatio-temporal configuration), precisely because Latour's avowed relationalism converts them into ersatz dependence relations (e.g., by making a node's identity dependent upon its relative location within the network). This enables Harman to castigate Latour for rendering impossible the diachronic causal interactions through which networks are rearranged, while simultaneously leveraging his model of ersatz dependence to portray all other relations as if they were synchronic causal dependencies, and thus amenable to analysis in intentional terms. By contrast, Whitehead's metaphysics of **prehension** already combines causal interaction and perception in a manner resembling Harman's intentional model, but it does not present this as an account of relationality *per se*.[205] However, those

---

204. However, as pointed out in our discussion of the argument from independence, that causal relations and intentional relations can both be portrayed as asymmetric does not mean that they can be portrayed as sharing the same direction (chapter 2.3, subsection II).

205. This is hardly surprising given Whitehead's contributions to modern logic.

who take up Whitehead's banner when Harman assimilates his relationalism to Latour's are not always so precise in making this distinction, and thereby acquiesce to his framing of the issue.[206] Though Harman's debate with Latour and Whitehead is not substantially affected by the conflation of interaction and relation that it tends to obfuscate, it nevertheless serves to distort his debate with Deleuze, DeLanda, and Ladyman and Ross by presenting them as more similar to Latour and Whitehead than they in fact are.

To demonstrate this point it is first necessary to rehearse the core complaint that Harman levels against relationism, namely, that it makes change impossible. As we hinted earlier, this complaint is prefigured in his engagement with Heidegger's supposed relationism in *Tool-Being*, which has two basic components: the claim that defining objects in terms of their relations inevitably collapses into some form of holism, and the claim that this holism precludes change.[207] Harman's argument is essentially that the indefinite ramification of functional dependence relations implied by their referential structure inevitably leads to a sort of functional saturation (a 'world-machine') that leaves no room for functional disruption, and therefore reconfiguration or change. However, though the complaint against Latour and Whitehead is the same, the argument cannot be, because Latour's relationism isn't *holist* and Whitehead's holism isn't *functional*. Harman thus needs a more robust argument to establish the conclusion that relationism implies stasis more generally. The argument he settles on approaches the same point—the inseparability of

---

206. Cf. Shaviro, 'The Actual Volcano', and 'The Universe of Things', <http://www.shaviro.com/Othertexts/Things.pdf>.

207. Chapter 2.1, subsection I.

an object's *identity* from its *effects* upon other objects—from two different angles.[208] On the one hand, he argues that this prevents objects from *instigating* change, because they cannot be exhaustively constituted by their current effects and yet capable of novel future effects. On the other, he argues that it prevents objects from *undergoing* change, because if they were to produce novel effects then they would no longer be the same objects. The problem with this argument is that the characterisation of relationism on which it rests does not apply either to Deleuze and DeLanda, or to Ladyman and Ross, albeit for different reasons.

I. RELATIONALITY AND VIRTUALITY

In the case of Deleuze and DeLanda's process metaphysics, the problem with Harman's argument is that it characterises relationism as reducing individuals to their relations *with one another*. The reason this is problematic is that both thinkers distinguish between *actual* individuals and the *virtual* multiplicities that provide the conditions of their individuation, and it is the *differential relations* constitutive of the latter which they take to have something like an ontological priority over the individuals constitutive of the former.[209] This is Deleuze

---

208. *Prince of Networks*, 186–7.

209. Cf. G. Deleuze, *Difference and Repetition*, tr. P. Patton (New York: Columbia University Press, 1994), chapters 4–5; M. DeLanda, *Intensive Science and Virtual Philosophy* (London: Continuum, 2002), chapters 1–3. It is worth noting that the precise strength of this ontological priority is disputed by interpreters. For example, following Badiou (*Deleuze: The Clamor of Being*, tr. L. Burchill [Minneapolis: University of Minnesota Press, 2000]), Peter Hallward criticises Deleuze for granting the virtual (*qua* unitary whole) a strong ontological priority over the actual individuals, or creatures, that emerge from it (P. Hallward, *Out of this World: Deleuze and the Philosophy of Creation* [London: Verso, 2006], chapter 3). By contrast, DeLanda's appropriation and development

and DeLanda's way of articulating Gilbert Simondon's idea that individuals must be understood in terms of the 'pre-individual' factors underlying their genesis. Harman does try to engage with these ideas to some extent:

> These positions try to enjoy the best of both worlds, defining a unified realm beneath experience that is not *completely* unified. Instead of a total lump-world, it is one animated in advance by different 'pre-individual' zones that prevent the world from being purely homogeneous. This position has the following supposed benefits: it prevents things from being overdetermined by their current actuality (an admirable object-oriented gesture), while also slyly bridging the gap between things without doing the required work (a merely 'radical' move in the sense that must be rejected). For instance, DeLanda wishes to establish the possibility of a 'continuous, yet heterogeneous space'. The same is true of Gilbert Simondon, that posthumous rising star. As Alberto Toscano describes Simondon's position, 'whilst [preindividual being] is yet to be individuated, [it] can already be regarded as affected by relationality. This preindividual relationality, which takes place between heterogeneous dimensions, forces or energetic tendencies, is nevertheless also a sort of non-relation [...]. Being is thus said to be *more-than-one* to the extent that all of its potentials cannot be actualized at once'. Simondon like DeLanda wants the world to be both heterogeneous and *not yet* parcelled out into

---

of Deleuze's metaphysics seems to treat actual individuals (and the intensive processes that produce them) as distinct from but not inferior to the virtual multiplicities they incarnate (cf. his remarks on 'flat ontology' in *Intensive Science*, 153–4). Regardless, it is clear that both Deleuze and DeLanda wish to reject the total assimilation of pre-individual differential relations to relations between actual individuals that Harman advocates.

individuals. In this way, specific realities lead a sort of halfhearted existence somewhere between one and many.[210]

173

RELATIONALITY AND VIRTUALITY

However, he does not actually consider the nature of 'preindividual relationality' and how the differential relations Deleuze and DeLanda take to be constitutive of the virtual might differ from the 'relations', or rather, causal interactions, that he deals with exclusively.

It is hard to do justice to this difference without providing a thorough survey of Deleuze's metaphysics (or its DeLandian variant), but it suffices to point out that differential relations (e.g., dx/dy) do not hold between individuals, but *variable quantities* (i.e., x and y). These variables may correspond to quantities of individuals (e.g., populations of foxes and rabbits, as in DeLanda's example of a predator-prey system),[211] but they can equally correspond to velocities, spatial orientations, temperatures, and the whole range of degrees of freedom characteristic of dynamic systems. Moreover, even in cases where they do correspond to quantities of individuals, they do not correspond to *specific* individuals or groups thereof (i.e., the differential relation between number of foxes and number of rabbits captures a tendency governing the relative rates of change in population that applies across successive generations of foxes and rabbits, without care for which particular foxes and rabbits these are). There is a legitimate metaphysical debate to be had about whether it makes sense to give this sort of relation ontological priority over individuals, but it is crucial to understand that this is *precisely not* the debate that Harman engages in:

210.   *Prince of Networks*, 188.

211.   DeLanda, *Intensive Science*, 166–8.

An obvious question to raise is why the relations between real attractors that build up a multiplicity are any less problematic than the relation between the real and the actual, or between two actual things. If no actual trajectory ever does justice to its underlying attractors, it should also be the case that no real multiplicity ever does justice to its own real components. In both cases it is a matter of relations, and relations are simply unable to exhaust their terms.[212]

This passage is little more than an attempt to sidestep the broader debate regarding the metaphysics of relations by converting it back into his preferred terms, or by portraying his own concern with 'relations' as more fundamental. It does this by treating the *attractors* (or singularities) that populate the *vector field* (or multiplicity) which is generated by the relevant differential relations as individuals that can be unproblematically separated from these relations, as if they were discrete components out of which the vector field was constructed, rather than *topologically invariant* features of a continuous curve.[213] This doesn't just presume what it means to establish—that description in terms of individuals is more fundamental than descriptions in terms of relations—it does

---

212. *Towards Speculative Realism*, 178.

213. In dynamic systems theory, a system is represented by a *phase space* whose dimensions correspond to its degrees of freedom (the system's variables). If a system has three dimensions [x, y, z], then its *vector field* is a manifold whose curvature is determined by the differential relations between their variables [dx/dy, dx/dz, dy/dz], and its *attractors* are the topologically invariant features of this curvature (e.g., cycles, saddles, points, etc.). For a more thorough overview of these ideas, consult DeLanda, *Intensive Science* (chapter 1), or Ian Stewart, *Does God Play Dice: The Mathematics of Chaos* (London: Penguin, 1989).

so by completely misrepresenting the logic of the mathematical structures in question.

Although Harman successfully avoids engaging Deleuze and DeLanda on their own terrain by obfuscating the extent of the difference between their relationism and that of Latour and Whitehead, the argument he deployed against the latter still lacks purchase upon them, not least because their avowed endorsement of the idea that 'relations are external to their terms' clashes with the characterisation of relationism upon which his argument turns.[214] He compensates for this by repurposing the strategy he deployed against Heidegger—he emphasizes the opposition between the *continuum* of virtual multiplicities (what Deleuze calls 'the plane of immanence/consistency') and the *discreteness* of actual individuals, and substitutes it for that between the *real absorption* of the world-machine and the *apparent distinctness* of its parts:

> We find then that DeLanda's *actual* world is made up of sterile nodules unable to affect one another or to relate in any way, while the non-actual zone of reality has no difficulty forming relations at all. There everything bleeds together in a continuum [...] and the fact that it was woven together from initial heterogeneity does not prevent it from being a *single* continuum.[215]

It is possible to take issue with Harman's characterisation of DeLanda's account of individuality here. DeLanda does hold that there is a sort of *quasi-causality* operating at the virtual

---

214. Cf. G. Deleuze, *Empiricism and Subjectivity: An Essay on Hume's Theory of Human Nature*, tr. C. V. Boundas (New York: Columbia University Press, 2001); M. DeLanda, *A New Philosophy of Society: Assemblage Theory and Social Complexity* (London and New York: Continuum, 2011).

215. *Towards Speculative Realism*, 177–8.

level that is responsible for the genesis of actual individuals and their behaviour, but he does not for all that deny that this behaviour is causal. It is perhaps better to look at this as a case of Harman putting the cart before the horse—his repurposed strategy is to show that the impossibility of change is an unintended consequence of Deleuze and DeLanda's holism. The idea thus seems to be that, if causal interactions between actual individuals emerge from their mutual envelopment within a virtual continuum, then it is sufficient to attack this envelopment to undermine causality and thereby the possibility of change.

However, it is not so easy to reconstruct precisely how Harman's attack on the virtual is supposed to work—although it is clearly directed at the claim that the virtual is *both* continuous and heterogeneous, it is less clear why this is a problem. The most in-depth presentation of this objection is to be found embedded in the narrative of Harman's *Circus Philosophicus*, during a fictional exchange between Harman and his erstwhile Deleuzian paramour, in which he recounts a dream wherein various famous metaphysical holists are punished for their intellectual errors by being submerged in a lake of molten lead. At the end of this exchange, he engages his interlocutor's Deleuzian holism explicitly:

> [Y]ou do not claim that the world is simply a united whole, as the full-blown thinkers of *apeiron* do. Rather, you contend that the world is both one and many at the same time. Any given object is already interwoven with all others in a sort of continuum. Whatever happens in the world does not result from contact between one individual entity and another, but happens at the level of a united *apeiron*, though you hedge your bets by calling it both heterogeneous and continuous. Since I am not fully myself,

and the shark and tree also not fully themselves, we are all laced with difference. No causal relation exists at the level of individual things; such individuals are not really cut off from each other in the first place. But the pernicious consequence is that the same thing will be simultaneously 'a battleship, a wall, and a human being,' in Aristotle's memorable phrase [...] [Y]ou always respond that the various individual things are not just 'potentially' distinct, but 'virtually' so. Yet here is the problem. Either the various beings dissolved in the lake of lead remain distinct, or they do not. If not then we have monism, and there is no reason that different entities would ever emerge from it. But if they do remain distinct, then there is the rather different problem of knowing why they are more than merely one. For how is the virtual *shark* different from the virtual *tree*? You want them to be a continuum, but this is a step that Aristotle knew could not be taken.[216]

The argument put forward in this monologue is essentially that individuals cannot be enveloped in a virtual continuum without ceasing to be distinct individuals, and that the *specific* relations of mutual envelopment (e.g., between populations of foxes and rabbits in a particular ecosystem) that are supposed to enable *specific* causal interactions between them (e.g., a particular fox eating a particular rabbit) are impossible without *distinct* relata.

The problem with this argument is perhaps best encapsulated by Harman's complaint that the virtual 'merely plays the double game of saying that true reality in the universe is both connected and separate, both continuous and heterogeneous'.[217] What this shows is that Harman equates heterogeneity

---

216. *Circus Philosophicus* (Winchester: Zero Books, 2010), 23–4.

217. *Prince of Networks*, 187.

with separation (or discreteness) and thereby takes the very idea of 'continuous heterogeneity' to be internally inconsistent (i.e., as tantamount to 'continuous discreteness'). This supposed inconsistency is presumably why the argument against the heterogeneity of the virtual is so rarely articulated. Nevertheless, this supposition plays a crucial role in the above argument, because it not only blurs the lines between discreteness, heterogeneity, and difference, but also confuses continuity, homogeneity, and identity. It is this latter confusion that enables Harman to argue that the mutual envelopment of distinct individuals within the same continuum inevitably results in them becoming identical. The irony looming behind this assumption is that Deleuze's *Difference and Repetition*—the key text for his metaphysics and DeLanda's appropriation of it—is best described as an attempt to articulate an account of difference that is not subordinated to the opposition between identity and distinctness, and thus to provide a consistent account of heterogeneous continuity. Moreover, the heart of this project is his interpretation of the significance of differential calculus, and the differential relations it describes. There is much to be said about this, but it is sufficient to observe that mathematical curves present the exemplary case of continuous heterogeneity, or difference that is not understood in terms of some prior discreteness. This is because they are not principally composed of distinct lines or infinitesimal points that differ from one another in their direction or position, but are first and foremost continuous lines that exhibit an equally continuous change in gradient.[218] Although it can be differentiated to

---

218. It is worth remembering that a line is just a one-dimensional surface, and that the vector field/virtual multiplicity is an *n*-dimensional surface whose curvature is determined by differential relations between many variables.

determine the gradient of a tangent to any arbitrary point along its length (x/y), this heterogeneous continuity can be exhaustively captured by a single differential relation (dx/dy). This is what it means to say that the difference (as captured by the differential relation) is *internal* to the curve, rather than a relation it bears to another line. It is important to emphasize that this does not necessarily establish the metaphysical applicability of the concept of continuous heterogeneity, let alone the consistency of Deleuze's account of the virtual as a whole. It simply shows that the concept is *prima facie* consistent, and cannot be simply dismissed without engaging in precisely the sorts of metaphysical debates that Harman sidesteps.

Of course, this does not constitute a complete response to Harman's worries about the relation between the virtual and the actual individuals that are enveloped in it. Such a response is not really possible without delving much deeper into Deleuze and DeLanda's projects than would be appropriate in the current context. It is no easy matter to outline how every variable characteristic of every physical system in the universe could in principle be incorporated as dimensions of a single continuum which would thereby informationally encode the complete actual state of those systems along with their virtual tendencies, let alone how this continuum can still be divided into discrete chunks corresponding to individual systems and their specific tendencies.[219] Nevertheless, it is worth making a final point about the relation between this form of holism and the possibility of change, given the general thrust of Harman's attack on relationism. It is important to see that whether we

---

219. See my paper 'Ariadne's Thread: Temporality, Modality, and Individuation in Deleuze's Metaphysics' (<http://deontologistics.files.wordpress.com/2011/03/deleuze-mmu.pdf>) for an attempt at an outline.

consider individual physical systems, or the totality of all such systems, the differential relations which constitute their virtual multiplicities essentially encode information about the way they change over time. They cannot be considered in isolation from change, even if they can be considered in isolation from the causal interactions between specific individuals that are involved in these changes. Harman might respond that these systems are *executing* a pattern through which they *persist* as the systems that they are, but that this does not thereby account for the possibility that this pattern could become otherwise. However, although there is something to be said about complicating the typology of change, one can only keep separate the two types of change this objection is predicated upon by framing them in functional terms (i.e., as either acting towards or against the system's end); the advantage of the dynamic systems approach that Deleuze and DeLanda adopt is precisely that it is capable of capturing complex behaviours without appealing to these terms (i.e., by means of the mathematics of attractors in phase spaces).[220]

II. RELATIONALITY AND STRUCTURE

In the case of Ladyman and Ross's ontic structural realism, the problem with Harman's argument is twofold. On the one hand, it characterises relationism as being concerned with specifically *causal* relations (albeit synchronic ones), so as to undermine the notion of causation more generally (by precluding diachronic ones); on the other, it characterises relationism as treating individuals as dependent upon *all* such relations.

---

220. It is worth noting that *catastrophe theory* was developed to provide mathematical tools to study precisely the sorts of changes that this objection takes to be outside of the scope of the dynamic systems approach.

It is quite easy to see the error underlying the first problem: the sorts of *mathematical structure* that Ladyman and Ross take to be realised in the *physical structure* to which they give ontological priority involve the whole range of types of relations alluded to earlier. For instance, the phase space descriptions of physical systems at the heart of Deleuze and DeLanda's metaphysics discussed in the last subsection are merely one example of such structures, and as we've seen, the differential relations between variables these involve simply aren't causal relations in Harman's sense. Furthermore, Ladyman and Ross examine the mathematical structures of systems described in the frameworks of both quantum mechanics and general relativity in some depth, in order to argue that they need not presuppose (and indeed, tell against) pre-individuated relata.[221] We need not even assess the validity of these arguments in order to point out that the mathematical structures in question are composed of relations whose logical features are completely different from those of Harman's 'relations'. This is aptly demonstrated by the following passage, in which they distinguish *relative* and *weak* forms of discernibility from the *absolute* form demanded by thorough-going substantialism:

> Two objects are 'relatively discernible' just in case there is a formula in two free variables which applies to them in one order only. Moments in time are relatively discernible since any two always satisfy the 'earlier than' relation in one order only. An example of mathematical objects which are not absolutely indiscernible but are relatively discernible include points of a one-dimensional

---

221. J. Ladyman and D. Ross, *Every Thing Must Go: Metaphysics Naturalized* (Oxford: Oxford University Press, 2007), §§3.1–3.2.

space with an ordering relation, since, for any such pair of points x and y, if they are not the same point then either x > y or x < y but not both. Finally, two objects are 'weakly discernible' just in case there is two-place irreflexive relation that they satisfy […] Clearly, fermions in entangled states like the singlet state violate both absolute and relative discernibility, but they satisfy weak discernibility since there is an irreflexive two-place relation which applies to them, namely, the relation 'is opposite spin to'. [222]

This should be enough to establish that any genuine debate with ontic structural realism over the ontological priority of relations must explicitly concern itself with the sorts of locative and comparative relations (e.g., 'earlier than' and 'is opposite spin to', respectively) that Harman's framing of the issue ignores.

When it comes to the idea that relationism reduces an individual to the totality of its relations, the problem is somewhat more complex. On the one hand, it is easy to show that this is not Ladyman and Ross's position: at worst, they reduce the individuals posited by the mathematical descriptions of physical structures to the specific relations that are involved in those descriptions—which is to say, to those that are considered scientifically relevant to capturing the phenomena in question. This means that any argument against relationism that proceeds by exploiting the apparent absurdity of an object's identity depending upon seemingly irrelevant relations to other things (e.g., the gravitational interaction between Mars and my shoe) cannot get off the ground here. On the other hand, the manner in which Harman exploits this misunderstanding in his criticism of ontic structural realism exemplifies his persistent conflation

---

222. Ibid., 137.

of epistemological and metaphysical issues under the heading of 'relations'. I do not aim to assess all of Harman's criticisms of Ladyman and Ross's position, some of which I am highly sympathetic to.[223] I will instead restrict myself to commenting on the objection contained in the following passage:

> A pattern, for these authors, is a bundle of relations no less than a bundle of qualities. The reasonable objection that there can be no relations without relata is quickly dismissed by the authors as an old-fashioned gimmick, in the eye-rolling spirit of 'here we go again'. And yet they must tacitly concede that our knowledge of specific subject matter is never exhaustive at any given moment; science changes and advances. For this difference between representational and extrarepresentational real patterns is the key to their whole position, since it is all that allows them to maintain realism against an idealism that would hold that whatever science thinks at any given moment is always true. Our knowledge of the planet Neptune is surely incomplete, and hence our current mathematization of that planet is at best a translation of the real pattern Neptune itself, even if it were granted that certain mathematical aspects of our current translation will survive into any future understanding of it. In short, the real pattern Neptune is something more than our or anyone else's *relation* to it. This means that they already accept a distinction between relation and relata at one level, at least. But as soon as representation is taken out of the picture

---

223. In particular, I think he is entirely right to criticise their refusal to account for the difference between mathematical and physical structure (*Every Thing Must Go*, §3.6). I am even willing to admit that there is something untoward about the manner in which they aim to derive metaphysical conclusions from epistemological premises, but this is of a piece with Harman's own methodological problems, rather than something his criticisms identify.

and we move to the realm beyond representation, we supposedly find that Neptune belongs to a giant relational structure
rather than being a discrete individual. In other words, although
Neptune cannot be dissolved into observers' current relations
with it, Neptune itself is supposedly dissolved into the relational
structure of the world, having no status as an individual except
when viewed by an observer from a specific scale.[224]

In order to see what is going on in this paragraph, it is necessary to understand that although ontic structural realism is a
metaphysical position, the motivation for it is epistemological.
It is meant to solve the problem of how successive scientific
theories can be understood as presenting incrementally better
descriptions of the same real phenomena even while the individual entities they purport to refer to differ (e.g., the phlogiston
and oxygen theories of combustion). It does this by holding
that there are strictly no individual entities to be *referred* to,
only physical structures to be mathematically *modelled*, and
that successive theories can preserve mathematical structure
that successfully represents this physical structure through
isomorphism despite permutations of reference.[225] What Harman does in the above passage is to posit a tension between
Ladyman and Ross's epistemological realism and the metaphysical relationism it motivates, by suggesting that whereas
the former demands that the thing modelled is *independent*
of the model *qua* mathematical structure, the latter makes
the thing *dependent* upon the model by incorporating the
representational relation within the thing *qua* physical structure.

---

224. 'I am also of the opinion that materialism must be destroyed', 786–7.

225. Ladyman and Ross, *Every Thing Must Go*, chapter 2.

It is important to understand why this objection doesn't survive the restriction of physical structure to relevant relations. For instance, the example of quantum mechanical systems might incline us to think that our observational relations to systems are relevant to understanding their behaviour, and so must be incorporated in our models of them, and thus, presumably, in the physical structures modelled thereby. However, this inclination misunderstands these relations in at least two ways. Firstly, not only does it erroneously infer that the need for a *general* model of observational effects upon a system (e.g., the system involved in the double-slit experiment) implies that the system's identity is dependent upon *particular* observation relations (i.e., that it is a different system when observed by me than when observed by you, or not observed at all); it illegitimately extends this dependence beyond those systems for which observational effects are relevant. Secondly, and perhaps more damagingly, it ignores the difference between observation and modelling: it treats the representational relation between mathematical model and physical structure as equivalent to the perceptual relation between an observer and what they observe. This is important, because even though quantum mechanics must account for the general effects of observing a system within the models it bases on these observations, there is no additional need for it to account for the effects of its models upon the systems they model.[226]

Ultimately, what this reveals is that the tension between epistemology and metaphysics that Harman locates in ontic

---

226. There is a case to be made that this sort of reflexivity occurs in certain areas of social science, such as economics, insofar as the availability of models of our own behaviour can lead to both self-fulfilling and self-refuting prophesy. However, these cases are hardly representative.

structural realism is based upon the same logic underlying the conflation of intentional and causal relations we addressed as the argument from independence.[227] However, we are now in a position to examine this logic in more depth, and to show how Harman's way of discussing 'relations' disguises it. As we saw in the last chapter, the account of representation at the heart of Harman's theory of intentional relations takes perception as its model, and this undermines its ability to account for the differences between observation and modelling in empirical investigation. Moreover, we saw that the central feature of this model is Harman's refusal to properly distinguish between perception and inference, or between what is directly given in observation and what is indirectly inferred from it. We are now in a position to recognise that this refusal to distinguish between perception and inference is crucial to maintaining the conflation between causal and intentional relations, because perceiving an object involves being both causally and intentionally related to that object (i.e., sensing *and* representing it), whereas inferring something about it does not (i.e., representing it *without* sensing). This exclusion of inference facilitates the non sequitur underlying the argument from independence, by allowing Harman to elide the difference between representational and causal success, but it equally underwrites the above objection against Ladyman and Ross, by giving the impression that mathematical models must be somehow causally enmeshed with the physical structures that they model.

Once more, it is Harman's choice of Latour as an interlocutor (and as an authority on the scientific enterprise) that works to disguise the assumptions about representation

---

227. Chapter 2.3, subsection II.

that motivate his arguments.[228] His use of Latour's notion of 'translation' in setting up the Neptune example is illustrative, because it enacts a sort of anthropological bracketing that dissolves the differences between epistemic activities such as perceptual observation and inferential modelling. Through this lens, the whole process of interacting with phenomena through observation and experiment, analysing the resultant data, constructing theoretical models, and elaborating their consequences, is collapsed into a single operation of translating those phenomena into theories.[229] However, Harman is not just exploiting the epistemological homogeneity of translation here, but also Latour's account of the 'networks' these translations compose. For example, Latour famously sees neutrons as essentially bound up in a network of relations that includes all the various elements of the historical process through which Joliot made them available as an object of technological manipulation and political action.[230] This process of translating between neutrons and politics constitutes a *particular* relation between neutrons and politics in which Joliot is the mediator—that is to say, a relation in which 'neutrons' and 'politics' are viewed as *individuals* in the same sense as is Joliot. This is in distinct contrast to the *general* relations that physics concerns itself with modelling, such as the relation between neutrons and protons viewed as *general kinds*. Through this lens, the metaphysical difference between individuals and general kinds is collapsed and subsumed into the function of network-node—a node in a network of slapdash references

---

228. Cf. R. Brassier, 'Concepts and Objects', in Bryant, Srnicek and Harman (eds), *The Speculative Turn*.

229. Cf. *Prince of Networks*, chapter 1, §A.

230. Ibid., 73–5.

deployed in anthropological descriptions of scientific practice, as opposed to those deployed in scientific explanation itself.[231] This metaphysical homogeneity of networks combines with the epistemological homogeneity of translation to obscure the difference between the representational relations involved in observing individual systems and modelling their general behaviour. Once we see past these Latourian distortions, the supposed tension between the epistemological and metaphysical sides of Ladyman and Ross's relationism disappears.

III. SPACE AND TIME

Now, we have already managed to locate a number of metaphysical blind spots in Harman's theory by tracing his peculiar usage of the term 'relation' through a number of different debates with other thinkers, but there is one particular blind spot that deserves special attention, both because it is so extreme and because it proves so central to his system as a whole. I did not mince my words when I described Harman's theory of qualities as a 'conceptual disaster', but I must be blunter still when it comes to his theory of space and time: it is in my opinion the most catastrophically inept aspect of his metaphysical system. This unapologetically harsh judgement is motivated by Harman's persistent inability to engage with the topic of *spatio-temporal relations*, on the one hand, and his consequent failure to thematise the essentially *temporal basis* of his theory of objects on the other. The remainder of this chapter is dedicated to examining these problems and their consequences.

---

231. Harman's failure to notice the elision of generality on Latour's part is hardly surprising given his own track record on the matter (see chapter 3.2, subsection II).

It is worth reminding ourselves of what Harman thinks about space and time before exploring why it is problematic. In *The Quadruple Object*, Harman introduces the topic by querying why space and time are simultaneously bound together and separated from other metaphysical structures in most philosophical speculation (e.g., Kant's division between space and time as pure forms of intuition and the categories as pure concepts of the understanding).[232] He goes on to argue that, in fact, space and time should be counted alongside essence and eidos as two of the four fundamental *tensions* implied by the fourfold split between the sensual, the real, objects, and qualities, and against the three *radiations* and three *junctions* that make up the remainder of the ten ontographic categories it demands.[233] What distinguishes these four tensions is that they are object-quality relations, as opposed to the quality-quality relations of the radiations and the object-object relations of the junctions. What distinguishes space and time from essence and eidos is that they involve *sensual* qualities: space consists in the tension between real objects and their sensual qualities (RO–SQ), and time consists in the tension between sensual objects and their sensual qualities (SO–SQ). What this means is that they *delimit* the bounds of experience (or vicarious relation): time enables relations of *confrontation* (time-fission) between real objects and the sensual facades that populate their experience, and space enables relations of *allure* (space-fusion) between them and their real counterparts hiding behind those facades. By contrast, the other tensions *individuate* these objects and their facades (the vicarious relata): eidos (SO–RQ) constitutes the identity of

232. *The Quadruple Object*, 99.

233. Chapter 1.2; see the diagram on p. 19.

a facade across variations within experience, and essence (RO–RQ) constitutes the identity of a hidden object between appearances in other objects' experience; these enable the remaining intra-experiential relation of *theory* (eidos-fission) wherein the real object moves from confronting an individuated facade to tracing the eidetic anchor that ties its individuation to an already individuated hidden object, and the sole extra-experiential relation of *causation* (essence-fusion) wherein a hidden object moves from alluding to its own depths through its facade's features to allowing its own features to modify the encountering object.

There are two points that we should take away from the above rehearsal of Harman's categorial schema. Firstly, with an eye to Harman's use of the term 'relation', it is now clear that although the tensions are the conditions under which certain complicated ranges of interaction occur (time: confrontation-theory and space: allure-causation), they are not themselves interactions, and thus not 'relations' in Harman's sense of the word. This is hardly surprising given his insistence that contiguity (SO–SO) and withdrawal (RO–RO) are not 'relations' either, despite their categorial status being discussed in the same putatively relational terms. Secondly, and more importantly, it is now equally clear how important the difference is between the three intra-experiential relations (confrontation, theory, and allure) and the extra-experiential one (causation). Although space remains a condition of causation insofar as causation proceeds via allure, it is not clear that the same holds for time. Even if allure must itself proceed via confrontation, and thus causation via confrontation, this would still grant space a priority with regard to causation that should be cause for concern. If we are to address the first of these points, it is important to explain what precisely it means to say that there is a 'tension' between an object and its sensual qualities. This is stated most concisely during the introduction of the concept of time in *The Quadruple Object*:

> When we speak of time in the everyday sense, what we are referring to is a remarkable interplay of stability and change. In time, the objects of sense do not seem motionless and fixed, but are displayed as encrusted with shifting features. Nonetheless, experience does not decay in each instant into an untethered kaleidoscope of discontinuous sensations; instead, there seem to be sensual objects of greater or lesser durability. Time is the name for this tension between sensual objects and their sensual qualities.[234]

It is clear from this passage that the tension proper to time consists in the fact that an intentional relation to a sensual object persists across variations in its sensual qualities. Harman has addressed these sorts of phenomenal shifts in his discussion of Husserl's notion of perceptual adumbration and the corresponding method of eidetic variation, wherein we encounter the same object from differing perspectives, be it really or imaginatively. The question is then whether the tension proper to space consists in a similar sort of variation. This is addressed further on in the same passage:

> When we speak instead of space, everyone will recall the old quarrel between Leibniz and Clarke over whether space is an absolute container or simply a matter of relations between things. But in fact it is neither: for space is not just the site of relation, but rather of relation *and* non-relation. Sitting at the moment in Cairo,

234. *The Quadruple Object*, 100.

I am not entirely without relation to the Japanese city of Osaka, since in principle I could travel there on any given day. But this relation can never be total, since I do not currently touch the city, and even when I travel to stand in the exact center of Osaka I will not exhaust its reality [...] This interplay of relation and non-relation is precisely what we mean when we speak of space [...].[235]

This 'interplay of relation and non-relation' consists in the fact that a real object persists across variations in which other objects are intentionally related to it by way of its sensual facades. The role of sensual qualities consists in the fact that, although a sensual facade can persist across minor variation in its qualities, there are major variations that it cannot persist across. Given that the intentional relation between two real objects cannot persist without the sensual object that mediates between them, these major variations are capable of altering the overall distribution of intentional relations between objects. As such, for Harman, space and time are not 'relations' because they are the conditions under which the connections between objects are created, maintained, and dissolved by eddies in the sensual ether that supports them.

The problem with this account is that it says nothing about specifically spatio-temporal relations (e.g., **x** is to the left of **y**, **x** has the same orientation as **y**, **x** happened before **y**, **x** had the same duration as **y**, etc.), because these are precisely the sorts of relation that Harman's idiom excludes. However, the situation is much worse than this. The above passage displays the point at which Harman's idiom moves from simply *excluding* types of relations to actively *conflating* them. This is his

---

235. Ibid.

invocation of the debate between Leibniz and Clarke, and subsequent framing of the spatio-temporal relations Leibniz is talking about as 'relations' or interactions. This mistake is repeated elsewhere with more explicitly absurd consequences:

> It would be mistaken to follow Leibniz literally and say that space is simply generated by the relations between things. For it is just as true that space is the site of *non*-relation between things. If space were simply made up of relations, we would have a systematic gridwork with each object utterly defined by its relations with all the others, and the universe would become a single lump interrelated to the point of homogeneity. Such a lump provides no room for anything like space, which by definition would contain only one position: that of the lump as a whole.[236]

This caricature of Leibniz's position is perhaps a result of confusing the idea that space and time are *epiphenomenal*—spatio-temporal relations can be derived from the non-spatio-temporal properties of monads—and the idea that each monad *mirrors* every other—the non-spatio-temporal properties of *every* monad can be derived from *any* monad. The result is the same crude accusation of radical holism Harman levels at Heidegger, Whitehead, and Deleuze, among others. The core of the debate between Leibniz and Clarke is whether we need to metaphysically distinguish between *locations* in space (i.e., the regions and points of space viewed as a coordinate system) and their *occupants* (i.e., the events, processes, and seemingly persistent objects that can be located within this coordinate system). Following Newton, Clarke held that this distinction is necessary to make sense of the

---

236. *Towards Speculative Realism*, 161–2.

mechanics of motion, and that these independently subsisting locations are part of an absolute space. By contrast, Leibniz held that this distinction is unnecessary, because the relations between locations out of which fixed coordinate systems are composed (e.g., in space [**x**, **y**, **z**], point <1, 2, 3> is located at -3 along the **x** axis from point <4, 2, 3>) are abstracted from spatio-temporal relations between objects (e.g., my table is to the left of my chair, which is to the right of my bed, and so on) and thus needn't presuppose an absolute space. The debate is very complex, and becomes even more so when it is extended to the advances in physics beyond Newtonian mechanics, and the contentious question of how to unite the differing conceptions of space presupposed by quantum mechanics and general relativity.[237]

However, we needn't resolve this debate to see that Harman's discussion of 'space' and 'relations' is at best entirely irrelevant to it, and at worst actively misrepresents it. That Harman is not in Osaka but can potentially travel to Osaka is not a 'non-relation' is Leibniz's sense, but a spatio-temporal relation that could be described in a variety of different coordinate systems abstracted from their spatio-temporal relations to their peers (e.g., by means of a three-dimensional planetary map that can account for distance through the earth, by means of latitude and longitude over the earth's surface, or by means of a network graph that restricts the available paths between the two nodes even further, etc.). Moreover, even if we decide that these various coordinate systems are pale reflections of an absolute coordinate system within which everything can be located, we still need not concede that the ability to specify unique spatio-temporal relations between everything

---

237. Cf. Ladyman and Ross, *Every Thing Must Go*, §3.2.

thereby makes them indiscernible, because it does precisely the opposite—it makes them *absolutely* discernible.

One might nevertheless want to champion Harman's account of space against the idea of absolute space on the basis that, as the condition under which relations of interaction can be formed and broken, it gives us a way of thinking about how these various coordinate systems are expressions of 'space' without reducing them to 'a' space. Although the general shape of this idea is unmistakably attractive, the problem with it is that there is no real account of *why* systems of spatial relations are expressions of 'space', or *how* it enables us to unify them. What needs to be thought through is the relationship between spatial relations and causal interactions: how proximity relations function as a condition of causal interaction (e.g., how 'touching' Osaka is dependent upon 'being in' Osaka), on the one hand, and how possible interactions function as a condition of coordinate systems (e.g., how different ranges of movement motivate different choices of map), on the other. Harman's account of space provides us with no resources to formulate, let alone address these questions, and so shouldn't be taken seriously.

If this is bad, the situation is much worse when it comes to Harman's account of 'time'. However, to see this, it's worth examining some of Harman's comments about the supposed difference between space and time, which requires quoting the relevant sections of *Guerrilla Metaphysics* extensively. To begin with, he makes a seemingly bold break with traditional thinking about space and time:

> Everyone puzzles over "time's arrow" and why and whether it only flows in one direction, but no one has ever asked about "space's arrow," since reversibility seems to belong to the very

essence of spatial movement. But we can now see a way in which the opposite is true. Namely, time is *always* reversible, because on the interior of a relation it makes no difference when the Taj Mahal cycles from pink to blue to yellow to orange to black and finally to pink again. The sequence can go in any order and reverse itself any number of times without shifting the regime of objects. But this is not so with space. When I move from Chicago to Davenport and back to Chicago, it is space that has changed, since objects are to some extent no longer what they were: houses have been torn down or rehabilitated, brain cells have developed or died, friendships have formed or decayed, old wounds have healed slightly [...] Time can always be reversed on the interior of an object, because the shifting gales of black noise within have no direct consequence for the regime of objects. But space can never be reversed, and we can never return to the same airport twice—the regime of objects will have shifted.[238]

When reading the above passage, one might, and indeed should, get the sense that something has gone awry in his discussion of space and time, such that what he calls 'space' and 'time' have become completely unmoored from their everyday reference. It is important to show that this is not some brilliant metaphysical rebellion against our common ways of thinking about space and time, but amounts, at best, to radically changing the subject of debate without changing its terms. The best way to make this clear is to quote Harman's elaboration of this passage, and to highlight the offending phrases:

---

238. *Guerrilla Metaphysics*, 251.

If someone now rephrases the traditional question and asks whether "space's arrow" can flow in both directions, the answer must be in the negative. The reason for this is interesting. When objects enter into a relation, the relation cannot necessarily decompose again into the same objects: two chemicals might necessarily mix to form a third, but this does not imply that the new fluid is able to break down into its original parts. There is an asymmetry of **cause and effect**, and this is why space is irreversible. There are **lasting** consequences to space, but none to time, that **transient** fulguration along the surface of things—or rather, in the molten cores of things. Time itself creates nothing, while **spatial changes** create lasting monuments.[239]

It should now be easier to see precisely what is wrong: Harman distinguishes space from time by means of *temporal terms*. Even if one disputes the idea that talk of cause and effect is inherently temporal, one cannot deny that the distinction between 'lasting' and 'transient' consequences is a temporal one; but it is the phrase 'spatial changes' that is most indicative, by condensing the conceptual confusion into a bitesize oxymoron—thinking about *change* presupposes *time*, which means one cannot oppose spatial changes to temporal ones. Moreover, this cannot be viewed as an isolated logical slippage—consider the reformulation of the question 'Is time finite or infinite?' in the conclusion to his essay 'Space, Time, and Essence: An Object-Oriented Approach':

"Is time finite or infinite?" Under the object-oriented model time unfolds only on the interior of an object. *As long as* objects exist,

---

239. Ibid., 252, my emphasis.

time must exist. The question can thus be rephrased as follows: "must objects *always* exist?"[240]

This subordination of time's *extent* to objects' *persistence* simply presupposes a deeper time in which they might or might not persist—a time whose logic is indistinguishable from the everyday time out of which this metaphysical question arises. Harman's 'time' is thus not only not what we usually mean by the word, but is actually parasitic upon it—'time' makes sense only insofar as we implicitly understand *time* but refrain from explicitly thematising it.

Once one sees the deep time lurking behind the surface 'time' in Harman's metaphysics, it cannot be unseen. Worse, one cannot help but see it everywhere. For instance, the contrast between types of variation through which we articulated the tensions constitutive of 'space' and 'time' is essentially about change, and thus presupposes deep time. However, if we pull on this conceptual thread it unravels Harman's system all the way back to the beginning. The contrasts between execution and causation, persistence and change, and synchronic dependence and diachronic affection, through which we have managed to make sense of Harman's system, are all fundamentally temporal. It is not simply that one term in each distinction is temporal (causation, change, diachronic affection), but that both terms denote types of *occurrence* (executing, persisting, depending, etc.). The twisted temporal logic underlying these distinctions was evident in the temporal tension in the argument from execution, but it is most prominent in Harman's repeated appeals to the reality of change in his arguments against relationism and holism in Heidegger,

---

240. *Towards Speculative Realism*, 166, my emphasis.

Whitehead, and Latour.[241] The whole trajectory of *Tool-Being* out of which the account of vicarious causation emerges turns around the recognition that things must change within the subterranean realm of withdrawn objects, even if we only experience the ripples these changes produce in the glimmering surface world. These real changes and the time they presuppose are explicitly not accounted for by what passes for 'time' at the level of sensual change, and are treated as mysterious enough to demand a whole new theory of causation. In essence, the rift between changes that belong to the seamless functioning of an existing apparatus (surface 'time') and the changes that belong to the erupting malfunctions that disrupt and reconfigure these regimes (deep time) is not a theoretical consequence of Harman's metaphysical system, but the pre-theoretic foundation upon which it is built.

IV. PHENOMENA AND NOUMENA

Having examined the problems with Harman's theory of space and time in detail, we are now left to extrapolate their consequences. This brings us at long last to the central claim of my interpretation of Harman's philosophy: namely, that it is not a *critique*, but rather a *consolidation* of correlationism. Harman's theory of space and time provides the most illustrative case of convergence between correlationism and object-oriented philosophy. To see this, we simply need to return to the initial problem out of which Meillassoux's discussion of correlationism grows in *After Finitude*—what he calls **ancestrality**, or the confrontation between empirical science and the **arche-fossil**:

---

241.   See chapter 2.2, subsection 1, and chapter 3.3.

The question that interests us here is then the following: *what is it* exactly that astrophysicists, geologists, or paleontologists are talking about when they discuss the age of the universe, the date of the accretion of the earth, the date of the appearance of pre-human species, or the date of the emergence of humanity itself? How are we to grasp the *meaning* of scientific statements bearing explicitly upon a manifestation of the world that is posited as anterior to the emergence of thought and even of life—*posited, that is, as anterior to every form of human relation to the world?* Or, to put it more precisely: how are we to think the meaning of a discourse which construes the relation to the world that of thinking and/or living—as a fact inscribed among others, inscribed in an order of succession in which it is merely a stage, rather than an origin? How is science able to think such statements, and in what sense can we eventually ascribe truth to them?[242]

As others have noted, this is not meant to provide an argument against correlationism (which comes later in the book), but to confront it with an unpalatable consequence of its restriction of knowing to the human-world correlate. Harman's presentation of this unpalatable consequence in his book on Meillassoux is admirably clear and concise:

The problem for correlationism is that it cannot give a *literal* interpretation of scientific statements [...] The literal claim that the earth dates to 4.56 billion years ago must give way to a second, more sophisticated interpretation of this statement. We have seen that, instead of saying the earth is 4.56 billion years older than humans, the correlationist says that the earth is 4.56

---

242. Meillassoux, *After Finitude*, 9–10.

billion years older than humans—*for humans*. No matter how skilled the sciences become at dating pre-human entities, the correlationist always has the trump card of turning all ancestral dates into dates *for us* [...] Correlationists do indeed *claim* that they are not merely trapped in a human interior, when they 'readily [insist] upon the fact that consciousness, like language, enjoys an originary connection to a radical exteriority (exemplified by phenomenological consciousness [...] transcending toward the world)'. But Meillassoux rightly calls this supposed exteriority 'a transparent cage', and notes that in this way 'contemporary philosophers have lost the *great outdoors*, the *absolute* outside of pre-critical thinkers [...] that outside which was not relative to us [...] existing in itself whether we are thinking of it or not'.[243]

The problem for Harman is that this is an equally clear and concise description of the consequences of his own theory of time. For him, the surface 'time' of all phenomenal experience (including empirical investigation) is not the deep time in which the real reconfigurations of objects occur (including the emergence of humanity), and this means that whatever systems of temporal relations empirical science employs to date such events are *for us* in precisely the sense he outlines, along with the systems of spatial relations in terms of which it locates them. To all appearances, this leaves Harman trapped in the same transparent cage as Kant and his successors.

Thus the question is what, if anything, differentiates Harman's supposed realism from the appeals to an 'originary connection with radical exteriority' that he and Meillassoux so rightly scorn. This question can only be answered by properly delimiting the convergence between object-oriented

---

243. *Philosophy in the Making*, 11–12.

philosophy and correlationism. The obvious way to begin this delimitation is by returning to the origin of correlationism in Kant's distinction between **phenomena** and **noumena**, and determining its proximity to Harman's distinction between the *sensual* and the *real*. There are obviously numerous parallels between these distinctions, but they are essentially united by their epistemological implications: we cannot know noumena/ real objects, because we only ever encounter phenomena/ sensual objects. The crucial point to take away from the above discussion is that Harman's theory of 'space' and 'time' implies that the particular spatio-temporal systems in terms of which we locate and date entities and events operate at the phenomenal/sensual level, in essentially the same way as forms of intuition in Kant's theory of space and time. Harman might wish to claim that he has regained the great outdoors, because his real objects exist in themselves 'whether we are thinking of [them] or not,' but he cannot articulate this inde- pendent existence in terms of any anteriority circumscribed by empirical science. He might insist that there is nevertheless some sort of *deep anteriority* that can be distinguished from surface anteriority, or a sort of primitive past that is demanded by the present but which can never be dated in relation to it.[244] However, not only would this involve precisely the sort of thematisation of deep time that his work eschews, but it is not clear how it could possibly be justified within his framework. This is made more problematic by the fact that merely insist- ing that real objects exist is insufficient to distinguish them from Kantian noumena, insofar as this claim is precisely what

---

244. This is not dissimilar to Iain Hamilton Grant's account of anteriority in Schelling (I.H. Grant, 'Does Nature Say What-It-Is?', in Bryant, Harman and Srnicek [eds], *The Speculative Turn*, 66–83).

distinguishes Kant's *weak* correlationism from the *strong* correlationism that follows it:

> We claimed above that Kantian transcendentalism could be iden-
> tified with a 'weak' correlationism. Why? The reason is that the
> Critical philosophy does not prohibit all relation between thought
> and the absolute. It proscribes any knowledge of the thing-in-
> itself (any application of the categories to the supersensible), but
> maintains the thinkability of the in-itself. According to Kant, we
> know *a priori* that the thing-in-itself is non-contradictory and
> that it actually exists. By way of contrast, the strong model of
> correlationism maintains not only that it is illegitimate to claim
> that we can know the in-itself, but *also* that it is illegitimate to
> claim that we can at least *think* it.[245]

If OOP is to avoid becoming indiscernible from this *weak* correlationism, we must be able to articulate the precise point at
which it radicalises the latter, just as Meillassoux's speculative
materialism radicalises *strong* correlationism. Meillassoux's
description of correlationism delimits this point of radical
divergence as well as it does the preceding convergence:

> [C]orrelationism is not a metaphysics: it does not hypostatize
> the correlation; rather it invokes the correlation to curb every
> hypostatization, every substantialization of an object of knowl-
> edge which would turn the latter into a being existing in and of
> itself. To say that we cannot extricate ourselves from the horizon
> of correlation is not to say that the correlation could exist by
> itself, independently of its incarnation in individuals. We do not
> know of any correlation that would be given elsewhere than in

---

245. Meillassoux, *After Finitude*, 35.

the human beings, and we cannot get out of our own skins to discover whether it might be possible for such a disincarnation of the correlation to be true.[246]

Harman's radicalisation of Kant turns upon this question of disincarnation: he insists, *pace* Kant, that we *do* in fact know that the correlation is 'given elsewhere than in human beings'. This is not a metaphysical *response* to weak correlationism, but the *conversion* of weak correlationism into a metaphysics. The difference between Kant's noumenon and Harman's real object is thus that, whereas the former is fundamentally an epistemological notion that *circumscribes* the limits of empirical knowledge, the latter is a metaphysical notion that *grounds* these limits. For Kant, the thinkability of the in-itself does not provide us with any positive knowledge of it; our knowledge of its existence and non-contradictoriness is merely a critical delimitation of what it means for there to be something-we-know-not-what. For Harman, the in-itself is not merely thinkable but genuinely knowable, even if all that can be known about it are the conditions that make it otherwise unknowable. Although this (metaphysical) knowability of (empirical) unknowability is entirely consistent, we are left to wonder what unique characteristic of metaphysical knowledge makes it possible when all else is impossible.

This wonder gets to the heart of the relation between *what* Harman thinks and *why* he thinks it, and thereby reignites the methodological worries that have plagued our attempt to make sense of his work from the beginning. We have seen several crucial points at which the development of Harman's meta-physics has been guided by appeals to certain fundamental

---

246. Ibid., 11.

facts about the real: the existence of real discreteness, the
existence of real change/causation, and most recently, the
existence of real time/anteriority. The important thing to
understand about these facts is that, even though the value
of Harman's fourfold schema depends upon its ability to make
sense of them, it does not, for all that, imply them: it is consistent with there being only phenomenal discreteness (*Apeiron*),[247]
it is consistent with there being only phenomenal change
(*world-machine*), and it is consistent with there being nothing
but a phenomenal past (*ancestrality*). There is a distinct lesson
to be learned from each of these appeals to metaphysical fact.

In the first case, we saw that Harman attempts to use
the 'glaring experiential fact' of discreteness to underwrite its
reality. This seems somewhat paradoxical given the incom-
mensurability between the real and the sensual, as his account
of individuation prevents us from inferring the number of real
objects from the number of sensual objects. This paradox is
indicative of the peculiar intersection of phenomenology and
metaphysics that defines Harman's work, as it suggests that
the reality of multiplicity is made manifest *by* the appearance
of multiplicity. The second case is similar to the first, insofar as
Harman seems to use the appearance of change and causal
interaction to underwrite their reality. This is complicated
somewhat by his tendency to associate these with the reality
of discreteness in his arguments against radical holism. However, there is more to this appeal, because Harman is able to
introspectively secure the reality of causation by using the
way that we are emotionally affected by experience as the
paradigm of real causal interaction and change. In both of these
cases there is an appeal to a peculiar sort of phenomenological

---

247.   See chapter 2.2, subsection III.

intuition capable of providing oblique access to the real. The final case is somewhat different from the others, because it is less an explicit appeal to metaphysical fact than an implicit dependence upon a metaphysical frame through which the other facts are understood. The reality of a deep time in which objects can come into being and cease to be provides the phenomenological background against which the intuitions of discreteness and causation emerge. Without this unthematised conception of time, his picture of vacuum-sealed objects that are nevertheless capable of violent interactions makes no sense.

So, what does this tell us about the form of metaphysical knowledge that Harman takes to be possible? It indicates that the oblique access to the structure of the real provided by his phenomenological method is of the same kind as the oblique access to real objects provided by *allure*: sensual multiplicity alludes to real multiplicity; causation is not merely alluded to, allusion is the very paradigm of causation; and time is the implicit and properly inexplicable background that is only ever alluded to. Of course, this is consistent with Harman's own thoughts about both the general importance of allure and the specific character of philosophical method as opposed to that of the sciences.[248] However, the idea that the only possible knowledge of the real and its structure depends upon allure as a mode of access, and thereby upon allusive language (i.e., metaphor) as a mode of expression, should give us cause for concern. The problem that ancestrality poses for correlationism is precisely that it is unable to take the claims of science *literally*. It makes their apparent truth compatible with the impossibility of knowing the real by redescribing them as

---

248. Cf. *Weird Realism*, 11–23.

true claims about appearance (i.e., as true-for-us). This is the semantic component of its epistemic scepticism. In defending the possibility of metaphysical knowledge against this semantic strategy, one might think that Harman had finally enabled us to take some claims about the real literally, but his interpretation of this knowledge as founded upon allure does precisely the opposite. We are left in a position where what we took to be literal claims about the world (e.g., 'the earth is 4.56 billion years older than humans') are *covertly figurative*, and what appear to be figurative claims about the world (e.g., 'the world is composed of vacuum sealed objects with molten cores') are *prototypically literal*. Seen aright, this is not a counterintuitive insight that is to be welcomed, but an intractable contradiction symptomatic of the deep and abiding influence of correlationism upon Harman's thought. If there is one overriding irony we have exposed in this chapter, it is that the supposedly metaphysical connection that Harman draws between correlationism and relationism has been very effective at concealing the far more significant epistemological convergence between correlationism and OOP.

4. WHAT ARE OBJECTS ANYWAY?: ON ONTOLOGICAL LIBERALISM

Since William of Occam introduced his eponymous razor, there has been a distinct tendency towards *ontological conservatism* in philosophy. This is to say that there has been a consistent pressure to demonstrate the explanatory worth of our *ontological commitments*, so that we are discouraged from littering our map of the world with superfluous entities.

This perennial conservatism went largely unchallenged until Meinong's controversial *The Theory of Objects*, which, as discussed above, insisted upon granting ontological status to every possible object of thought, including those that merely *subsist* because they do not genuinely *exist* (e.g., the present king of France, the largest prime number, the younger sister I never had, etc.).[249] This challenge was motivated by the project of circumscribing the full range of possible intentional relations, a task that animated the Austrian school of philosophy that emerged out of Brentano's work. However, this project was developed along divergent lines: metaphysically, by explicitly differentiating between existence and subsistence (Meinong and his successors), and phenomenologically, by explicitly bracketing questions of existence (Husserl and his successors).[250] Let us call this the *noetic challenge* to ontological conservatism.

---

249. A. Meinong, *The Theory of Objects*, tr. I. Levi, D.B. Terrell, R.M. Chisholm, in R.M. Chisholm (ed.), *Realism and the Background of Phenomenology* (New York: The Free Press, 1960), 76–117, <http://www.hist-analytic.com/Meinongobjects.pdf>.

250. With regard to Meinong and his successors, we have explained the motivations of his theory and their effect upon Harman's metaphysics in more depth in

When the tendency toward ontological conservatism converged with the paradigm of explanatory reductionism in the twentieth century, a different response emerged, which refused to withhold existence from any entities whose features could in principle be derived from more fundamental entities (e.g., reducing economic systems to individual actors, reducing mental episodes to neurological states, reducing macroscopic objects to microscopic particles, etc.). Rather than being motivated by a particular explanatory problem such as intentionality, this response was motivated by more general concerns with explanation as such. However, these concerns were also developed along divergent lines: metaphysically, by developing a positive account of *emergence* in contrast to reduction (Deleuze and his allies), and methodologically, by diluting the relevant criteria of explanatory worth (Latour and his allies).[251] Let us call this the *anti-reductionist* challenge to ontological conservatism.

More recently, a new generation of thinkers has synthesised these challenges in a way that no longer merely rejects the virtues of ontological conservatism, but actively articulates

---

the 'Sense and Sensuality' chapter (chapter 3.1). With regard to Husserl and his successors, it is important to note that Heidegger differs from much of the rest of the phenomenological tradition in attempting to use the bracketing provided by the phenomenological method to methodologically ground metaphysics. See my *The Question of Being* for further details.

251. With regard to Deleuze, the important reference is his and Guattari's *A Thousand Plateaus*, tr. B. Massumi (Minneapolis: Minnesota University Press, 1983); his allies include figures such as Manuel DeLanda, Isabelle Stengers, and the proponents of complexity theory (cf. Ian Stewart and Jack Cohen, *The Collapse of Chaos: Discovering Simplicity in a Complex World* [London: Penguin, 1994]). With regard to Latour, the crucial reference is his 'Irreductions' (second part of *The Pasteurization of France* [Cambridge, MA: Harvard University Press, 1993]); his allies include figures such as Michel Serres, Jane Bennett, and the adherents of actor network theory (ANT) who draw upon him.

and espouses the virtues of **ontological liberalism**. This is to say that there has been growing pressure to reject the traditional worry about *excessive* ontological commitment in favour of a contemporary concern with *comprehensive* ontological commitment, so that we are encouraged to account for the full range of possible objects of thought, experience, and explanation. In drawing upon all of the above influences—uniting Husserl and Meinong in his account of representation,[252] exploiting the homogeneity of Latour's explanatory networks,[253] and appealing to the spatio-temporal levels of DeLanda's theory of emergence[254]—Harman is the paragon of this liberal synthesis. Although the banners of 'flat ontology' (Bhaskar and DeLanda) and 'the democracy of objects' (Latour) had already been raised before it, the banner of object-oriented ontology (OOO) raised by Harman and flown by others (Bryant, Bogost, and Morton) has proved to be a rallying point for those drawn to ontological liberalism, and its manifesto is contained in the opening lines of *The Quadruple Object*:

> Instead of beginning with radical doubt, we start from naiveté.
> What philosophy shares with the lives of scientists, bankers,
> and animals is that all are concerned with *objects*. The exact
> meaning of "object" will be developed in what follows, and must

---

252. Chapter 3.1.

253. Chapter 3.3, subsection 2.

254. This aspect of DeLanda's influence on Harman is not something we have addressed in any depth. It is evident from his discussion of DeLanda's multi-layered 'flat ontology' (*Towards Speculative Realism*, 178–82) and his subsequent adoption of this term (albeit with a slightly modified meaning, cf. 'Response to Garcia', *Parrhesia* 16 [2013], 27). This expands upon the concept of 'levels' that he had already drawn from Alphonso Lingis's work (*Guerrilla Metaphysics*, chapter 5).

include those entities that are neither physical nor even real. Along with diamonds, rope, and neutrons, objects may include armies, monsters, square circles, and leagues of real and fictitious nations. All such objects must be accounted for by ontology, not merely denounced or reduced to despicable nullities. Yet despite repeated claims by both friends and critics of my work, I have never held that all objects are "equally real." For it is false that dragons have autonomous reality in the same manner as a telephone pole. My point is not that all objects are equally real, but that they are equally *objects*. It is only in a wider theory that accounts for the real and the unreal alike that pixies, nymphs, and utopias must be treated in the same terms as sailboats and atoms.[255]

This is the archetypical form of the demand for comprehensiveness that animates ontological liberalism. On the one hand, it deploys the favoured rhetorical device of anti-reductionism: extensive lists of objects ranging from the everyday to the extraordinary, which seem to collapse barriers between divergent explanatory registers simply by including diverse terms alongside one another.[256] On the other, it invokes the vast noetic expanse of the Austrian school: menageries of fantasms and fictions whose lack of 'reality' is no good reason to ignore them. These are the two expressive strategies through which Harman endeavours to encapsulate the idea that ontology must account for 'everything'.

Nevertheless, there is more to contemporary ontological liberalism than OOO. In particular, thinkers such as Tristan Garcia and Markus Gabriel have championed the demand for

---

255. *The Quadruple Object*, 5.

256. This device has been dubbed the 'Latour litany' by Ian Bogost.

comprehensiveness in their own ways: the former systematically in his *Form and Object*, and the latter more sporadically under the heading of *Transcendental Ontology*.[257] Garcia best captures the curious affect that seems to motivate this demand:

> Our time is perhaps the time of an epidemic of things.
>
> A kind of 'thingly' contamination of the present was brought about through the division of labour, the industrialisation of production, the processing of information, the specialisation of the knowledge of things, and above all the desubstantialisation of these things. In Western philosophical traditions, things were often ordered according to essences, substrata, qualities, predicates, *quidditas* and *quodditas*, being and beings. Precluding anything from being equally 'something', neither more nor less than any other thing, thus becomes a rather delicate task. We live in this world of things, where a cutting of acacia, a gene, a computer-generated image, a transplantable hand, a musical sample, a trademarked name, or a sexual service are comparable things. Some resist, considering themselves, thought, consciousness, sentient beings, personhood, or gods as exceptions to the flat system of interchangeable things. A waste of time and effort. For the more one excludes this or that from the world of things, the more and better one makes something of them, such that things have this terrifying structure: to subtract one of them is to add it in turn to the count.[258]

---

257. T. Garcia, *Form and Object : A Treatise on Things*, tr. M. A. Ohm and J. Cogburn (Edinburgh: Edinburgh University Press, 2014); M. Gabriel, *Transcendental Ontology: Essays in German Idealism* (London: Bloomsbury, 2013).

258. Garcia, *Form and Object*, i.

Moreover, in discussing his proximity with Harman, Garcia successfully pinpoints the crucial commitment underpinning the liberal synthesis:

> *Form and Object* and Harman's object-oriented ontology are thought-experiments on the "equality" of all things. Both see philosophy as having an imperative to combine knowledge and morality so that they cannot be separated. The role of philosophy is to understand what composes the world and the way to divide and order its elements on an equal plane by refusing to attribute any ontological privilege to anything in particular. It is therefore a question of grasping the equal ontological chance that every thing has, whether it is material, immaterial, possible, necessary, true, or false.[259]

In essence, what binds these new ontological liberals together is a commitment to some form of *ontological egalitarianism*: their demand to account for *all* things is fundamentally connected to the demand to account for them *equally*. This shows us that not only does the motivation for Harman's metaphysics hang upon whether this conceptual connection can be made coherent, but so does the motivation for the liberal trend to which it belongs. If we are to analyse this connection then we must look deeper than Harman's fairly superficial strategies for encapsulating 'everything' and the supposedly egalitarian notion of 'thing' (or 'object') that this implies.

The remainder of this chapter is devoted to this task. If we are to examine the notion of ontological commitment

---

259. T. Garcia, 'Crossing Ways of Thinking: On Graham Harman's System and My Own', tr. J. Cogburn and M. Ohm, in *Parrhesia* 16 (2013), 15.

in more detail, it will first be necessary to clarify what we mean by 'ontology'. This will provide the necessary historical background to explain Quine's famous analysis of ontological commitment in 'On What There Is',[260] which establishes the crucial link between ontological commitment and quantification, on the basis of which it will be possible to explain the logical connection between the problem of *defining existence* and the problem of *unrestricted quantification*. This will provide us with the necessary conceptual background to explain the final and in many ways most significant influence upon contemporary ontological liberalism: Alain Badiou's set-theoretical approach to ontology in *Being and Event*. This detour into the *logical role* of ontological commitment will enable us to locate the precise point at which Harman's ontological egalitarianism falls short of the noetic challenge to ontological conservatism. This will then be supplemented by a discussion of the *explanatory role* of ontological commitment that locates the corresponding point at which Harman's egalitarianism falls short of the anti-reductionist challenge to conservatism. These fault lines within Harman's project will then be traced back to a conceptual problem with his formulation of the metaphysics of 'objects', and a corresponding methodological problem with his formulation of the 'metaphysics' of objects. The chapter will close by addressing the wider conceptual problem with ontological liberalism, and how this emerges from the wider methodological problem regarding the relation between logic and metaphysics that has defined the last four sections.

---

260. W. V. O. Quine, 'On What There Is', in *From a Logical Point of View* (New York: Harper, 1953).

I. ONTOLOGY AND METAPHYSICS

Using the word 'ontology' in mixed philosophical company can prove challenging. The origin of the term lies in the scholastic division of metaphysics into its various sub-disciplines, in which ontology—as the science of beings *qua* beings—comprises *metaphysica generalis*, or the attempt to articulate the structure of beings *as such*, as opposed to cosmology, psychology, and theology—the sciences of natural beings, rational beings, and the highest being—which form the tripartite division of *metaphysica specialis*, or the attempt to circumscribe the structure of beings *as a whole*.[261] However, gradually freed from these methodological shackles by the slow collapse of scholasticism, the sense of the term began to wander in divergent directions. As such, it is worth briefly tracing its wandering significance before delving into the discussion of ontological commitment, if only so as to avoid the various terminological confusions that are likely to arise. We will first explore the evolution of the term 'ontology' in the 'Continental' tradition, focusing upon Heidegger's project of fundamental ontology and its influence, before examining the independent reintroduction of the term into 'analytic' discourse by Quine and its consequences.[262] However, the discussion of each tradition will require a preparatory analysis of how the relevant problems emerge out of Kant and

---

261. It is important to note that the scholastic division between *metaphysica generalis* and *metaphysica specialis* is older than the term 'ontology', which was only introduced in the seventeenth century (cf. A. Baumgarten, *Metaphysics*, tr. C. D. Fugate and J. Hymers [London and New York: Bloomsbury, 2013]; H. Caygill, *A Kant Dictionary* [Oxford: Blackwell, 1995], 307–8).

262. I shall have more to say about the historical and sociological dimensions of the split between the 'analytic' and 'Continental' traditions of Western philosophy below (chapters 3.5 and 4.1).

their divergent appropriations of his work. Overall, this will enable us to articulate the parallels between the two traditions and thereby clarify what is at stake in our discussion of 'ontological commitment'.

In tracing the development of 'ontology' in the Continental tradition, it is useful to begin with the observation that the tradition is often delineated historically as well as geographically—as 'Post-Kantian European philosophy'. Although this attests to the general importance of Kant's thought within this tradition, it is essential to grasp the specific influence it has had upon the appropriation of scholastic 'ontology' and its subsequent development. Kant is very sensitive to the scholastic methodological framework in articulating his delimitation of the possibility of metaphysical knowledge in *The Critique of Pure Reason*: he dedicates the transcendental analytic and transcendental dialectic to the critical demarcation of the problems of *metaphysica generalis* and *metaphysica specialis* respectively. Although Kant initially presents the transcendental analytic and its account of the categories of pure understanding as replacing 'ontology', he subsequently adopts the term and treats the analytic as redefining its scope.[263] Moreover, this redefinition is carried out as part of a wider engagement with the scholastic interpretation of the meaning of 'metaphysics', which no longer simply groups those works of Aristotle that *come after* his physics, but names the study of that which is *beyond physics* because it is *beyond experience*.[264] Although Kant's critical demarcation rejects the possibility of such *transcendent* knowledge of the Being

---

263. Caygill, *A Kant Dictionary*, 307–8.

264. Heidegger traces this shift in the meaning of the term in *Fundamental Concepts of Metaphysics* (§§11–14).

of 'things' (*Dinge*) outside experience, insofar as it is discon-nected from empirical (or *immanent*) knowledge of 'objects' (*Objekte*) as they appear within it, he nevertheless secures the possibility of *transcendental* knowledge of their conditions of possibility. In essence, this means that Kant redefines ontology as the study of *objects as such* (phenomena) as opposed to *things as such* (noumena). Notoriously, the distinction between phenomena and noumena that underwrites this move is attacked by subsequent German idealists (e.g., Hegel and Schelling), but we will refrain from discussing how this leads to the reincorporation of Kant's ideas within more classical metaphysical projects.

Instead, we will turn to Husserl's phenomenological trans-position of the noetic challenge to ontological conservatism, because it marks the explicit dissociation of 'ontology' from 'metaphysics'. For Husserl, *formal ontology* concerns itself with the eidetic structures of intentionality in much the way that formal logic does, differing only insofar as it addresses the objects rather than the contents of intentional relations; whereas *regional ontology* concerns itself with delimiting the various domains of possible intentional objects (e.g., physical, mathematical, historical, etc.).[265] This distinction reconstitutes the scholastic division between the study of beings as such (formal ontology = *metaphysica generalis*) and as a whole (regional ontology = *metaphysica specialis*), while segregating them from 'metaphysical' questions regarding the existence and coexistence of these beings within the world. However, this methodological segregation is precisely what Heidegger takes issue with in his critique of Husserl, insofar as it amounts to systematically excluding a fundamental sense of 'Being'

---

265. Husserl, *Ideas I*, §§148–149.

(*Sein*)—existence (*Daß-sein*)—from the formal ontological analysis of beings (*Seienden*) that is nevertheless foundational for this very analysis. In essence, although Husserl rejects Kant's distinction between phenomena and noumena, he is only able to transpose *ontology* into *phenomenology* by presupposing a parallel distinction between *reality* and *appearance* (or *Being* [*Sein*] and *seeming* [*Schein*]) that he is thereby unable to thematise.[266] Heidegger's own *fundamental ontology* is concerned with overcoming this problem by completely thematising the Being of beings (*das Sein des Seienden*) on the basis of nothing but the pre-theoretical understanding of Being that we (*Dasein*) share in virtue of our ability to understand any beings whatsoever.

However, there is more to Heidegger's project than compensating for Husserl's lack of methodological self-consciousness in discussing 'Being', precisely because he sees this lack as endemic in the Western philosophical tradition, as exemplified by the scholastic appropriation of Aristotle's 'first philosophy' (*prote philosophia*) under the name of 'metaphysics'. Heidegger locates the original division and articulation of the study of beings *as such* and *as a whole* in Aristotle's definition of first philosophy.[267] Although Aristotle also defined

---

266. Heidegger discusses this distinction in detail in *Introduction to Metaphysics* (103–22).

267. *Fundamental Concepts of Metaphysics*, 33. Heidegger also shows the way in which these two different inquiries emerge out of a single concern with *physis*, which is interpreted as both beings as such and beings as a whole. This develops into Heidegger's later analyses of *physis* as the initial form that Being takes at the beginning of the history of metaphysics. Cf. *Introduction to Metaphysics*, 14–19; *Contributions to Philosophy (From Enowning)*, tr. P. Emad and K. Maly (Bloomington, IN: Indiana University Press, 2000), part III; and 'The Onto-Theo-Logical Constitution of Metaphysics', in *Identity and Difference*, tr. J. Stambaugh (Chicago: University of Chicago Press, 42–74: 66).

first philosophy as theology, or that which concerns itself with the divine first cause, this characterisation is derivative, because the first cause (God—*theos*) is supposed to be that *through which* we think beings as such and as a whole. This division is the foundation of Heidegger's whole critique of the metaphysical tradition, insofar as he holds that Aristotle never actually explained the underlying unity of the two halves of his definition of first philosophy, but merely posited an ad hoc theological principle to hold them together. Heidegger claims that the defining characteristics of the metaphysical tradition are all consequences of this move. The first consequence is the beginning of what he calls the *forgetting of Being*—the increasing lack of methodological self-consciousness that creeps into metaphysics over the course of its history (e.g., the Husserlian exclusion of existence from ontology). The second consequence is the birth of what he calls *onto-theology*—the systematic ignorance of what he calls the *ontological differ-ence*, or the distinction between Being (the structure of beings as such and as a whole) and beings themselves (e.g., the scho-lastic account of beings as *ens creatum* in relation to God as *ens increatum*). The final consequence is the convergence of the previous two—the historical tendency to think Being (*Sein*) as substance (*ousia*).[268] The tortured relationship between the terms 'ontology' and 'metaphysics' in the Continental tradition emerges out of the ways in which later thinkers appropriate and/or react to these insights.

It is a common assumption in Continental circles that Heidegger's renewal of the question of Being in the face of its historical forgetting amounts to a decisive rejection of 'metaphysics' in favour of 'ontology'. However, the truth is far

---

268. Cf. *Introduction to Metaphysics.*

more complicated. In *Being and Time*, Heidegger describes his project as 'fundamental ontology' not so as to distinguish it from 'metaphysics', but in order to emphasise its continuity with Husserl's project of formal ontology.[269] Although many of Heidegger's criticisms of the metaphysical tradition can be found in this work, it does not identify the tradition's problems with metaphysics as such. Moreover, there is a distinct period following *Being and Time* in which he presents his project as a renewal of metaphysics.[270] It is only later on that he begins to view these problems as inherently metaphysical, and that the word 'metaphysics' takes on the pejorative sense it has in so much post-Heideggerian discourse; at the same time, the word 'ontology' also begins to disappear from his work, precisely as its continuity with Husserl's project fades.[271] Nevertheless, those who come after Heidegger tend to treat 'metaphysics'

---

269. The project of fundamental ontology is sometimes read as identical with the inquiry into the Being of Dasein. In *Being and Time*, Heidegger seems to deny this, explicitly stating that: 'The analytic of Dasein [...] is to prepare the way for the problematic of fundamental ontology—*the question of the meaning of Being in general.*' (*Being and Time*, 227) However, in *Basic Problems of Phenomenology* he states: 'We therefore call the preparatory ontological analytic of the Dasein *fundamental ontology* [...] It can only be preparatory because it aims to establish the foundation for a radical ontology.' (224) It thus appears that what Heidegger means by 'fundamental ontology' shifts between these two works. I choose to use the term as it is used in *Being and Time*, where it names the project of grounding regional ontology by attempting to provide a concept of Being in general.

270. Cf. Heidegger, *Fundamental Concepts of Metaphysics, Introduction to Metaphysics*, 'What is Metaphysics', in W. McNeill (ed.), *Pathmarks* (Cambridge: Cambridge University Press, 1998), and *Metaphysical Foundations of Logic* (Bloomington, IN: Indianapolis University Press, 1984)

271. The last substantive and indicatively minimal engagement with ontology is to be found in 'The End of Philosophy and the Task of Thinking' (in *Basic Writings*, ed. D. F. Krell [London: Routledge Classics, 1993]).

as inherently degenerate, and often treat 'ontology' as what the inquiry into Being (the structure of beings as such and as a whole) becomes once it has been divested of the baggage of the metaphysical tradition. Leaving the orthodox Heideggerians to one side for the moment, we can distinguish three distinct post-Heideggerian rejections of metaphysics according to the aspect of the concept of substance they hold responsible for its onto-theological legacy: *presence* (Derrida), *unity* (Badiou), or *ground* (Meillassoux).

Derrida focuses upon Heidegger's reading of substance as presence (*Anwesenheit*)—according to which the essence of metaphysics is the privileging of the temporal present.[272] It is on this basis that he introduces the supposedly pleonastic phrase 'metaphysics of presence' that is so common in orthodox discourse. This phrase signals a deeper affinity between the Heideggerian orthodoxy and its Derridean progeny, which consists in their mutual refusal to renew the project of ontology after 'the end of metaphysics': they concur in demanding a practical reorientation of our relation to the subject matter of metaphysics (the attitude of *Gelassenheit*, or the operation of *deconstruction*), rather than a theoretical resolution of its problems (which would lapse back into metaphysics); they merely differ on the question of whether this reorientation is capable of overcoming metaphysics (so as to pass over into a 'second beginning') or is condemned to remain within it (as an endless engagement with its 'limits').[273] In each case, the reorientation is prepared by subsuming Husserl's unthematised

---

272. J. Derrida, 'Ousia and Gramme', in *Margins of Philosophy* (Chicago: University of Chicago Press, 1982), 29–68.

273. Cf. Heidegger, 'On the Essence of Truth', in *Pathmarks*, 126–7; *Basic Questions of Phenomenology*, §§31–3 ; *Contributions to Philosophy*, §85, §87, §91; Derrida, 'Ousia and Gramme', 63–7.

distinction between reality and appearance within a more fundamental historical/temporal structure (*Ereignis* or *différance*) through which beings come to presence (*clearing* or *presencing*) within a structured horizon (*Da-sein/world* or *arche-writing/text*) in a manner that simultaneously erases and hints at its origins (*withdrawal* or *trace*); as such, the refusal is enacted by sublimating the opposition between Being and seeming, thereby denying any role to 'ontology' that could be separated from their pragmatically reoriented 'phenomenology' of historical/temporal coming-to-presence.

Badiou instead focuses upon the traditional link between substance and unity most clearly espoused by Aristotle (for whom substances are *units* to be counted) and Leibniz (for whom 'that which is not *one* being is not a *being*')—presenting the essence of metaphysics as this subordination of Being to the normative force of the one.[274] Unlike Derrida and the later Heidegger, he uses this diagnosis to cleave ontology from metaphysics: he takes his axiomatic rejection of the one (or units) to imply the identity of ontology and mathematical set theory *qua* theory of pure multiplicity (or multiples without units); this does not so much foreclose ontology to philosophy as require a philosophical supplement ('meta-ontology') that can interpret the significance of its results.[275] Badiou's commitment to the identity of ontology and mathematics inaugurates this supplement—not only is it a philosophical rather than a mathematical thesis, but its intelligibility hinges upon a precise reformulation of the opposition between Being (as *inconsistent* multiplicity) and appearing (as *consistent* multiplicity) that Heidegger and

---

274. A. Badiou, 'The Question of Being Today', in *Theoretical Writings*, ed., tr. R. Brassier and A. Toscano (London: Continuum, 2006).

275. A. Badiou, *Being and Event*, tr. O. Feltham (London: Continuum, 2005), 9–16.

Derrida sublimate.[276] Badiou's definition of Being's appearance as its *presentation* in the form of countable units (or *objects*) is essentially a refinement of Husserl's transposition of the noetic challenge: it cleanly separates phenomenology as the *logic of appearance* (or the formal/regional circumscription of the range of possible objects) from ontology as the mathematical *presentation of presentation* (or the *subtraction* of what is presented in every situation [inconsistent multiplicity] from its presentation [consistent multiplicity]).[277] On the one hand, this makes phenomenology into a genuinely logical enterprise by unbinding it from any constraints imposed by 'consciousness' or 'intuition' and looking to category-theory for a formal analysis of the (*transcendental*) conditions governing the relations of self-identity that constitute regions of countable objects (or *worlds*).[278] On the other hand, this overcomes the problems of phenomenological bracketing by confining existence to inconsistent multiplicity (Being) and positing an archimedean point—the empty set ($\emptyset$ or *the Void*)—to which its existential import is indexed.[279]

Finally, Meillassoux focuses upon the conceptual link between substance and ground most clearly developed in Spinoza and Leibniz's systematic extrapolations of the *principle of sufficient reason* (in terms of a single substance or infinite substances)—locating the essence of metaphysics in its search for an absolute ground (of existence and/or intelligibility) in the form of a necessary entity (paradigmatically, the

---

276. Ibid., Meditation I.

277. Badiou, 'Being and Appearance', in *Theoretical Writings*.

278. A. Badiou, *Logics of Worlds*, tr. A. Toscano (London: Continuum, 2009).

279. Badiou, *Being and Event*, Meditation IV.

God of onto-theology).[280] Like Badiou, he uses his account of metaphysics to secure the possibility of a non-metaphysical ontology: he provides a proof of the necessity of contingency that simultaneously precludes all metaphysical absolutes (necessary entities) and provides a non-metaphysical absolute (the *principle of factiality*); not only does this restrict the scope of ontology from 'what is' to 'what could be'—it also posits mathematics (the systematic extrapolation of the *principle of noncontradiction*) as that which thinks this pure contingency (as opposed to pure multiplicity) and philosophy as that which interprets its significance (the *figures of factiality*).[281] This means that, although ontology is concerned with what *necessarily* exists (something), it is unconcerned with what *actually* exists (everything). The philosophical circumscription of the various regions of actuality (or *worlds*)—types of objects, their qualities, and the laws that govern them—is thus not a phenomenological analysis of appearance, but a speculative exploration of reality.[282] That this speculative supplementation of ontology amounts to something like a return to *metaphysica specialis* can be seen from the three

---

280. Meillassoux, *After Finitude*, 32–4 and 125–6.

281. 'Speculative Realism' in *Collapse* vol. 3, 393; *After Finitude*, chapter 6; P. Wolfendale, 'The Necessity of Contingency', in P. Gratton, P. J. Ennis (eds), *The Meillassoux Dictionary* (Edinburgh: Edinburgh University Press, 2014).

282. This is not to say that there are not important connections between Meillassoux's treatment of the distinction between *possibility* and *actuality* and the distinction between *reality* and *appearance* (or *Being* and *seeming*) that is implicit in Husserl, problematised by Heidegger and Derrida, and explicitly reformulated by Badiou. Importantly, the way that Meillassoux uses the emergence of worlds from one another *ex nihilo* to underwrite the distinction between primary and secondary qualities (cf. *After Finitude*, chapter 1; *Philosophy in the Making*, appendix B) can be seen as grounding his account of appearance in his account of actuality.

worlds Meillassoux takes to be extant—*matter*, *life*, and *thought* (cosmology/biology and psychology)—and the fourth world whose *advent* his speculative philosophy anticipates—*justice* (theology).[283]

What can we learn from this trajectory we have traced? To begin with, it is worth recognising the transition from Kant to Husserl as the crucial moment in the evolution of correlationism. Husserl's formal ontology modifies *metaphysica generalis* in essentially the same manner as Kant's transcendental analytic, replacing its concern with beings *qua* beings (understood as things *in themselves*) with objects *qua* objects (understood as the *correlates* of thought); but he opposes this to metaphysics rather than redefining it (replacing *metaphysica specialis* with regional ontology). This opposition is responsible not only for the split between ontology and metaphysics in the Continental tradition, but also for the emergence of correlationism as an anti-metaphysical stance. Husserl distances himself from Kant not so much by rejecting the distinction between phenomena and noumena (as the German idealists do), but by practically subsuming it within the phenomenological reduction: he extracts the phenomenal by repressing the noumenal. This repression is responsible not only for the Heideggerian critique of metaphysics that subsequently shapes the tradition, but also for the emergence of strong correlationism as an alternative to Kant's weak correlationism.

In bracketing the existence of objects, Husserl's phenomenological reduction suspends the epistemological limit that Kant placed upon the correlation between subject and object—the existence and noncontradictoriness of things in themselves—and thereby facilitates its reabsorption into the correlation.

---

283. *Philosophy in the Making*, appendix D.

The historical/temporal sublimation of the phenomena/nou-mena distinction enacted by Heidegger and Derrida (through *Ereignis/différance*) should be seen as a radicalisation of this suspension, and their corresponding practical reorientation towards metaphysics (in *Gelassenheit/deconstruction*) as the resultant transmutation of Husserl's methodology. There are other forms of strong correlationism, some of which have inde-pendent origins, but this Heideggero-Derridean form is without doubt the most influential in the Continental tradition.[284] The mathematical reformulation of the Being/appearance distinc-tion carried out by Badiou should be seen as breaking with this strong correlationism and returning to a form that is in many ways weaker than Kant's: reinstituting the existence of the in-itself (as indexed to *the Void*) and thereby deducing ontological constraints upon the logic of appearance beyond mere noncontradiction (the meta-ontological analysis of the relation between set theory [ontology] and category theory [phenomenology]).[285] This contrasts with the radicalisation of strong correlationism performed by Meillassoux, which should be seen as converting its practical suspension of the in-itself (de-absolutisation) back into theoretical knowledge of it (an absolute): demonstrating the absolute contingency of the

---

284. Meillassoux explicitly acknowledges Wittgenstein as the founding figure of strong correlationism in analytic philosophy (*After Finitude*, 41–51), whose *Tractatus Logico Philosophicus* is undoubtedly inspired by Kant's correlation-ism. However, he also draws a useful distinction between universalist and anti-universalist strains of strong correlationism, which differ on whether there is a universal structure of correlation (e.g., language, consciousness, etc.). Husserl, the early Wittgenstein, the early Heidegger, and perhaps Habermas exemplify the former strain, and the later Wittgenstein, the later Heidegger, Derrida, and the loose agglomeration of thinkers who self-identify as 'postmodernists' ex-emplify the latter.

285. Cf. Badiou, 'Kant's Subtractive Ontology' in *Theoretical Writings*.

in-itself and thereby deducing both its existence (as something rather than nothing) and its submission to non-contradiction (as the applicability of mathematics).

We are now in a position to show why the difference in usage between the terms 'ontology' and 'metaphysics' in the Continental tradition has progressively narrowed since Husserl first placed them in opposition. On the one hand, what constitutes 'ontology' in the tradition has gradually become more like the 'metaphysics' it was originally opposed to: the initial exclusion of existential questions from ontology (Husserl) gave way to a demand to thematise the notion of existence implicit in it (Heidegger), which in turn enabled the gradual reinclusion of these questions within a broader philosophical project (Badiou and Meillassoux). Meillassoux's speculative philosophy exemplifies this trend, insofar as it treats ontology as the core of a larger speculative enterprise that has more than a passing resemblance to the programme of scholastic metaphysics. On the other, this shift has been accompanied by the decline of the 'end of metaphysics' narrative that was dominant in twentieth-century Continental philosophy after Heidegger.[286] Of course, metaphysics never entirely went away: there was always interest in self-avowed metaphysicians such as Hegel and Bergson, or in figures whose thought harboured an unexplored metaphysical dimension, such as Nietzsche and Bataille; but it wasn't really until Deleuze's self-avowed

---

286. Although it is in decline (or remission) it is far from dead, and has in fact been radicalised into a more general 'end of philosophy' narrative by François Laruelle, whose non-philosophy aims to axiomatically extend philosophical practice in much the way that Heidegger and Derrida aimed to pragmatically reorient it (cf. F. Laruelle, *Principles of Non-Philosophy*, tr. A. P. Smith [London and New York: Bloomsbury, 2013]; F. Laruelle, *From Decision to Heresy*, tr. M. Abreu et al. [Falmouth and New York: Urbanomic and Sequence Press, 2012]).

'metaphysics' became popular in Anglo-American Continental philosophy that the term began to lose its pejorative edge.[287] What one sees at the intersection of these two trends is an increasing pressure to place purportedly antimetaphysical figures such as Heidegger and Badiou and explicitly metaphysical figures such as Hegel and Deleuze into dialogue, and this results in the term 'ontology' being used as the lowest common denominator of their joint enterprise. However, this diplomatic usage elides the traditional difference between ontology as species (*metaphysica generalis*) and metaphysics as genus (also including *metaphysica specialis*). We can only hope that the increasing popularity of 'metaphysics' helps reverse this confusion by allowing 'ontology' to return to its more specific meaning.[288]

In tracing the development of 'ontology' in the analytic tradition we must return to a different part of Kant's critique of metaphysics: his famous response to the ontological argument that God's *existence* follows from his *essence*.[289] This argument, which lies at the heart of both scholastic theology (e.g., Anselm) and early rationalist metaphysics (e.g., Descartes), essentially attempts to infer the actual existence of a possible

---

287. It is important to note that Deleuze is sensitive to Heidegger's critique of the metaphysical tradition: he acknowledges the problems of onto-theology and incorporates the idea of ontological difference into his work (cf. *Difference and Repetition*, 77–9); he simply rejects Heidegger's identification of onto-theology and metaphysics; and on that basis continues to draw upon the tradition (e.g., Spinoza and Leibniz).

288. It is worth noting that Badiou has warmed to the term 'metaphysics' over time, precisely because it provides a better index of the relation between his project ('meta-ontology') and that of figures such as Deleuze ('Political Perversion and Democracy', talk given at the European Graduate School 08/12/2004: <https://www.youtube.com/watch?v=AcKdPzB3gYQ>).

289. Kant, *Critique of Pure Reason*, B620–30, B660–70.

entity (*that* it is, or its *Daß-sein*) from the properties that are predicated of it *qua* possibility (*how* it is, or its *Sosein*), or from those determinations that are internal to its concept. Kant's negative thesis is that we can disqualify all such inferences on the basis that existence is not a real predicate: to predicate existence of something is not to add anything to it *qua* possibility, but merely to posit its actuality, and therefore existence is a determination that is external to its concept. Kant's positive thesis is that positing the actuality of the thing is locating it within the intuitive bounds of experience, or situating it within the spatio-temporal realm of nature. The influence of these ideas upon the analytic tradition begins with Frege, who accepts the negative but rejects the positive dimension of Kant's account of existence. Frege cashes out Kant's negative thesis that existence is not a 'real' predicate by interpreting it not as a (first-order) predicate of *objects* but as a (second-order) predicate of *concepts*: to make a *general* existential claim is to say of some concept that it is instantiated (e.g., 'horses exist' is understood as 'the concept <horse> has at least one instance'). Russell then refines this account by explaining *singular* existential claims in terms of his theory of definite descriptions (e.g., 'my horse exists' as 'there is a unique instance of the concept <horse that belongs to me>') and his associated descriptive theory of names (e.g., 'Trojan exists' as 'there is a unique instance of the concept <horse that belongs to me, is black, is swift, is...etc.>').[290] However, although this does much to clarify the *form* of existential claims, it is not clear that it does much to clarify their *content*—

---

290. See chapter 3.1, subsection 2 for a more thorough description of Russell's theory of descriptions and the controversy over its extension into a theory of proper names.

the concept of *instantiation* is no less opaque than the concept of *existence* it is supposed to explain.[291]

In order to show how this relates to the evolution of 'ontology' in the analytic tradition, it is necessary to say something about the evolution of 'metaphysics'. It is important to understand that neither Frege nor Russell were anti-metaphysical thinkers. Frege's mathematical platonism, which treats mathematical objects and senses as existing independently of thought about them, is explicitly metaphysical, as is Russell's logical atomism, which treats the propositions that provide the content of thoughts as actually composed by the individual objects and universals to which they refer.[292] The rejection of 'metaphysics' in the analytic tradition begins with Wittgenstein's *Tractatus Logico-Philosophicus*, and its appropriation by the logical positivists of the Vienna Circle. Though in many ways a development of Russell's logical atomism, the *Tractatus* posed the first *semantic* challenge to metaphysics: it did not reject the possibility of knowing things in themselves, but the possibility of saying anything meaningful about them.[293]

---

291. Frege is more perspicuous than Russell in this regard. He rejects Kant's positive thesis because he is concerned to provide an account of the existence of numbers, which are abstract objects and therefore non-spatio-temporal. He derives the existence of abstract objects from concrete ones by means of an operation of abstraction (e.g., [abstract] orientations must exist because the relation '...is parallel to...' holds between [concrete] lines, such that 'the orientation of x' is identical to 'the orientation of y' iff x is parallel to y). This does not provide a complete alternative to Kant's positive account, but it does present an important conceptual link between existence and criteria of identity (cf. Brandom, *Making It Explicit*, chapter 7).

292. B. Russell, 'On Propositions: What They Are and How They Mean', *Proceedings of the Aristotelian Society, Supplementary Volumes*, vol. 2, *Problems of Science and Philosophy* (1919), 1-43.

293. This is the origin of strong correlationism in the analytic tradition. See p. 227 n. 284.

This challenge was then developed and popularised by the Vienna Circle, who replaced Wittgenstein's account of meaning as picturing with an account of meaning as verifiability, so that metaphysics is meaningless not because it cannot picture the structure of states of affairs, but because it cannot be empirically verified.[294] Though this idea famously collapsed under its own weight—one cannot empirically verify the principle of verifiability—its sceptical inertia infused the tradition that coalesced after the breakup of the Vienna Circle and the resulting diaspora of logical positivism.[295] Nevertheless, this inertia is consolidated and focused by Carnap in a gesture that parallels Husserl's methodological suspension of the existence of things in themselves, determining the fate of 'ontology' in the analytic tradition much as Husserl did in the Continental tradition.[296]

In Carnap's logical empiricism, the mere fact that existential claims share the same *syntactic form* (e.g., 'horses exist', 'societies exist', 'transfinite cardinals exist', etc.) does not mean that they share the same *semantic content* (e.g., horses, societies, and transfinite cardinals can 'exist' in different senses). He holds that existential questions are relative to the *linguistic framework*—or the set of rules governing the relevant terminology (e.g., the frameworks of biology, sociology, and mathematics)—in which they are posed. It thus makes sense to ask questions that are *internal* to a given framework (e.g., 'is there a transfinite cardinal larger than the set of rational

---

294. M. Schlick, 'Meaning and Verification', *Philosophical Review* 45:4 (1936): 339–69.

295. The influence of this diaspora is why the analytic tradition is sometimes referred to as 'Anglo-Austrian' as much as 'Anglo-American'.

296. R. Carnap, 'Empiricism, Semantics, and Ontology' in *Revue Internationale de Philosophie* 4 (1950), 20–40.

numbers but smaller than the set of real numbers?' in a mathematical context), but not to ask questions that are *external* to a given framework (e.g., 'do transfinite cardinals exist in the same way that horses exist?'); metaphysical questions about existence are thereby replaced with pragmatic questions about our choice of linguistic frameworks.[297] Carnap is thus even more radical than Husserl: not only does he pragmatically suspend 'metaphysical' questions about the existence of things in themselves, he reduces anything like 'formal ontology' to syntactic analysis of language in general and anything like 'regional ontology' to the semantic analysis of specific theoretical languages. This reduction has had an important influence on the meaning of 'ontology' in the sciences, where it is used to talk about the typology of entities implicit in a given theoretical framework (e.g., anatomy, cosmology, economics, etc.).[298] However, much as the meaning of 'ontology' in the Continental tradition is indexed to Heidegger's critique of Husserl, so is its meaning in the analytic tradition indexed to Quine's critique of Carnap.

It is important to emphasise just how much Quine agrees with Carnap's views on metaphysics. Not only is he willing to accept Carnap's choice of semantics as the terrain on which the battle over the possibility of metaphysics is fought; he is also willing to accept that most of the substantive claims

297. See H. Price, 'Metaphysics After Carnap: The Ghost Who Walks?' and M. Eklund, 'Carnap and Ontological Pluralism', in D. Chalmers, D. Manley and R. Wasserman (eds), *Metametaphysics* (Oxford: Clarendon Press, 2009), 320–46 and 150–56.

298. The explicit cultivation of such 'ontologies' is most popular in computer science and biomedical science. For a useful discussion of the terminology see Werner Ceusters, 'Biomedical Ontologies: Toward Sound Debate', <http://www.referent-tracking.com/RTU/sendfile/?file=CeustersCommentaryOnMaojoLongVersion.pdf>.

made by all sides in the history of metaphysics are strictly meaningless. He also shares Carnap's staunch commitment to the priority of natural science, which, as we shall see, ultimately leaves an untidy thread hanging from the account of 'ontological commitment' he provides. Where Quine demurs is simply on the question of the meaningfulness of *univocal* existential commitments.[299] Quine thinks that there are good semantic reasons to think that there must be a single and privileged domain of objects in terms of which the meaning of 'exists' is to be understood, precisely because the external existential question par excellence—'What is there?'—has an obvious and even trivial answer: 'Everything'. It is important to see that this rejection of Carnap's ontological pluralism functions by invoking the very connection between beings *as such* and beings *as a whole* from which metaphysics as a discipline originates.

This goes some way to explaining the unintended consequence of Quine's critique: the gradual reconstruction of metaphysics within the analytic tradition on the foundation of 'ontology'—no longer understood as the study of beings *qua* beings ('What is a being?'), but as the study of beings as a whole ('Which beings exist?'). Quine's aim was *deflationary*: he aimed to defend Frege and Russell against the instantiation objection by showing that there simply is nothing more to be said about existence/instantiation than what is provided by the logical analysis of the syntax of existential claims. However, his influence was ultimately *inflationary*: not only did he enable analytic philosophers to argue for the (univocal) existence of naturalistically intractable entities—beginning with Quine's

---

299. Quine, 'On What There Is'.

own minimalistic commitment to the existence of numbers[300] and leading to David Lewis's extravagant commitment to the existence of fully formed possible worlds[301]—he inadvertently legitimated more substantial analyses of the semantics of existential claims (so called analytic 'meta-ontology')[302] and with it a range of more classical metaphysical problems beyond the scope of ontology: the metaphysics of relations (e.g., Ladyman and Ross) modality (e.g., Lewis), universals (e.g., Armstrong)[303] and beyond.[304] This return to 'metaphysics' via 'ontology' curiously mirrors the progression of Continental philosophy in the twentieth century.

What remains is to try to synthesise the two stories just told, and to see how the notion of ontological commitment with which we began this chapter fits into the unified narrative. We have already seen that each tradition rejects 'metaphysics' only to revive some form of 'ontology', which then paves the way for its return; but we have not yet articulated the crucial difference between their uses of 'ontology' and thus precisely how their paths diverge before they converge once more. This crux is the concept of *existence*: Husserl and Carnap

---

300. See Quine, *The Roots of Reference* (La Salle, IL: Open Court, 1973), part III.

301. See D. Lewis, *On the Plurality of Worlds* (Oxford: Wiley-Blackwell, 2001).

302. The *Metametaphysics* collection (see p. 233 n. 297, above) is an excellent survey of contemporary work in this field. Kit Fine's essay ('The Question of Ontology', 157–77) provides the best example of the sort of substantial analysis that Quine himself rejects.

303. See D. M. Armstrong, *Universals: An Opinionated Introduction* (Boulder, CO: Westview Press, 1989).

304. Of course, there are figures in the analytic tradition who entirely ignore the Viennese rejection of metaphysics (e.g., substance theorists such as E.J. Lowe and David Wiggins), and there are others who stick with Carnap against Quine (e.g., neo-Carnapians such as Eli Hirsch and Huw Price).

suspend it and Heidegger and Quine critique this suspension, but their attempts to explicitly thematise the concept develop in opposing directions. On the one hand, the tradition that follows Heidegger treats 'ontology' as the study of what existence is—or what it is to be a being—retaining the core theme of *metaphysica generalis* (e.g., fundamental ontology) and ultimately reconstructing the themes of *metaphysica specialis* on this basis (e.g., regional ontology). It is nevertheless resisted by an enduring correlationism that continues to reject unqualified existential claims until the work of Deleuze and Meillassoux. On the other hand, the tradition that follows Quine treats 'ontology' as the study of what exists—or which beings there are—retaining the core theme of *metaphysica specialis* (as applied ontology)[305] and eventually regressing to the themes of *metaphysica generalis* on this basis (as meta-ontology). Quine's introduction of the term 'ontological commitment' to designate the unqualified existential claims to which our theories commit us is thus opposed to the correlationist vision of 'ontology' that is still alive in parts of Continental philosophy. We shall now proceed to examine Quine's account of ontological commitment and its importance for the debate between ontological conservatism and ontological liberalism.

II. EXISTENCE, QUANTIFICATION, AND MULTIPLICITY

In order to understand Quine's account of ontological commitment it is necessary to explain how Frege and Russell's idea that existence is a second-order predicate is formalised by

---

305. This term is introduced by Dale Jacquette in his book *Ontology* (Montreal: McGill-Queen's University Press, 2002) and is contrasted to 'pure ontology' which covers both Heideggerian fundamental ontology and analytic meta-ontology.

contemporary logic. We have already explained how predicates are usually understood as mathematical functions (e.g., **Fx**) or open sentences (e.g., '...is red'), in which the variable must be given a determinate value (e.g., **Fa**) or the sentence must be completed with a singular term (e.g., 'the apple is red') in order to express a determinate proposition. We now have to introduce the notion of a *quantifier*, which is understood either as a mathematical function that takes predicates as arguments and returns truth-values (e.g., $(\forall x)(Fx)$ and $(\exists x)(Fx)$, read as 'for all **x**, **x** is **F**' and 'for some **x**, **x** is **F**', respectively), or as the main component of a *quantified noun phrase* that takes the place of a singular term in completing an open sentence (e.g., 'not all...' in 'not all apples', completing 'not all apples are red'; 'most...' in 'most integers', completing 'most integers aren't primes'; or even 'exactly four...', in 'exactly four planets', completing 'exactly four planets in the solar system are gaseous').[306] The obvious way to understand

---

306. The standard account of quantifiers is called the *objectual* interpretation (cf. J. Barwise and J. Etchemendy, *Language Proof and Logic* [Stanford, CA: CSLI Publications, 1999], part II), because it treats variables as ranging directly over sets of objects. This is contrasted with the *substitutional* interpretation, in which variables ranges over sets of *singular terms* that purportedly refer to objects, rather than the objects themselves (cf. *Making It Explicit*, chapters 6–7; M. Lance, 'Quantification, Substitution, and Conceptual Content', *Nous* 30:4 [December 1996], 481–507; and J. Tomberlin, 'Objectual or Substitutional', *Philosophical Issues* vol. 8 [1997], 151–67). It is also sometimes contrasted with the interpretation of the quantifiers provided by *free logic*, which standardly uses two domains: an *inner* domain of existing objects and an *outer* domain of either non-existing objects or the singular terms that refer to them (cf. K. Lambert, 'The Philosophical Foundations of Free Logic', in *Free Logic: Selected Essays* [Cambridge: Cambridge University Press, 2003]). However, as Lance shows, it's possible to reconstruct objectual quantification in substitutional terms (using substitution-inferential semantics as opposed to model-theoretic representational semantics), and as Tomberlin shows, Brandom's own way of doing this is essentially a variant of free logic. This shows that there are more

quantifiers is as devices for *quantification*, or for expressing the number of things in a given set that meets a certain criteria (e.g., 'there are nine planets in the solar system', 'there are no unicorns on earth', 'every electron has a negative charge', etc.). However, the best way to understand them is in terms of their role in *binding* the free variables of syntactically well formed *formulas* (e.g., the quantifier ($\forall$...) binds the variable **x** in the formula **Fx∧Gx** to form the proposition ($\forall$**x**)(**Fx∧Gx**)), or in progressively *completing* open sentences by closing the *grammatical openings* left for singular terms (e.g., the quantified noun phrase 'most apples' completing '...are green and sharp' to form the grammatically complete sentence 'most apples are green and sharp').

This allows us to draw three overlapping distinctions between types of predicates. Firstly, we can make our earlier distinction between *monadic* and *relational* predicates more precise, as we can see that some predicates contain more than one free variable/grammatical opening (e.g., **Fxy**, or '...loves...') which can be bound/closed by different quantifiers (e.g., ($\forall$**x**)($\exists$**y**)(**Fxy**), or 'everybody loves somebody') even if they needn't be (e.g., ($\forall$**x**)(**Fxx**), or 'everybody loves themselves').[307] Secondly, we can introduce the distinction between *simple* and *complex* predicates, or between predicates whose corresponding formulas/open sentences contain nothing but free variables/openings (e.g., **Fx** and **Gxy**, or '...is red' and '...loves...') and predicates whose corresponding formulas/sentences are composed out of simple predicates and logical operators (e.g.,

---

complex interactions between the different interpretations of the quantifier than a simple threefold distinction might indicate. Nevertheless, I will remain neutral on these issues until specified otherwise.

307. See chapter 3.3.

Fx ∧ **Gx** and ¬(**Fxy** ∧ **Fyx**), or '...is green and sharp' and '...and... don't love each other'). Finally, we can introduce the distinction between *first-order* and *higher-order* predicates, or between those predicates whose variables can only take objects as their values (e.g., **Fx** where **x** takes objects {**a**, **b**, **c**, ...}) and those predicates whose variables can also take *lower-order* predicates as values (e.g., **Kφ** where **φ** takes first-order predicates {**F**, **G**, **H**, ...}). This is the founding gesture of *type theory*, which distinguishes the types of *values* that free variables can have: either by being given a *determinate value* (e.g., **a** for **x** in **Fx**: **Fa**) or by being bound to a *determinate range* of values (e.g., {**a**, **b**, **c**, ...} for **x** in **Fx**: (∀**x**)(**Fx**)). This enables the generation of a *type hierarchy*, beginning with a primary type of objects that are not functions (individuals) and a secondary type of functions whose arguments are of the primary type (first-order predicates) and then recursively enumerating new types of functions (higher-order predicates) whose arguments may be drawn from previously generated types.[308] This means that we can treat an open sentence (e.g., '...has an arrity of 2') as a second-order predicate if its grammatical openings can be closed with the name of a first-order predicate (e.g., 'the relation '...loves...' has an arrity of 2') or some suitable nominalisation thereof (e.g., 'love is a two-place relation'). We will return to the importance of type theory as a strategy for dealing

---

308. There are a number of complexities involved in the formulation of type theories that I have deliberately glossed over in the above presentation (e.g., the distinction between type and order necessitated by the ramification of types once relational predicates are considered, and the successor theories proposed by Church and others). For a detailed historical overview of these issues, beginning with Frege's hierarchy of concepts and its development in Russell and Whitehead's hierarchy of propositional functions, see W. Kneale, *Development of Logic* (Oxford: Clarendon Press, 1962), 652–72; and C. Chihara, *Ontology and the Vicious Circle Principle* (Ithaca: Cornell University Press, 1973).

with Russell's paradox and other so-called impredicative definitions later.[309]

For now, it is important to explain why quantifiers are not higher-order predicates in the sense just defined, even though they are functions from predicates to truth-values. This is because quantifiers don't specify variable types: the same quantifier (e.g., ($\forall$...) and 'most...') can be used to bind free variables ranging over different types of values (e.g., ($\forall x$)(Fx) and ($\forall \varphi$)($K\varphi$), and 'most mammals are quadrupeds' and 'most simple predicates are monadic'). It is for this reason that first-order logic contains quantifiers even though it excludes second-order predicates: first-order quantifiers take first-order predicates as their arguments by binding their first-order variables (x), not by containing additional second-order free variables (φ). The grammatical distinction between quantifiers (e.g., 'most...') and quantified noun phrases (e.g., 'most mammals' and 'most simple predicates') makes this separation between quantifiers and variable types clear, insofar as the noun (e.g., 'dog' and 'simple predicate') that gets added to a quantifier to create a quantified noun phrase is needed to specify the types of values the variable ranges over. This point is crucial for understanding Quine's defence of Russell and Frege from the instantiation objection. This is because their idea that existence is a second-order predicate is often understood as meaning that it is

---

309. In explaining type theory as the classic solution to these paradoxes, I am not thereby advocating the idea that it is the definitive solution. There has been much useful work done that tries to get beyond this approach (cf. Ø. Linnebo. 'Plurals, Predicates, and Paradox: Towards a Type-Free Account', <http://semantics.univ-paris1.fr/pdf/ppp-description.pdf>; J.-Y. Girard 'Locus Solum: From the Rules of Logic to the Logic of Rules', <http://iml.univ-mrs.fr/~girard/0.ps.gz>).

equivalent to the *existential quantifier* (∃...), which appears to conflict with the definition of 'second-order' just provided.[310] Quine's defence of Frege and Russell exploits the difference between first-order existential quantifiers and second-order predicates in order to show that grasping the meaning of the former is quite a different matter from grasping the meaning of the latter, such that '...has an instance' need not be defined in the same way as an ordinary second-order predicate. Although it is possible to use the existential quantifier to define existence predicates for both singular cases (i.e., $Ex \equiv (\exists y)(x = y)$, so that $Ea \equiv (\exists y)(a = y)$ or 'there is something identical with fido') and general cases (i.e., $E\varphi \equiv (\exists y)(\varphi y)$, so that $EF \equiv (\exists y)(Fy)$ or 'there is something that is a dog'), there is no more to understanding these predicates than understanding the syntactic role of the existential quantifier in binding the relevant first-order variables: 'To be assumed as an entity is, purely and simply, to be reckoned as the value of a variable.'[311]

It is also important to explain why understanding the syntactic role of variable binding isn't just a matter of understanding the existential quantifier, but quantification per se. We can show this simply by pointing out that the existential and universal quantifiers are interdefinable (i.e., $(\exists x)(Fx) \equiv \neg(\forall x)\neg(Fx)$, which is to say 'there is something that is a dog' is equivalent to 'not everything is not a dog'; and $(\forall x)(Fx) \equiv \neg(\exists x)\neg(Fx)$, which is to say 'everything is material' is equivalent to 'nothing isn't material'). However, it is better shown by echoing Frege's famous claim that '[a]ffirmation of existence is nothing but the

---

310. This conflict arises from the terminological differences between Frege's hierarchy of concepts (which quantifiers are internal to) and Russell's hierarchy of propositional functions (which quantifiers are external to).

311. Quine, 'On What There Is', 13.

denial of number nought'.[312] This means that the existential quantifier is equivalent to the numerical quantifiers 'more than zero...' or 'at least one...' and as such demands nothing more than a practical grasp of *counting*. It is also important to explain that Quine adopts Russell's anti-Meinongian solution to the problem of negative singular existential claims (e.g., ¬**Ea**, or 'Pegasus does not exist'), namely, treating proper names (e.g., the constant **a**, or 'Pegasus') as covert definite descriptions (e.g., a unique descriptive predicate **F**, or 'the winged horse of Perseus'), so as to remove reference to objects that don't exist (e.g., $Ea \equiv (\exists x)(\forall y)(Fx \wedge (Fy \rightarrow x = y))$ and $\neg Ea \equiv \neg(\exists x)(Fx)$, or 'there is one and only one winged horse of Perseus' and 'there is no winged horse of Perseus'). Once both of these points are recognised we can see that Quine essentially defends Frege and Russell's explanation of existence in terms of instantiation by showing that there is nothing more to understanding instantiation than being able to count: if you know how to count individuals, then you know what it is for them to exist.

We have now explained the logical foundations of Quine's account of ontological commitment, but there is still more to it than this. One way of bringing the remaining issues to light is by considering the claim that 'two out of three little pigs lost their houses to the big bad wolf'.[313] There is an obvious sense in which this claim is true, and in which it is the result of an accurate counting procedure. It would make sense to ask a child who had been told the story of the three little pigs 'how many of them lost their houses?' in order to test their counting

---

312. G. Frege, *The Foundations of Arithmetic*, tr. J. L. Austin (Oxford: Blackwell, 1950), 65.

313. No relation. See p. 29 n. 17.

ability, and to treat the above claim as a correct response. However, this implies the claim that 'there are some little pigs that lost their houses to the big bad wolf', which we are supposed to treat as synonymous with 'there *exist* little pigs that lost their houses to the big bad wolf', and this seems to ontologically commit us to the existence of some well-known fictional pigs. Quine thus has to methodologically differentiate *ontological* commitment from mere *existential* commitment if he is to avoid including fictional pigs in his ontology.

It is at this point that Quine invokes Occam. He claims that we are only ontologically committed to those entities that are *explanatorily indispensable*: meaning those entities that are within the range of the variables bound by the sentences composing our best scientific theories, once those theories have been translated so as to be as referentially frugal as possible.[314] We are thus not ontologically committed to the existence of fictional pigs, even though we can count them, because counting them makes no contribution to the natural-scientific enterprise. However, Quine never properly thematises and justifies this restriction of ontological commitment to the natural sciences. Although he comprehensively articulates ontological conservatism from a naturalist perspective, he does not fully articulate this perspective, nor the reasons for adopting it. This uncritical naturalism is the untidy thread hanging from his account I alluded to earlier. To show why it is so unsatisfactory

---

314. For a comprehensive overview of just how referentially frugal Quine thinks we can be, see *The Roots of Reference*. It is worth pointing out that Quine rejects higher-order logic in favour of set theory, meaning that he is committed to the numbers and sets ranged over by the first-order variables of mathematical discourse as much as the concrete individuals ranged over by the first-order variables of empirical discourse (x), but is not committed to the existence of anything ranged over by supposedly second-order variables (φ) such as concepts, properties, etc.

it is necessary to return to the initial gesture that Quine makes in his dispute with Carnap: invoking the conceptual connection between 'what exists' and 'everything', or the link between ontological commitment and unrestricted quantification.

To do this, it is necessary to explain what we mean by *restricted quantification*. On the standard interpretation of quantifiers, the bound variable ranges over a set of objects called the *domain* of quantification.[315] This is naïvely understood as the set of everything that exists, or the *unrestricted domain*. To restrict this domain is to only allow the variable to range over some subset of the unrestricted domain (e.g., the set of dogs that exist). In practice, the vast majority of quantificational claims are restricted in some way, though these restrictions may be more or less explicit. For instance, when I say to my guests that 'there is no beer' I do not mean that all of the beer in the world has been consumed or otherwise eradicated; I am *implicitly* restricting my claim from the domain of everything to that of those things in my house (which is a subset of everything), or even that of things in my fridge (which is a subset of things in my house). This restriction can be made *explicit* by adding '...in my house' or '...in my fridge' to the original quantificational claim. Conversely, when I say 'there is nothing in the fridge' I am not denying that there are shelves, stains, oxygen molecules, and even light in there; I am implicitly restricting my claim to food (or perhaps just safely edible food). We have already seen how this sort of restriction gets made explicit, by combining the quantifier (e.g., 'no...') with a noun (e.g., 'food') to form a quantified noun phrase (e.g., 'no food') that specifies the range of the bound variable (e.g., 'no food is in my fridge'). It is important to understand

---

315. This is the objectual interpretation mentioned in p. 237 n. 306.

that quantifying with the noun 'thing' signals an absence of explicit restrictions, meaning that the associated quantifier (e.g., 'no...', 'some...', 'every...', etc.) is either implicitly restricted (e.g., 'there is no*thing* in the fridge') or explicitly unrestricted (e.g., 'some*thing* exists').

It is with regard to this question of unrestricted quantification that Quine's ontological conservatism and contemporary ontological liberalism cross paths: both take themselves to be entitled to the seemingly unrestricted claim that 'every*thing* exists', though they disagree about its significance. The problem is providing a precise interpretation of what either side means when they make this claim; though the crucial difference between them lies in what they mean by 'everything', this difference cannot easily be made explicit, because one is *implicitly restricted* and the other is *implicitly unrestricted*. On the one hand, although Quine takes 'everything exists' to be a trivial claim, insofar as he defines existence (*qua* instantiation) as belonging to the set of everything, he nevertheless wants to exclude some 'things' (e.g., fictional pigs, round squares, universals, etc.) from this set. This indicates that his account of ontological commitment depends upon an implicit restriction of 'everything' that he delegates to natural science. On the other hand, although ontological liberals take 'everything exists' to be a profound injunction, insofar as it indexes the ontological circumscription of the whole range of possible objects of thought in accordance with the noetic challenge to conservatism, they nevertheless experience difficulty defining 'thing' (or 'object') broadly enough to circumscribe 'everything' in the completely unrestricted sense. To appreciate this difficulty we must delve deeper into the logic of unrestricted quantification.

Although it might seem that quantifying without any restrictions would be the most simple form of quantification, its possibility is a highly controversial topic in philosophical logic. The most famous problems for unrestricted quantification are posed by the set-theoretical paradoxes formulated by Cantor and Russell.[316] Cantor's paradox shows that there cannot be a set of all sets (**U**) on pain of contradiction, because its cardinality (|**U**|) would have to both be lesser and greater than that of its power set (|$\mathcal{P}$**U**|): a power set—the set of all subsets of a given set—must always have a greater cardinality than its corresponding set (|**U**| < |$\mathcal{P}$**U**|), and a set must always have a cardinality greater than or equal to its subsets (|$\mathcal{P}$**U**| ≤ |**U**|).[317] Russell's paradox constructs another seemingly comprehensible set that cannot exist on pain of contradiction: the set of all sets that don't contain themselves (**W**), which contains itself if it doesn't contain itself (**W** ∉ **W** → **W** ∈ **W**), and doesn't contain itself if it does (**W** ∈ **W** → **W** ∉ **W**). The general form of reasoning these paradoxes display rests upon *impredicative definitions*, or functions defined in such a way that they can take themselves as arguments (e.g., **Fx** where **F**(**Fx**) is syntactically well formed). This is the same sort of problematic self-reference that lies behind the liar paradox

---

316. For a slightly less brief summary of these paradoxes, consult Glenn W. Erickson and John A. Fossa's *Dictionary of Paradoxes* (Lanham, MY: University Press of America, 1998). For a thorough exposition cf. Kneale, *The Development of Logic*, and Chihara, *On the Vicious Circle Principle*.

317. Cantor's paradox has become popular in recent Continental philosophy because of the work of Badiou. It has been appropriated by various other thinkers (e.g., Meillassoux, Slavoj Žižek, Adrian Johnston) as evidence for the non-existence of the Whole. However, unlike Badiou, they tend not to explain how we are to deduce the nonexistence of a totality of entities as such from a claim about the totality of sets.

(e.g., '...is false' where 'this sentence is false' is grammatical).[318] Russell's theory of types was formulated as a way of preventing such paradoxes of self-reference by hierarchically segregating functions into orders whose variables can only range over types in the orders beneath them.

One might object at this point that these paradoxes are concerned with sets and not 'things', and thus pose no problems for thinking about 'every *thing*' even if they cause problems for thinking about 'every *set*'. We can respond to this by pointing out that sets are well-defined objects of mathematical thought, such that ontological liberalism ought to include whatever sets can be coherently specified within its comprehensive circumscription of what there is. However, if 'everything' should thus contain 'every set', then it seems that the set of everything (E) should include the set of all sets (U) as a subset ($U \in E$), and Cantor's paradox precludes this. Similarly, for the set of objects that constitutes any given domain of quantification (D), one can exploit the reasoning of Russell's paradox to construct a set that is not contained within it: the set of everything in D that doesn't contain itself ($R_D = \{x : x \in D \land x \notin x\}$). This means that one can never define an absolutely unrestricted domain, because the very act of defining it enables one to construct an object that is not present within it, and thereby to define a more expansive domain that includes it ($E' = \{x : x \in E, R_E\}$).[319] Once liberalism allows sets in, sets of things quickly get out of hand.

---

318. Cf. Kneale, *The Development of Logic*.

319. For a detailed exploration of this move and its potential pitfalls, see K. Fine, 'Relatively Unrestricted Quantification' in A. Rayo and G. Uzquiano (eds), *Absolute Generality* (Oxford: Oxford University Press, 2006).

One might further object that the problem is not with sets *qua* objects, but with the attempt to circumscribe 'everything' by means of a determinate set of objects over which the bound variables of unrestricted quantifiers range. This objection is important, but we must be careful not to interpret it in a trivial manner: if one treats set theory as merely one mathematical formalism among others, so as to emphasise the sense in which it is concerned with a specific type of object (sets), rather than an attempt to formalise thinking about collections of objects as such, then one has merely stipulated one's way out of the challenges it poses. One need not treat a given formalism as binding in order to see the significance of the problem that these paradoxes pose.[320] They suggest that the capacity for self-reference (or the reflexivity of *sense*) is an internal obstacle to the circumscription of the totality of possible objects of thought demanded by the noetic challenge to ontological conservatism. Our ability to think about the very manner in which we think about objects (or to *refer* to senses) puts us in a position to generate an endlessly ramifying network of new objects of thought, the delimitation of which only offers further opportunities for ramifying beyond those limits.

The non-trivial form of the objection is that it is not merely the manner in which set theory articulates the idea of 'everything' as a determinate collection that is problematic, but the very notion that to think 'everything' is to think some determinate collection. However, it is possible to interpret the problematic feature of this notion either as *reification* or as

---

320. Whether one chooses to work within the confines of some form of type theory, a system that allows for a distinction between sets and classes such as Quine's New Foundations, or a typeless system such as 'pure' Zermelo-Fraenkel set theory, one has been forced to navigate the noetic obstacles thrown up by the possibility of self-reference.

de-absolutisation. So, one might hold that thinking 'everything' as a collection treats it as an additional *object* we are both obliged to include within itself ($U \in U$) and permitted to use in constructing further objects (e.g., $\mathcal{P}U$ and R_U) that cannot be so included. This interpretation of the objection seems to be favoured by ontological liberalism, which on this basis follows Badiou in denying the existence of anything like *the Whole* that could be thought as such.[321] However, one might instead hold that thinking 'everything' as one collection among others prevents us from grasping what differentiates it from all other such collections (e.g., 'every dog', 'every number', etc.)—its unique *absoluteness*. This interpretation of the objection is suggested by Kant's positive account of existence: his distinction between the appearance of spatio-temporal objects within experience and the pure forms of space and time through which they appear amounts to a distinction between the *specific contents* and the *general structure* of 'absolutely everything' in relation to which objects *qua* objects are defined (ontology). Furthermore, this provides a way of demystifying the self-containment of 'everything': space and time appear within themselves insofar as they are coextensive with themselves. The spatio-temporal manifold need not appear as an object within a more expansive manifold.

This distinction between the structure and contents of 'everything' is taken up and articulated by the early Heidegger, who uses it to thematise the connection between beings as

---

321. Markus Gabriel provides the clearest formulation of this objection and the liberal response to it, explicitly defending the idea that the totality of what exists is the only thing which does not exist ('The Meaning of "Existence" and the Contingency of Sense', in *Speculations* vol. IV [2013], <http://www.spec-ulations-journal.org/storage/Gabriel_Meaning%20of%20Existence_Specula-tions_IV.pdf>).

such and beings as a whole that simultaneously defines and escapes the metaphysical tradition. This is the significance of his discussion of 'the Nothing' (*das Nichts*) and its relation to what he calls the fundamental question of metaphysics: 'Why is there something rather than nothing?'[322] This discussion is famously ridiculed by Carnap, and taken to exemplify the way that seemingly profound but essentially vapid metaphysical theses can be derived from basic misunderstandings of the underlying logic of language.[323] Explaining what Heidegger means and why Carnap's criticism is wrong is a good way of getting a grip on the difference between the reification and de-absolutisation objections to set-theoretical approaches to 'everything' and their relation to the ontological difference.

To do this properly, it is necessary to frame the issue in terms of our discussion of quantificational restriction. Carrying on the earlier example: in a more philosophical mood I am entirely capable of asking the question 'Why is there beer?', and of making explicit its unrestricted scope (as opposed to 'Why is there beer *in the fridge*?') by saying 'Why is there beer *rather than none*?'. This kind of construction has two effects. Firstly, it contrasts the state of affairs for which we are demanding a reason (the existence of beer) with an alternative state of affairs that is prima facie possible (the non-existence of beer). Used literally, all the 'none' does here is to pick out a state of affairs in which there is some number of beers (zero). We could ask very similar questions contrasting different states in which we varied this number (e.g., 'Why are there *two* beers rather

322. Heidegger 'What is Metaphysics?' in *Basic Writings*; and *Introduction to Metaphysics*.

323. R. Carnap, 'The Elimination of Metaphysics Through Logical Analysis of Language', in S. Sarkar (ed.), *Logical Empiricism at its Peak: Schlick, Carnap, and Neurath* (New York: Garland, 1996), 10–31.

than *three*?', 'Why are there *no* beers rather than *two*?', etc.). However, zero is the *limit-case* of the various possible states of affairs we can produce by varying the number of some kind of things. It is what we will call an *empty state of affairs*, or *a* nothing. We can contrast this limit-case with all *non-empty states of affairs*, i.e., those in which there are *some* of the kind of object in question. Secondly, it is an additional quirk of our language that this kind of contrast can be used to signal a lack of implicit restrictions on the quantifier (e.g., '...in my fridge', '...in Saudi Arabia', '...that I like', etc.). When we combine these two features in the case of the fundamental question, we see that the qualification '...rather than nothing' makes explicit a possible state of affairs (there is nothing) to which the actual state of affairs (there is something) is contrasted, and the fact that this is a *unique* limit-case (the limit-case of limit-cases). The quantifier is not explicitly restricted, nor is it supposed to be implicitly restricted—it is explicitly *completely unrestricted*. The qualification thus forces us to think the *absolutely empty* state of affairs, or *the* Nothing.

Carnap's criticism of Heidegger works by treating his use of the singular term 'the Nothing' as naming a special meta-physical object, and thus as internally inconsistent insofar as it implies that there is something after all. This reification of 'nothing' directly parallels the reification of 'everything' which ontological liberalism by necessity opposes. It is clear from our above explanation of the Nothing that Heidegger rejects any such reification. This rejection is the foundation of Heidegger's thesis that Being *is* Nothing: the fundamental question of metaphysics enables us to think the *structure* of 'absolutely everything' (beings as a whole) as distinct from its *contents* (beings) by identifying it with the structure of 'absolutely nothing' (the Nothing); this amounts to thinking Being as the unitary structure of beings *as such and as a whole* by understanding existence (beings as such) as the content of this structure (beings as a whole).[324] Just as for Kant space and time do not appear as objects within themselves, so for Heidegger Being is not a being, but literally no-thing. This is the essential statement of the ontological difference between Being and beings that he takes to be elided by onto-theology.[325]

It is important to emphasise that Heidegger does not transcend the bounds of logic in drawing this connection between Being and Nothing, so much as slip the restraints of Carnap's preferred logic. This is clear if we consider another controversy in the philosophy of logic that their debate skirts: the problem of *empty domains*. Classical logic and most forms of predicate logic cannot allow the domains over which their variables range to be empty. *Relatively* empty states of affairs (nothings) are perfectly acceptable (e.g., the cases where there is no *beer*, there are no *unicorns*, or there is nothing *in the space between galaxies*) insofar as they restrict the quantifier in some way, thus allowing there to be something *in general* despite there being nothing of a *specific type* or in a *specific locale*. But the *absolutely* empty state of affairs (the Nothing) is logically impermissible. The reason for this is that the truth conditions of the quantifiers are defined in terms of the way that the well formed formulas whose variables they bind are *satisfied* by objects in the domains they range over

---

324. Heidegger, *Introduction to Metaphysics*, 2–3.

325. It is worth pointing out that the early Heidegger's project was essentially to provide an account of this structure within which beings appear as content (the worldhood of the world) in terms of the primordial temporality (*Temporalität*) involved in Dasein's projection of a world. For a more thorough discussion of this project and its failure, consult chapters 4 and 5 of my *The Question of Being*.

(e.g., $(\forall x)(Fx)$ is true iff every object in the domain $\{a, b, c, ...\}$ maps Fx to truth if taken as its value: Fa, Fb, Fc, ...), and this makes even self-evident propositions false when the domain is empty (e.g., $(\forall x)(x = x)$ is false when there are no objects in the domain $\{\}$, or when the domain is $\varnothing$). This problem is rectified by *free logics*, which allow the introduction of *non-referring singular terms* (e.g., 'the present king of France', 'Pegasus', etc.).[326] Although not all free logics can handle empty domains, the only logics that can (so called *universally free* or *inclusive* logics) are free in this sense. They do so by partially suspending Quine's bond between quantification and existence: distinguishing between quantifiers that can range over existents (e.g., 'there are *no* little pigs who lost their houses to the big bad wolf' and '*no* unicorns have horns'), and those that can also take non-referring singular terms (e.g., '*two out of three* little pigs lost their houses to the big bad wolf' and '*all* unicorns have horns'). This constitutes a distinction between the existential quantifier ($\exists$...) and the particular quantifier ($\char"0295$...) by differentiating those uses of 'some...' that imply existence from those that don't.

The crucial point is that, however the particular quantifier is defined (e.g., as taking both referring and non-referring singular terms, or as ranging over an *outer domain* that includes both existent and subsistent objects), the corresponding existential quantifier is defined by means of an *inner domain* that only contains existents: existence (beings as such) is understood as the content of this domain structure (beings as a whole).[327]

---

326. See p. 237 n. 306.

327. The definition of existence predicates proceeds exactly as we discussed earlier (e.g., $Ex \equiv (\exists y)(x = y)$). The only difference is that Russell's theory of descriptions is not needed to parse its application to non-referring singular terms (e.g., $Ea \equiv (\exists y)(a = y)$).

It is on this basis that the possibility of an empty inner domain can be thought consistently.

Lest this be seen as simply one more detour into irrelevant logical theory, let us explicitly articulate its significance for thinking about the ontological difference. Just as the set-theoretical paradoxes of self-reference trace an ontological obstacle internal to the project of noetic circumscription, so do free logic's sundered quantifiers trace a noetic caesura internal to the project of ontological circumscription. This caesura is the manifestation of the ontological difference in thought: the singular difficulty of thinking beings as such and as a whole without thinking them in terms of some highest being (e.g., God) or some genus of beings (e.g. Ideas, subjects, etc.), or of thinking their structure (Being) as distinct from its content (beings). What this means is that, if we are to think beings comprehensively, then we must draw a distinction within thought between thinking about beings and thinking about Being. However, this distinction can be developed in two directions, depending on how one interprets the relation between noetic circumscription and ontological circumscription. Ontological conservatism is in a position to distinguish between beings and objects of thought because it does not identify noetic and ontological circumscription. This means that it can distinguish between thinking about beings *qua* objects and thinking about Being *qua* object, and thus does not need to radically dissociate the latter from the former. This is not to say that this is what ontological conservatism does in practice: Quine refuses to fully thematise thinking about Being, and defers to whatever implicit grasp the natural sciences have upon it in practice. Ontological liberalism is forced to identify beings and objects because it folds noetic into ontological circumscription. This means that it must radically dissociate thinking about beings *qua* objects from thinking about Being. This is the significance of the later Heidegger's turn to poetry as a medium of thinking that escapes the objectifying power of literal discourse.[328]

We are now in a position to describe the ontological egalitarianism that binds ontological liberalism together: the connection between the demand to account for *all* things and the demand to account for them *equally*. The de-absolutisation objection to treating 'everything' as a determinate collection opens up the possibility of defining existence in terms of unrestricted quantification. This is because it identifies the whole to which the latter refers as a general structure whose specific content is provided by existents. In aiming to provide a comprehensive account of beings as such by comprehensively defining beings as a whole, it grasps the *equality* of things by way of the *totality* of things. However, this is not egalitarian enough for ontological liberalism, because it refuses to treat whatever objects we can think beyond the bounds of this totality as things in their own right. By contrast, the reification objection to treating 'everything' as a determinate collection suggests the converse possibility of defining unrestricted quantification in terms of existence by treating the latter as the general structure of the objects of thought. In aiming to provide a comprehensive account of beings as a whole by

---

328. Cf. M. Heidegger, *Poetry, Language, Thought*, tr. A. Hofstadter (New York: HarperCollins, 1981). It is worth pointing out that this puts the later Heidegger in the unique position of endorsing the de-absolutisation objection to the idea that beings as a whole can be grasped as a determinate collection (as opposed to the reification objection endorsed by most ontological liberals) while nevertheless refusing the conservative move of decoupling noetic circumscription from ontological circumscription. However, this is best understood as the result of a more thorough annihilation of the distinction between the noetic and the ontological performed by the notion of *Ereignis*.

comprehensively defining beings as such, the objection grasps the *totality* of things by means of the *equality* of things. In essence, ontological egalitarianism dismisses any attempt to define the whole as reifying it, because it insists on treating whatever objects we can think beyond the bounds of any proposed totality as things in their own right. By denying existence to the Whole, the ontological egalitarian keeps their options perpetually open, enabling them to gesture towards ever larger samples of myriad and mythical entities. However, the role of these gestures is purely negative—they strip away predicates often illicitly attached to Being (e.g., not 'spatio-temporality' because we include non-locatable things, not 'materiality' because we include immaterial things, not 'persistence' because we include transitory things, etc.)—and there must be a corresponding positive account of Being. It is at this point that the need to radically dissociate thinking about Being from thinking about objects implied by the ontological difference becomes pressing. How are we supposed to think the equality of objects in a manner radically dissociated from thought about their differences? How are we to think their structure as radically alienated from their content? There are roughly two ways of approaching this question, but to understand them we must return to the logic of quantification one last time.

There is a further objection to the possibility of absolutely unrestricted quantification that is quite different from those based on the set-theoretic paradoxes: that it only makes sense to quantify over a domain that is *sortally restricted*.[329] This is a special form of restriction using what are called *sortal predicates*, and although there is some disagreement

---

329. This is the view adopted by Brandom in *Making It Explicit* (chapters 6–7).

over precisely what these are, it is commonly accepted that they are predicates that provide *criteria of identification*. For instance, the predicate '...is a natural number' is defined in such a way that we have a clear criterion for whether two natural numbers are identical: if they are located at the same point in the succession of numbers, then they are the same number (e.g., if **x** is the successor of 2, then **x** = 3). The objection is then that it is impossible to count any kind of object without such a criterion of identity (e.g., it makes no sense to ask 'how many *instances* of red are there in this street?' unless one specifies that one is counting instances of red *cars*, red *flashes of light*, or red *areas*, etc.).[330] In natural languages, sortal restriction is performed by the noun added to the quantifier in composing a complete quantified noun phrase (e.g., 'cars', 'flashes of light', or 'areas' in 'there are some...that are red'), but not all such nouns correspond to sortal predicates (e.g., 'food' in 'there is some food in my fridge'), because some do not specify a complete *counting procedure*. On the one hand, some nouns leave much of the counting procedure implicit (e.g., it might be easy to determine that we've got 'some food' rather than 'none', or 'enough food' rather than 'not enough', but this doesn't mean that there are generic units of food that can be applied to both apples, oranges, and half-eaten tubs of yoghurt). On the other, some nouns correspond to rigorous counting procedures with conventional units (e.g., it is easy to determine that we've got '100ml of yoghurt', and that this is comparable to '100ml of water', but these generic units are conventional measurements of volume, not natural units of number).

---

330. The same idea is approached from the opposite direction by Peter Geach, who famously claims that there is no absolute identity, only identity relative to a sortal predicate ('Identity', *Review of Metaphysics* 21 [1967], 3–12.)

The idea behind this objection is similar to the idea behind type theory: the variables bound by quantifiers must always correspond to a specific range of values, and there simply is no way to specify a range that includes every possible value that could be specified, not only because we use these specifications to produce new values that they don't include, but because they correspond to a whole plethora of more or less determinate counting practices that can be indefinitely elaborated. This implies that the nouns 'object' and 'thing' that we use to signal an absence of *explicit restrictions* do not for all that signal an *explicit absence* of restrictions. They do not correspond to a sortal predicate that provides some special procedure for counting everything we could possibly think of. They are *pseudo-sortals*, and they must always be implicitly restricted by some genuine sortal.[331] The consequence of this objection is that the sort of thinking that is made explicit by quantificational logic cannot possibly provide a positive account of the Being of objects. Ontological liberalism essentially embraces this consequence, albeit with variable levels of self-consciousness. The crucial point is that this provides it something to contrast its own form of thinking against, so as to clarify the methodological status of ontology. The difference between the two ways of approaching the methodological question lies in the way in which they contrast themselves with thinking that can be made explicit using quantifiers: Does ontology think something *more* than it, or something *less*?

---

331. Brandom, *Making It Explicit*, 437–8.

III. SUBTRACTION AND ALLUSION

This brings us to Badiou's role in the emergence of ontological liberalism. Although Badiou's work is not directly influential upon Harman in the same way as either the Austrian school or Latour, its influence upon Garcia, Gabriel, and Bogost[332] is a synecdoche of its influence upon the philosophical discourse as a whole, such that it indirectly enables the liberal paradigm of which Harman is the paragon. It is no secret that the primary motivation for Badiou's philosophy is political. Even if politics is only one of philosophy's four conditions (along with art, science, and love), it is clear that the principal contribution of Badiou's meta-ontology is its account of the emergence of subjects as instances of truth-procedures initiated in fidelity to an Event (*l'événement*) that is 'trans-Being' or undecidable in the context of the situation in which it emerges (e.g., the French Revolution, Sophoclean tragedy, Cantorian set theory, an amorous encounter, etc.), and that this is specifically addressed to the problem of political agency.[333] I raise this motivation not to make any critical comments about it or its consequences, but to explain Badiou's affinity to the antireductionist challenge to ontological conservatism.[334]

We have already noted that Badiou follows Husserl in sublimating the noetic challenge in his study of the logic of appearance, transforming the task of circumscribing the full range of possible objects of thought into an exploration of the *Logics of Worlds* within which these objects appear. This is

---

332. Cf. I. Bogost, *Unit Operations: An Approach to Videogame Criticism* (Cambridge, MA: MIT Press, 2006).

333. See P. Hallward, *Badiou: A Subject to Truth* (Minneapolis, MN: University of Minnesota Press, 2003).

334. I owe this point to Ray Brassier.

strictly different from ontology for him, but it remains close enough to the ontology of the liberal paradigm that one can see the affinity between them.[335] However, one cannot appreciate Badiou's proximity to anti-reductionism without seeing it as a result of his commitment to an account of political agency that is strictly irreducible to the economic, sociological, and biological dimensions upon which it is predicated. Though he is an avowed 'materialist' in the Marxist tradition, his rejection of the principle of sufficient reason in order to secure the trans-ontological supplement provided by the Event should indicate the extent of his anti-reductionism. His category-theoretical phenomenology should thus be seen as the noetic counterpart to this ontological anti-reductionism, providing a basis for the detailed circumscription of the political life-worlds within which political agency can emerge.

Given this, the most important thing to understand about Badiou's philosophy is that he understands and embraces the sortal objection to unrestricted quantification more thoroughly than anyone. Badiou's rejection of substance as unity is essentially a rejection of the idea that there are natural units: nothing is *one* until it is *counted-as-one*, or until it appears as an object within the quantificational domain specificied by a particular counting procedure. This explains his rejection of type theory, insofar as the hierarchy of types must always begin with a primitive type of natural units (objects) that can be unproblematically quantified over. It also explains why he retains Kant's use of the term 'object' to designate what *appears* (units), as opposed to what *is* (multiples without units). However, this means that ontology cannot be the

335. It is that part of Badiou's work that could be legitimately described as 'object-oriented'.

study of *objects qua objects*. As we have already explained,
that is the province of phenomenology, or the study of the
transcendental structures within which objects can appear as
self-identical (i.e. *worlds* as domains of quantification). The
province of ontology is the study of what is counted-as-one
before it is unified by the count, or *multiplicity qua multiplicity*.
This explains Badiou's choice of Zermelo-Fraenkel (ZF) set
theory over type theory, insofar as the former quantifies over
sets without supposing that these sets must be composed
by things that are not themselves sets. His meta-ontological
identification of mathematics and ontology is more precisely
the claim that ZF set theory is ontology.

It is important to understand why the thesis that mathematics is ontology cannot be articulated within the austere
realm of mathematical inscription. For Badiou, mathematics
does not think *about* objects—there strictly *are no* mathematical objects, but only a deductive practice that methodically
(albeit sometimes brilliantly) extrapolates the consequences
of an initial decision regarding axioms. However, it is this very
austerity that enables mathematics to inscribe Being:

> [B]eing *qua* [B]eing does not in any manner let itself be
> approached, but solely allows itself to be *sutured* in its void to
> the brutality of a deductive consistency without aura. Being
> does not diffuse itself in rhythm and image, it does not reign over
> metaphor, it is the null sovereign of inference.[336]

This is the essence of Badiou's concept of *subtractive ontology*: mathematics can dissociate the structure of multiplicity
(Being) from its apparent contents (objects) by quantifying

---

336. Badiou, *Being and Event*, 10.

over nothing but Nothing itself (∅) and whatever multiplicities can be constructed out of it (i.e., {∅}, {∅, {∅}}, {∅, {∅}, {∅,{∅}}}, etc.).[337] Badiou fundamentally sunders Heidegger's claim that Being is Nothing by refusing to identify the Nothing and the Whole *qua* Whole. In contrast to Heidegger's claim that the Nothing *qua* Whole does not exist (the de-absolutisation objection), he claims that the Whole *qua* set of all sets does not exist (the reification objection), but that the Nothing *qua* Void exists as the sole index of existence (∅ as the name of Being). This scission marks his retreat from the strong correlationism of Husserl and Heidegger to one even weaker than that of Kant—a retreat that is simultaneously a consolidation and radicalisation of Kant's own subtractive gesture: it converts the thing-in-itself as *external limit* of empirical knowledge into the Void as *internal limit* of mathematical knowledge.[338]

Badiou's subtractive ontology uncovers the structure of beings *qua* beings by taking the objects that constitute the content of thought and stripping them of every possible predicate—and thereby even their objectivity—leaving nothing but multiplicities without unity. However, he refuses to explicitly define multiplicities as such, because this would be to treat '...is a set' as one more sortal predicate by means of

---

337. This is the consequence of Zermelo's axiom schema of separation, which limits the scope of the operation of abstraction through which sets are constructed to sets that already exist, combined with the axiom of the Void which stipulates the existence of the empty set as a fixed point from which other sets can be constructed (*Being and Event*, §3 and §5).

338. Cf. Badiou, 'Kant's Subtractive Ontology', in *Theoretical Writings*; and the introduction to *Being and Event*. This might be seen as Badiou's mathematical synthesis of Kant and Lacan, insofar as he has always identified the Void with the Lacanian Real, or thought's constitutive impossibility.

which to count objects. Badiou navigates the noetic caesura of ontological difference by implicitly defining sets (and thereby beings) in terms of the membership relation between them and their elements (...∈...): instead of stating what sets *are*, he demonstrates what set membership *implies*. This reveals an interesting parallel between Badiou and Quine: whereas Badiou implicitly defines beings *as such* by indexing them to the axioms of ZF set theory and the mathematical practice founded upon them, Quine implicitly defines beings *as a whole* by indexing them to the parsimonious syntactic reformulation of our theories about the world and the natural-scientific practice it is founded upon. Both take a subtractive approach that dissociates thought about Being from thought about objects by harnessing the power of formalism (ZF set theory/first-order quantificational logic) against positive definition, but they approach it from opposite directions (as such → as a whole/as a whole → as such). Both secure the implicitness of Being by deferring its content to a choice (between axioms/between explanations) that they delegate to another form of thought (mathematics/natural science), but they thereby foreclose the conditions under which that choice is made to philosophical reflection: whereas Badiou ignores issues regarding the semantics of quantifiers that determine the space of possible mathematical axioms,[339] Quine ignores issues regarding

---

339. It is important to understand that axiomatics has been gradually superseded by semantics in the history of mathematical logic, insofar as the latter represents an attempt to map the use of the relevant terms (e.g., connectives, quantifiers, modal operators, etc.) onto other mathematical structures (e.g., models, proof structures, strategies, etc.) that explain the range of choices between axioms encoding their inferential behaviour (e.g., mapping modal operators to sets of possible worlds so as to explain axiom choice [K, S4, S5, etc.] in terms of the algebraic properties of the accessibility relation between worlds). Understood in this way, axiomatic set theory represents the last bastion of

the semantics of causal explanation that determine the space of possible scientific theories.[340] However, despite this, their subtractive methodologies do effectively circumscribe what remains implicit in their meta-ontologies.[341]

We must now explain the alternative to subtraction, which takes thought about Being to access something *more* than thought about objects, rather than something *less*. Badiou provides an eloquent description of the way this alternative appears in Heidegger's later work:

> Heidegger still remains enslaved, even in the doctrine of the withdrawal and the un-veiling, to what I consider, for my part, to be the essence of metaphysics; that is, the figure of [B]eing as endowment and gift, as presence and opening, and the figure of ontology as the offering of a trajectory of proximity. I will call this type of ontology *poetic*; ontology haunted by the dissipation of Presence and the loss of origin [...] For poetic ontology, which—like history—finds itself in an impasse of an excess of presence, one in which [B]eing conceals itself, it is necessary to substitute a mathematical ontology, in which dis-qualification and unpresentation are realised through writing.[342]

---

axiomatics against semantics, which should ultimately replace it with a complete semantics of quantifiers (incorporating plural and predicate quantifiers). The main reason this is often overlooked is that the dominant semantic paradigm for analysing other forms of logical vocabulary (model theory) is founded upon axiomatic set theory, so that the standard semantics of generalised quantifiers turns in a tiny explanatory circle.

340. See my *Essay on Transcendental Realism*.

341. It is curious that this word is entirely appropriate to both Quine and Badiou here.

342. Badiou, *Being and Event*, 9–10.

Although the later Heidegger no longer thinks that there can be an account of Being (*Sein*) outside of its particular historical manifestations (e.g., *Physis*, *Logos*, *Hen*, *Idea*, *Energeia*, Substantiality, Objectivity, Subjectivity, the Will, the Will to Power, the Will to Will, etc.) much as Badiou thinks that there is no objectivity outside of its manifestations within particular worlds, he nevertheless thinks that there can be an account of the singular structure (*Seyn/Ereignis*) through which these epochs come about. Heidegger's poetic ontology aims to think this structure by means of the noetic supplement that poetry provides to literal discourse, as opposed to the noetic remainder that formalism subtracts from it.[343] This is the poetic mirror image of Quine's subtractive methodology: it aims to say what little can be said about beings (beings as such) by appealing to the unitary structure that withdraws behind every particular attempt to grasp them (beings as a whole) in a manner that can never become fully explicit.

We are now in a position to precisely articulate the proximity between Badiou and the ontological liberalism of which OOO is the exemplar. If Heidegger's historical poeticism is the mirror image of Quine's subtractive naturalism, then ontological liberalism is the shattered mirror reflecting jagged fragments of Badiou's subtractive mathesis. Without the formal anchor provided by the deductive suture of the Void, the project of encapsulating 'everything' (beings as a whole) by means of a poetics of 'objects' (beings as such) fractures along metaphoric lines. The attempt to navigate the noetic caesura of ontological difference by transcending the expressive constraints of

---

343. The term 'poetic ontology' conflicts with my earlier characterisation of Heidegger as rejecting 'ontology' in describing his later project, but I think the term is useful enough to adopt as long as this conflict is borne in mind.

literal discourse inevitably turns to metaphor as its means of transcendence. We have seen this in the way in which Harman overcomes the gap between phenomenology and metaphysics not merely through the *tactical* use of metaphors to leap from phenomenological to metaphysical chains of reasoning and back again, but through the *strategic* use of metaphor in methodologically founding his metaphysics upon *allusion*. It is easy enough to see the tactical use of metaphor as a common theme in ontological liberalism, but it is important to see that this strategic move is what binds it together. The strategy is presented casually but revealingly by Ian Bogost in *Alien Phenomenology*:

> In short, *all things equally exist, yet they do not exist equally.* The funeral pyre is not the same as the aardvark; the porceletta shell is not equivalent to the rugby ball. Not only is neither pair reducible to human encounter, but also neither is reducible to the other [...] This maxim may seem like a tautology—or just a gag. It's certainly not the sort of qualified, reasoned, hand-wrung ontological position that's customary in philosophy. But such an extreme take is required for the curious garden of things to flower. Consider it a thought experiment, as all speculation must be: what if we shed all criteria whatsoever and simply hold that everything exists, even things that don't?[344]

Here we see ontological liberalism in its most innocuous form: don't worry that 'everything exists' is *literally* a tautology, because it is required for *figurative* goals ('for the curious garden of things to flower'); don't worry that it isn't

---

344. I. Bogost, *Alien Phenomenology, or What it's Like to Be a Thing* (Minneapolis: Minnesota University Press, 2012), 11.

philosophically precise, because it is a *speculative experiment* in imprecision ('everything exists, even things that don't'). It is precisely insofar as it is bound together by a commitment to figuration (allusion) rather than formalism (subtraction) that ontological liberalism fractures itself: the strategic use of metaphor inevitably splinters into a multitude of metaphorical strategies.[345] These strategies may borrow from, intersect, and overlap with one another, but, in the absence of *formal devices* for indexing and delimiting what is implicit in them (e.g., set theory or first-order logic) let alone making it explicit (i.e., in literal discourse), they are little more than an expressive patchwork of resonant metaphors held together by a common pool of *rhetorical devices* (e.g., 'everything exists', 'the Whole does not exist', and the increasingly bizarre lists of things that flank them).

We can see this complicity between metaphor and rhetoric in Harman's version of the reification objection, which rejects the existence of the Whole *qua* holism by *strategically alluding* to the reality of multiplicity by means of its appearance. This strategy is realised less by a litany of *expressive tactics* than by the expression of *tactical litanies*—the deeper truth

---

345. Once again, Markus Gabriel presents perhaps the clearest example of this logic at work, even if he does not articulate it himself (cf. *Transcendental Ontology*, 'Introduction'; and 'The Meaning of "Existence" and the Metaphysics of Sense'). His transcendental ontology rejects the possibility of providing a *general* formalisation of the 'fields of sense' within which 'objects' are defined as appearing, because it accounts for metaphors as *specific* fields of sense that resist such formalisation. It is then reduced to using formalism *as a metaphor*, which conveniently allows Gabriel to pick and choose between those features he takes to allude to important metaphysical truths (e.g., Cantor's and Russell's paradoxes) and those that he can dismiss as mere precision for precision's sake (e.g., the need for a precise equivalent of the axiom of extensionality for fields of sense, if they are to analogically inherit these extensional paradoxes).

about objects to which metaphysics refers is secured by referencing and rhetorically ramifying the superficial diaspora of non-metaphysical sense: pupils and Popeye; muons and moods; the holy spirit and flatulence; Zimbabwe and lambda functions; misogyny and melanomas; klingons and car crashes; lists of lovers and lovers of lists; spells and spookiness; Being, time and *Being and Time*; the Big Mac™ and the empty set (Ø); The Big Bang and The Homosexual Agenda; Proustian experiences and Cthulhu; the best of all possible worlds and the perfect sandwich; boredom and Boris Johnson's famous haircut; Microsoft and Minesweeper; Bruno Latour and Latour litanies; true contradictions and false tautologies; evil and Elvis; something that cannot be referred to in this list and everything else that can; Gödel's famous theorems and his infamous paranoiac fantasies; qualia and quiche; whatever I am currently alluding to and the sublime excess over our collective imagination thereby invoked; transfinite sets and the slow, creeping, horrific, but nevertheless inevitable and in truth almost Lovecraftian realisation that none of us understand the implications of their usefulness in mathematical practice; ambiguity and aubergines; lists of (lists of (lists of [...])) and the uncomfortable reflexivity of this phrase; the dawning realisation that litanies such as this one are at best rhetorically grandiose and at worst cognitive anaesthetics with performative pretensions, and the corresponding hope that they will fade from the pages of history like an exhausted simile.[346]

Nevertheless, it is important to acknowledge that, while this alliance of strategic metaphor and tactical rhetoric is insufficient, there is always more to ontological liberalism than mere metaphor and rhetoric. If there were no explicit metaphysical

---

346. To this list I add, for the sake of Benedict Singleton, 'your mum'.

supplement, then there could be no useful metaphysical debate between it and other such positions, much as there can be no such debate with the later Heidegger's anti-metaphysical position. The problem is that its explicit metaphysics is always in conflict with the implicit metaphorics it is founded upon. The demand for a positive concept of 'object' sufficient to encapsulate an expressive allusion to 'everything' requires that we curtail the expressive power of this metaphorics to allude to objects that don't fit the concept. The conflict between metaphysics and metaphorics can only ever resolve itself in the form of a representational blockage.

In Harman's work, the principal site of this conflict is the temporal underpinnings of his renewed concept of substance. This conflict and the resulting temporal blockage is perfectly articulated by Tristan Garcia in contrasting his own work with Harman's OOP:

> Time is a tribunal deciding between a theory that treats everything as equal objects, but transforms these objects into purely formal things, and a theory that treats its objects as objects, but excludes some things and transforms them into secondary objects.
>
> I choose a path that leads me to treat no-matter-what as a thing and to explode the spatio-temporal constraints in order to define a formal system [...] But there is a price to pay. My thing hardly has anything to do with objects of common sense or at least the objects that 'object-oriented ontologies' would like to account for. No-matter-what being something, my thing is too formal: each instance of something, each event, and each part of each thing are so many things. And in this way, my thing slips through my fingers. My world is populated not only with football teams, words, ghosts, falsities, golden mountains, and

square circles, but also and above all parts of ghost fingers, parts of parts, and parts of these parts at any time *t*, and in the following moment, and the hundred moments before, and ten seconds before that [...] On the other hand, Harman chooses to remain at the level of objects and not to break with the common sense notion of objects, that is, spatio-temporal identifiable and re-identifiable entities. In this way, his objects are more concrete, more easily discernible. The price to pay for his ontology is that it presupposes time and space as specific constraints, internal to the object [...] He borrows from the classical model of substantiality and endows it with an innovative meaning. Internally, his model is strengthened by space and time. But in this way, he gives up considering many things like full-fledged objects.[347]

Despite the fact that we can think the temporal parts of objects (e.g., a person as infant and as adult) as distinct from the temporally enduring objects they compose (e.g., the person who was once an infant and is now an adult), Harman refuses to count them as distinct objects. Although he diverges from classical substance theorists by insisting that fleeting occurrences and events (e.g., a birth, a death, a gamma ray burst, etc.) can be thought as substances in their own right, he nevertheless refuses to allow the division of substances into discrete temporal events. In essence, Harman diverges from Badiou, Garcia, and Gabriel by refusing to take the noetic challenge to its extreme—his unthematised dependence upon deep time curtails the representational dimension of his ontological egalitarianism.

---

347. Garcia, 'Crossing Ways of Thinking', 9–10. It is worth noting that Harman concurs with this analysis of the difference between his and Garcia's work ('Tristan Garcia and the Thing-in-itself', in *Parrhesia* 16 [2013]).

This temporal blockage is peculiar to Harman (and OOO to a lesser extent),[348] yet the self-limiting character of the alliance between metaphysics and metaphorics makes similar blockages in other strands of ontological liberalism inevitable. Subtractive ontology may leave too much unsaid, but *allusive ontology* tries to say too much—to say the *unsayable*—and becomes tangled in its own ambitions. It is a cautionary example of the importance of recognising the difference between meaningfulness and the experience of meaningfulness, or between genuine profundity and the affect of edification. Badiou provides the best account of the dangers of confusing philosophical insight and poetic allusion:

> Now, to abandon the rational mathematical paradigm is fatal for philosophy, which then turns into a failed poem. And to return to objectivity is fatal for the poem, which then turns into didactic poetry, a poetry lost in philosophy [...] Let us struggle then, partitioned, split, unreconciled. Let us struggle for the flash of conflict, we philosophers, always torn between the mathematical norm of literal transparency and the poetic norm of singularity and presence. Let us struggle then, but having recognized the common task, which is to think what is unthinkable, to say what is impossible to say. Or, to adopt Mallarmé's imperative, which I believe is common to philosophy and poetry: 'There, wherever it may be, deny the unsayable—it lies.'[349]

---

348. It is certainly present in Levi Bryant's processual fork of OOO in *The Democracy of Objects* (Ann Arbor, MI: Open Humanities Press, 2011), but Bryant's subsequent reversion to a more classical materialism (under the heading of 'machine-oriented ontology' or MOO) seems to abandon the noetic challenge to ontological conservatism in favour of a more Deleuzian anti-reductionism, which would suggest that he has abandoned the radical ontological egalitarianism characteristic of the rest of OOO.

349. Badiou, 'Language, Thought, Poetry' in *Theoretical Writings*, 233–41.

We need not follow Badiou in his attempt to mathematically trace the edges of the unsayable to agree that philosophy cannot but lose itself in the attempt to transgress these limits: the methodological foundation of allusive ontology is built on the shifting sands of insincerity.

IV. EXPLANATION, NETWORKS, AND PARSIMONY

What lesson should we learn from all this? I think that we must realise that ontology—both in the sense of defining ontological commitment in general (meta-ontology) and that of articulating our specific ontological commitments (applied ontology)—has an important representational function, and that this function should be understood in terms of its epistemological role in our practices of explanation. This is the essential truth revealed by the way 'ontology' is approached by both natural and informational science: there is a practical need to organise the systems of reference through which we index and identify both the *explanandum* of our theories and their *explanans*.[350] There is a connection here with type theory, which is an attempt to formally circumscribe mathematical reference by means of a system of variable types, but is sometimes misunderstood as an attempt to formally circumscribe reference as such. This is a misunderstanding because, although there is a primitive type of non-mathematical objects, it does not distinguish between non-mathematical types. We can see that the interface between the explanatory tools that mathematics provides and the non-mathematical domains in which they are applied is provided by the more or less implicit counting procedures corresponding to interconnected

---

350. See p. 233 n. 298.

systems of predicates: including sortal predicates (e.g., [dog →
mammal → animal], [flathead → screwdriver → tool], [network
interface → daemon → program], etc.) and quasi-sortal predicates (e.g., [electron → lepton → fermion],[351] [gouda → cheese
→ food], [water → liquid → volume], etc.). This reveals a similar
insight underlying Husserl's phenomenological sublimation
and Badiou's subsequent category-theoretical reorientation
of the noetic challenge to ontological conservatism. Though
their respective suppression and suturing of existence obvi-
ates anything like a global set of ontological commitments
(*metaphysica specialis*), their attempts to internally delimit the
phenomeno-logical structure of different domains of objects
(regions/worlds) should be seen as performing the crucial
epistemological role of organising reference within the areas
of theory and practice that correspond to those domains
(e.g., computer science, sociology, and anatomy, along with
database design, social organising, and forensics). Moreover,
Badiou sees this precisely as a matter of articulating the
logical regimes of counting procedures within which objects
can appear as units. In essence, they aim to facilitate *intra-*
disciplinary organisation, even if they thereby preclude *inter-*
disciplinary organisation.

How exactly does the appeal to metaphor undermine
this representational function? It is best to approach this
question from the opposite direction, and explain how metaphors can contribute to the systematisation of reference
within given domains.[352] This means saying something about

---

351. These predicates are quasi-sortal for the reasons pointed out by Ladyman and Ross: they permit the counting of particles but not their absolute
individuation (see *Every Thing Must Go*, §§3.1–3.2).

352. This amounts to giving something like an account of how metaphors
compose 'fields of sense' in Gabriel's terms (see p. 267 n. 345).

how metaphors enable *semantic grafting* between sortal and quasi-sortal predicates, without getting too deep into the corresponding semantics of singular terms.[353] This might best be described as *referential transport*, or the transposition of counting procedures and the referential infrastructure they implement from one system of predicates to another. For example, by describing musical genres as 'families' we can begin to describe their subgenres and the artists that compose them in terms of 'lineages', and to refer to them on this basis (e.g., 'the father of free jazz', 'the children of blues and rock music', etc.) and even to anticipate their as yet nonexistent 'progeny' (e.g., 'the descendants of the union of progressive rock and contemporary folk music'). The metaphors underlying referential transport can be transformed into analogies in the same manner as other metaphors, by precisely delimiting the relations between objects that are transposed from one domain to another (e.g., '...is father of...', '...descends from the union of ... and ...', etc.). These analogies can even become systems of predicates in their own right, potentially constituting relatively autonomous domains of objects. For example, the metaphor of corporate personhood has developed from a suggestive way to look at group enterprises through multiple iterations of analogical pruning into a constitutive legal framework for individuating corporations and managing their rights and responsibilities.

Alternatively, relevant metaphors can remain inchoate, providing a reservoir of conceptual resources for organising and extending our referential capabilities within a given domain: for example, Wilfrid Sellars's famous metaphor of 'the space

---

353. For my earlier explanation of the concept of semantic grafting, see chapter 3.1, subsection IV. For a more detailed discussion of the semantics of singular terms, see Brandom (*Making It Explicit*, chapters. 6 and 7).

of reasons', which licenses more or less open-ended transport from the geometric/topological domain to the logical/discursive domain (e.g., 'concepts in the same neighbourhood as...', 'the inferential maps one needs to navigate...', etc.). It is this ability of inchoate metaphors to perpetually extend the range of possible objects we can refer to by licensing new referential transports that undermines the representational function of any ontology founded upon them—the dissemination of sense prevents the organisation of reference. However, this problem with metaphors reveals a deeper problem with the noetic challenge to ontological conservatism: the egalitarian drive to ontologically *encapsulate* every possible object of thought is incompatible with the epistemological demand to ontologically *organise* thought by articulating a fixed referential framework. One necessitates ontological expansion while the other necessitates ontological contraction. This tension can only be kept at bay by binding the epistemological demand within the domains themselves, refining and reorganising their internal referential systems, while freeing the egalitarian drive to roam between domains, generating new and stranger modes of reference. This differs from Husserl and Badiou's patchwork of regions and worlds only insofar as its insistence on reality over appearance (*metaphysica specialis* over phenomeno-logic) requires that thought's referential profligacy is metaphysically significant.

It is this space between domains of objects, and the *hierarchical* and *transversal* explanatory connections it enables between them (e.g., reducing the domain of chemistry to the domain of physics, or explaining changes in artistic domains through interactions between economic, sociological, and psychological domains), with which the anti-reductionist challenge to ontological conservatism is concerned. This is because reductionism as an ontological schema is essentially a representational paradigm for organising reference *globally* (between domains), rather than *locally* (within domains). The challenge to reductionism must thus be formulated at this global level (as being concerned with 'everything'). This enables us to explain the difference between the *methodological* (Latour) and *metaphysical* (Deleuze) forms of antireductionism outlined at the beginning of this chapter.

However, the names I have given to these two strands might seem counterintuitive, so it is important to explain why I have chosen them. The reason for this counter-intuitive character is that Harman's engagement with Latour consists in treating his methodology (ANT) as a metaphysics (OOO). This engagement has been a dialogue, and Latour has in many ways embraced Harman's reframing of explicitly methodological issues as implicitly metaphysical ones.[354] However, this reframing is only possible on the basis of something like a shared commitment to the noetic challenge to ontological conservatism. This is to say that methodological issues regarding the organisation of explanatorily transversal reference are converted into metaphysical ones by treating the senses that determine these references as entities in their own right (e.g., sensual objects, fictions, theories, etc.). This solves the relevant methodological issues by subsuming sense within ontology, rather than using ontology as a means to organise reference. The former strategy (Latour/ANT/OOO) is merely methodological because it disarticulates the functional role of ontology in mediating between explanation and representation; whereas the latter strategy (Deleuze/Delanda/emergentism) is properly metaphysical because it proposes a genuine

---

354. Cf. *The Prince and the Wolf* (Winchester: Zero Books, 2011) and *An Inquiry into Modes of Existence* (Cambridge, MA: Harvard University Press, 2013).

alternative to the ontological schema of reduction—namely, *emergence*—and thereby provides an alternative global representational paradigm.[355]

To understand this contrast between Latourian methodological anti-reductionism and metaphysical emergentism we must return to Latour's anthropological bracketing of differences between epistemic activities, because his account of transversal explanation is fundamentally motivated by his own work in the anthropology of science.[356] It is because Latour has a *specific* interest in representing science as a domain of objects (e.g., experiments, theories, paradigms, etc, *qua explanandum*) to be explained in terms of its relations to other domains of objects (e.g., experimental equipment, the referents of theories, the sociological environment of paradigms, etc., *qua explanans*) that he ends up disarticulating the *general* relation between explanation and representation encoded by ontology. This disarticulation can be seen most clearly in his theory of *circulating reference*, which he introduces by describing a device that scientific researchers use for storing, organising, and comparing soil samples:

> [T]he pedocomparator will help us grasp the *practical* difference
> between abstract and concrete, sign and furniture. With its
> handle, its wooden frame, its padding, and its cardboard, the
> pedocomparator belongs to "things." but in the regularity of
> its cubes, their disposition in columns and rows, their discrete
> character, and the possibility of freely substituting one column

---

355. See Stewart and Cohen, *The Collapse of Chaos* for a thorough discussion of what this alternative paradigm involves, especially their notions of *simplexity* and *complicity*.

356. See chapter 3.3, subsection II.

for another, the pedocomparator belongs to "signs." Or rather, it is through the cunning invention of this hybrid that the world of things may become a sign [...].

Notice that, at every stage, each element belongs to matter by its origin and form by its destination; it is abstracted from a too-concrete domain before it becomes, at the next stage, too concrete again. We never detect the rupture between things and signs, and we never face the imposition of arbitrary and discrete signs on shapeless and continuous matter. We see only an unbroken series of well nested elements, each of which plays the role of sign for the previous one and of thing for the succeeding one.[357]

Here Latour turns an empirical practice of referential organisation into an object that is itself to be examined empirically. He thereby aims to understand the practical basis of referential organisation internal to the sciences (e.g., the counting procedures implicit within the relevant systems of predicates as used by a given discipline) by treating reference as the operation of a sequence of increasingly rarified *signs*—understood as naturalistically tractable *representational vehicles* or referents—embedded within our explanatory practices.[358] However, by explaining the process through which signs are *abstracted* from the things they refer to as the production of new concrete things in their own right, he essentially suspends the gesture of *abstraction*, by refusing to understand these signs *qua signs*— as bearers of *representational contents* or senses.

357. B. Latour, *Pandora's Hope* (Cambridge MA: Harvard University Press, 1999), 47–56.

358. See chapter 3.2, subsection I for a discussion of the distinction between the vehicles and contents of representation. It is also worth noting that this is not entirely dissimilar from Kripke's causal theory of reference (chapter 2.2, subsection III).

We are now in a position to see that the concept of translation is essentially a metaphysical generalisation of Latour's concept of circulating reference that makes explicit the epistemological and metaphysical homogeneity hiding within it. This generalisation proceeds in two steps: *reflexively subsuming* itself by referentially expanding its anthropological focus from specific practices of representation to representation in general, before *de-anthropocentrising* itself by unilaterally cancelling the difference between its own specifically referential chains and chains of causal interaction in general. This radicalises the initial anthropological bracketing of the difference between epistemic practices into an *anthropomorphic reduction* of the difference between explanatory connections and causal connections, homogenising its own activity of explanation with what it aims to explain. It is harder to find a methodology more diametrically opposed to Husserl's phenomenological reduction, not just because Latour refuses to bracket the existence of things, but because he actively projects his understanding of himself onto their existence. This flight from anthropocentrism into anthropomorphism is the essence of Latour's *amodernism*, or his elision of the divide between culture and nature (or norms and causes).[359]

However, in collapsing this divide, he has equally collapsed the distinction between sense and reference. This is no longer the local collapse with which we began, in which he permits himself to incorporate scientists' means of reference alongside their referents within his models of scientific practice, but a global collapse, which makes *concepts* interchangeable with their *objects*—making them nodes in representational

---

359. Cf. B. Latour, *We Have Never Been Modern* (Cambridge, MA: Harvard University Press, 1993).

networks of explanatory connections that are indiscernible from the real networks of causal interactions they supposedly represent. Latour essentially inverts the relationship between explanation and representation (putting the epistemological cart before the metaphysical horse): he solves the problem of transversality not by providing an alternative ontological schema for organising representation of causal interactions between disparate domains, but by ensuring us that they can interact because *we* can refer to them. Ray Brassier describes the metaphorical underpinnings of this move in the most eloquent terms:

> In dismissing the epistemological obligation to explain what meaning is and how it relates to things that are not meanings, Latour, like all postmodernists—his own protestations to the contrary notwithstanding—reduces everything to meaning, since the difference between 'words' and 'things' turns out to be no more than a functional difference subsumed by the concept of 'actant'—that is to say, it is a merely nominal difference encompassed by the metaphysical function now ascribed to the metaphor 'actant'. Since for Latour the latter encompasses everything from hydroelectric powerplants to toothfairies, it follows that every possible difference between powerplants and fairies—i.e. differences in the mechanisms through which they affect and are affected by other entities, whether those mechanisms are currently conceivable or not—is supposed to be unproblematically accounted for by this single conceptual metaphor.[360]

---

360. Brassier, 'Concepts and Objects', 52.

The metaphysical homogeneity of networks is deeper than we previously realised. Not only does the concept of 'act-ant' elide the ontological difference between individuals and general kinds (e.g., between Joliot and neutrons), but it does so by eliding the difference between general kinds and the concepts that refer to them (e.g., between neutrons and the concept <neutron>). However, although Harman effectively exploits Latour's conflation of individuality and generality, and otherwise praises his willingness to incorporate fictions, phan-tasms, and other senses in his explanatory networks, he does not follow Latourian anti-reductionism in conflating sense and reference—his corresponding metaphysical distinction between sensual and real curtails his ontological egalitarianism from the explanatory direction.[361]

What alternative does metaphysical emergentism provide to this referential catastrophe? It can obviously account for hierarchical explanation insofar as it provides a complementary ontological schema for reduction between domains, but how does it account for the transversal explanations that motivate Latour's anti-reductionism? There is no single answer to this question, but Deleuze and DeLanda's metaphysics provide an illustrative example. As we noted in the last chapter: 'it is no easy matter to outline how every variable characteristic of every physical system in the universe could in principle be incorporated as dimensions of a single continuum which would thereby informationally encode the complete actual state of those systems along with their virtual tendencies, let alone how this continuum can still be divided into discrete chunks corre-sponding to individual systems and their specific tendencies.'[362]

361. See chapter 3.1.

362. p. 179.

However, this is precisely what Deleuze and DeLanda aim to do: to articulate a global representational paradigm capable of situating every entity within this continuum (as individualising loci of pre-individual variables), and to thereby enable the explanation of every causal interaction between those entities (as actual trajectories across virtual surfaces), including transversal interactions between those traditionally confined within the quantificational domains of disparate disciplines.[363]

Deleuze's account of *the plane of immanence* is an exquisite formulation of the de-absolutisation objection to the Whole—an attempt to reimagine Spinoza's Substance through the lens of the ontological difference—aiming to re-articulate *universals* as dimensions of qualitative and quantitative variation within a dynamically unfolding informational surface.[364] DeLanda's notion of *flat ontology* is a radical experiment in ontological univocity—an attempt to universalise dynamic systems theory through population theory—aiming to reconceive *individuals* as intensive indices within a unitary causal-mereological nexus of reciprocally constraining processes, in which populations of populations evolve and effervesce out of one another and their interwoven environments across a manifold of spatio-temporal scales.[365] In essence, although

---

363. The classic statement of this transversality is contained in Deleuze and Guattari's *A Thousand Plateaus* (chapter 3).

364. Cf. Deleuze and Guattari, *A Thousand Plateaus*, chapters 3 and 10; *What is Philosophy*, tr. G. Burchell and H. Tomlinson (London: Verso, 1994), chapter 2. See my 'Ariadne's Thread: Temporality, Modality and Individuation in Deleuze's Metaphysics' for a detailed discussion of this point. It is also worth pointing out that Deleuze's emergentism is often misinterpreted along the lines of Latour's catastropic anti-reductionism by means of a failure to distinguish between 'the' plane of immanence and 'a' plane of immanence, and the 'Ideas' composing the former from the 'concepts' composing the latter.

365. Cf. DeLanda, *Intensive Science and Virtual Philosophy*, chapter 4; *A New*

they work in opposing directions (universal → individual and individual → universal), they both aim to understand beings *as such* (the univocity of Being)[366] through beings *as a whole* (the plane of immanence) in the same manner as Quine.

Nevertheless, they diverge from Quine in refusing his subtractive suturing of the Whole to the referential systems implicit in the supposedly unified enterprise of natural science, but aim to intervene in this enterprise by explicating and revising these referential systems. It is for this reason that their anti-reductionism is properly metaphysical: it adopts an active role in the global organisation of scientific representation.[367] Yet this is the same reason that their anti-reductionism should not be opposed to ontological conservatism: in adopting this role it reaffirms the explanatory value of *parsimony*, rejecting only the twisted form of parsimony popularised by the propagandists of metaphysical reductionism. It is clear that *everything* has a place within Deleuze and DeLanda's worlds except *those things that don't* ('everything exists' is trivial), and that these *placeless things* are placeless not because they are *strictly unthinkable*, but because they are *explanatorily irrelevant* (precisely, 'some things don't exist insofar as they give us no reason to suppose they do'). Although ontological liberalism might appear to be an

---

Philosophy of Society (London and New York: Bloomsbury Academic, 2006). This term has unfortunately become somewhat of an etymological car crash after its appropriation by OOO. As Harman himself points out (*Towards Speculative Realism*, 180) it was initially used by Roy Bhaskar but with an opposing sense to DeLanda's usage. However, whereas DeLanda quite explicitly uses it to withhold existence from certain entities (i.e., universals such as 'Lionhood'), the proponents of OOO use it to mean the rejection of all such gestures (cf. Bogost, *Alien Phenomenology*, 11–19).

366. Cf. Deleuze, *Difference and Repetition*, 377–378.

367. Cf. Deleuze, 'I Feel I am a Pure Metaphysician' in *Collapse* vol. 3.

alliance between the noetic and anti-reductionist challenges to ontological conservatism, this alliance is more fragile than it seems. Metaphysical anti-reductionism is less an attack upon ontological conservatism in general than upon the specific form allied to metaphysical reductionism in the twentieth century. Once ontological conservatism abandons reductionism, it can make its peace with emergentism.

V. ASPECTS, TYPES, AND REALITY

It is now time to consolidate our understanding of Harman's OOP and attempt a serious answer to the question with which this chapter (and perhaps this whole book) is concerned: What *are* objects? However, our dissection of ontological liberalism has revealed that answering this question is far from simple, principally because it must be prefaced by a more subtle question: What does 'object' *mean*? The popularisation of this term, as a (pseudo-sortal) alternative to 'thing' (*Ding*, *res*, entity, being, etc.) emerged directly from Kant's development of the Cartesian opposition between the 'subject' and 'object' poles of the noetic relation. This noetic connotation of the term was retained in its appropriation by the Austrian school and the Husserlian phenomenology that developed out of it—both of which aimed first and foremost to circumscribe all possible *noetic foci* (intentional objects). It was later openly resisted by the numerous critiques of the subject-object relation that emerged from Heidegger's critique of this Cartesian tradition—all of which invariably seek to free 'things' from the theoretical/practical constraints imposed upon them by the thinking/acting subject.[368] That Harman's demand to return to the objects themselves positions itself

---

368. Not to mention the parallel critiques of the 'objectification' of subjects.

to inherit both of these traditions is thus somewhat peculiar, but it is clear that his distinction between *sensual* and *real* is supposed to bind these seemingly conflicting enterprises together, by granting each their own half of the concept <object>. However, this feeds back into our initial question, as it is unclear whether this binding is a mere terminological trick, or a genuine conceptual synthesis.

Harman's divergences from the noetic and anti-reductionist challenges to ontological conservatism frame this issue on either side: he curtails the representational dimension of ontological liberalism by refusing to extend the term 'object' to absolutely everything we can think about (i.e., not all noetic foci are sensual objects); and he curtails the explanatory dimension of ontological liberalism by refusing to treat every 'object' as a legitimate *explanans* (i.e., some sensual objects don't have corresponding real objects). This means that the term 'object' has a positive content that excludes some things we can think about (e.g., non-enduring *time-slices* of objects), although it isn't clear how this positive content is shared by both real and sensual objects (e.g., whether sensual objects and real objects *endure* in the same sense). It is thus absolutely crucial to make explicit what is common to both types of 'objects', because it is this generic notion of 'object' that Harman appeals to in differentiating himself from his opponents:

> Some of these objects are physical, others not; some are real, others not real in the least. But all are *unified* objects, even if confined to that portion of the world called the mind. Objects are units that both display and conceal a multitude of traits. But whereas the naive standpoint of this book makes no initial claim as to which of these objects is real or unreal, the labor of the intellect is usually taken to be *critical* rather than naive.

Instead of accepting this inflated menagerie of entities, critical thinking debunks objects and denies their autonomy. They are dismissed as figments of the mind, or as mere aggregates built of smaller physical pieces. Yet the stance of this book is not critical, but sincere. I will not reduce some object to the greater glory of others, but will describe instead how objects relate to their own visible and invisible qualities, to each other, and to our own minds—all in a single metaphysics.[369]

Whether they are *underminers* who downwardly reduce objects to something more fundamental (e.g., physical systems, atoms and void, or formless *Apeiron*), *overminers* who upwardly reduce objects to something less tangible (e.g., sensations, textual effects, or bundles of qualities), or both simultaneously (e.g., by means of an epistemologically Janus-faced 'materialism'), Harman thinks philosophers have not been sincere in their theoretical dealings with objects.[370] They have overlooked the middle ground (or 'mezzanine level') of the universe in their rush to theorise their favoured fundament.[371]

Yet one cannot *sincerely* demand that they return their attentions to objects without being willing to explain what one means by 'object', and, for all his protestations to the contrary, Harman remains surprisingly elusive on this point. Of course, this *elusiveness* goes hand-in-hand with his *allusiveness*. However, as we have seen, the confluence of metaphysics and metaphorics in allusive ontology is, if anything, a breeding ground for philosophical insincerity. Our aim should thus be

---

369. *The Quadruple Object*, 7.

370. Ibid., chapter 1.

371. Cf. 'I am also of the opinion that materialism must be destroyed'.

to extract as much precision from Harman's allusions as possible, so as to reconstruct his determinate commitments, or *what he sincerely believes*. The locus of this precision—the metaphysical innovation hinted at in the above passage—is almost certainly the fourfold schema; yet it is also in this titular *quadruplicity* that the elusiveness of the 'object' is most clearly manifest: does the schema confront us with a single *genus* of objects that are genuinely quadruple (sensual/real and object/quality), or two distinct *species* of objects (sensual/real) that are merely double (object/quality)?

Seemingly subverting its title, *The Quadruple Object* only ever *explicitly* describes 'objects' as belonging to mutually exclusive species (sensual objects *or* real objects); yet it constantly invokes the allusion embedded therein by *implicitly* suggesting that 'objects' somehow unite the two sides: 'I will not reduce some object to the greater glory of others, but will describe instead how objects relate to *their own* visible and invisible qualities'[372] ('objects' with both sensual *and* real qualities). The allusion is concentrated in the categorial connections that span the two sides of the schema: the sensual object is in tension with *its own* real qualities (eidos), the real object is in tension with *its own* sensual qualities (space), and sensual qualities radiate from their real *counterparts* (duplicity), while the sensual object is encountered by a potentially *distinct* real object (sincerity). In the first three categories (eidos, space, duplicity) the implicit unity of 'objects' is encoded in the hypostatized referential relation between the sensual object (*qua* sense) and the real object (*qua* reference).[373] On the one hand, the referential relation between a specific

---

372. *The Quadruple Object*, 7 , my emphasis.

373. See chapter 1.2, above.

sensual object and a specific real object is what enables the counterpart relation between their specific qualities. On the other hand, this specificity is itself hypostatized in the form of the 'it' to which both sensual and real qualities can belong. But it is telling that the final category (sincerity) does not address this unity at all, but displaces the concern with the *reference relation* between sensual object (*qua* sense) and real object (*qua* reference) with a diametric concern for the *referring relation* between sensual object (*qua* sense) and real object (*qua* referrer). This forces the unity to which the fourfold schema alludes to remain implicit, by occupying the only schematic location where it could be made explicit. This leaves us hovering between the species interpretation explicit in the fourfold schema and the genus interpretation implicit in its categorial allusions.

Although this tension between implicit and explicit is intricately woven into both the form and the content of the fourfold schema in *The Quadruple Object*, it is already present in an inchoate form in *Tool-Being*. We can even trace its genesis to a specific passage:

> To say that every entity is both tool and broken tool is to say that every entity is half physically real and half merely relational. No entity can be assigned unequivocally to one side of the equation or the other. But this implies something more than we have seen so far. It is not only the case that every entity has a deeper essence—rather, every *essence* has a deeper essence as well. This will be simpler if we revert to our own earlier terminology: not only does an object have tool-being, but this tool-being *in turn* has its own tool-being [...]
>
> The preceding paragraph has a rather strange implication. The initial argument of this book was that *Vorhandenheit* and

Zuhandenheit are not two distinct classes of entity, but two *modes* of being that belong to every entity. But we have now pushed Heidegger's insight far enough that the situation has reversed into its opposite. In a sense, it has now turned out that the hammer in use and the hammer in its tool-being are not simply two sides of the same coin, but two different coins altogether. In an unexpected sense, presence-at-hand and readiness-to-hand turn out to be *two distinct beings*.[374]

This passage provides us with three insights into the genesis of Harman's system. The first insight is that the 'objects' which unify the two halves of the fourfold are descended from the reading of Heidegger with which his metaphysics begins, which insisted upon treating the ready-to-hand (substance) and the present-at-hand (relation) as two *aspects* of the same object, rather than two *types* of distinct objects. The second insight is that, in clawing its way out of the belly of this reading, his metaphysics transitions from the aspect view to the type view, even if it never entirely cuts the cord between them that its allusions to unity depend upon. The final insight is that the catalyst for this transition is the collision between his Husserlo-Meinongian account of representation and the reflexivity of sense—the realisation that in referring to the object-for-us and the object-in-itself independently from one another, he has converted them into distinct objects that must themselves be sundered between the for-us and the in-itself (i.e., the for-us-*in-itself*, the for-us-*for-us*, the in-itself-*in-itself*, and the in-itself-*for-us*).

It is this final insight that concerns us, because this newly discovered reflexivity heralds a runaway recursive doubling of

---

374. *Tool-Being*, 258–9.

every 'object' through which even the referents of metaphysical thought (i.e., sensual objects and real objects) perpetually evade us, escaping across fractal senses (i.e., [sensual [sensual [sensual [...]]]] or [[[[...] for us] for us] for us]). It thus seems as if the reflexive transubstantiation of aspects into types should make metaphysical knowledge of these types impossible in the same way that the initial distinction between aspects made knowledge of 'objects' impossible. This would mean the total and utter collapse of Harman's metaphysical edifice. He briefly addresses this worry in a different section of the previous passage:

> Will this lead to an "infinite regress" of tool-beings? For now, we can simply call it an "indefinite regress", and move on to other problems that arise from the emerging concept of substance.[375]

It is first worth pointing out that the substitution of 'indefinite' for 'infinite' is, at best, a clarification of what makes the regress problematic, and, at worst, a mere terminological sleight of hand designed to dismiss the severity of this problem. It is next worth pointing out that the tacit promise to return to this regress after addressing other problems is never actually fulfilled. Although *Guerrilla Metaphysics* stumbles through the same conceptual terrain at various points, it fails to reformulate the problem, let alone solve it.[376] The type view is simply restated in *The Quadruple Object*, as

---

375. *Tool-Being*, 259.

376. This stumbling takes two forms: (a) Harman's fleeting dalliance with 'elements', which does little but blur the lines between qualities and objects, and (b) his disastrous attempt to defuse the distinction between an object and its essence, which results in a complete collapse of the distinction between objects and their qualities (see chapter 3.2, subsection II).

a seemingly stable axis harbouring no hidden regress. This blocks the recursive doubling of objects into sense/reference branches in a manner parallel to the temporal blockage upon the division of objects into time-slices, but it also erases the genesis of the type view. This erasure is responsible for both its *allusiveness*—by securing its continued indiscernibility from the aspect view—and its *elusiveness*—by concealing the continued absence of a distinct justification for it.

Ultimately, the seemingly diagrammatic precision of the fourfold schema is nothing but an alibi for a more insidious conceptual vagueness.[377] Its neat numerological derivation of *ontographic categories* conceals the intractable obscurity of the elementary *metaphysical categories* they are founded upon: object, quality, and relation. We have progressively traced the pathologies of Harman's deployment of these categories across the three preceding sections, but having contextualised his concern with 'objects' and shown how this concern is embedded in his mature categorial schema, we are now in a position to integrate those insights into a comprehensive epidemiology of obfuscation.

Harman can never give the concept <object> a determinate positive content *qua genus* to which sensual and real objects belong as *species*, because our grasp of the latter is still tethered to understanding them as *aspects* of a unified 'object'. Conversely, he can never give the concept a determinate positive content *qua universal* of which these unified objects are *instances*, because the allusion to them which the fourfold schema encodes cannot be made explicit without contradicting its axial division of 'objects' into mutually exclusive *types*. This conflict within the concept is the ultimate consequence of

---

377. See diagram on p. 19, above.

the hypostatization of reference explained in chapter 3,1, 'Sense and Sensuality'. The catastrophic contradictions of Harman's representationalism are only contained by the representational blockage allusively encoded in the fourfold diagram, which disguises the choice between the *de-reification* of sense—refusing the ontological distinction between the object-for-us and the object-in-itself—and its *fractal proliferation*—allowing the recursive branching of objects-[...]-for-us that is seemingly indistinguishable from anti-metaphysical correlationism. As ever, only the invocation of allusion as an oblique mode of reference immune to the ontological bifurcation of sense and reference is sufficient to cut the gordian knot this choice presents us with: we avoid contradiction by thinking in a manner that is supposedly beyond such logical niceties.

The resultant vacuousness of the concept <object> is positively virulent, infecting and evacuating the concept <quality> of its determinate content by means of their opposition within the second axis of the fourfold schema. The orthogonal opposition between real and sensual precludes understanding <quality> as a genus to which both sensual and real qualities belong in much the same way it precludes understanding <object> as a genus. However, in this case it is a consequence of the hypostatization of predication (as explained in chapter 3.2, 'Qualities and Qualia', above). Harman severs the representational connection between reference and predication and thereby establishes the duplicitous relationship between the qualities of the object-for-us and the object-in-itself that absolutely segregates them. This segregation prevents us from abstracting anything common to them that is not already supplied by Harman's implicit account of the predicative dimension of representation. Harman's qualitative haecceitism is less an attempt to fill this conceptual void than its recognition *qua void*: the 'vacuous actuality' of real qualities is simply the projection of the *sheer thisness* of sensory qualities onto their representational counterparts, constrained by a duplicitous filter that permits no commonality beyond *mere thisness*. It is thus hardly surprising that Harman complements this explicit recognition of vacuousness with an implicit allusion to mereology, because he has nothing else with which to shore up the axial distinction between the *referential thisness* of objects and the *predicative thisness* of qualities.

Nevertheless, it is the concept <relation> that incorporates the most fascinating paradox. As explained above (chapter 3.3, 'What are Relations Anyway?'), the very possibility of categorially circumscribing the various possible 'relations' that can obtain within Harman's world (confrontation, theory, allure, and causation)—by means of the 'tensions' between the four poles of the schema (time, eidos, space, and essence) as their 'fission' (confrontation-time and theory-eidos) and 'fusion' (allure-space and causation-essence)—is dependent upon not counting these tensions (nor the junctions and radiations) as the *relations* between poles that they so obviously are (SO–SQ, SO–RQ, RO–SQ, and RO–RQ). Distilling the paradox: the concept <relation> is used to restrict itself in a way that would preclude this very use. Once more, Harman's only way to navigate paradox is by harnessing the power of metaphor to evade inconvenient reflexivity: the sense in which tensions are relations must be a metaphorical appropriation of the sense in which their fusions and fissions are relations. This evasion turns in a metaphorical circle that is not so much vicious as it is absurd: a metaphor that is parasitic upon the very concept it is constructed to define. Nevertheless, as absurd as this is, it is not the most egregious obfuscation diagrammatically embedded in the fourfold, an honour which belongs to the category of sincerity.[378] Not only does sincerity occupy the only place in the schema in which its underlying unity could be articulated (SO-RO), but in doing so it equally suppresses the crucial factor that distinguishes the 'surface relations' of confrontation and theory from the 'deep relations' of allure and causation—namely, the referential connection between the sensual object and real object that enables us to *vicariously* encounter the latter *through* the former.

All of these considerations bring us back to the Husserlo-Meingonian account of representation from which Harman's metaphysics unfurls, and the primitive relation between the object-for-us and the object-in-itself that defines it. We have already said much about this account, both in trying to wrest it from its lair, hidden deep between the lines of Harman's texts, and in trying to dissect it, unveiling its limited explanatory skeleton; we have even situated it within a broader lineage of noetic challenges to ontological conservatism; but we have yet to really consider what motivates these challengers to ground representation in metaphysics. The best way of bringing out this motivation is to consider the case of fictional objects, such as Eldorado, Popeye, or the three little pigs. It is even better to return to the sort of claims about fictional objects that proved problematic for Quine (e.g., 'Eldorado has a golden king', 'Popeye has a girlfriend', and 'two out of three little pigs lost their houses to the big bad wolf'). Intuitively, these claims seem to be true, but they cannot be interpreted as true unless we take them to quantify over fictional objects, and this seems to suggest that these fictional objects exist. However, and just as intuitively, these fictional objects don't seem to exist in

---

378. That the most obfuscatory category within Harman's schema is called 'sincerity' is an irony that is not lost on me. I will have more to say about Harman's invocation of the virtue of sincerity in chapter 3.6.

the same way as non-fictional objects such as London, Boris Johnson, or the 650 elected members of the House of Commons. Of course, just as there are ontological conservatives who deny the former intuition (e.g., Quine), there are ontological liberals who deny the latter (e.g., Gabriel), but there are others who try to affirm them both (e.g., Meinong). Meinong aims to synthesise them by means of a distinction between modes of Being—some things do not *exist* but merely *subsist*—whereas Harman holds that everything *exists*, but that everything is not therefore *real*. For Harman, the difference between Popeye and Boris Johnson is not that, as generic 'objects', they have different modes of Being, but rather that, as encountered sensual objects, only one of them conceals a corresponding real object.

It is a useful exercise to consider whether there is another way to synthesise these intuitions, or an alternative to both Meinong and Harman's Husserlo-Meinongian hybrid. Consider the following suggestion: what if we agree that it is true that 'Popeye has a girlfriend' and thus that there is some sense of 'existence' in which it is true that 'Olive Oyl exists', but that nevertheless there is a univocal sense in which 'Olive Oyl doesn't *really* exist'. This is precisely the sort of talk that free logic formalises, by enabling us to introduce non-referring terms that we can nevertheless use in quantification.[379] On this view, what 'really exists' is what lies within the inner quantificational domain (the Whole)—the content (beings) corresponding to its structure (Being/Nothing). But how does this differ from Harman's view? Surely, they both agree that 'Popeye has a girlfriend' and that 'Olive Oyl isn't real'? The crucial difference is that this view—my view—denies

---

379. See chapter 3.4, subsection II.

the need to provide a metaphysical explanation for how we can think about Olive Oyl even if she isn't real. This *non-metaphysical* approach to fictions is not for that matter *anti-metaphysical*: it simply maintains that metaphysics begins and ends with *reality*, and that we can happily think and talk about *unreal* things that lie entirely beyond its scope. In endorsing this view I am an unabashed ontological conservative, albeit one who is more drawn to Deleuze's metaphysical emergentism than to Quine's subtractive naturalism.

How can we resolve the conflict between my non-metaphysical approach to fictions and Harman's object-oriented metaphysics? I think it is worth drawing some inspiration from Hegel's account of Sense-Certainty: 'But language, as we see, is the more truthful; in it we ourselves directly refute what we *mean* to say'.[380] That is, we should aim to explicitly articulate the motivation for Harman's approach, and see if this very attempt leads to its refutation. This means capturing what it is about the non-metaphysical approach that Harman would find so inadequate. Harman might insist that 'Olive Oyl exists!', to which I would respond with qualified agreement. He would then try to leverage my qualification into a disagreement, claiming that 'But you don't think she *really* exists!', to which I would most certainly agree, and add 'But surely, neither do you?' At this point, Harman would want to say something like 'I mean that Olive Oyl really exists *qua sensual object* even if she doesn't really exist *qua real object!*' This is the point at which language is more truthful—the natural way to counter my 'really' qualification is to posit a different sense of 'really', but this sense must split apart

---

380. G.W.F. Hegel, *Phenomenology of Spirit*, tr. A. V. Miller (Oxford: Oxford University Press, 1977), §97.

from the sense in which real objects are 'real', so that we distinguish between 'really unreal' objects and 'really real' ones. However, it is crucial to understand that this bifurcation of 'reality' is nothing but the other fork of the recursive sense/reference branching engendered by the reflexive application of Harman's account of representation. In the attempt to talk about the object-for-us-*in-itself*, our metaphysical referent escapes us along the edge of a ramifying pathway: object-for-us-[[[...]]-in-itself]in-itself]-in-itself or really-[really-[really-[...]]]-unreal. Harman would no doubt insist that his allusive escapology secures the possibility of metaphysics against the trivial reflexive gymnastics of literal thought, but this can never compensate for the fact that he cannot *say what he sincerely believes*, even if he can allude to it. What are objects? If you ask Graham Harman, expect a gesture, not an answer.

5. WHAT IS METAPHYSICS ANYWAY?

I have now thoroughly circumscribed OOP as an exercise in *first philosophy*—an attempt to provide an ontological and categorial foundation for non-metaphysical explanation—and vindicated my contention that it is both *explanatorily impotent*—since it ignores explanatory anti-representationalism in favour of brute representationalism—and *explanatorily regressive*—since it precludes any positive analysis of properties in favour of gastronomic mysticism. Moreover, I have thoroughly articulated the sense in which OOP is *methodologically uncritical* in its use of basic metaphysical concepts—*quality, relation*, and even *object* itself—and the manner in which this is both engendered and obfuscated by its prioritisation of *aesthetics* as first philosophy—the mixture of metaphors, diagrams, and rhetoric that allusively position the ontological circumscription of thought as its own constitutive exception. However, although I have tentatively outlined the role that *ontology* has played within the history of metaphysics—as the study of the types of things which exist (regional/applied ontology) and as the study of what it is for them to exist (fundamental/meta-ontology)—and tentatively explained how it intersects with two distinct forms of *metaphysical scepticism*—Husserlian phenomenology (and its Heideggerian legacy) and Carnapian semantics (and its Quinean legacy)—I have yet to say anything about what *metaphysics* is, if it is not first philosophy.

The aim of this section, departing from the profoundly negative path we have walked so far, is to try to articulate some positive insights about what metaphysics is and how we should go about it. In doing so, I do not aim to say anything about what results metaphysics should achieve (what an adequate alternative to OOP would look like) but simply to try to see what Harman's cultivated obliviousness to methodology can teach us about the process of constructing such an alternative.

So, what is metaphysics? As I have already noted, this important question does not get asked often enough, and gets answered even less. We can imagine Socrates prowling through contemporary philosophy departments demanding to know just what it is metaphysicians are up to, only to be confronted with *examples* of metaphysical problems (e.g., personal identity, the nature of change, the existence of the Divine, etc.) rather than *definitions*.[381] This is not a new predicament though. Unlike logic, epistemology, semantics, or even ethics, metaphysics has always been a loosely defined grouping of problems in search of a definition. To repeat the story told earlier, even the term 'metaphysics' is an accident of the way in which Aristotle's works were catalogued. It originally referred to those books which came after the books on physics, and only later came to denote a subject matter loosely understood to *transcend* the physical. There is of course a more detailed history of this development to be told, but I shall reach a little further back into the origins of the Western philosophical tradition before I come to it.

Wilfrid Sellars famously defined philosophy as that enterprise that aims to 'understand how things in the broadest possible sense of the term hang together in the broadest possible sense of the term.'[382] This quote is sometimes reached

---

381. This is invariably the way that metaphysics is taught to undergraduate students, a fact which is attested to by the lack of a solid definition in many basic textbooks on metaphysics. In its place, we find a loose taxonomy of problems, arranged by family resemblances.

382. W. Sellars, 'Philosophy and the Scientific Image of Man', in *Science, Perception, and Reality* (Reseda, CA: Ridgeview Humanities Press, 1991), §1.

for when the question of defining metaphysics is raised, but it is a poor stopgap. This is not to say that it is a bad definition of philosophy, just that we should not be so quick to identify metaphysics with the discipline of philosophy as a whole, which such appeals inevitably do. To do so is to undermine the whole point of defining metaphysics as a *specific* philosophical discipline. However, the legitimate intuition underlying this move is that there is something eminently *general* about metaphysics, even in its specificity. The results of metaphysical inquiry are supposed to have an expansive, if not infinite, range of impact across other disciplines (both philosophical and extra-philosophical). Let us call this issue **the question of generality**.

If we return to the origin of Western philosophy in the presocratics, we see that Sellars's definition describes what they are doing pretty well. They are engaged in the first great attempts at *synoptic* thinking, trying to bring together the various elements of their cultural understanding by means of unitary principles: water, air, fire, etc. However, their thinking is not yet *systematic*, insofar as they have yet to differentiate the numerous theoretical tasks into which philosophy will eventually divide itself (e.g., logic, ethics, aesthetics, etc.), let alone articulate the various relations between these tasks. The presocratic who deserves special mention is Parmenides, who inaugurates the first and foremost foundational philosophical distinction: that between *thought*—which includes what we are doing in philosophising—and *Being*—which names the bare unity of whatever it is that his compatriots were trying to identify with their respective primal elements. This is the conception of metaphysics, if not yet its birth, insofar as its core *subject matter* (Being) is separated off from the study of the *means* through which it is to be grasped (thought). It is thus equally the conception of **logic**, in its most general sense.[383] This distinction inaugurates the questions regarding the *methodological* relation between logic and metaphysics (itself a logical matter, broadly construed) and the *substantive* relation between thought and Being (itself a metaphysical matter, broadly construed). These questions haunt the history of metaphysics, most clearly in the never-ending and progressively more complicated debates regarding *realism* and *idealism* (along with *anti-realism*, *correlationism*, and the other positions spawned by this debate).[384] We will lump all these issues together under the heading of **the question of thought**.

Given the conception of metaphysics in Parmenides, we might say that Plato's work is where it gestates. Moreover, if Socrates was the first thinker within the tradition to begin the task of thinking about the structure of thought (with his pragmatic, dialectical approach to logic), then Plato is the first to begin real systematic thinking about *both* the structure of thought and the structure of Being, and their relation to one another. This does not yet amount to an explicit differentiation of the systematic task of metaphysics, which is only truly born in the work of Aristotle. However, as we have already noted, the term 'metaphysics' appears nowhere within Aristotle's work.

---

383. It is this broad sense of 'logic' that Hegel is referring to in the title of his *Science of Logic*. It should not be confused with formal or mathematical logic, which is an important part of the broader study of thought. I shall have more to say about the latter in chapters 3.6 and 4.1.

384. The framing of these issues in terms of the debate between realism and anti-realism (principally in logical terms) obviously emerges out of Dummett's work (cf. *The Logical Basis of Metaphysics* [Cambridge, MA: Harvard University Press, 1991]), whereas the framing of these issues in terms of the debate between correlationism, realism and idealism (principally in metaphysical terms), emerges out of Quentin Meillassoux's work (cf. *After Finitude*).

Instead, Aristotle talks of *first philosophy* (*prote philosophia*),
which is what ultimately becomes the template for metaphysics as it is practised by subsequent philosophers. As such, we can legitimately claim that Aristotle presents the first definition of metaphysics, insofar as he does go to some lengths to define its scope and subject matter. We have already explained this definition (the study of beings as such and as a whole) and its subsequent development (scholasticism and onto-theology),[385] but it is useful to point out a further issue that Aristotle's definition of first philosophy raises, and which I shall call **the question of priority**. We have already indicated that the tradition is concerned with the question of how metaphysics is related to other disciplines in terms of its generality, and how it is related to the discipline of logic more specifically, but what we have in our sights here is the issue of priority involved in all such relations. Are the results of metaphysics to be *foundational* for all other forms of inquiry, for some such forms, or for none at all? Those who aim to inherit the title of first philosophy lay claim to some variant of Aristotle's answer to this question: metaphysics is the foundation of everything else.

I. THE DIALECTIC OF DEMARCATION

If we take only one insight about the metaphysical tradition from Heidegger, it is that there is something important about its own lack of self-consciousness regarding its defining question (**the question of Being**) and that this 'forgetfulness' structures the way metaphysics develops throughout its history. In particular, this forgetting of Being has a complicated relationship to the more or less implicit answers to the questions of *generality*, *thought* and *priority* that the tradition

---

385. Chapter 3.4, subsection I.

provides for itself as it develops. It is this that we must bear in mind as we return to examining the development of metaphysics after Aristotle's inaugural definition.

It is perhaps rather hasty to treat scholasticism as a unitary body of doctrine emerging out of the Christian appropriation of Aristotle's work, but this is precisely what I intend to do. During the scholastic period there is obviously a massive amount of work done in fleshing out Aristotle's metaphysics, producing numerous variants and several distinct alternatives.[386] More importantly, a vast collection of specifically *metaphysical problems* emerge, creating and tying together the various debates that both constitute the scholastic tradition and provide the backdrop against which the rationalist and empiricist programmes that kick off the modern philosophical era are formulated. Many of these problems emerge out of the specifically theological character of the scholastic appropriation of Aristotle (e.g., the problem of evil), and they are carried forth into the rationalist metaphysics of Descartes, Spinoza, and Leibniz even as they kick away the Aristotelian methodological scaffolding within which they were initially constructed. Here then is the question: which of these purportedly metaphysical problems are *genuine problems*, and which are *pseudo-problems*? Once there is a loosely defined metaphysical tradition, whose problems are related by various historically configured relationships of family resemblance, any really novel metaphysical inquiry is faced with a demarcation problem. It must once more undertake to define metaphysics, so as to choose which of the 'metaphysical' problems it inherits from its forebears can be retained, and which can be regarded as mere historical artefacts.

---

386. Neoplatonism and nominalism deserve special mention here.

However, as we see in the case of the rationalists, as brilliant as these thinkers are (e.g., Spinoza and Leibniz still set the terms of today's metaphysical debates regarding the nature of modality), it is entirely possible for them to simply ignore the demarcation problem, at least in the form of the demand for a principle of demarcation. They just choose the problems they find most compelling and run with them. This strategy is the essence of what Heidegger calls the forgetting of Being. We will call it the **mainstream strategy**, because it is most certainly the dominant approach, even in the present day. However, there are two other strategies that also emerge at this point, and which are importantly interlinked: the **sceptical strategy** and the **revisionary strategy**. We will introduce these by continuing our dramatisation of the history of metaphysics, beginning with the first (or at least most pronounced) proponent of metaphysical scepticism: David Hume.

Hume is the first philosopher to define metaphysics simply in order to demonstrate its impossibility.[387] His principled answer to the demarcation problem is that there are *no* genuine metaphysical problems. It is interesting to consider this response in terms of the questions of thought and priority we discussed above. Firstly, Hume uses resources from his account of thought to provide an *epistemological* definition of metaphysical inquiry as that which transcends scientific inquiry grounded in experience. This picks up on the scholastic reinterpretation of metaphysics as that which is concerned with what transcends the physical. He then aims to show that metaphysical questions so understood (most famously those

---

387. Cf. David Hume, *An Enquiry Concerning Human Understanding*, in *Enquiries Concerning Human Understanding and the Principles of Morals* (Oxford: Oxford University Press, 1975), §1.

concerning the nature of *causality* and *normativity*, or *alethic* and *deontic* modality) are strictly *impossible* to answer outside of the framework of empirical inquiry, and thus should be abandoned as false problems.[388] Secondly, Hume gives the first (or most prominent) instance of a particular answer to the question of priority, which comes to define the subsequent tradition of empiricism and its naturalist offshoots: the idea that the results of metaphysics, whatever it is, must be subordinated to those of empirical (or natural) science.[389] This position is one that will be articulated in more or less consistent ways following Hume, but it is no exaggeration to say that it has come to dominate the philosophical field, at least in the analytic tradition.[390]

If Hume is the paradigmatic example of a metaphysical sceptic, then Kant is his metaphysical revisionist counterpart. Kant takes Hume's various epistemological challenges seriously, and he recognises that, against mainstream metaphysics, the only way to preserve the legitimate parts of traditional metaphysical inquiry that Hume overzealously amputates is to confront the problem of demarcation head on. This is the goal of his project in the *Critique of Pure Reason*: to carry out a critical delimitation of the problems of metaphysics which thereby articulates the constraints under which any future metaphysical inquiry should be carried out.[391] Moreover, not

---

388. See chapter 3.2, subsection III.

389. Precisely how one defines philosophical naturalism is a difficult question. However, at minimum, I would suggest that it is precisely the disentangling of this response to the question of priority from the particular epistemological prejudices of empiricism.

390. Cf. Brandom, *Between Saying and Doing*, chapter 1.

391. Sadly, few people read Kant's *Metaphysical Foundations of Natural Science*, which is meant to be his positive contribution to metaphysics (along with the *Opus Posthumum*), rather than his negative delimitation of which positions are impermissible.

only does Kant attempt to respond to the specific problems Hume raises for metaphysical inquiry (most famously defending the legitimacy of causal and normative theorising);[392] he adopts the choices that frame Hume's own attempt to define metaphysics: he provides an epistemological definition of metaphysics that gives priority to the natural sciences.[393]

What is fascinating here is the historical interplay between the three strategies. Hume's epistemological challenge to mainstream metaphysics leads to a revisionary epistemological response from Kant. This then leads to a gradual mainstreaming of Kant's approach, in which problems from the tradition prior to Hume/Kant are slowly reintegrated into his framework (e.g., Schelling's metaphysics of Freedom and Hegel's theology of Absolute Spirit), ultimately resulting in the excesses of German Idealism against which the next round of metaphysical sceptics will react. What is also interesting is that these excesses are largely caused by a shift in focus from the methodological to the substantive form of the question of thought: the relationship between thought and Being ceases to be *epistemologically* prescribed (*transcendental idealism*) and instead becomes *metaphysically* prescribed (*absolute idealism*). The real value of looking at the history of metaphysics in this way extends beyond giving us a clearer insight into the specific metaphysical (or anti-metaphysical) positions involved in this period: it gives us a loose dialectical schema in terms of which to understand the developments in the twentieth century that are the main topic of the present section.

---

392. Again, see chapter 3.2, subsection III.

393. It is because of this that eminent Kantians such as Sellars can legitimately claim a prominent naturalist pedigree.

II. DEFLATIONARY REALISM

Returning to the analytic tradition first, it is important to see that the anti-metaphysical correlationism of Wittgenstein and Carnap that we discussed earlier is a sceptical response to both the excesses of German idealism *and* the metaphysical rejoinders of British realism (e.g., Russell and Moore).[394] Given our dialectical schema, we can now see that the relationship between Carnap and Quine is analogous to the debate between Hume and Kant, even though it is specifically concerned with *existence* rather than *modality*. The real difference between the two debates is that Carnap mounts a *semantic* challenge to the possibility of metaphysics, rather than an *epistemological* one. This is to say that not only does he think it impossible to determine the truth of metaphysical claims (as Hume does), but *a fortiori* that they make no sense whatsoever. We have already explained that Quine concurs with the greater part of Carnap's critique of metaphysics: he agrees that metaphysics must be semantically delimited, he agrees that doing so renders most of traditional metaphysics meaningless, and he shares Carnap's commitment to the priority of science over metaphysics; he demurs merely in providing a revisionary semantic definition of ontology that secures a tiny sliver of traditional metaphysics against Carnap's sceptical assault. However, it is worth explaining the alternative to anti-metaphysical correlationism inaugurated by this slight divergence—what I call **deflationary realism**—insofar as it is this Quinean innovation that heralds the return of metaphysics within the analytic tradition.[395]

---

394. This relationship to German idealism is mediated by British idealism, to which Russell and Moore were responding, and German neo-Kantianism, which was the principle reference point for the Vienna Circle in conceiving their break with the tradition.

395. For an extended discussion, see my 'Essay on Transcendental Realism'.

Deflationary realism is defined by a certain dialectical strategy for intervening in metaphysical debates between realists and anti-realists. Quine implements this strategy in relation to the traditional debate between platonism (realism) and nominalism (anti-realism) over the existence of numbers and other mathematical objects. Whereas the platonist holds that numbers 'really' exist in the same sense as the familiar middle-sized physical objects littering the everyday world, the nominalist denies this, holding that only the latter 'really' exist. Quine's intervention is to claim that neither side knows what it means by 'really', and *a fortiori* that this meaning cannot be extracted from the confused intuitions that drive metaphysical speculation. This is the dialectical significance of Quine's subtractive suturing of existence to the syntactic regimentation of quantificational variables deployed in natural-scientific theorising. A similar move is made by McDowell in relation to the debate between realism (e.g., Mackie) and expressivism (e.g., Blackburn) over the reality of value properties.[396] Whereas the realist holds that the sunset 'really' is beautiful in the same sense that it is caused by the diffraction of light through the atmosphere, the expressivist denies this, holding that only the latter is a 'real' property. McDowell's intervention is to claim that there is no way of distinguishing between the truth-aptness of the claims 'the sunset is beautiful' and 'the sunset is caused by the diffraction of light through the atmosphere' that would not beg the metaphysical question, and thus that their truth or falsity can't be used to distinguish 'real' properties

---

396. Cf. J.L. Mackie, *Ethics: Inventing Right and Wrong* (London: Penguin, 1990); S. Blackburn, *Spreading the Word* (Oxford: Oxford University Press, 1984); and J. McDowell, 'Values and Secondary Qualities' and 'Projection and Truth in Ethics', in *Mind, Value, and Reality* (Cambridge, MA: Harvard University Press, 1998), 131–50 and 151–66.

from 'unreal' ones. What unites these deflationary moves is the attempt to articulate a realism (or anti-anti-realism) about things in themselves without appealing to a substantive 'reality' that must be secured by means of a special supplement (*meta*-physics) to our ordinary description of them (physics). Deflationary realism thereby abandons the radical scepticism of anti-metaphysical correlationism for a more circumspect suspicion of metaphysics as a positive project.

Given this lingering suspicion, why does the lush garden of analytic metaphysics blossom in the methodological desert of Quinean ontology? This unanticipated reinflation of metaphysical debate is the dialectical parallel of the resurgence of speculative idealism in the wake of Kant's critical idealism— the *mainstreaming* of the revisionary moment, in which its methodological purpose is gradually forgotten and traditional problems are slowly reimported into the new framework. To understand why this happens, it is necessary to draw out the answer to the question of thought implicit within deflationary realism, and to see how this slides from a methodological to a substantive conception of the relation between Being and thought, much as transcendental idealism slides into absolute idealism. We must first explain how deflationary realism collapses metaphysics into semantics: its answer to the question of thought is that there is no more to metaphysics—the study of the structure of Being—than semantics—the study of the structure of thought.[397] This is made explicit to some extent in Davidson's account of the relationship between metaphysics and semantics: he moves us from the mundane Quinean

---

397. This position is actually best articulated by Brandom as what he calls *objective idealism* ('Holism and Idealism in Hegel's Phenomenology', in *Tales of the Mighty Dead*, 178–209).

ontology of the entities implied by natural science to a relatively innocuous categorial ontology derived from assumptions about universal grammatical categories beyond simple quantifier phrases.[398] This is the basis of his deflationary metaphysics of events.[399] Quine disagrees with this,[400] but he does not find it as horrific as the metaphysical menagerie that Lewis unleashes in the second half of the twentieth century. What happens in the latter is that Quine's commitment to the priority of the natural sciences is loosened (despite the ubiquity of 'naturalism') to allow for greater *semantic speculation*—admitting naturalistically intractable entities so long as they can be used to make sense of the meaning of the claims made by the natural sciences themselves.[401] In essence, once Quine allows us to deploy indispensability arguments derived from the claims of the natural sciences, he opens up the possibility of deploying indispensability arguments derived from the analyses of these claims provided by philosophical and formal semantics.

However, the reason why the real horrors of modern analytic metaphysics emerge with Lewis rather than Davidson is that Lewis's semantic methodology abandons the residual

---

398. Cf. D. Davidson, 'The Method of Truth in Metaphysics', *Midwest Studies in Philosophy* 2:1 (1977), 244–54; and 'On the Very Idea of a Conceptual Scheme', *Proceedings and Addresses of the American Philosophical Association*, Vol. 47 (1973–74), 5–20.

399. D. Davidson, 'The Individuation of Events', in N. Rescher (ed.), *Essays in Honor of Carl G. Hempel* (Dordrecht: Reidel, 1969), reprinted in *Essays on Actions and Events* (Oxford: Clarendon Press, 2001).

400. Cf. W. V. O. Quine, 'On the Very Idea of a Third Dogma', in *Theories and Things* (Cambridge, MA: Harvard University Press, 1991).

401. This is enabled by the paradigm of *model-theoretic semantics* that grew out of Tarski's work, whose applicability to natural language semantics was initially championed by Davidson but taken in very different directions by Kripke, Lewis, and Montague, amongst others.

pragmatism Davidson inherits from Quine and the constraints upon permissible assumptions this supplies. Quine and Davidson not only espouse the priority of natural science over *metaphysics*, but also the priority of natural science over *semantics*. They are very scrupulous about the entities they allow explanatory roles within their (consequently very austere) semantic frameworks. The abandonment of these scruples in the transition to Lewis's possible world semantics is the catalyst for the metaphysical explosion that follows. On the one hand, Lewis is ontologically committed to a plurality of possible worlds containing a menagerie of possible objects existing *alongside* the actual world and its actual objects. On the other, he is categorially committed to understanding the actuality of the actual world in *indexical* terms (i.e., 'actually...' is equivalent to '*here* in this world...'), and the trans-world identity of individuals in terms of *counterpart relations* between individuals in different worlds (e.g., 'I could have been a boxer' is equivalent to 'I have counterparts that are boxers'). He justifies these commitments on the basis that they enable him to interpret the semantics of the modal language deployed by natural science in terms of implicit quantifiers over worlds and objects (e.g., '1N of force will always accelerate 1kg of mass at a rate of 1m/s²' can be parsed as 'there is no 1kg mass in any possible world *accessible* from our own that when subjected to a force of 1N did not accelerate at a rate of 1m/s²').[402] This subtly inverts

---

402. This example is obviously an oversimplification of both the relevant physical law (it takes an instance of the law [1 = 1/1], rather than the law itself [$F = ma$]) and Lewis's semantics (it ignores both the issue of tense and temporality, and the issue of potential defeasors). However, it gives a rough idea of how the quantificational machinery underlying Lewis's modal semantics works, and importantly, just what work is done by the accessibility relations that restrict these quantifiers. For more details, see *On the Plurality of Worlds* (Oxford: Blackwell, 1986) and *Counterfactuals* (Oxford: Blackwell, 1973).

the deflationary collapse of metaphysics into semantics, such that instead of providing novel semantic answers to traditionally metaphysical questions (e.g., 'to be is to be the value of a bound variable'), one provides novel metaphysical answers to traditionally semantic questions (e.g., 'to have a propositional attitude is to stand in a relation to a set of possible worlds'). In essence, despite his claims to naturalism, Lewis indirectly returns metaphysics to the position of first philosophy, by using it as a dumping ground for supposedly indispensable ontological and categorial assumptions needed for his semantic framework to function.[403] Lewis remains a faithful deflationary realist insofar as he denies the claim that possibilia 'really' exist, but simply insists that there isn't any sense of 'existence' that we could use to contrast the actual with the possible. Nevertheless, his inversion of deflationism's priorities constitutes a shift from a methodological to a substantive conception of the relation between thought and Being, wherein this relation is to be articulated by metaphysics itself, rather than being delimited by an antecedent logic. This goes some way towards explaining the more drastic methodological laxity of those he inspires, whose mainstreaming of his ideas gradually unmoors them from the minimal constraints of semantic explanation under which he operates. If metaphysics is first philosophy then it is licensed to define itself, inviting a range of vicious circles (e.g., model-theoretically defining models, appealing to a primitive metaphysical notion of 'reality',[404] alluringly defining allure, etc.) whose conceptual flexibility allows their proponents to contort

---

403. Unconstrained model theory *just is* metaphysics as first philosophy.

404. Cf. K. Fine, 'The Question of Ontology', in Chalmers, Manley and Wasserman (eds), *Metametaphysics*, 157–77.

their way out of whatever methodological constraints the last round of revisionists imposed upon them.[405]

III. METAPHYSICAL CORRELATIONISM

Returning now to the Continental tradition, it is important to see how the Heideggerian responses to Husserl's anti-metaphysical correlationism diverge from the Quinean responses to Carnap's anti-metaphysical correlationism. It is all too tempting to suggest that the former provide a *deflationary idealism* that mirrors the deflationary realism of the latter. This symmetry is not unappealing: Heidegger and his heirs are most certainly more indebted to German idealism (e.g., Hegel and Schelling) than to British realism (e.g., Russell and Moore), and there are many deflationary appropriations of its ideas on display in their work (e.g., Derrida's *tantric dialectics* of deconstruction without synthesis and Heidegger's *poetic ungrounding* of freedom in the ur-event of *Ereignis*). However, the essence of this philosophical lineage lies in its attempt to revive the Kantian thing-in-itself in response to its dismissal by German idealism and its suspension by Husserlian phenomenology. Seen in this light, the various appropriations of the noumenal that it spawns (e.g., earth/*Ereignis*, *différance*, inconsistent multiplicity, Hyperchaos, and real objects) are in

---

405. It is worth pointing out that there is a more recent metaphysical dialectic in the analytic philosophy of science. This begins with Bas van Fraassen's constructive empiricism, which presents a distinct epistemological challenge to the possibility of metaphysics (*The Scientific Image* [Oxford: Oxford University Press, 1980]). Ladyman and Ross's rejection of the mainstream analytic metaphysics represented by Lewis can be seen as a revisionary response to van Fraassen, one that attempts to engage with his epistemological framework in order to demarcate a scientifically informed metaphysics (*Every Thing Must Go*, chapter 1). There is more that could be said about the novelty of Ladyman and Ross's definition of metaphysics, but I will have to leave that for another time.

many ways more *inflationary* than deflationary. Although it begins as a critique of metaphysics *qua* onto-theology, this lineage is more accurately described as **metaphysical correlationism** than as deflationary idealism, insofar as it aims to metaphysically circumscribe the correlation between thought and Being. This is true even of Heidegger and Derrida, who, in attempting to practically re-orient metaphysics and historically/temporally sublimate the distinction between reality and appearance, inevitably found this reorientation upon a conception of appearance (clearing/presencing) as belonging to a deeper historical/temporal reality (*Ereignis/différance*). This metaphysical remainder is the seed that germinates in the more obviously metaphysical projects of Badiou and Meillassoux, before blossoming into Harman's avowedly metaphysical correlationism.

To situate this development within our guiding dialectical schema (metaphysical scepticism → metaphysical revisionism → mainstream metaphysics) it is necessary to reemphasise the distinction between Heidegger's early revisionism and his later scepticism, in order to explain how Heidegger's early attempt to redefine metaphysics ultimately develops into a paradoxically *metaphysical* anti-metaphysical correlationism.[406] To this end, it is necessary to specify the type of sceptical challenge to metaphysics posed by Husserl, and to see how it shapes both Heidegger's initial revisionist response and his ultimate return to scepticism. Although it may initially seem as if Husserl echoes Hume's epistemological challenge by disavowing knowledge that transcends experience, we have shown that he does not disavow this knowledge so much as practically suspend it: he presents a *pragmatic* challenge to

---

406. See chapters 3, 4, and 5 of my *The Question of Being*.

metaphysics that proceeds not so much by positing a definition of metaphysics as by foreclosing anything that could be used to define it (reality/existence). However, although Husserl's project is eminently *logical* in the broad sense of the term, it does not present an account of the pragmatic dimension of thought, and this leaves his sceptical challenge implicit in his methodology. Heidegger's revisionary response to Husserl's scepticism consists not in articulating a *better* definition of metaphysics, but in providing the pragmatic supplement to phenomenology required to go about defining it *at all*. It is the failure of this attempt to ground metaphysics in a pragmatic phenomenology of the unitary temporal horizon of experience (*Temporalität*)[407] that convinces him of the impossibility of revisionism, and thereby leads him to reconceive this temporal horizon as the ur-historical event (*Ereignis*) through which we are given unto different metaphysical epochs.

However, although this shift in Heidegger's work constitutes a sceptical rejection of metaphysics, it is no longer based upon a *pragmatics* of thought from which this ur-historical structure could be derived, so much as an *imperative* to pragmatically reorient thought towards it. Heidegger's abandonment of his earlier metaphysical project is at the same time an abandonment of Husserl's logical project—he rejects the possibility of a transhistorical account of Being by rejecting the possibility of a transhistorical account of the structure of thought. However, this leaves him with nothing to appeal to but the *ur-historical reality* of the *historical appearance* of Being (*Ereignis*), and no way to appeal to it but through a reorientation of the attitude of philosophy (*Gelassenheit*) and a reconfiguration of its practice (poetics). The paradox of

---

407. Cf. *Basic Problems of Phenomenology*.

Heidegger's correlationism is that it defines metaphysics (the epochal sending of Being) in a manner that outright refuses to define itself (practical reorientation), and thereby alludes to a deeper (metaphysical) reality that the tradition failed to grasp. This paradoxical gesture plays the same role as the methodological circularity encoded in the idea of metaphysics as first philosophy, but it performs the escapological trick more directly, by supposedly situating itself outside of metaphysics while usurping and renaming its role (*das seynsgeschichtliche Denken*). This usurpation is repeated at each point in the post-Heideggerian lineage that follows: Derrida's performative evisceration of metaphysics in invoking *deconstruction*, Badiou's axiomatic displacement of metaphysics in favour of *meta-ontology*, and Meillassoux's tactical subversion of correlationism in the name of *speculation*.[408] The consequence of all this is that the return of metaphysics in the Continental tradition is very much a return of the repressed—the expression of something that was always implicit in the series of partial definitions through which it was disavowed. What makes Harman's metaphysics so unusual is that it is a return of the repressed without an end to repression—the implicit is announced but forced to remain implicit, as allusive circularity is substituted for paradoxical usurpation.

IV. THE CRITIQUE OF METAPHYSICS

Taking these dialectical developments into account, then, the question of what metaphysics is becomes an invitation to revise the discipline by providing a response to the demarcation problem. I cannot provide a comprehensive solution to

---

408. We might also include Laruelle's axiomatic suspension of philosophy's sufficiency in opening up the domain of non-philosophy. See p. 228 n. 286.

the problem here, but I will attempt to provide an outline of a response that synthesises the historical story just told with the various insights provided by my engagement with the conceptual roots of Harman's metaphysics.

Returning to the parallel between traditions, we can now see that each lineage traces an arc from anti-metaphysical correlationism back to mainstream metaphysics, and that, although the intermediary positions this arc passes through are different (deflationary realism/metaphysical correlationism), it always begins with a methodological concern with the role of *reality* in traditional metaphysics (the deflation of 'real'/the 'reality' of appearance), before performing a methodological sleight of hand in which the status of reality is apparently secured without its ever being *defined* (circularity/usurpation), and concluding with the methodological unravelling of the *constraints* implicit in the initial concern (semantic speculation/pragmatic allusion-subtraction). Given this, we can see that Harman's metaphysics does not so much stand outside this trajectory as present its inevitable conclusion: it simultaneously *announces* the implicit essence of metaphysics by invoking the 'real', and *subsumes* it within a metaphysical opposition (with the 'sensual') while allusively containing the recursive bifurcation of sense unleashed by this deceptive gesture (e.g., really-[sensually-[really-[sensually-[...]]]]). I have already suggested a putatively non-metaphysical alternative to Harman's use of 'real', but I have yet to situate it within my broader historical narrative. In doing so, I aim to show how it is possible to provide a non-metaphysical account of 'reality', and how this enables us to define metaphysics without resorting to either circularity or usurpation. I will do this by returning to the questions of generality, thought, and priority from within this perspective.

To begin with, I think that the generality of metaphysics is encapsulated by Aristotle's original invocation of the connection between beings *as such* and beings *as a whole*, and Heidegger's attempt to formulate the question of Being as the inquiry into the unitary structure of beings *as such and as a whole*. We have seen that there are roughly two strategies for addressing this connection/structure, corresponding to two different ways of objecting to the onto-theological conception of the whole: the *reification objection*, which encourages us to think beings as a whole in terms of beings as such (Badiou and ontological liberalism) and the *de-abolutisation objection*, which encourages us to think beings as such in terms of beings as a whole (Heidegger and ontological conservatism). Moreover, we have seen that each of these strategies can be pursued either *subtractively* (Badiou and Quine) or *allusively* (Heidegger and Harman), and that the common element they thereby share is an appeal to something that cannot be made explicit (i.e., Badiou: deference to axioms; Quine: deference to science; Heidegger: use of poetics; Harman: use of diagrammatics).

The task of defining metaphysics demands that we overcome these appeals to the implicit, but the question is whether it is possible for either strategy to do so without reverting to onto-theology. I doubt whether it is possible to think beings as such directly without either implicit definition, metaphorical allusion, or a reversion to thinking in terms of a highest genus of beings, although I hesitate to claim that it is strictly impossible. However, we have seen that not only is it possible to think beings as a whole directly without conceiving this whole as a being, but that extant attempts to do so (Deleuze and DeLanda) actively aim to explicate, integrate, and revise the systems of reference implicit in natural science to which

Quine subtractively deferred. This sort of approach aims to think the Whole not as the totality of what can be thought (*objects*), but as the totality of what really exists (*beings*), or to think the Whole as **Reality**. I propose that metaphysics is eminently general precisely insofar as it is concerned with *the fundamental structure of Reality*, and that it therefore need not say anything about those objects that *aren't real*.

Of course, this distinction between objects and beings assumes that we can provide a sufficient definition of 'real' in non-metaphysical terms, but it equally suggests that this problem is to be understood in terms of the relation between thought and Being. The claim that not all objects of thought are beings implies that the study of objects *qua* objects (logic) is independent of the study of beings *qua* beings (ontology). It is this independence of logic from metaphysics that promises to free us from circularity, insofar as it opens up the possibility of using logic to define metaphysics by *logically* distinguishing thought about the real (beings) from thought about the unreal (nonbeings) rather than *metaphysically* distinguishing the real from the sensual (as types of beings). This sort of separation and articulation of the relation between logic and metaphysics occurs in each of the revisionary moments we have so far considered (Kant, Quine, and Heidegger), but varies as to the manner in which the logical task is approached: in terms of *knowledge* about objects (epistemology); in terms of the *content* of this knowledge (semantics); or in terms of the *practices* through which these should be understood (pragmatics). These revisionary moments are mainstreamed when their initial separation/articulation comes to be conceived metaphysically rather that logically, or when metaphysical assumptions are incorporated into their account of knowledge, content, or practice.

It is worth noting that Heidegger is unique not only in mainstreaming his own revisionary moment, but in instigating the turn to usurpation as an alternative to circularity in the process. His Nietzschean insistence that theory is a form of practice enables him to stipulate that his own practice of theorising metaphysics is distinct from the practice of metaphysical theorising; this practical difference enables the former to usurp the latter without circularity. It is the same Nietzschean pragmatism that enables him to assert the impossibility of providing a transhistorical account of Being (metaphysics) by asserting the impossibility of providing a transhistorical account of thought (logic); the latter assertion is responsible for the degeneration of his earlier pragmatic phenomenology into his later poetic thinking, and therefore also responsible for the repression of metaphysics within his poetic allusions to *Ereignis* (as the reality of appearance). In dissolving logic into historicised pragmatics, Heidegger eschews the only way to define metaphysics that has enough reflexive purchase upon itself to avoid collapsing back into metaphysics either by *embracing* it (circularity) or *displacing* it (usurpation). If we are to avoid both of these pitfalls, our only option is to secure logic's independence from metaphysics—and this means considering the relationship between epistemology, semantics, and pragmatics with which the revisionary moments confront us.

The truth in Heidegger's turn to pragmatics is that it provides the only way to avoid circularity and the forgetting of Being that results: the only way to differentiate between forms of thought (i.e., logic and metaphysics) that cannot be reinterpreted as a (metaphysical) difference between their objects is to differentiate them as forms of practice. This methodology parallels Fichte's foundational insight that the difference between practical reason and theoretical reason is itself a practical one.[409] The problem with Heidegger's turn to poetics is that it severs the link between practice and practical reason through which logic can reflexively secure itself: Heidegger abandons his attempt to ground epistemology and semantics in pragmatics by describing how knowledge and its content is situated in practice, and in so doing transforms 'thought' into a mysterious practice that no concrete pragmatics can describe. The alternative is to reconnect epistemology, semantics, and pragmatics in a unified **logical pragmatism**, and to use the account of thought this provides to define *metaphysical knowledge* by means of its *specific content*, and the *specific practices* that constitute this content. Given our answer to the question of generality, this means providing a pragmatic response to the semantic challenge posed by deflationary realism: we can escape the choice between circularity and usurpation by developing a pragmatically grounded semantics for the term 'real' that is sufficient to explain what we mean when we ask metaphysical questions (e.g., 'What is the fundamental structure of Reality?'). This is what I have elsewhere described as moving beyond deflationary realism to **transcendental realism**.[410]

Providing this semantics is beyond the scope of the present work, but I will try to say something about how it relates to the question of priority. The important thing to understand is that the metaphysical project of organising a unitary system of reference through providing a unified account of Reality

---

409. Cf. J.G. Fichte, *The Science of Knowledge* (Cambridge: Cambridge University Press, 1982), first and second introductions; and J. Dunham, I. H. Grant, and S. Watson, *Idealism: The History of a Philosophy* (Durham: Acumen, 2011), chapter 6.

410. See my 'Essay on Transcendental Realism' for a more complete (if early) version of this story.

(Deleuze and DeLanda) essentially aims to make explicit, to integrate, and to revise what Quine either leaves implicit in scientific practice, or defers to the syntactic regimentation of its quantificational variables. This is to say that metaphysics and natural science both describe the same unitary structure: Reality is **Nature**. However, this does not mean that Reality is to be explained in terms of some antecedent conception of Nature (e.g., as material/energetic, mechanistic/vital, corpuscular/flux etc.), which would simply be more implicit metaphysics, but that we are to understand what 'Reality' means in terms of the pragmatic structure of natural science, and what 'real object' or 'being' means in terms of what it is to be referenced within natural-scientific explanation.[411]

This enables us to draw a threefold distinction between the *implicit metaphysics* that is more or less passively effected by natural science, the *explicit metaphysics* that aims to actively intervene in natural science, and the **critique of metaphysics** that enables us to move from the former to the latter by articulating the questions through which we explicate, integrate, and revise the fundamental structural assumptions

---

411. One might wonder why 'natural' science is privileged (including physics, chemistry, biology, and other sciences founded upon experiment), and not 'mathematical' science (including the various areas of pure mathematics, formal logic, and computer science that are independent of experiment). There is a more complicated answer to this question, but the simple version is that Badiou is right to say that mathematics is not strictly concerned with *mathematical objects*, even if his choice of set theory cuts against this insight to some extent. Rather, mathematics is concerned with *mathematical structure*, which, as Fernando Zalamea has pointed out, is far better viewed from the perspective of category theory than set theory (*Synthetic Philosophy of Contemporary Mathematics* [Falmouth and New York: Urbanomic and Sequence Press, 2012]). Mathematics is neither excluded from metaphysics nor the whole of metaphysics (or ontology), but is rather a crucial component of the project of describing the fundamental structure of Reality *qua* structure.

of natural science (e.g., 'What are beings?', 'What is essence?', 'What is causality?', etc.). It is in terms of this relation between metaphysics and its critique that the methodological relation between Being and thought is to be articulated. Although there is certainly more to metaphysics than logic, there is an important sense in which logic *constrains* metaphysics. Metaphysics seeks to understand what Nature *is* (the question of Being), whereas logic seeks to understand what 'Nature' *means* (the question of the meaning of 'Being'). This extends to the discussion of particular metaphysical categories and the problems that correspond to them: identity, difference, individuality, universality, quantity, quality, relation, essence, space, time, part, whole, causation, etc. Each of these corresponds to a metaphysical problem (e.g., 'What are relations?'), the scope of which is determined by the logical analysis of the relevant category in each case (e.g., 'What does "relation" mean?'). These metaphysical categories are derived from logical categories by means of the concept of reality, such that the metaphysics of relations is distinguished from the logic of relations insofar as it is concerned with 'real relations' much as ontology is concerned with real objects (beings).[412] The broader range of categorial questions this opens up expands the scope of metaphysics beyond ontology by transforming its account of Reality/Nature from a system for organising *scientific reference* to a system for organising *scientific explanation* as such. This gives us some theoretical purchase upon the balance between

---

412.   The other way of parsing this is to use 'really' as a copula modifier that makes the metaphysical character of categorial questions explicit: 'What are properties?' could be read as 'What *really are* properties?' as easily as 'What are *real properties*?' It is also worth pointing out that my account of the relation between logical and metaphysical categories parallels Kant's distinction between general and transcendental logic (*Critique of Pure Reason*, A55–57).

continuity and *autonomy* in the relation between metaphysics and science.

The continuity between metaphysics and science consists in the fact that metaphysical ideas are already implicit in the scientific enterprise. Natural science always proceeds with some implicit understanding of what beings are, what essence is, what causality is, and so on; and this implicit understanding is itself subject to revision in the ongoing process of scientific inquiry, in more or less explicit ways. Einsteinian relativity fundamentally challenged our implicit metaphysical understanding of space and time, and the subsequent developments in physics have raised serious questions regarding how we should understand causality. The Darwinian revolution in biology has forced us to rethink the very way in which we understand the idea of types, and thus the notion of essence. Dynamic systems theory has provided us with alternative ways to conceive of the modal features of entities, and its development and extension in the field of complexity theory is forcing us to rethink our understanding of mereological relations. And this is all before we even begin to consider the conceptual puzzles generated by the counterintuitive logic of quantum mechanics.[413]

Thus, metaphysics is already present in natural science, it just hasn't been made *explicit as* metaphysics. It is the possibility of doing metaphysics explicitly which preserves its relative autonomy *within* natural science. There are two features which distinguish the proper practice of metaphysics from its implicit form: *criticality* and *systematicity*. Metaphysics proper is critical insofar as it properly delimits the various questions with which it is concerned and the ways they are related, from an *a priori* standpoint (logic). Metaphysics proper is systematic insofar as

413.   See p. 273 n. 351.

it attempts to provide a unified answer to all of these questions which takes into account the whole variety of *a posteriori* considerations provided by the various natural sciences. This is just to say that it attempts to unify the various metaphysical debates implicit within the natural sciences as a whole. The autonomy of metaphysics stems from these two features. On the one hand, metaphysics has a distinctive relation to *a priori* considerations that are independent of the natural sciences (the critique of metaphysics). On the other hand, it is the most abstract form of *a posteriori* discourse, situated *within* the natural sciences only insofar as it plays a unifying and organisational function in relation to them. Conceived this way, metaphysics stands in a reciprocal relationship with science: it is in a position to provide the abstract conceptual foundations which organise them, while at the same time it must be sensitive to their subject matter, insofar as it is through this sensitivity that its concepts remain open to revision. This complex reciprocity is my alternative to the blunt foundationalism proposed by those who treat metaphysics as first philosophy.

6. WHAT DOES IT ALL MEAN?

Having extensively mapped the failure of Harman's metaphysics to provide a coherent explanatory programme, demonstrating both its impotence and regressiveness, and its proximity to the dogmatic correlationism it purportedly opposes, we are now in a position to see the true significance of these failures. This requires examining one last extended quote from Harman's work, which I think most explicitly articulates the essence of his thinking, and thereby distills the fundamental error upon which it is based. The following passage provides a condensed version of the chapter titled 'The Inherent Stupidity of All Content' from *Weird Realism*, which elaborates and generalises Žižek's thoughts on 'the inherent stupidity of all proverbs'.[414] Žižek's original point is that proverbs can be reversed into their opposites (e.g., 'seize the day!' and 'consider eternity!') without losing their seeming profundity. This mutates into something much more virulent in Harman's hands:

> While the annoying reversibility of proverbs provides a convenient target for his comical analysis, the problem is not limited to proverbs, but extends across the entire field of literal statement. Indeed, we might speak of the inherent stupidity of all *content*, a more threatening result than the limited assault on proverbial wisdom [...].
>
> Now, it might be assumed that we can settle the issue in each case by giving "reasons" for why one proverb is more accurate than its opposite. Unfortunately, all reasons are doomed to the

---

414. S. Žižek and F. W. J. Schelling, *The Abyss of Freedom/The Ages of the World* (Ann Arbor, MI: Michigan University Press, 1997).

same fate as the initial proverbs themselves [...]. The point is that no *literal* unpacking of their claims can ever settle the argument, since each remains an arbitrary Master for as long as he attempts to call upon literal, explicit evidence. There may be an underlying true answer to the question, assuming that the dispute is properly formulated, but it can never become directly present in the form of explicit content that is inherently correct in the same way that a lightning flash is inherently bright [...].

There is no reason to think that any philosophical statement has an inherently closer relationship with reality than its opposite, since reality is not made of statements. Just as Aristotle defined substance as that which can support opposite qualities at different times, there is a sense in which reality can support different truths at different times. That is to say, an absolutism of reality may be coupled with a relativism of truth [...]. [All] content is inherently stupid because *reality is not a content*.

There are two strands of 'argument' in this passage. The first has only been partly quoted, as it consists in an attempt to show that one cannot use reasoning to decide between any two conflicting propositions by narrativising a hypothetical debate regarding two conflicting proverbs ('a penny saved is a penny earned' and 'penny wise, pound poor'). The fact that Harman holds to the example of conflicting proverbs while implying that it can be usefully extended to all cases of rational conflict (e.g., conflicting theories of quantum gravity) is indicative of both the poverty of his theoretical resources for dealing with these cases and his willingness to substitute rhetoric in their place. There is nothing further to be said about it. The second is the argument that epistemic relativism follows from the fact that 'reality is not a content.' This is nothing but a bare assertion of the argument from identity—an argument that I have already spent more time unpacking and analysing than Harman has expounding in all of his works.[415] It should be clear that neither of these arguments is remotely plausible; but they are not what is interesting about the passage. What is interesting is that it reveals that the true essence of Harman's scepticism is semantic.

It is important to understand that Harman has not developed an analysis of the nature of semantic content in order to justify the core correlationist conceit that knowledge is irredeemably contaminated by its semantic conditions (e.g., forms of sensibility, language games, cultural practices, etc.), but has instead rejected the very possibility of semantic analysis at all. The background for this move is that the unprecedented progress made in semantics in the twentieth century (following the logical revolution of Frege, Russell, Tarski and Gentzen) has slowly chipped away at the bond between *meaning* and *the experience of meaning*, to the point at which radical semantic holism (as found in the otherwise diverse works of Hegel, Saussure, Quine, Derrida, and Brandom) threatens to completely dissociate semantic content from either external (representational) or internal (phenomenal) correlates. Harman's radical haecceitism is a reactionary response to this trend, which, in the name of defending our authority over what we mean, retreats to *primitive* conceptions of external (reference) and internal (quality) correlation, in which what we mean becomes a *pure thisness* to which no one else has any access. This is precisely the sort of haecceitism ('Sense-Certainty') that Hegel strips to its bare essence and systematically undermines at the beginning of the *Phenomenology of Spirit*.[416]

---

415. Chapter 2.1, subsection III.

416. Hegel, *Phenomenology of Spirit*. Harman shrugs off this critique of *im-*

In essence, Harman presents us with a semantic parallel of Descartes's defence of our epistemic access to our own representational states. Such *semantic cartesianism* comes at the price of the possibility of knowledge, or a complete and irremediable disjunction between what these states represent and their phenomenal manifestation (or the external world and the internal world). We are once more monarchs of our own mental domains, not in the sense that we have privileged access to ourselves *qua* real objects, but in the sense that nothing is hidden in our sensual contact with anything *qua* sensual object but *the truth*. Returning to Hegel's dialectical dramatisation of this problematic, in unfolding the implicit contradictions present within Sense-Certainty, he confronts anyone who wishes to occupy this position with a choice: either move beyond it (into 'Perception') and start doing genuine semantic analysis of the relations between concepts,[417] or abandon the search for truth. Those who stay within Sense-Certainty are thus naïve sceptics who are unable to see anything but the *nothingness* of the self-undermining of their own position, entirely missing the *determinacy* of its negation and the way this motivates the continued pursuit of certainty.

Harman has openly embraced this epistemic void. He has not motivated the core epistemological idea that he shares with correlationism, so much as accepted it as the price of his phenomenal kingdom. Far from being the metaphysical messiah, destined to liberate philosophers from the horrors

---

mediacy without much further analysis in *Guerrilla Metaphysics* (147–8). See chapter 3.2, subsubsection III for our earlier discussion of the implications of Hegel's ideas for the theory of qualities.

417. See Brandom, *Tales of the Mighty Dead*, chapter 7.

of correlationism, Harman is the Fisher King of its sceptical community. He has been nominated to the post not by the multitude of *oppressed* realists seeking wise philosophical rule after the dark days of correlationism, but by the legions of *oppressive* sceptics seeking a new justification for their prejudices after sacrificing the previous occupant (as they are wont to do with surprising regularity).

This rejection of semantic analysis goes hand in hand with Harman's wilful disregard of philosophical logic. There is a reason why the various advances in semantics throughout the history of philosophy have accompanied the development of new logical tools (e.g., Aristotle's *term* logic (and the Port-Royal revisions of it), Kant's *propositional* logic (and Hegel's extension of it), Frege's *functional* logic (and Russell, Tarski, and Gentzen's advances upon it), Kripke's *modal* logic (and its deployment by Lewis, Montague, Creswell, etc.), and the ongoing *substructural* revolution...).[418] This is because, as Brandom says: 'logic is the linguistic organ of *semantic self-consciousness*'.[419] To put it another way: logic is what lets us move from *meaning what we say* (sincerity), to *saying what we mean* (explicitness). The various forms of logical vocabulary that we have naturally evolved (e.g., 'if... then...', 'Some, but not all...', 'It could be that...', etc.) and the various formalisations and extensions of these that we have subsequently developed (e.g., differentiated conditionals, iterated quantifiers, nested modal operators, etc.) provide us with the expressive resources

---

418. See G. Restall, *An Introduction to Substructural Logics* (London: Routledge, 2000).

419. R. Brandom, *Articulating Reasons* (Cambridge, MA: Harvard University Press, 2000), 149 (emphasis added). This is what Brandom refers to as his *logical expressivism*.

needed to make explicit what we mean. The precision that this vocabulary makes possible when used correctly is useful in all forms of rational enquiry.[420] The acquisition of these resources is thus a hard-won communicative victory (or series of victories in the long war on *semantic false-consciousness*), which has come at the cost of a great deal of difficult work and experimental fumbling by our philosophical forebears, and thus should not be cast aside lightly.[421]

The upshot of this is that Harman subordinates the expressive virtues associated with the logical regimentation of communication (e.g., clarity, precision, etc.) to the expressive virtues associated with its aesthetic dimension (e.g., style, vividness, etc.). This is because the only linguistic resources that let us move beyond simply *pointing* at the various sensual haecceities presented to us are the resources of literature, poetry, and aesthetic discourse. His semantic cartesianism thus gives way to a *semantic romanticism*, It is for this reason that metaphor enjoys such a privileged place in both Harman's philosophical system and in the writings that present it. It is the expressive

---

420. It is all too possible to have too much of a good thing here, and to move from confusion to precision and back again by means of obfuscatory formalism. This is a serious problem in certain circles.

421. Harman is far from unique here. There is a widespread tendency to reject the logical tools that have been made available to us (at great cost) as somehow shackling the ways we may express ourselves, as if they are the components of some great logical gulag designed to imprison and ultimately extinguish all expressive creativity. This is total nonsense. It may be that certain *stylistic* norms that encourage the excessive use of logical formalism are currently in vogue in some areas, and that these do cause expressive maladies, but this hardly warrants the widespread equivocation of *logical form* with *literary style* that has accompanied much orthodox correlationism. In fact, it warrants precisely the opposite approach: the rigorous analysis of style as something distinct from semantic content and its logical expression. See chapter 4.1.

exemplar of his semantic picture: an expressive form whose content cannot become explicit without ceasing to be what it is. One cannot explicate a metaphor without transforming it into a simile, or worse, a full-blown analogy. It seemingly allows one to mean what one says without saying what one means, or to be sincere without being explicit.[422] However, this picture simply misunderstands the expressive role of metaphor. It refuses to let metaphors grow, mature, and ultimately die, preferring to keep them in a perpetual expressive adolescence. To become similes, analogies, and ultimately even concepts in their own right (e.g., the classic dead metaphors: the river's *mouth*, the *bottleneck* of the system, *falling* in love, etc.) is their expressive lifecycle. Metaphors are a part of a larger expressive ecosystem, and their role is to be consumed by roaming explanatory predators seeking new conceptual forms. If they are precluded from partaking in this cycle, then they play no genuinely expressive role at all.[423]

In the end, it is no coincidence that Harman's scepticism in the epistemological domain is accompanied by romanticism in the semantic domain. It all amounts to an attempt to protect sincerity from anything that might challenge it, or to insist that *we mean what we say* regardless of any attempts on behalf of others to *say what we mean*, and thereby show us that we cannot both *understand* and *endorse* it. Once the possibility

---

422. This is the view that Harman defends against both Davidson and Derrida in *Guerrilla Metaphysics* (121–4).

423. It is important to point out that there is more to the use of metaphor than its *expressive role*. If nothing else, metaphor plays an important *aesthetic role* in the production of literary and poetic affects, which although it may overlap with its expressive role is not to be assimilated to it. Just how the expressive and aesthetic dimensions of metaphor are to be understood, both independently and in relation, is a topic worthy of another book entirely.

that anything we mean might actually be true is thrown out of the window, the relationship between understanding and endorsement gets defenestrated along with it. If we know that *nothing* we mean will ever be true, then the revelation that what we happen to mean is internally inconsistent can have nothing but an *ironic* hold upon us.[424] We are thus *free* to mean what we like. It is then but a small step to the idea that the only access to the real is provided by the *most free* form of expression. We liberate ourselves from the myriad constraints placed upon us by our language (and our culture, biology, etc.), by playing with the limits of expression (or living, life, etc.). It is only by liberating ourselves thus that we can commune with the real *directly*, without being *mediated* by these constraints. In essence, the idea that no form of discourse which aims to speak the truth about the real can achieve this truth (*scepticism*) is converted into the idea that the only form of discourse that can actually grasp the real is that which abandons any claim to truth (*romanticism*).

This is OOO's inverted world: what it takes for freedom is in truth mere caprice, what it takes for self-consciousness is in truth pervasive self-deception, and, most importantly, what it takes for sincerity is in truth nothing but a sense of entitlement to mean whatever one wants. By contrast, I maintain that if something cannot (at least in principle) be made explicit, then there is nothing implicit in the first place. There is no content without expression. One can sincerely mean what one says if one is *unable* to explicitly say what one means, but not if one is merely *unwilling* to do so. On this basis, the refusal of the

---

424. Recall Bogost's ironic appropriation of contradiction in his formulation of the liberal demand: 'everything exists, even the things that don't' (*Alien Phenomenology*, 11).

myriad expressive resources that philosophers and logicians have carefully cultivated over the past two and a half millennia in favour of purposely stunted metaphors can only be called insincere.[425] The philosophical virtues of sincerity and explicitness have thereby been traded for the sophistic vices of insincerity and implicitness.[426]

---

425. This is to deny Harman's own opposition between *sincerity* and *critique* (*Tool-Being*, 226). To refuse the critical injunction to make our meanings explicit, and thereby ensure that they are consistent, is to refuse to be sincere. This is also to deny Harman's own metaphysics of sincerity: 'Everyday life is laced with sincerity through and through, in the sense that I really am doing right now whatever it is I am doing—delivered over to that activity rather than to any of the possible others that might be imagined.' (*Guerrilla Metaphysics*, 135) To say that the chair I am currently sitting on is 'sincere' in supporting me is to devalue the term to the point at which it completely ceases to name a *virtue* in accordance with which we could live (or fail to).

Sincerity is never simply a matter of being oneself. Any*one*, and indeed, any*thing* does this by default. Sincerity is a matter of *owning* one's commitments and *engaging* in the process through which these commitments are tried, tested, corrected, and possibly abandoned. If these commitments are part of *who* one is, then sincerity involves a *willingness* to become other than one is, to be pushed outside one's comfort zone in the name of *truth*. Putting this point another way: *pace* Harman, sincerity is not *naiveté*.

426. Harman's relationship to the historical sophists is an interesting one, insofar as he champions much of Latour's work (cf. *Prince of Networks*, 85–95), which explicitly attempts to rehabilitate the reputation of sophism against the attacks upon it by Socrates and his followers (*Pandora's Hope*, chapters 7–8). However, he thinks that Latour is too harsh on Socrates, and that the latter's skill as an ironist, along with his professed ignorance, make him a superior philosophical role model. Harman interprets Socrates's famous dialectical practice as a matter of performatively demonstrating that definitions are always inadequate, and thus championing his own idea that things withdraw from our knowledge of them (*Guerrilla Metaphysics*, 152).

This is a parody of Socrates as bad as Aristophanes's infamous *The Clouds*. It champions Socrates only by transforming him into an exemplar of sophism. This is because it transforms Socrates's dialectical practice into nothing but an ironic gesture. The demand for definition becomes completely *insincere*, insofar as it is no longer one part of an expressive dialectical process (the practice of *explicitness* and *consistency*) aimed at *truth*, but a rhetorical trick employed to undermine every *sincere* attempt to achieve it. We may remember Socrates mainly for his refutations of other thinkers, but he equally had positions (and definitions) of his own, even beyond those that Plato puts into his mouth (cf. Xenophon, *The Memorable Thoughts of Socrates* [New York: Kaplan, 2009]). Harman's Socrates is not a master dialectician, but a mere rhetorician; not the archetypal philosopher, but the sophist par excellence. This is perhaps worse than his reading of Heidegger, insofar as it does not merely radically misread Socrates, but transforms him into his antithesis.

4

SPECULATIVE
DYSTOPIA

Having examined Harman's work in as much detail as possible, we are finally in a position to carry out the promised hyperbolic projection of a world in which it has achieved absolute victory over its competitors. Unfortunately, unlike the more or less rosy pictures Harman paints of a world dominated by DeLandian, Latourian, or even Meillassouxian philosophy, my hyperbolic portrait is remarkably bleak. This is not a function of spite on my part, but simply an attempt at honest prediction, faithfully extrapolating from the data so far provided. Nor is it a deliberate attempt at hyperbolic hyperbole. If you accept the conclusions already drawn, then the conclusions that follow from the hyperbolic hypothesis cannot but be *dystopian*. A world of object-oriented dominance could not be judged as anything but a philosophical *regression* of the lowest order: a new philosophical *dark age*, in which we could only hope that the knowledge of the present day was hallowed and preserved, as was the knowledge of antiquity, in order that it might emerge on the other side as the seed of a new philosophical renaissance. The real disanalogy here is that this would not be a dark age of conceptual *austerity*, limited by the theological dogmas of the church, but a dark age of conceptual *abundance*, in which a dogmatic refusal of all critical limits would unleash a torrent of speculative noise so great as to drown out any coherent philosophical signal.

The crux of this dystopian vision is the central claim of this book: that OOP should be seen as the natural successor of correlationism, rather than the radical critique of correlationism it presents itself as. It has established itself as the torchbearer of the epistemological scepticism that has dominated much of twentieth-century Continental philosophy, in the face of renewed epistemological challenges to this dominance from within Continental philosophy itself. In order to properly elaborate this point, it is necessary to trace the historical trajectory of which OOP is a part back into the heart of the twentieth century, before drawing it forward through OOP's manifestation in the present day, and finally into the stark future in which it reigns supreme. The following three sections will concern themselves with the different parts of this narrative, dealing with the *past*, the *present* and the *future*. Moreover, they will endeavour to account for the *theoretical*, *historical*, and *sociological* dimensions of correlationism in the past and present, in order to project them into the future.

1. THE SPECTRE OF THE PAST

To put a twist on Alexander Pope's famous epitaph for Isaac Newton: 'Nature and Nature's laws lay open to sight; God said "Let Kant be" and brought back the night.'[427] For all of the powerful and enduring positive contributions that Kant made to philosophy, he is undoubtedly the father of correlationism. I have already traced the germination and growth of the noumenal seed he plants in the European philosophical tradition into the various branches of the mighty oak of correlationism—both analytic and Continental—in the twentieth century. The noumenon begins as a minimal epistemological limit upon empirical knowledge that is reified by its opposition to the phenomenon, giving it a minimal metaphysical consistency sufficient to shelter Kant's faith in Freedom, God, and the Soul, before being practically repressed by anti-metaphysical correlationism (Husserl, Wittgenstein, and Carnap) and reemerging in metaphysical correlationism and its myriad mutant descendants: earth/*Ereignis* (later Heidegger), *différance* (Derrida), the Real (Lacan/Žižek), inconsistent multiplicity (Badiou), the One (Laruelle), Hyperchaos (Meillassoux), and real objects (Harman). However, I have yet to say much about the wider motivations governing this proliferation of noumena in the Continental tradition. Meillassoux has already shown how strong correlationism has tended to revive and radicalise Kant's **fideism**—securing a place for faith beyond the bounds of reason while simultaneously assaulting its territory, so as to

---

427. The original reads: 'Nature and Nature's laws lay hid in night: God said, "Let Newton be!" and all was light.' This parallel between Newton and Kant is all the more appropriate given Kant's philosophical debt to Newton.

claim more and more ground for faith and its cognates.[428] Yet open religiosity is only the final phase in a longer correlationist lifecycle that begins with the seemingly reasonable demand for **epistemic humility** and ends in the philosophical graveyard of **negative theology**.[429] To understand the development of correlationism in the Continental tradition it is thus important to explain the historical origins of the demand for epistemic humility and to trace its sociological effects.

Although the origins of the split between analytic and Continental traditions lie in their divergent relations to Kant,[430] the split is articulated by the first post-Kantian figures claimed largely by one tradition or the other: Russell and Frege on one side, and Hegel and Husserl on the other.[431] In locating

---

428. Meillassoux, *After Finitude*, 48–9.

429. This lifecycle is most obvious in Heidegger's own later work (Heidegger, 'Only a God Can Save Us', interview with *Der Spiegel*, 1966), its subsequent appropriation by theology (cf. J. Wolfe, *Heidegger and Theology*, [London: Bloomsbury and T&T Clark, 2014]), and the so-called 'theological turn' in French phenomenology that occurred after him (cf. *Phenomenology and the 'Theological Turn'*, [New York: Fordham University Press, 2001]). But the same dynamic is evident in the theological development and appropriation of Derrida's work (cf. Derrida, *Acts of Religion* [London and New York: Routledge, 2001]; Steven Shakespeare, *Derrida and Theology* [Edinburgh: T&T Clark, 2009]; John D. Caputo. *The Prayers and Tears of Jacques Derrida: Religion without Religion* [Bloomington and Indianapolis, IN: Indiana University Press, 1997]), and the gradual filtration of the other figures in this lineage into a renewed discourse of Continental theology. As an additional point, I will admit that the sense of 'negative theology' is quite disparate within this discourse, and that I intend less to capture any one specific sense than the intellectual diaspora to which they belong.

430. See chapter 3.4, subsection I.

431. This schema is obviously quite reductive, not only because it ignores the relevant interactions between Russell and Hegel (via the British Idealists) and Husserl and Frege (more directly), but because it leaves out independent influences upon the traditions that are merely less prominent: American pragmatism,

the common themes in Hegel's and Husserl's work from which the Continental tradition springs, it is all too tempting to grant significance to the fact that they both use the word 'phenomenology' to describe at least a part of their philosophical practice.[432] However, this commonality is superficial, because they interpret its meaning in different ways: as the immanent unfolding of the concept of consciousness (Hegel) and as the immanent description of the given in its givenness (Husserl).[433] Their real commonality lies rather in their use of the word 'logic' to index their ambition to articulate the universal structure of thought and its content.[434] It is important to see that this ambition is not merely *epistemic*, but profoundly *semantic*: Hegel aims to account for the content of thought in terms of the dialectical dynamics through which concepts mediate and negate one another, whereas Husserl aims to account for the same content in terms of intuitive fulfilment and its eidetic invariants. If this manner of describing Hegel's and Husserl's projects sounds closer to the work of Russell, Frege, and their descendants than it does to much of the work in the Continental tradition that follows, it is because there is a logical dimension to Kant's thought that the latter tends to discard. Whatever other epistemic virtues

---

ordinary language philosophy, Marxism, psychoanalysis, Saussurian structuralism, and the French tradition of philosophy of science (e.g., Bachelard and Canguilhem), to name but a few. Nevertheless, if we can only pick a pair for either tradition, Russell-Frege and Hegel-Husserl are the obvious choices.

432. Cf. Hegel, *Phenomenology of Spirit*; and Husserl, *Ideas I*.

433. See my 'The Greatest Mistake: On the Failure of Hegel's Absolute Idealism', <http://deontologistics.files.wordpress.com/2011/04/dundee-paper.pdf>, for a more thorough discussion of Hegel's *Phenomenology* and its difference from Husserl's phenomenological method.

434. Cf. Hegel, *Science of Logic* and Husserl, *Logical Investigations*.

one can ascribe to Hegel, the sheer scope and raw ambition of his philosophical system indicate that humility is not one of them; and whatever epistemic humility one can ascribe to Kant and Husserl, it is strictly limited: they are more concerned with critically circumscribing and securing the possibility of knowledge (transcendental epistemology) than they are with critically demonstrating its impossibility (transcendental scepticism). This means that, although Kant provides the theoretical seed which grows into strong correlationism, the true source of the epistemic humility that nourishes it is to be found in the reaction to Hegel's and Husserl's radicalisation of his logical ambitions.

It is at this point that we must turn to the historical context of twentieth-century philosophy and the broader sociological trends with which it is enmeshed. Here we have no choice but to explore the connection between philosophical and political developments. From this perspective, although Heidegger's philosophy of freedom (*Freiheit*) represents a bridge between the *Enlightenment ideals* of German idealism and the *modernist methods* of Husserlian phenomenology, it equally represents a bridge between the *counter-Enlightenment* thinking of German romanticism and the *anti-modernism* of German nationalism.[435] One might say that Heidegger ends both the tradition of German idealism and the original project of Husserlian phenomenology by disconnecting them from the progressive **universalism** that defined both the theoretical project of Enlightenment and the practical project of modernity (their concern with Truth

---

435. There has been plenty of ink spilled regarding Heidegger's Nazism, and so I will restrict myself to discussing the conservative elements of Heidegger's philosophy that undoubtedly attracted him to the ideas and rhetoric of national socialism, rather than the details of his involvement in the Nazi party.

as *Logos*).[436] In its place, he constructs a sophisticated yet conservative **historicism** that supplies the hyperbolic nostalgia motivating both his philosophical obsession with the origins of the Western tradition and his disastrous political involvement with Nazism (his concern with Truth as *Kampf*).[437] Perhaps the greatest irony of twentieth-century philosophy is that so many came to see universalism as a conservative doctrine responsible for the horrors of Nazism, and therefore to advocate some form of historicism, relativism, or similar **pluralism** as a progressive alternative in the domains of theory and practice. It is for this reason that Heidegger remains an important influence upon many whose politics could hardly be more diametrically opposed to his own. Moreover, it is this pervasive rejection of universalism in

---

436. Karl Otto Apel aptly describes this aspect of Heidegger's thought as the origin of a forgetting of the Logos (*Logosvergessenheit*) comparable to the forgetting of Being (*Seinsvergessenheit*) that Heidegger locates in the metaphysical tradition ('Meaning constitution and justification of validity: has Heidegger overcome transcendental philosophy by history of being?', in H. Dreyfus and M. Wrathall [eds], *Heidegger Reexamined Vol. 4: Language and the Critique of Subjectivity* [London: Routledge , 2002]).

437. Cf. M. Heidegger, *Being and Truth* (Bloomington, IN: Indiana University Press, 2010). This collects two lecture courses, 'The Fundamental Question of Philosophy' and 'On the Essence of Truth', delivered during Heidegger's brief rectorship of Freiburg University, at the height of his political involvement in Nazism (1933–1934). These courses are useful both because they provide a detailed reading of the metaphysical tradition culminating in Hegel (as the highest point of onto-theology) and because they contrast this with his attempt to retrieve a more primordial conception of truth from the inception of Greek philosophy. Moreover, the latter course is interesting because it reveals the genesis of his account of truth as strife, along with the obvious influence of Nietzsche's early work on the conflict between the Dionysian and the Apollonian and the deliberate resonances its early formulation (strife as struggle, or *Kampf*) has with the political language of German nationalism and Nazism (see the translator's foreword for a discussion of this).

the wake of the crimes of Nazism, colonialism, patriarchy, and associated structures of **domination**, from which the demand for epistemic humility that nourishes strong correlationism emerges, insofar as it sees epistemic arrogance as a crucial component of the attitudes that animate these structures.[438]

Returning to the theoretical register briefly, to explain how pluralism motivates strong correlationism it is necessary to isolate the non-universal element underlying Kant's weak correlationism: namely, his account of space and time as pure forms of intuition in the transcendental aesthetic. Kant's corresponding account of the categories as the pure forms of conception in the transcendental analytic is strictly universal, insofar as it is meant to apply to every *finite* thinking being. For Kant, our finitude consists in our need for *specific* forms of sensibility to supplement our limited, but *general*, form of understanding, as opposed to the infinite divine intellect which unites the two in an unlimited intellectual intuition that is thoroughly *universal* insofar as it spontaneously creates its objects, rather than passively receiving them. In essence, the phenomenal realm is separated from the noumenal realm by its filtration through the myriad limitations and imperfections of our parochial modes of sensation.

We briefly mentioned this core conceit of correlationism at the beginning of the last chapter: the idea that knowledge is

---

438. It is important to point at that I do not reject the idea that universalism and domination have been historically enmeshed in a variety of ways. Moreover, I support the theoretical concern with studying these connections and the practical concern with resisting them that motivates so much work from the Second World War to the present day. However, I do believe that the anti-universalism that is often inferred from this enmeshment is misguided, and that it has been responsible for a number of problematic philosophical (not to say political) developments.

irredeemably contaminated by its semantic conditions. We are now in a position to see how pluralism radicalises this conceit, by enabling strong correlationism to claim that the separation of the *for-us* from the *in-itself* is effected not simply by the inherent plurality of *sensibility* (e.g., forms of intuition, sensory mechanisms, etc.), but by the inherent plurality of *thought as such* (e.g., historical thrownness, language games, etc.). It is this pluralistic dissolution of semantics into a diaspora of historical, cultural, linguistic, and even biological forms that mutates Husserl's phenomenological suppression of the noumenon into the quasi-mystical celebration of **radical alterity** that is the mainstay of strong correlationism in the Continental tradition. Strong correlationism ceases to strategically ignore the minimal logical constraints Kant places upon the noumenon (existence and non-contradiction) and begins to attack them as remnants of a historically pernicious universalism (*logocentrism*).

This gives us some purchase upon the historical and sociological developments through which Kantian critique—the *transcendental* delimitation of the domains of theory and practice—evolves into a larger and more diverse critical ecosystem—incorporating the analytical tools of Nietzschean genealogy, Marxian ideology critique, and Saussurian structuralism.[439] There are numerous specific examples of these theoretical strains that we could isolate (e.g., Lyotard, Adorno, and Lacan) and various specific hybrids that index their connections (e.g., Foucault, Althusser, and Derrida). A complete

---

439. For those wondering why I have not included psychoanalysis in this list, it is principally because its incorporation is filtered through one of these other frameworks (e.g., Klossowski, Marcuse, and Lacan). There is obviously more to be said about the integration of psychoanalytic ideas within this extended historical tradition and its anglophone sociological nexus, but I will not endeavour to tackle the topic here.

map of these ideas and their intersections is beyond the scope of this brief historical survey, but what really concerns me is their envelopment in the peculiar sociological nexus of anglophone Continental philosophy and its affiliated disciplines (e.g., literary criticism, art theory, sociology, cultural studies, etc.). The move beyond the transcendental in considering the biological, psychological, sociological, linguistic, economic, political, and otherwise cultural conditions of thought and action is an entirely natural and philosophically significant extension of the project of critique. However, in its appropriation by anglophone Continental philosophy this significant extension has all too often been misconstrued as a wholesale rejection of the transcendental foundations of the critical project—as an intellectual paradigm shift in which the seemingly necessary structures of thought and action are finally unmasked as contingent empirico-historical configurations.[440] The parallel

---

440. By far the best example of this is the dominant interpretation of Foucault's thought, precisely because Foucault was explicitly concerned with unmasking seeming necessities as historical contingencies. Moreover, his empirico-historical critiques self-consciously paralleled the structure of Kant's transcendental critiques (see the pseudonymous dictionary article 'Michel Foucault' in P. Rabinow [ed.], *Aesthetics* [London: Allen Lane, 1998], 460): (a) the historical *a priori* is the empirico-historical correlate of Kant's synthetic *a priori*, and (b) the architectonic of his overall critical project (knowledge, power, and ethics/'aesthetics of existence' ('What is Enlightenment?' in *Ethics* [London: Penguin, 1994], 317–18) is correlated with the architectonic of Kant's three critiques (theoretical reason, practical reason, and aesthetics). However, these correlations should not be taken as a rejection of Kant's transcendentalism (as [a] might initially suggest) so much as a revision and extension of his transcendental project into the social sphere (as [b] more precisely indicates). Foucault's later work on subjectivity and ethics provides the best demonstration of this point: his idea that there are different forms of subjectivity is usually interpreted as a radical pluralism, when in fact it provides an account of the universal structure of such forms of subjectivity (again, see 'Michel Foucault'). Foucault's unified account of knowledge, power, and subjectivity provides us with universal structures in terms of which to understand particular empirico-

between this *critical shift* from universalism to pluralism and the *sceptical shift* from weak to strong correlationism indexes the reigning *doxa* of the Continental tradition in the latter half of the twentieth century.

Of course, it is perhaps somewhat simplistic to lay the blame for the misconstrual of critique at the feet of Heideggerian historicism, its Derridean synthesis with structuralism (*poststructuralism*), or its Lyotardian synthesis with modernism (*postmodernism*), but it is hard to dismiss the role this **orthodox correlationism** has played in encouraging the systematic misappropriation and conflation of the different elements of the critical ecosystem. It is perhaps better to see orthodox correlationism as a lens through which critical philosophy was diffracted and distorted by the anglophone world—it certainly existed as an aspect of the European philosophical tradition, but it came to define this tradition in its appropriation by the sociological nexus of anglophone Continental philosophy. The other crucial factor involved in this distortion is the misinterpretation of the term 'critique' itself, which, in a perfect example of **academic idle talk**,[441] has

---

historical social configurations, complicating the transcendental account of thought and action rather than dissolving it in pure historicism.

441. I am here alluding to Heidegger's account of idle talk (*Gerede*) in *Being and Time* (§35), which refers to the fallen mode of discourse (*Rede*) in which one is able to use a word without really understanding what it means. From the perspective of semantic pragmatism, this means having a sufficient understanding of the word's usage to get by in certain limited everyday contexts (e.g., being able to discuss *economic inflation* at a dinner party), without understanding the broader usage which constitutes mastery of the corresponding concept (e.g., without being able to explain the complicated relationships between *inflation*, *interest rates*, *monetary policy*, *currency circulation*, etc., or rather, without having any grasp of the various theories about these relationships). In this example, one can talk idly about 'economic inflation', even though one has no grasp of economic inflation.

been systematically conflated with 'criticism' both in the aca-demic sense of literary and artistic criticism (two disciplines thoroughly entwined in the anglophone Continental nexus) and in the ordinary sense of the discursive process of disagree-ment (academically enhanced by the unrelenting negativity of Adornian *critical theory*). This critical idleness is responsible for a twofold degeneration of critique in the anglophone world. On the one hand, it has instilled a concern with *style over substance*, or more concretely, a focus on *style over form*—ignoring the structure of argumentation in favour of the mode of its presentation—and *symbolism over content*—ignoring the implications of a position in favour of the connotations of the words in which it is expressed. On the other hand, it has perverted the *conceptual tools* of *critique*—whose function is to *open* discourse onto its own conditions, so as to enable more nuanced and complicated forms of disagreement, challenge, and correction—into *rhetorical tools* of *criticism*—whose function is to *close* discourse to more nuanced and complex engagements, so as to enable more simple and convenient forms of dismissal, deflection, and incorrigibility. Style, sym-bolism, and rhetorical strategy are neither unimportant nor expressively inert, but they cannot supplant form, content, and conceptual substance in the expressive evolution of theoretical discourse.

We can index the **degeneration of critique** by exam-ining a specific perversion of the core analytical concepts extending the original project of critique: *practice* (Nietzsche), *materiality* (Marx), and *structure* (Saussure). Initially, each concept names a form of *concreteness* whose analysis is intended to subvert the *abstractness* of dogmatic theory: the manifestation of thought in social practices (e.g., the genealogical analysis of ascetic ideals in terms of practices maintaining social cohesion); the embedding of culture in the economy of material needs (e.g., the ideological analysis of political liberalism in terms of bourgeois class interests); and the realisation of idealisations through contextualisation in relational structures (e.g., the linguistic analysis of ideal meanings [signifieds] in terms of networks of relations between the words used to express them [signifiers]). However, they become progressively unmoored from concreteness as they are divorced from *specific analyses* and deployed in *overarching generalisations*: the pluralisation of thought through the homogenisation of practice (e.g., the Heideggerian practical reorientation of philosophy);[442] the demonisation of culture through the ubiquity of economy (e.g., the kitsch-Marxist insistence that everything within capitalism is contaminated by the value-form);[443] and the idealisation of reality through the de-hierarchisation of structure (e.g., the Derridean insistence that the ur-structure of iterability precludes the functional differentiation and articulation of literal and non-literal language).[444] This amounts to pragmatism without pragmatics, materialism without matter, and structuralism without structure. Continuing along this trajectory, the critical demand to get concrete/specific becomes hyperbolically abstract/general—philosophical critique reaches its lowest energy state in the reflexive gestures of dogmatic criticism. These **critical reflexes**—learned techniques of dismissal, deflection, and incorrigibility—frequently

---

442. See chapter 3.4, subsection I, and chapter 3.5.

443. I am indebted to Reza Negarestani for the term 'kitsch Marxism', which quite wonderfully captures the hyperbolic cultural cynicism that has somehow evolved out of the rich theoretical tradition of Marxism over the last few decades ('The Labor of the Inhuman', in R. Mackay and A. Avanessian [eds], *#Accelerate: The Accelerationist Reader* [Falmouth; Urbanomic, 2014]).

444. Cf. J. Derrida, *Limited Inc* (Evanston, IL: Northwestern University Press, 1998).

deploy the original critical concepts we began with—practice, materiality, and structure—as **critical shibboleths** that function to distinguish those who understand and endorse their *esoteric abstraction* from those who do not and therefore must be cowed by their *exoteric concreteness*.[445] The irony here is that the demand to attend to the specific structures of concrete material practices is all too often an exercise of discursive power of precisely the kind it supposedly suggests we should analyse and subvert.[446]

However, although this sceptico-critical alliance of strong correlationism and radical pluralism constitutes the *reigning doxa* of the Continental tradition in the latter half of the

---

445. This section is concerned with the past and its effects upon the present, but it is worth making a further point about the present and its potential effects upon the future. The terms 'embodiment' and 'lived experience' seem to be travelling the same degenerative trajectory as 'practice'/'materiality'/ 'structure'. This seems to be driven by a desire to recuperate certain methodological privileges of phenomenology (especially with regard to the affective dimension of experience) that were critically stripped from it by the dominant strains of Continental theory. This affective phenomenological dimension is presented as an immanent concreteness to which philosophical, ethical, and political thinking must bow, and is invoked to this effect, but it is hard to find a purer abstraction than immanent concreteness *qua* immanent concreteness ('thisness-in-thisness'), as Hegel's discussion of Sense-Certainty most amply demonstrates.

446. I consider myself a pragmatist, a materialist, and a structuralist (not to mention an advocate of 'embodied' cognition), but these terms are increasingly denied to me not because of the theoretical content of my specific endorsements of them (e.g., semantic pragmatism, sociological materialism, mathematical structuralism, etc.), but because of a range of seemingly unrelated commitments (e.g., ethical, political, aesthetic, etc.) that they are implicitly taken to index. Often, these are not even commitments I disagree with (e.g., the distortive effects of patriarchy upon the sociological organisation of mathematical practice), but which I simply take to be irrelevant to establishing the point at hand (e.g., the unique epistemic warrant provided by the procedural structure of mathematical proof).

twentieth century, that is not to say that it is the *only doxa*. There have always been Continental thinkers whose work runs counter to the image of thought that guides the anglophone appropriation of Continental philosophy, but there have sometimes also been counter-images in the anglophone world that contest these appropriations, encouraging divergent interpretations of accepted figures and legitimating the work of counter-hegemonic thinkers. The turn of the century was characterised by the ascendancy of one such counter-image: the philosophical couplet of Deleuze and Badiou. There are obviously many crucial differences between these two thinkers, but it is important to understand the manner in which the dialogue between them (and its echoes in the dialogue between their followers) enabled them to be extracted from the reigning narrative of anglophone Continental philosophy.[447] On the one hand, it had previously been all too easy to overemphasise the Nietzschean themes in Deleuze's thought and his stylistic experiments with Guattari in order to subsume him within the poststructural/postmodern nexus. On the other, it had been all too easy to overemphasise the Heideggerian themes in Badiou's thought and his engagement with Sartrean, Maoist, and Lacanian discourses in order to collapse his opposition to poststructuralism/postmodernism back into alternative forms of historicism. The debate between these thinkers not only breached the heavily policed border between classical metaphysics (Deleuze) and post-Heideggerian ontology (Badiou), but the central and crucially non-metaphorical role

---

447. The correspondence between Deleuze and Badiou was never published, at Deleuze's request; but the edges of the debate can be traced implicitly in the comments on Badiou in Deleuze and Guattari's *What is Philosophy?* [London:Verso, 1994], 151–3) and explicitly in Badiou's *Deleuze: The Clamor of Being*. There has since been no end of secondary literature comparing the two.

played within it by mathematics (i.e., differential calculus and set theory) flaunted the taboos of much anglophone discourse by stubbornly refusing reduction to either style or symbolism. Taken together, the work of Deleuze and Badiou provided an island of hermeneutic stability from which the philosophically curious could set out to explore those conceptual waters foreclosed by sceptico-critical hegemony.

It is important not to overemphasise the unity and consistency of this counter-image. Its novelty stemmed less from any implicit agreement than from a series of explicit disagreements that could not be framed in terms of orthodox concerns. Nevertheless, there are at least two important philosophical trends associated with the popularity of Deleuze and Badiou that we should note. Firstly, there is an additional dimension to their peripheral involvement in the genesis of ontological liberalism, namely, the emergence of a demand for **ontological humility** that parallels the demand for epistemic humility discussed above. The essence of this demand is a refusal to understand ourselves as possessing a unique metaphysical status (e.g., as ensouled creatures or thinking substances) that would explain our difference from everything else (e.g., our capacities for thought and action) and perhaps justify treating ourselves differently from other things (e.g., animals, plants, etc.). This is a form of ontological egalitarianism motivated less by the noetic and anti-reductionist challenges than by a commitment to what constitutes proper causal explanation (e.g., there must be a causal genesis of thinkers/agents within the world) and normative justification (e.g., there must be non-arbitrary grounds for ethical judgements). Deleuze's work is more obviously in tune with these motivations, insofar as his panpsychist metaphysics dissolves any distinction between thinking and non-thinking beings in a univocal account of Being as information processing/problem solving, and his neo-Spinozist ethics eschews any transcendent imposition of norms in favour of a universal drive to become ever more adaptable. Badiou's work is more often criticised from this perspective, insofar as his laudably impersonal account of the subject nevertheless depends upon a meta-ontological supplement (the Event) which raises suspicions of illicit transcendence. However, the point remains that the nascent opposition to ontologically arrogant modes of explanation and justification already present in anglophone Continental discourse could only be articulated as an ontological constraint once metaphysical/ontological issues once more became legitimate concerns.

The second trend associated with the rising popularity of Deleuze and Badiou is a methodological shift in the way in which philosophy relates both to itself and to other practices (e.g., science, politics, art, etc.), namely, a renewed emphasis upon **construction** as opposed to critique. This is significant insofar as it marks a return to cultivating novel theoretical and practical projects based on philosophical ideas, as opposed to the delimitation of possible projects and the elimination of actual projects that had become synonymous with critique and criticism. Again, Deleuze is more obviously aligned with this shift, insofar as his theoretical and practical approach to philosophy as *conceptual creation* both enabled his own experimental interactions with other fields (e.g., painting, cinema, political economy, psychoanalysis, mathematics, etc.) and encouraged others to pursue similar experiments. Badiou is perhaps more sober in his articulation of the relations between philosophy and its four conditions (art, science, politics, and love), but this does not prevent him from both drawing philosophical insight from them (e.g., his ontological engagement with mathematical set theory and his psychoanalytic engagement with the amorous encounter) and applying these philosophical insights to them (e.g., his literary works and his Maoist political activism). Moreover, there is an important sense in which the very feature of Badiou's work that raises suspicions of illicit transcendence—his account of the constitution of a political subject through its *fidelity* to an Event—has certainly encouraged a more active approach to politics than its critical precursors, even if the effectiveness of the resultant activism is open to question. Finally, the resurgence of metaphysics in the anglophone Continental world inspired by Deleuze and Badiou is equally bound up with this constructive trend, insofar as the construction of new metaphysical systems is, for better or worse, largely motivated by the potential use to which they can be put in other domains.

At this point one might be tempted to conclude that the conjunction of epistemic humility and critique is entirely regressive, and the conjunction of ontological humility and construction entirely progressive. However, just as the critical tradition gradually degenerated into sceptico-critical hegemony, so its constructive counterpart has begun to spawn its own pathological tendencies. On the one hand, despite the sobering effect of his opposition to Badiou, Deleuze's stylistic experiments with Guattari in *Capitalism and Schizophrenia* have continued to warp the reception of his account of conceptual creation, unfortunately encouraging the production and proliferation of philosophical jargon more concerned with affective resonance than conceptual function.[448] This is merely

---

448. There is simply too much terrible literature that could be referenced here. However, it is worth mentioning the Cybernetic Culture Research Unit (CCRU), insofar as they explored this expressive trajectory with more discipline and self-awareness than many of those who followed them. Nevertheless, even if their original 'hyperstitional' praxis was not without results, the misunderstandings and oversimplifications generated by their attempt to achieve 'maximum

one example of the way in which the constructive tendency has both fed off, and been fed into, the sociological nexus of poststructuralism/postmodernism to which it is nominally opposed, reinforcing the concern with style over substance evidenced by the worst excesses of the latter. On the other hand, despite the qualified character of his own ontological humility, Badiou's work has catalysed the growth of ontological liberalism, engendering an enthusiasm for metaphysical speculation not merely unconcerned with its explanatory worth but entirely willing to undermine the edifice of explanation itself. This is nowhere more evident than in the increasing popularity of Latour's work, whose avowed hostility toward critique[449] is little more than an alibi for substituting spurious metaphysics for substantive methodology, enabling him to bootstrap even more virulent forms of epistemic scepticism out of constructive pluralism.[450] We must recognise that both the critical and constructive dimensions of the anglophone tradition have become pathological, and that these pathologies have in fact selectively reinforced one another in various ways. It is only on the basis of this admission that we can understand the true significance of Harman's OOP—as the point at which this mutual reinforcement reaches its synthetic nadir.

---

slogan density' attest to its insufficiency (CCRU, 'Swarmachines', in Mackay and Avanessian [eds], *#Accelerate*).

449. B. Latour 'Why has Critique Run out of Steam?', in *Critical Inquiry* 30 (2004).

450. See chapter 3.4, subsection IV.

We cannot discuss the emergence of OOP or its sociohistorical significance without beginning with Speculative Realism.[451] Obviously, Harman was in the process of developing his metaphysical system long before the 2007 workshop from which SR takes its name, but his work only became popular after, and largely as a result of, its association with the exciting new trend in Continental philosophy that SR supposedly represented.[452] It is important to understand that the somewhat unexpected excitement (and derision) with which SR was greeted in anglophone Continental circles was a direct result of the intellectual climate examined in the previous section. Not only did it represent an attempt to break with the dynamic of translation and commentary upon Continental thinkers within which much anglophone scholarship was trapped, announcing the possibility of doing original philosophical work that was nevertheless in dialogue with the Continent, but it also seemed to reinforce and extend the break with the sceptico-critical hegemony begun by the ascendance of Deleuze and Badiou in the anglophone canon. The reason for this was precisely that the four thinkers grouped by SR (Quentin Meillassoux, Ray Brassier, Iain Hamilton Grant, and Graham Harman) had rallied around a diagnosis and criticism of the conceptual core of this hegemony—orthodox correlationism—as laid out in Meillassoux's *After Finitude*. However, although this involved a common commitment to

---

451. For a more detailed reflection on SR, see Ray Brassier's postscript below.

452. This wider popularity followed the 2007 publication of the transcript of this workshop in *Collapse* Vol. 3.

metaphysics[453] in opposition to the avowedly antimetaphysical orthodoxy, there were not only substantive divergences between their metaphysical projects, but perhaps even more serious divergences in the extent to which their projects broke with the other elements of this orthodoxy.

Meillassoux's work must be understood not only as resurrecting themes from modern philosophy (e.g., primary/secondary qualities, necessary connection, why there is something rather than nothing, etc.), but equally as reinforcing Deleuze and Badiou's philosophical engagement with mathematics as a literal discourse rather than a figurative resource. Brassier's work should be seen not only as forcing Continental philosophy to confront the necessity of epistemology (e.g., in articulating the relationship between cognitive science and the philosophy of mind), but equally as demanding that it overcome its dismissive attitude toward the work already done in the analytic tradition. Grant's work can be interpreted not only as refusing the assimilation of German idealism to the canon of correlationism (e.g., in championing Schelling over Fichte), but equally as encouraging a direct engagement with the *content* of the natural sciences comparable to Meillassoux's engagement with mathematics and consonant with Brassier's insistence on understanding their *form*. By contrast, Harman's work must be interpreted not only as metaphysically re-inscribing the orthodoxy's scepticism, but equally as sociologically consolidating its other philosophical prejudices. Harman sides with the orthodoxy against the other three figures in almost every case: he outright denies the literal significance of mathematics,

---

453. Although Meillassoux rejects the term 'metaphysics' in favour of 'speculation', we have already explained the extent to which this is more terminological than substantive. See chapter 3.4, subsection I, and chapter 3.5.

recklessly liquidates epistemology, flagrantly caricatures analytic philosophy, reliably collapses idealism into correlationism,
and proudly ignores the results of natural science.

On this basis, it is hard not to see OOP as a natural out-
growth of the orthodoxy in both content and character, but it
does break with the sceptico-critical hegemony in one important respect: Harman repeatedly rejects the project of critique
in favour of the sorts of constructive philosophical intervention
performed by Deleuze, Badiou, and (paradigmatically) Latour.
Already in *Tool-Being*, he opposes his own 'sincere' approach
to entities to the 'critical' approach of orthodox Heideggerians:

> Instead of structural aloofness and quasi-transcendental doubt,
> what philosophy now needs above all else is an injection of sheer
> naiveté—not the pathetic innocence of a burglary victim, but
> the innate candor with which circus clowns handle everything
> from cowbells to puppies to dynamite.[454]

This clownish naïveté is Harman's alibi for his methodological
obliviousness: an excuse to return to precritical metaphysics while simultaneously preserving a number of distinctly
postcritical attitudes concerning knowledge, meaning, mathematics and science. Essentially, he separates the sceptical
terminus of the trajectory of critique from its methodological origin, freeing Kant's noumenal legacy from any residual
universalism once and for all. However, it is worth exploring
how this move relates to the conflation of 'critique' with
'criticism' discussed earlier,[455] because Harman's rejection of
critique has less to do with any positive engagement with its

---

454. *Tool-Being*, 238.

455. See chapter 4.1.

methodological origins than with his exclusive focus upon 'criticism' in both its argumentative and literary/artistic (or cultural) senses.

To elaborate: it is important to see that Harman's attacks upon critique are not so much concerned with the practice of delimiting possible positions as with the the practice of disagreement as such—his cultivated naïveté is more of a response to philosophical *cynicism* than to excessive methodological *caution*.[456] Now, I have already discussed the ways in which the degeneration of critique has engendered this sort of cynicism through the proliferation of a number of discursive pathologies, for instance, enabling the evasion of difficult disagreements by facilitating easy dismissal. Yet it is not these pathologies with which Harman takes issue. Rather, he challenges the presumption that the worth of philosophical positions is to be gauged primarily in terms of the strength of the arguments presented for and against them. We have already come across this particular feature of Harman's position, in his attempt to generalise Žižek's point about the stupidity of all *proverbs* into a claim about the stupidity of all *content*—a naked rhetorical gesture in which all explicit claims, no matter how precise, no matter whether they concern philanthropy, philosophy, or physics, are reduced to the level of vague folk wisdom.[457] Of course, insofar as this constitutes an attack upon the value of argumentation in favour of the value of rhetoric, it is admirably performative; but it is not the only arrow that Harman has let fly on the topic. He elaborates his views on the role of argument more extensively in *Prince of Networks*:

---

456. See p. 29 n. 17.

457. See chapter 3.6.

I reject the suggestion of Meillassoux and many analytic thinkers that philosophy plays out primarily at the level of explicit, deductive argument from clear first principles. With Whitehead I hold that 'logical contradictions [...] are the most gratuitous of errors; and usually they are trivial. [And that] after criticism, systems do not exhibit mere illogicalities. They suffer from inadequacy and incoherence' [...] Neither Meillassoux nor anyone else in philosophy simply follows a remorseless chain of deductions without stepping back from time to time and looking at whether these deductions describe the world accurately. Mathematics may proceed in this way, but I agree with Whitehead that philosophy cannot. And as for the natural sciences, not only do they not proceed through sheer logical deduction—they do not even acknowledge contradiction as their major principle of discovery.[458]

The first thing to notice here is that Harman associates explicitness not only with deductive reasoning, but *a fortiori* with deduction from first principles (or axioms). The second is that he understands this deductive approach to argumentation as essentially mathematical. The third and final point to note is that he implies that this approach takes logical contradiction as its 'major principle of discovery'. Taken together, these constitute a rather extreme caricature of the role of argument in philosophy, suggesting that the rejection of either of two non-equivalent claims—(a) that philosophy proceeds by deduction from first principles, or (b) that philosophy proceeds in the same manner as mathematics—entails that one should weaken (or even abandon) the rational constraints of

---

458. *Prince of Networks*, 173–4.

explicitness and *consistency*.[459] This results in a decrease in the value of argument, which Harman attempts to leverage into a corresponding increase in the value of rhetoric:

> Rhetoric has as much power as argument in establishing new paradigms in both science and philosophy. This is not because 'people are not always rational and you sometimes have to appeal to their emotions to make them see the light'. Instead, it is due to Whitehead's point about the inability of arguments, propositions, explicit evidence, or tangible qualities to do full justice to the world. [...] To say that a philosophy is made of arguments is like saying that an apple is nothing but a bundle of qualities—that there is nothing more to the apple than the sum of its explicit traits. [...] Against this 'bundle of qualities' theory, I have said that we must uphold *objects*. And against the idea of philosophies as 'arguments', we must defend a model of philosophy as object-oriented. Analytic philosophy has given us more 'knockdown arguments' than the human race has ever known, yet it is not clear that we have achieved a Golden Age of philosophy in return.[460]

By now Harman's strategy should be familiar: just as he inflates Žižek's observation that conflicting proverbs are equipollent into the claim that the justification of every statement is undecidable, so he inflates Whitehead's advice not to treat philosophy as if it were mathematics into the claim that philosophies are something other than statements and their justifications. The real meaning of both gnomic proverbs and intricate philosophies always withdraws behind their

---

459. Which, as I have argued earlier, amounts to abandoning *sincerity* (chapter 3.6).

460. *Prince of Networks*, 175.

words—as an implicit insight that can never be explicitly expressed, but only allusively invoked.

In dissecting Harman's caricature of argument, we should begin by noting that even mathematics does not proceed by means of 'a remorseless chain of deductions'. This is because there is a practical difference between its context of *discovery*—in which imaginative variation and abductive experimentation are paramount—and its context of *justification*—in which formal explicitness and deductive consistency are paramount.[461] The distinction between these contexts is operative outside mathematics, even if it is differently articulated in philosophy—whose mode of discovery involves bringing axioms into question (e.g., exploring the reasons why we might accept or reject the principle of sufficient reason)—and natural science—whose mode of discovery underwrites its mode of justification (e.g., defending the standard model on the basis of the experimental discovery of the Higgs boson). Moreover, these differences modify the requirements of explicitness and consistency: the explicitness of philosophical theories can no more be secured by the stipulation of axioms than the consistency of natural-scientific theories can be secured without experimental testing.[462] Regardless, explicitness and consistency are principally constraints upon justification, rather than discovery. Although it is undoubtedly the case that the dialectical process of making explicit and revising our theoretical

---

461. A particularly nuanced account of the creativity involved in mathematical discovery is provided by Zalamea in part three of his *Synthetic Philosophy of Contemporary Mathematics*.

462. Brandom gives an illuminating account of the objectivity of empirical discourse based on the ability of experiment to force us to revise inconsistencies in the inferential commitments that constitute the content of our empirical concepts (*Between Saying and Doing*, chapter 6).

commitments by divesting ourselves of their contradictions *can* play an important role in practices of discovery,[463] the motive force of these contradictions derives from the role they *must* play in procedures of justification, namely, withholding warrant from the theories that contain them.[464]

The claim that many, if not most, contradictions we actually uncover are trivial and uninteresting in the context of discovery is no reason to weaken the ideal of consistency in the context of justification, and *a fortiori* no reason to weaken the ideal of explicitness, because these ideals are constitutive features of the normative structure of justification itself. This is certainly not the conclusion that Whitehead is trying to draw from this claim. It is worth quoting the relevant section of *Process and Reality* at length:

> The second condition for the success of imaginative construc-
> tion is unflinching pursuit of the two rationalistic ideals, coher-
> ence and logical perfection. [...] Logical perfection does not here
> require any detailed explanation. An example of its importance
> is afforded by the role of mathematics in the restricted field of
> natural science. [...] The requirement of coherence is the great
> preservative of rationalistic sanity. But the validity of its criticism

---

463. Imre Lakatos's masterful *Proofs and Refutations* (Cambridge: Cambridge University Press, 1976) presents an excellent analysis of the way this dialectical process plays out in mathematics, by means of an exquisite reconstruction of the history of the Euler conjecture and the associated definition of polyhedra.

464. Brandom has an illuminating account of the pragmatics of this procedure in terms of the normative statuses of commitment and entitlement (*Making It Explicit*, chapter 3), wherein incompatibility between commitments (which results in contradiction when they are jointly held) is defined as commitment to one precluding entitlement to the other (such that commitment to both precludes entitlement to either).

is not always admitted. If we consider philosophical controversies, we shall find that disputants tend to require coherence from their adversaries, and to grant dispensations to themselves. It has been remarked that a system of philosophy is never refuted; it is only abandoned. The reason is that logical contradictions, except as temporary slips of the mind—plentiful, though temporary— are the most gratuitous of errors; and usually they are trivial. Thus, after criticism, systems do not exhibit mere illogicalities. They suffer from inadequacy and incoherence. Failure to include some obvious elements of experience in the scope of the system is met by boldly denying the facts. Also while a philosophical system retains any charm of novelty, it enjoys a plenary indulgence for its failures in coherence. But after a system has acquired orthodoxy, and is taught with authority, it receives a sharper criticism. Its denials and its incoherences are found intolerable, and a reaction sets in.[465]

If we parse this passage carefully, we can see that Whitehead's point has nothing to do with 'the inability of arguments, propositions, explicit evidence, or tangible qualities to do full justice to the world'. Although he distinguishes *adequacy and coherence* (or simply 'coherence') from *explicitness and consistency* (or simply 'logical perfection'), he does not oppose the former to the latter as Harman opposes rhetoric to argument. One need only attend to Whitehead's definition of incoherence as 'the arbitrary disconnection of first principles'[466] to see that it is a matter of inferential economy

---

465. A.N. Whitehead, *Process and Reality* (New York: Free Press, 1978), 5–6.

466. Ibid., 6. Whitehead helpfully discusses the metaphysical trajectory from Descartes, through Spinoza, to himself as an example of increasing systemic coherence.

rather than persuasive presentation.[467] Whitehead's point is that coherence is a distinct feature of the normative structure of justification, and that appeals to it are more frequent in philosophical argument than appeals to consistency, despite being more difficult to formulate and carrying less immediate force. While we must not tolerate inconsistency, it is relatively easy to correct it by abandoning the offending commitments, whereas we can and do tolerate incoherence to some extent, partly because it is a matter of degree, and partly because it is not so easily corrected. This means that, although incoherence cannot give us the brute reason to reject a theory that inconsistency does, coherence can give us subtle reasons to favour one theory over another that consistency cannot.

It is important to see that Harman's attack on argumentative criticism aligns him with the *epistemological scepticism* of the hegemony, even while it distances him from its *affective cynicism*. However, it is equally important to see that he performs a corresponding defence of cultural criticism (e.g., Clement Greenberg, Marshall McLuhan, and Cleanth Brooks)[468] that aligns him with the *semantic romanticism* of degenerate critique, even while it feeds into the *affective enthusiasm* of unconstrained construction.[469] Harman deploys his metaphysical resources to free the expressive dimensions of style, metaphor,

---

467. It is worth pointing out that Kant defines reason as the faculty of inference, and its cognitive role as establishing an economy of principles of precisely the kind that Whitehead is discussing (*Critique of Pure Reason* A299–302).

468. Cf. Harman, 'The Revenge of the Surface: Heidegger, McLuhan, and Greenberg' (http://dar.aucegypt.edu/bitstream/handle/10526/3640/harman-1.pdf?sequence=1); and Harman's own extensive remarks on literary criticism and their application to Lovecraft in *Weird Realism*.

469. See chapter 3.6 for a detailed discussion of the conceptual connection between epistemological scepticism and semantic romanticism in Harman's work.

and rhetoric from their subordination to the content of explicit arguments, going so far as to radicalise the hegemonic concern with style *over* substance by converting style *into* substance, and thereby transforming content into its accident:

> We can say of any object that it is not a bundle of specific qualities, nor a bare unitary substratum, but rather a *style*.[470]

> What we are here calling content can be identified with what we have also called the sensual realm. While real objects and qualities always withdraw from access, and are incommensurable with any form of presence, we are always pressed up against sensual objects and qualities just as the faces of children are pressed against the windows of toy stores and pet shops. This is the world of content, and content is a world of *sincerity*.[471]

We have already examined this metaphysics of sincerity in some detail, but we are only now in a position to describe its role in severing the association between cultural criticism and critique, and thereby transposing the former to a new constructive register: its purpose is not just to protect cultural criticism from the *naïve seriousness* of philosophical literalism, but equally to liberate it from the *suffocating irony* that has persisted since the advent of postmodernity.[472] In Harman's work, the seemingly counter-hegemonic desires for

---

470. *Guerrilla Metaphysics*, 55.

471. *Weird Realism*, 254.

472. The return to sincerity in the face of postmodern irony is by now a well established gesture in cultural criticism, as evidenced by 'The New Sincerity', but it is not for that matter unwarranted. Its best advocate in literary criticism remains David Foster Wallace ('E Unibus Pluram: Television and U.S. Fiction', *Review of Contemporary Fiction* 13:2 [Summer 1993], 151).

constructive philosophical intervention *in* and sincere critical engagement *with* practices such as science, politics, and art converge to produce a form of **philosophical criticism** opposed to critical philosophy. The hypothesis that aesthetics is first philosophy ultimately results in philosophy relating to everything in aesthetic terms, such that the already fine line between philosophy of art and art criticism collapses, and the constructive interventions of political philosophy and the philosophy of science are substituted for critical appraisals of political and scientific developments as if they were intellectual fashions. This essentially replaces the standards of argumentative criticism with those of cultural criticism: valuing refinement of taste over sensitivity to reasons, feel for holistic shape over attention to devilish details, and—above all— imaginative elegance over rational coherence. If this is where serious naïveté leads us, then perhaps naïve seriousness is preferable.

Nevertheless, it is worth briefly entertaining Harman's aesthetic hypothesis as applied to the criticism of philosophy, as this can potentially reveal more about how his own work functions sociologically. If nothing else, it can help us answer the following question: Given that the arguments for OOP are, at best, simply underdeveloped and, at worst, blatant non sequiturs, why has it become so popular? Let us approach this question by considering the extension of his account of style as substance into the area of philosophical writing, in *Prince of Networks*:

> This suggests a good definition of a minor author, minor charac-
> ter, minor concept, minor invention, or minor argument: one that
> is reducible to *content*. The more a person, object, or idea can be
> summarized in a list of univocal assertions, the less substantial

they are, since substance always wears different costumes when seen from various angles. This has important stylistic implications for philosophy. Against the programme for philosophy written in 'good plain English', I hold that it should be written in good *vivid* English. Plain speech contains clear statements that are forgotten as soon as their spokesman closes his mouth, since they have already said all that they are capable of saying. But vivid speech forges new concepts that take on a life their own, like good fictional characters. It ensures that Leibniz's monad and Kant's *Ding an sich* will haunt the dreams of the future despite endless 'refutations' of both. Here we find the sole but towering advantage of continental philosophy over its analytic rival—the awareness that a philosophy is more than a list of true and false arguments.[473]

This opposition between *clarity* and *vividness* transposes that between *argumentative explicitness* and *rhetorical potency* into a stylistic key. I have spent a good deal of this book trying to redress the lack of clarity in Harman's writings by making the ideas and arguments contained in them explicit, but I have yet to really address the surfeit of vividness that he takes to compensate for it. Doing this provides precisely the sort of holistic purchase upon Harman's work that he suggests is peculiar to style; yet this is not a purchase upon some deeper coherence of its principles, but rather upon the systemic cohesion of the literary machinery that works to disguise their incoherence.[474]

---

473. *Prince of Networks*, 140.

474. Having striven for clarity in redressing Harman's insufficient clarity, I reserve the right to be vivid in addressing his excessive vividness. Fair is fair.

We cannot simply ignore Harman's vividness, if only because we cannot prevent it from seeping into our cognitive processes whenever we attempt to engage the intellectual content of his work, his unctuous prose leaving a sticky residue of *extraneous adjectives* (e.g., 'piles of vacuous inert matter that swarm through empty space', 'a starry, windy space of transcendent vision', 'either a colourful swarm of disjoined qualities, or unitary lumps of inarticulate pulp') and *superfluous similies* (e.g., 'radiating over us like a black sun', 'sunk beneath the surface like the hull of a venetian galley', 'resemble escape pods that jettison clear of their original environments') that adheres to our critical faculties and threatens to immobilise them entirely.[475] If the vividness of Harman's writing is supposed to give his thought a life of its own, then it has succeeded, but only by supporting a thriving imaginary ecosystem that shrouds the conceptual terrain much as the Amazon's amorphous fecundity masks its changing geography. The most difficult aspect of writing this book has been cutting a path through this voluminous stylistic overgrowth: disentangling the controversial historical narratives and questionable phenomenological analyses coiled around the ruins of Harman's arguments, evading the confusing herds of examples unleashed by his insatiable lust for lists, all the while capturing and domesticating the predatory metaphors he has left lying in wait for unwary critics.

The purpose of the expedition catalogued in these pages has been to explore the theoretical landscape thoroughly

---

475. The stylistic examples are taken from a broad selection of Harman's works, but I have deliberately not taken any from *Circus Philosophicus*, precisely because it takes Harman's stylistic vices to their logical extreme. As such, it deserves to be read independently, as a sort of cautionary tale.

enough to prove that the philosophical paradise Harman promised us is nowhere to be found therein; that it was never more than a metaphysical mirage, another lost city of gold luring the avaricious to their doom. However, in the process we have seen that Harman's writing style effects more than mere obfuscation. This emerged most clearly in our analyses of the argument from execution[476] and the fourfold diagram,[477] whose cultivated tensions do more than disguise gaps in argumentation, generating paradoxes whose constitutive irreducibility to expressible content *simulates* precisely the sort of depth Harman aspires to. These paradoxes are the heart of Harman's literary machine: they interlock with his rhetorical armamentarium and metaphorical menagerie to form an engine which, lubricated by stylistic snake oil, projects the withdrawn essence of withdrawn essence beyond any possible presentation, oriented by a conceptual vanishing point at which coherence converges with inconsistency. If nothing else, Harman's writing is proof that vividness can be used to conjure the illusion of conceptual substance as easily as it can be used to secure the persistence of genuine innovation.

It is thus no mystery that Harman's writing style is a crucial element of OOP's popularity. Its easygoing accessibility is deceptive: it lures us into his grandiose metaphysical picture by enticing us with paradoxes, while its literary excesses distract us from the fact that these paradoxes are never really resolved. However, there is more to Harman's work than his remarkable ability to fabricate affective edification. If we are to provide a complete explanation of its popularity, we must acknowledge that his philosophy displays a certain seductive coherence

---

476. See chapter 2.1, subsection II.

477. See chapter 3.,4, subsection V.

that transcends mere rhetorical cohesion, precisely because it overcomes an 'arbitrary disconnection of first principles' of the sort that Whitehead criticises. The reason this is not always obvious is that the 'first principles' in question are not usually presented as such, either by Harman or those seduced by his work. Nevertheless, we can begin to sense their outlines in the following passage:

> Human knowledge may indeed be something quite special, but this does not mean that it is something philosophically basic that creates a vast gap between humans and nonhumans, any more than noteworthy objects such as backbones and glass create such a gap between themselves and other things. No ontologist would ever dream of dividing the world into objects with spines and those without (though for zoology this might be illuminating). If we shift to the case of glass, the human-centred philosopher is ontologically fundamental, while the vitalist is like someone who says that everything in the world is actually already glass, though perhaps in a "weaker" form than windows. What is lacking is the most sensible alternative, which is to say that human knowledge, just like glass, backbones, reptiles, music, and mushrooms, arises at a certain point in the history of the universe, but without necessarily forming some sort of root metaphysical dualism in the world. I see no convincing reason to regard human knowledge as of such pivotal importance in the universe.[478]

This paragraph exemplifies the trend toward ontological humility we traced in the wake of Deleuze and Badiou. The demand for humility infuses the argument without ever being raised to the status of an explicit principle; it remains implicit in the

---

478. *Guerrilla Metaphysics*, 84.

denunciation of hubris, much as it did in Harman's rejection of anthropocentric readings of Heidegger.[479] However, whereas the latter rejection was the crucial step in *generalising* Heidegger's account of understanding to encompass all encounters between objects, the purpose of this denunciation is to *particularise* human knowledge, and thereby to sever the connection between understanding (*qua* general metaphysical relation) and knowledge (*qua* particular cultural institution). We need not rehearse what is problematic about this separation any further than we already have.[480] What concerns us is the line it draws from the *ontological humility* of the speculato-constructive counterimage back to the *epistemic humility* of the sceptico-critical hegemony. If it would be ontologically hubristic to claim that we had some special epistemic access to things in themselves, and ontologically absurd to claim that everything has such access to everything else, then we are left with the conclusion that nothing has access to anything, and that things appear to us only as they appear to one another. This particular brand of epistemic humility may be couched in far more metaphysical terms than the hegemony is used to, but it is no less amenable to the latter's sceptical predilections. The seductive coherence of OOP lies in this synthesis of the different demands for humility animating the main strands of anglophone Continental thought: deflating the cosmological significance of humanity's seeming capacity for knowledge by downgrading it to a capacity for knowledge *of seeming*.[481]

---

479.   See chapter 2.1, subsection I.

480.   The crucial problem is the attempt to separate the normative dimension of understanding (as correct/incorrect) from the normative dimension of knowledge (as true/false), which we have discussed under the heading of the argument from independence (chapter 2.3, subsection II).

481.   See the introduction to chapter 3.

It is my considered opinion that this synthesis of ontological and epistemic humility is the principal source of OOP's popularity. The main reason many find Harman's metaphysical radicalisation of correlationism so tempting is that it neatly integrates certain foundational intuitions that already overlap in Continental circles: *we aren't really anything special and we can't really know anything.* If one already shares these intuitions, then it is easy to care little about whether Harman has properly articulated and justified them, so long as he has made them cohere in an elegant fashion. This alliance of existing intuitions reinforces the convergence of critical engagement and constructive intervention that we have already identified in Harman's work, establishing a conceptual and practical connection between the pathological extremes of degenerate critique and unconstrained construction. On this basis, OOP emerges as a bizarre sceptico-constructive hybrid that exemplifies the worst traits of Continental philosophy in the anglophone world: it enables anyone to carry out speculative analyses of whatever they like (e.g., dark matter, direct action, or disco), analyses whose seeming significance is derived from empty metaphysical language (e.g., 'political science has so far failed to grasp the *vicarious causation* inherent in so-called direct action'), and whose effective unassailability is guaranteed by evasive sceptical manoeuvres (e.g., 'mathematical physics can never access the *withdrawn essence* of dark matter'). Thus its attraction lies not merely in the fact that it is *believable* (the combined effect of its rhetorical cohesion and seductive coherence), but also in the fact that it is *useful* (the combined effect of its speculative enthusiasm and sceptical conservatism).

Given that this perverse utility is what secures OOP's popularity in the last instance, it is worth saying something more about how it can be exploited to intervene in non-philosophical theory and practice. I will now try to examine the ways in which OOP has begun to cultivate an **ersatz interdisciplinarity** by infiltrating the disciplinary nexuses of science, politics, and art. It is impossible to consider every intellectual offshoot of Harman's thought here; it is more important to trace the manner in which his work interfaces with and bolsters existing trends than to catalogue everything it has inspired. As such, I will only consider the most significant confluences in each case.

Science. It is important to see that Harman's metaphysical twist on phenomenology (panpsychism/polypsychism) is an attempt to defend the authority of philosophical introspection after the collapse of the Husserlian project's anti-psychologism. This collapse was heralded by Merleau-Ponty's admission of empirical research into the phenomenological programme, but its actuality is the cascading methodological separation of anti-psychologistic epistemology from empirical psychology that followed. This continuing shift in the philosophy of mind is evidenced by the epistemological subtraction of givenness performed by Sellars's critique of the myth of the given[482] on the one hand, and the (neuro)psychological reduction of consciousness to the functional architecture of the brain promised by cognitive science[483] on the other. What we see here is a

---

482. The most famous statement of this critique remains that given in *Empiricism and the Philosophy of Mind* (Cambridge, MA: Harvard University Press, 1997), but it has since influenced many to pursue the sort of anti-psychologistic epistemological project Husserl began in a distinctly non-phenomenological register (e.g., Daniel Dennett, Jay Rosenberg, Richard Rorty, et al).

483. It is no coincidence that the most famous advocate of eliminative materialism, Paul Churchland, was a student of Sellars. However, he is far from alone in forcing the philosophy of mind to confront the results of psychological research, a list including at least: Patricia Churchland, Daniel Dennett, Ruth Millikan, and more recently Thomas Metzinger.

gradual pulling away of the *transcendental* from the *empirical* that gradually cedes more and more ground (e.g., sensation, emotion, selfhood) to the latter, leaving no room for philosophical introspection or those whose projects are founded upon it. Harman's rebranding of phenomenology as introspective metaphysics is a convenient escape route for those who prefer their psychological reflection unconstrained by empirical research.

Seen from the opposite direction, this phenomenological twist on metaphysics is an attempt to defend the authority of philosophical speculation against the ramifying methodological demands imposed by Kant's critical turn. The progressive differentiation of the transcendental from the empirical has been accompanied by a more extreme convergence between *metaphysics* and *physics* that has tended to disenfranchise those speculative metaphysicians unwilling or unable to keep up with developments in the latter.[484] However, in this case, Harman's introspective metaphysics provides more than an escape route for those who have been left behind by physicists' penetrating investigations of traditionally metaphysical topics (e.g., space/time, order/chaos, causality, etc.); it provides an elaborate excuse to suggestively dabble in physics (e.g., uncertainty, superposition, non-locality, etc.). This excuse is wielded most boldly by Tim Morton, whose repeated invocations of theoretical physics in his book *Realist Magic* are framed in the following way:

> If objects are irreducibly secret, causality must reside somewhere
> in the realm of relations between objects, along with things like
> number, qualities, time, space and so on. This is congruent with

---

484. Ladyman and Ross's *Every Thing Must Go* is still the best discussion of this convergence and its effects.

the last century of physics. For Einstein, space and time are also emergent properties of objects: objects don't float in a neutral void but emanate waves and ripples of spacetime. Clocks run faster in orbit above Earth than they do on Earth's surface. This congruency is a good sign that an object-oriented theory of causality is on the right track. But it's not strictly necessary: if anything the necessity goes the other way around. In other words, quantum theory and relativity are valid physical theories to the extent that they are object-oriented.[485]

This passage exemplifies the highly opportunistic attitude that Harman's metaphysics encourages towards natural science. OOP allows one to claim the support of physics whenever it seems consistent with one's views, while eschewing the reciprocal responsibility to make one's views cohere with physics. This is what happens to metaphysics once *science criticism* is substituted for the *philosophy of science*: it becomes more important to cultivate a *taste* for the weird and wonderful in scientific research than to develop an *understanding* of its consequences.

Politics. There is a peculiar pressure in Continental circles to secure the worth of one's philosophical insights by demonstrating their political applicability. It is thus entirely unsurprising that Harman's vocabulary of 'objects' has been experimentally adopted and even hybridised with more familiar political vocabularies in certain cases.[486] However, the only significant relation between OOP and politics derives from

---

485. T. Morton, *Realist Magic: Objects, Ontology, Causality* (Open Humanities Press: 2013), 30.

486. Cf. I.G.R. Shaw and K. Meehan, 'Force-Full: Power, Politics, and Object-Oriented Philosophy' in *Area*, 45:2 (June 2013), 216–22; S. Mussell, 'Object Oriented Marxism?', <http://www.metamute.org/editorial/articles/object-oriented-marxism>.

its role as the paragon of contemporary ontological liberalism. This has nothing to do with the political connotations of the words 'liberal' or 'conservative', which cannot be simplistically transposed to their use in describing opposing philosophical approaches to ontological commitment. Rather, what concerns us is the fact that Harman's metaphysics has catalysed the development and appropriation of Latour's social theory,[487] and the way this has begun to mingle with the so-called New Materialism of Jane Bennett, Karen Barad, and others.[488] We have already discussed the first aspect of this—namely, the manner in which Harman has successfully transposed Latour's methodological concerns into a metaphysical key.[489] This transposition threatens to let a methodological mutation in one area explode into full-blown methodological metastasis across the social sciences, spreading to every essential organ of political thinking and dissolving any foundational distinction it comes into contact with: object/concept, nature/culture, cause/reason, might/right, and accident/action.[490]

It is the elision of the final distinction—the insistence that everything that happens is an expression of *agency*, or

487. Cf. The ANTHEM group (<http://anthem-group.net/>); B. Latour, G. Harman, and P. Erdélyi, *The Prince and the Wolf: Latour and Harman at the LSE* (Winchester: Zero Books, 2011); and G. Harman, *Bruno Latour: Reassembling the Political* (London: Pluto Press, 2014).

488. Cf. J. Bennett, *Vibrant Matter: A Political Ecology of Things* (Durham, NC: Duke University Press, 2010); K. Barad, *Meeting the Universe Halfway: Quantum Physics and the Entanglement of Matter and Meaning* (Durham, NC: Duke University Press, 2007); and D. H. Coole and S. Frost (eds), *New Materialisms: Ontology, Agency, and Politics* (Durham, NC: Duke University Press, 2010).

489. See chapter 3.,4, subsection IV.

490. Once more I must refer the reader to Ray Brassier's comments on Latour's work in 'Concepts and Objects' for a more thorough analysis of the corrosive power of his irreductionism.

that everything that exists is an *actant*—that characterises
the emerging nexus of OOO, ANT, and New Materialism.
From the perspective of Harman's OOP/OOO, there is a
natural symmetry in treating every causal output as an action
in the same sense as it treats every causal input as a perception. From the perspective of Latour's ANT, there is not
simply explanatory convenience in imbuing everything with
agency (i.e., unconstrained transversal linkages), but also
political convenience in reducing every social situation to a
series of interlocking trials of strength (i.e., a resurrected
and rebranded *will to power*). From the perspective of the
new materialists, the animation of nature provides a potent
alternative to the Marxist materialisms that have dominated
leftist academic discourse (e.g., dialectical materialism), and a
new way to frame political and ethical issues posed by environ-
mentalism (e.g., preventing climate change) and posthumanism
(e.g., empathy for nonhuman animals). Of course, there are
crucial disagreements between these orientations—most
importantly Harman's open hostility to materialism—but they
converge in their attempts to project some form of *ontological
egalitarianism* into the political sphere. The problems involved
in doing so can be seen most clearly by considering Jane Bennett's justification of her project in *Vibrant Matter*:

> Why advocate the vitality of matter? Because my hunch is
> that the image of dead or thoroughly instrumentalized mat-
> ter feeds human hubris and our earth-destroying fantasies of
> conquest and consumption. It does so by preventing us from
> detecting (seeing, hearing, smelling, tasting, feeling) a fuller
> range of the nonhuman powers circulating around and within
> human bodies. These material powers, which can aid or destroy,
> enrich or disable, ennoble or degrade us, in any case call for our

attentiveness, or even "respect" (provided that the term be stretched beyond its Kantian sense). The figure of an intrinsically inanimate matter may be one of the impediments to the emergence of more ecological and more materially sustainable modes of production and consumption. My claims here are motivated by a self-interested or conative concern for human survival and happiness: I want to promote greener forms of human culture and more attentive encounters between people-materialities and thing-materialities.[491]

The important thing to take away from this is that Bennett is addressing a problem of *motivation*. Bennett's book is not meant to establish the need for 'more ecological and more materially sustainable modes of production and consumption', but to *motivate* us to bring them about by reframing our relationship to the world. Bennett's goal is certainly admirable and her strategy seems reasonable, so what is wrong with it?

There are two interconnected issues. Firstly, treating matter as 'vital' is at best a useful analogy encapsulating those aspects of complex dynamic systems ignored by the mechanistic paradigm of nineteenth-century physics and engineering (e.g., nonlinearity, deterministic chaos, emergence, etc.). There is something to be said about the way in which this mechanistic picture has persisted in the popular consciousness,[492] but it has long since been superseded in science by a paradigm in which complexity and dynamism are readily appreciated and analysed non-analogically.[493] The 'figure of an intrinsically

---

491. Bennett, *Vibrant Matter*, ix–x, my emphasis.

492. It is worth recalling Harman's tendency to talk about causation in terms of things smashing together (see chapter 2.3, subsection III).

493. Cf. Stewart and Cohen, *The Collapse of Chaos*.

inanimate matter' has been overcome not by injecting life into it, but by refusing to treat the opposition between the living and the dead as a guiding principle. This means that, although the analogy is well established, it retains little more than a pedagogical function, as one way of bridging the conceptual gap between natural science's past and its present. Secondly, to move from treating matter as 'vital' to treating material things as 'agents' is to turn this defunct analogy into an unruly metaphor that confuses our understanding of the very problem we are supposed to be solving. This move is supposed to emphasise the practical complexity that follows from the theoretical complexity stressed by vitalism: things have agency because they can surprise us, undermining our plans for action in intricate and unpredictable ways. However, the metaphor is supposed to resonate beyond this emphasis, suggesting the possibility of extending relations of sympathy and respect from human agents to the nonhuman realm, with no obvious limit (should we sympathise with the plight of smallpox, and if not, why not?). This weakens our grip on the problem of motivation that we started with, by undermining our ability to think *politically* about the conditions underlying the constitution of agency—in the same way that Harman's panpsychism undermines our ability to think *psychologically* about the conditions underlying the constitution of experience. If every occurrence counts as an action, then there is no difference between *motivating* us to action and *causing* us to behave in a certain way, and this evacuates the concept of motivation of any useful content that might distinguish it from the concept of cause. The OOO/ANT/NM axis thus solves the pressing political problem of cultivating collective agency by dissolving it.

Art. The greatest influence that OOP has had lies, no doubt, in its appropriation by artists, architects, curators and the discourses that cater to their theoretical needs. The rapid spread of novel Continental philosophy through gallery bookshops and press releases alike is nothing new, but even by the usual standards OOP has caused a stir, precipitating a renewed interest in 'objects' and even some avowedly *object-oriented art*.[494] I think that there are a number of connected reasons for this beyond the deceptive accessibility and perverse utility we have already discussed, the most obvious of which is the foundational status that Harman grants to aesthetics. Beyond providing art with a seeming metaphysical significance, the convergence of philosophical speculation and artistic appreciation in the category of allure suggests that artists can do philosophy *simply by doing art*. This is not a new idea for artists, many of whom have been attempting to realise this convergence for some time, but for philosophers to collude in eliding their differences is a new and welcome development. This practical convergence of philosophy and art is complemented by the theoretical convergence of philosophy and art criticism we have already discussed. Although the critical tradition has historically defended the importance of art, or at least obsessed about the question of its importance in a manner that is functionally indistinguishable from such a defence, it simply cannot offer the seat at the metaphysical table that OOP provides.

---

494. E.g., Bruno Latour's *Making Things Public*, ZKM, Karlsruhe, 2005; Joanna Malinowska, *The Time of Guerrilla Metaphysics*, Canada Gallery, New York, 2010; *Animism*, curated by Anselm Franke, 2010; *The Universal Addressability of Dumb Things*, curated by Mark Leckey, Hayward, 2013; *Speculations On Anonymous Materials*, curated by Susanne Pfeffer, Fridericianum, Kassel, September 2013 to January 2014; *Thingworld: International* Triennial of New Media Art, National Museum of China, June to July 2014; *Disobedient Objects, Victoria and Albert Museum*, London, July 2014 to February 2015. For one among many art-theoretical overviews, see Katy Siegel, 'Worlds With Us', <http://www.brooklynrail.org/2013/07/art/words-with-us>.

However, there are reasons for OOP's artistic influence that have more to do with the current state of contemporary art than with OOP's orientation towards art as such. The most obvious of these is the way in which an 'object-oriented art' can be conveniently opposed to the *relational aesthetics* of Nicholas Bourriaud.[495] Whatever the worth of the relational paradigm, its ascendancy has quite naturally generated antagonism in the art world, and this organic resistance has eagerly adopted whatever theoretical weapons it can wield against its aesthetic nemesis. However, the opposition this resistance encourages between OOP and relational aesthetics is as opportunistic as that which Harman encourages between OOP and relational metaphysics,[496] precisely because the concept of relation is being deployed differently in each case. Relational aesthetics is certainly influenced by a sort of poststructuralist hostility to essence that could be classified as metaphysical relationalism in Harman's sense,[497] and OOP is certainly more aesthetically concerned with artworks that are not relational in Bourriaud's sense, but this does not mean that the metaphysical and aesthetic uses of the term meet in any significant way. The sociological case for pursuing contextualised interactive art and the metaphysical case for appreciating decontextualised object-centred art fundamentally talk past one another.[498]

The genuine connection between Harman's philosophy and contemporary art lies in the way it resonates with the legacy

---

495. N. Bourriaud, *Relational Aesthetics* (Paris: Les presses du réel, 2002).

496. See chapter 3.3.

497. Consider the opening lines of the book: 'Artistic activity is a game, whose forms, patterns and functions develop and evolve according to periods and social contexts; it is not an immutable essence.' (Bourriaud, *Relational Aesthetics*, 11)

498. See 'Art Without Relations', *ArtReview*, September 2014, 144–7.

of Marcel Duchamp's famous 'readymades', which cascaded through Andy Warhol's pop art objects, before ramifying into a whole range of strategies for generating aesthetic affects by framing unexpected objects in curated contexts rather than composing technical works that integrate the sensory, emotive, and even conceptual dimensions of experience.[499] Obviously, to justify this point properly would require presenting a much more thorough narrative regarding the development of art in the twentieth century than I can provide here, but the core idea can be communicated simply: OOP provides a pseudo-aesthetic justification for the Duchampian gesture after its conceptual innovativeness has waned. The artistic power of Duchamp's initial intervention lay in its conceptual component, the aesthetic potency of which was guaranteed by its reflexive invocation of the complex of concepts (e.g., art, value, work, etc.) constitutive of the context in which it was displayed. This inspired a general approach to artistic production—summarised by the equation: object + concept = art—the dependable staple of which was the conceptual repertoire of art practice and criticism itself. The reason this repertoire remained at the core of the object+concept paradigm is that mastering and using concepts that are interesting enough to support a genuine aesthetic encounter is not easy (either for

---

499. For an account of the decline of the aesthetic and the rise of the semantic dimension of art in the twentieth century that takes Warhol's objects as its central example, see Arthur Danto's *The Abuse of Beauty* (Chicago: Open Court, 2003). For a parallel account of the decline of compositional technique and the associated sundering of art into a *conceptual* strand increasingly obsessed with its own concept (the art-loop) and an *aconceptual* strand concerned with the immediacy of aesthetic experience (the tyranny of feeling), consult Sinead Murphy's *The Art Kettle* (Winchester: Zero Books, 2013) and/ or my review thereof ('The Ends of Beauty: Sinead Murphy's *The Art Kettle*', in *Pli: The Warwick Journal of Philosophy* 24 [2013]).

the artist or the spectator), especially without the representational resources which poetry and literature are able to deploy in order to invoke concepts. The conceptual context of artistic production and display is more easily mastered by artists than anything else. Once the exhaustion of this conceptual staple becomes obvious, and the easier conceptual alternatives (e.g., obvious ethical/political gestures) have become tiresome, it seems that the paradigm must either return to compositional technique, or cultivate a new conceptual technique.

However, there is a third strategy: the retrenchment of *curatorial technique*. The object+concept paradigm functions by framing an encounter with an object or series of objects within a curated space, facilitating a peculiarly conceptual cognitive affect that is distinguishable from the sensory and symbolic affects associated with more traditional compositional artforms. However, the cultural inertia of the gallery as an institution allows one to counterfeit this cognitive affect, not merely by bypassing the specific conceptual frame the artists themselves intend, but by making any determinate conceptual frame unnecessary. This **placebo affect** is generated by encouraging the spectator to supply their own cognitive stimulation, on the basis that *this is how one is supposed to think/feel when one encounters an artwork*. The spectator thus comes to supply the conceptual content of their encounter with the artwork to an increasing degree, running with whatever meagre hints are supplied by the gallery catalogue, the professional thinker, or whoever else has been wheeled out to referee their engagement with the objects in question. The result of this retrenchment is that art is no longer that which 'makes you think', but simply *whatever you are made to think about in the right setting*.

The aesthetic novelty of OOP consists in providing a retroactive justification of this artistic/curatorial practice: the conceptual paucity that might be interpreted as laziness if it were not thinly veiled in various ways can now be openly portrayed as admirable restraint, insofar as it does no more than highlight the object's own allusiveness. OOP's role in increasing curatorial interest in diverse arrays of intriguing objects transplanted from their native contexts has been to remove concepts from the paradigmatic equation altogether, reducing it to the bland equivalence: object = art (in suitable contexts). However, it is important to note that this metaphysical reframing of our aesthetic engagements with art objects does not eliminate the minimal conceptual infrastructure needed to engender the placebo affect, and that Harman is entirely happy to supply his own brand of sugar pills. OOP provides both an alibi and a handy toolkit for a ruse in which spectators become complicit in their own aesthetic deception. After the conceptual desaturation of objects, all that is left is **stuff**, which we are then encouraged to find our own affective resonance with. Object-oriented art exemplifies the technical shift from composition to framing: from skill in producing genuine *works* of art to skill in interfacing autonomous *objects* with the artworld matrix. There is a surprising amount of money to be made and prestige to be garnered in the supposedly self-effacing enterprise of letting things speak for themselves.

In addressing the spread of Harman's ideas in these areas we are inevitably moving beyond the scope of OOP and into the more general realm of OOO. Unfortunately, I cannot consider the more systematic variants of OOO presented by Bryant, Bogost, and Morton without expanding this book beyond its already considerable length. However, I can say something more about the enticing adjective 'object-oriented' and why it almost begs to be attached to nouns such as 'architecture', 'ethics', 'geography', and who knows what else.

The origin of the term 'object-oriented' in computer programming connotes a certain contemporary character, familiarity, and practicality, even though object-oriented programming and object-oriented philosophy share nothing beyond a common acronym. Yet this doesn't quite account for the temptation to 'go OO-' in other domains. The real source of this allure is the word 'object' itself, insofar as it simultaneously suggests a *specific* orientation that would distinguish an 'object-oriented geography (OOG)' from other geographical approaches, while being so *general* that it doesn't explicitly exclude any alternative orientation (other than perhaps 'subject-oriented geography', whatever that might be). Harman's work has transformed the term 'object' into a new constructive shibboleth whose exoteric concreteness ('to the objects themselves!') is *openly vacuous* ('everything is an object'). This enables it to play a similar sociological role to the critical shibboleths of 'practice', 'materiality', and 'structure' identified earlier, except that it enables solidarity in flaunting constraints rather than enforcing them. Ultimately, this new shibboleth displays an almost poetic symmetry, having synthesised the theoretical and practical dimensions of its critical counterparts in an explicitly **abstract concreteness**, as if the interacting pathological dynamics of Continental philosophy had finally achieved self-consciousness.

Metaphysics is explanatory dynamite. It is good for blasting foundations, but it is downright dangerous if not handled carefully. You can just as easily blow holes in existing explanatory frameworks as clear the ground for building new ones. To translate this metaphor into a full-blown analogy:

the pervasive appeal to metaphysical primitives without care for methodological scruples is very much like the increasing cinematic obsession with complex special effects without care for aesthetic scruples. In each case, one sacrifices structure (explanatory structure and narrative structure, respectively) in favour of cheap thrills. One might call the propagation of metaphysical principles without philosophical justification 'style', and the wholescale substitution of metaphorics for methodology 'vividness', but in truth these are nothing but thinly veiled excuses to blow things up. It is **pyrotechnic scepticism** packaged as systematic philosophy. To capitulate to Harman's aestheticisation of philosophical narratives for a brief moment: Harman may see himself as Lovecraft, Picasso, or even Coltrane—a bold innovator reshaping the cultural terrain—but he is really Michael Bay: a conservative authority continually churning out ever more explosive (and unfortunately popular) cultural products, which serve only to exemplify the vices of his artform rather than its virtues.[500]

---

500. In philosophy as much as art, one must be careful to avoid associating *popularity* with vice as much as virtue. Popularity is *quality neutral*, even if it can sometimes be *indicative*. It is of course possible that some readers will disagree with my assessment of the aesthetic worth of Michael Bay's contributions to cinema. This is not the place to go into such agreements in detail. I shall simply say that watching *Transformers: Dark of the Moon* was one of the least pleasant experiences of my aesthetic life. Its only value lies in its compression of all the worst excesses of contemporary cinema into a single place (and I use the term 'compression' loosely, given its truly tedious length). Give me the *Die Hard* series over *Transformers* any day.

Finally, the time has come to cast ourselves into an object-oriented future. Everything that could reasonably have been done to prepare us for the hyperbolic reading of Harman's philosophy has been done, and so the promise made in the very first pages of this book must now be fulfilled. In accordance with the rules of the hyperbolic procedure,[501] we must imagine a world in which the trivial flaws in Harman's work have been overlooked and the embrace of his philosophical picture is so thorough and widespread that even his few remaining opponents must concede its inestimable worth.[502] Let us begin with the following hypothetical scenario:

> By the year 2050, Harman's self-pronounced philosophical virtues have triumphed: rhetoric has thwarted argument, vividness has humbled clarity, and aesthetic taste has finally overcome rational sobriety; his methodological mixture of historical dramatisation, phenomenological performance, and metaphysical speculation has coalesced into a new norm of thought; and his threefold doctrine of withdrawal, the fourfold, and vicarious causation have become the pillars of a new intellectual orthodoxy as powerful and enduring as scholasticism. Harman's legacy as the Aristotle of his era is secured, his influence singlehandedly undoing Kant's Copernican turn, demolishing the regrettable

---

501. Laid down most clearly in *Philosophy in the Making*, 126 and 152–3.

502. I will assume that the present book was either left unpublished or largely scorned by my philosophical contemporaries. I myself am either dead, or locked in an asylum ranting about the dangers of *gastronomic mysticism*, *semantic romanticism*, and *pyrotechnic scepticism* to any who will listen. It is safe to say that I will not have gone down without a fight.

monuments of Hegelian thought, wiping the historical slate clean and refounding the tradition on a lineage running from Leibniz through Whitehead, Heidegger, Lingis, and Latour. Critique is dead. Analytic philosophy is no more. Copies of *Das Kapital* and *Word and Object* are hidden away from prying eyes and exchanged only in secret. The age of objects is upon us.

This gives us a rough outline of the object-oriented future, but we must fill in the details if we are to draw any interesting conclusions. Perhaps the best way to do this is to work out how this state of affairs could possibly come about. What follows is an attempt to do just that, by constructing a plausible narrative leading to Harman's absolute victory.

The first APA conference panel composed entirely of inanimate objects is held in 2023, to much applause. The ensuing audience discussion unanimously agrees that the contribution of a small half-eaten pot of jam—whose unknown organic composition, ruptured purplish surface, and burgeoning film of green-grey mould present a haze of interacting ecological qualities that perfectly infuse their collective musings on the ethical implications of the ever-worsening environmental crisis—is the highlight of the whole event. The practice quickly becomes a fixture of humanities conferences, though the funding never comes through for object-only meetings. In 2026, a small number of American philosophy departments expand their commitment to interdisciplinary education by insisting that, alongside studying a human language such as German or Spanish, each graduate student must specialise in a nonhuman substance (e.g., graphite, silk, or nematode worms), whose features they learn to commune with and cultivate through a series of immersive practical and theoretical studies. This too becomes popular, and is the de facto standard within a decade, with some PhD students taking out whole semesters to mine tin, perfect their custard recipes, or wallow in their own filth, preceded by a thorough methodological survey of the area and followed by a detailed research report. By the end of the third decade of the twenty-first century the object-oriented craze has spread to all but the most conservative bastions of the humanities, its increasing philosophical dominance and its proliferating extra-philosophical applications mutually reinforcing on another.

OOO's major foothold on culture remains the artworld, which has been increasingly dominated by object-oriented theory and practice since the early 2020s. Some specialised curators have even abandoned the constraints of the white cube entirely and begun to lead paying visitors on excursions to view objects in their native locations, cultivating innovative and tasteful selections of everything from industrial electrical transformers, to piles of medical waste about to be incinerated, to the half-excavated remnants of abandoned quarries, while providing critical appraisals of the nuances of the many genres of things. Other guerrilla practitioners specialise in removing objects from these spaces and juxtaposing them with new contexts, producing strange encounters with antelope in New York's Central Park and volcanic ash on the London Underground, or, most famously, stealing the extant replicas of Duchamp's *Fountain* and refitting them for use in public toilets. Furthermore, the possibility of aesthetic value completely unmoored from any artistic origin generates a new and even more bizarre market for financial speculation, a generalised and quantified allure pulling free of its origins and spinning into complex webs of object futures. By 2035 it is possible to invest in pools of collateralised mystique composed of randomly selected thing-tranches whose diverse inner mysteries await discovery.

Meanwhile the political pull of the nonhuman has only intensified. Against the backdrop of economic and ecological catastrophe, the demand to empathise with the myriad and misunderstood components of our social and environmental infrastructure takes root, generating an expanding reservoir of feeling *that* something must be done, while further splintering our understanding of precisely *what* this is and *how* it should be achieved. The affective impetus towards conservation pulls in divergent directions, with those determined to respect the animate and the natural (e.g., ecological diversity, animal rights, genetically unmodified plant life, etc.) increasingly in conflict with those determined to establish the autonomy of the inanimate and the artificial (e.g., geological diversity, electronics rights, fandom-unmodified fictional life, etc.). The triumph of Latour's amodernism leaves no principled distinction between the two, and warring factions emerge whose conflicts are won or lost through strength of feeling alone. By 2040 this indirect democracy of objects has produced half a dozen underground coalitions of sympathy who claim to represent divergent constituencies of people, things, and people-things. These mostly fail to have any effect on the political policy of organised democratic states, though the coalitions dedicated to entertaining the feelings and desires of corporations and states themselves are a notable exception.

For a long time scientists are indifferent to or hostile to OOO. However, its increasing pervasiveness gradually wins them over, though at first they are only inspired by it in the same way they are inspired by poetry, art, and speculative fiction. They do not grapple with the arguments of the object-oriented pop-philosophers who come into vogue in the 2030s, but simply let the ideas flow over them, so as to commune with the alluring magma that flows beneath the surface of the universe their mathematical models trace. Philosophy finally wrests its independence from science, by ceasing to talk to it in any meaningful way. Things begin to change in the 2040s as the spiralling budget for public research erodes access to the experimental resources needed to test hypotheses at the edge of physics. Those research programmes whose ties to falsifiability are already tenuous seize the opportunity to become fashionably untestable, drawing upon the philosophical weight of OOO in the process. *Rhetorical string theory* emerges as a bold new synthesis of physics and metaphysics, diving headlong into abstract theory construction with naught but aesthetic constraint, generating unusually eloquent debates regarding how many variations of supersymmetry can pulsate in the heart of the standard model in the process. Not to be outdone, rogue mathematicians inspired by Tim Morton's visceral rejection of the principle of non-contradiction[503] decide that π is insufficiently irrational, and devote their energies to the study of a new set of flamboyantly irrelevant *withdrawn numbers*, whose haunting symbolism is matched only by their utter uselessness. By 2050 the pathological peer-review system can no longer maintain the fragile link between the theoretical and applied dimensions of the natural and mathematical sciences, and the culture of science has begun to revert to the premodern configuration it enjoyed in the heyday of scholasticism.

What conclusions does this narrative suggest? Crucially, that Harman's work could achieve absolute victory in the only manner a philosophy unconcerned with justification can: by birthing a **dogma** that supplies the ideological infrastructure of more expansive social system. It is this that reveals the age of objects for a new dark age. It also suggests the true

---

503. Morton, *Realist Magic*, 25–32.

significance of the parallel between Harman and Aristotle: if we ask ourselves how Harman's work could birth such a dogma, it seems almost obvious that it could provide the core of a neo-animistic theology around which contemporary hostilities toward both scientific and human hubris could converge, much as Christian theology crystallised around Aristotle's monotheistic metaphysics. To be truly victorious, OOO must resurrect scholasticism and reinvent the social order that supported it, weaving together cultural, political, and scientific trends so as to undo modernity and prosper in its wake. We are still left to wonder: what would this authentically postmodern world look like?

Under the reign of **negative animism** we would no longer be restricted to *effing the ineffable* nature of God, Being, *Ereignis*, or whichever principle encapsulates universal mystery, but would be free to ponder the unspeakable essence of anything and everything: toasters, lint, neutrinos, and the unsettling reflexivity of sentences such as this. A new breed of philosopher-shamans would rise to guide us through these encounters, teaching us the secret of making the everyday as mystifying as the phenomenological extremes of human experience. Even scientists would come to accept that their own pronouncements are not to be taken literally—their claims about the great pre-human past naught but caresses upon its sensual face—and the faithful among them would turn to writing hymns to the arche-fossil, so as to penetrate its glittering folds, striving toward the warm dark recesses beneath. All this is to say that Harman's metaphysics would inspire acts of intellectual onanism more extreme than the worst excesses of the Heideggerian orthodoxy: failed romantic overtures to noumenal intimacy doomed to wallow in the most pathetic mysticism; a sort of theoretical suicide akin to death by auto-erotic asphyxiation—lonely, and mildly embarrassing for everyone who hears about it.

If we ask ourselves the ultimate question of hyperbolic reading—what would be missing from this world?—it is hard to answer, simply because so much has been washed away by the tide of object-orientation. However, there is one crucial thing that is missing, notable above all others, namely, the love of wisdom named philosophy.[504] *Pace* Harman, this love is not supposed to be unrequited. Its object is not supposed to be placed upon a pedestal beyond our reach. Its satisfaction is to be embraced as a genuine possibility, even if, as in life, its actuality is far more complicated than our desires ever anticipate.

---

504. I am not the first to express this idea. See Amy Ireland's 'Ontology for Ontology's Sake: Object-Oriented Philosophy as Poetic Metaphysics', <http://aestheticsafterfinitude.blogspot.fr/2013/04/ontology-for-ontologys-sake-object.html>.

5

SPECIOUS
REALISM

At last, we come to the point where I reveal the moral of the story. This book does indeed have such a moral, remarkably like that of the children's fable at which its title hints. The fable is never just about a specific emperor, or the particular finery in which they claim to be attired. It's really about people in general, and the way our shared wishes and prejudices cause us to buy into certain ideas against our better judgement, whether we be those standing naked or those who look on idly, unwilling (or unable) to state the obvious. What I have attempted to do in this book is not just to show that a certain fashionable garment is threadbare to the point of nonexistence (the *poverty* of OOP as a philosophical system), but also to analyse why many people are tempted to don it regardless (its simple yet powerful blend of *radical humility* in both the epistemological and ontological domains), and why others stand awestruck, unsure of what to say or do in response (a combination of *historical* circumstance, clever *rhetorical* defences, and surprisingly effective *branding*).

Maybe it is presumptuous for me to paint myself as the innocent youth speaking truth to power, but I genuinely feel that someone had to write a book like this—for the sake of my sanity if nothing else. I say this as someone who was intrigued by the loose confluence of themes brought back to prominence in anglophone Continental philosophy circles by Speculative Realism, who was ultimately weaned off his dependence upon Deleuze by working through these themes, and yet who finds himself thoroughly disappointed by what its initial promise has given way to, largely because of the need to accommodate the undeservedly prominent precepts of Object-Oriented Philosophy.

One of the founding myths of SR is that what di̶
OOP from the philosophies of Quentin Meillassou̶

materialism), Iain Grant (transcendental materialism/speculative idealism), and Ray Brassier (speculative nihilism/transcendental realism), is its rejection of materialism.[505] However, the word 'materialism' is used so differently by these three thinkers that it is useless as a line of demarcation between their ideas and Harman's. The real reason that OOP is the odd man out of the initial SR group is not that it refuses materialism, but rather that it refuses to have any truck with positive epistemology whatsoever. Regardless of the supposed ontological realism in which it dresses itself up, its epistemological anti-realism is pervasive and corrosive to the realist spirit that the other approaches, for the most part, represented. Most tellingly, the rallying cry of Meillassoux's arche-fossil narrative and its demand that we take the literal pronouncements of the sciences seriously is completely rebuffed by OOP, despite its claims to the contrary. In the end, it is speculative in only the most facile way, and realist in only the most impoverished fashion. It has diluted Speculative Realism until nothing is left but Specious Realism, and thereby destroyed any promise that the original grouping might have had.

Although the other constituents of SR were all opposed to the correlationist approaches that did indeed begin with Kant, they did not for that matter take this to warrant a return to precritical metaphysics.[506] All of them in different ways champion as essential elements of their work philosophical manoeuvres, devices, and strategies that are distinctly post-Kantian. OOP is the exception, insofar as its only debt to Kant is its fetishization of the noumenal—which is precisely the

---

505. See Harman's narrative of SR in *Philosophy in the Making*, 77–80.

506. Harman's pre-SR narrative regarding his return to such pre-Kantian themes is explained best in—and indeed as—*Guerrilla Metaphysics* (75).

aspect of Kant responsible for the genesis of correlationism. It is not Kant's focus on the transcendental conditions of knowledge that makes him the father of correlationism, but his insistence that these conditions somehow *colour* or *irreparably distort* our grasp of the real. The elaborate way that Harman takes this misguided epistemological claim and transforms it into a **sceptical cosmology** capable of justifying any and all personal prejudices in the face of reasoned debate, scientific or otherwise, is truly amazing to behold. He takes the core intuition driving correlationism—that epistemic access is internally undercut by its own semantic mediation (e.g., forms of sensibility, language games, cultural practices, etc.)—*simplifies* it by stripping away any need for an account of this mediation, and *weaponizes* it into a doctrine capable of filling the **sceptical niche** left in the wake of the continuing collapse of orthodox correlationism.

OOP is leaner and meaner than traditional correlationism. It is capable of taking up the traditional role that the loose grouping of ideas referred to by non-philosophers as 'postmodernism' played in legitimating **selective doubt** (i.e., the easy dismissal of conclusions one does not like as 'metaphysical', 'logocentric', 'dogmatic', or even 'proto-fascist'—relayed by OOO's trigger-words such as 'scientistic', 'anthropocentric' and even 'epistemicist'). But it also fulfils the more recent role that certain extreme appropriations of Deleuze and Guattari have played in encouraging **capricious speculation** (i.e., the 'deterritorialization' of our philosophical culture in favour of unconstrained, transdisciplinary 'conceptual creation'). OOP is willing to give a whole new generation of theorists what they *want* at the expense of what they *need*. This makes it the intellectual equivalent of high-sugar, low-nutrition junk food.

If you listen closely, you can already hear the clacking of keyboards as a plethora of new Object-Oriented essays are written: 'An Object-Oriented Approach to Tattoos as a Means of Cultural Expression', 'Object-Oriented Solutions to Urban Gentrification', 'Angels and Vicarious Causation', 'Are Hipsters Independent of their Relations?', 'Sensual Objects, Quantum Consciousness, and Meister Eckhart: Towards an Object-Oriented Mysticism'... or so I fear. The hard question that anyone tempted to add to this hypothetical litany has to ask themselves is this: Do you like OOO because you *agree* with its basic tenets, or do you like it because it lets you do *whatever you want*? Are the concepts you are borrowing from it placing explanatory constraints upon your project that lead you to draw more interesting and powerful explanatory connections, or are they simply permitting you to pick and choose whichever constraints you want, while at the same time signalling your affiliation with a new and exciting theoretical trend? If your use of OOO has less to do with constraint than permission, and less to do with explanation than affiliation, then you are repeating a pernicious social dynamic that has been festering at the core of anglophone Continental philosophy and the disciplinary groupings that lie intellectually downstream from it for decades.[507]

---

507. At this point I expect to be subject to two divergent objections from self-identified anglophone Continental philosophers: (a) that I am failing to show the *solidarity* with my Continental brethren that is required if we are to stand up to standard analytic challenges (e.g., 'obscurantism', 'logical ignorance', 'excessive historicality', etc.); or (b) that I have *betrayed* them by throwing in with, or having always secretly been part of, analytic philosophy, and can thus justly be ignored insofar as I am merely echoing its characteristic prejudices (e.g., 'obsessive clarity', 'superfluous formalism', 'spurious trans-historicality', etc.). There was a point at which I accepted some variant of the standard analysis of the 'Continental/analytic divide', but I find it increasingly counterproductive, as my response to these challenges will attest.

This, then, is the moral of the story: **theoretical flexibility** is not always a virtue. When it is, it comes from a *determinate thesis* that matches very specific reasons with very general consequences. When it's not, it comes from a *vacuous thesis* that mirrors the inclinations of whoever gazes upon it.

In essence, this book is one long obituary for Speculative Realism. The only thing that could possibly bind SR together as a coherent intellectual movement was Meillassoux's intellectual call to arms in the fight against correlationism, but it has become increasingly apparent that if we are at indeed at war with this pervasive epistemological scepticism that metastasised across the humanities in the latter half of the twentieth century, then OOP is our manchurian candidate. Putting it in the most stark terms, if OOP is included within SR, then whatever thematic unity SR *might* have been able to muster is annulled in advance. Moreover, it is important to

---

In response to (a), I think that solidarity has become a weight around the collective necks of Continental philosophers that encourages the very problematic social dynamic at issue. To break with it, Continental philosophers have to be both able and willing to denounce *bad philosophy* sold under the same heading as their own. In response to (b), I certainly draw upon a lot of traditionally 'analytic' figures (e.g., Wittgenstein, Quine, Sellars, Brandom, etc.) and themes (e.g., pragmatics, logic, epistemology, semantics, etc.) within in my own work, but I aim to do so in a way that seamlessly switches between them and more traditionally 'Continental' figures (e.g., Hegel, Husserl, Heidegger, Deleuze, etc.) and themes (e.g., historical dialectics, methodological immanence, ontological difference, metaphysical immanence, etc.). We should all endeavour to do 'post-divide' philosophy to the extent that we should paint our own philosophical pictures with the broadest conceptual palette the history of our discipline can provide, and not restrict ourselves to more or less arbitrary groupings of figures or themes.

Finally, for those worried that my criticisms are somehow one-sided, there are equally pernicious social dynamics in the rival analytic camp, some of which are geographically and linguistically specific, and some of which are not. However, this is not the place to go into the deep waters of the 'divide debate', as it is very easy to drown one's substantive commitments therein.

recognise that, beyond this, SR presented us with an opportunity to overcome the pernicious **intellectual dandyism** that has thrived in the wake of correlationism. The other aspect of its tragicomic transformation into Specious Realism is that this opportunity was not only squandered, but that, through its association with OOO, it has become precisely the kind of vapid philosophical fashion that exemplifies this trend.[508]

Still, despite everything, the call to arms has not been silenced, and there are many still keen to respond to it in earnest. But their voices have been drowned out by the inrush of erstwhile correlationists permitted by the ascendancy of OOO. Those who enthusiastically leapt into the melée, enthused by the renewal that SR seemed to promise, have found themselves at once unwillingly conscripted into a dubious 'movement' promoted by an efficiently-organised PR operation, and continually reprimanded for stepping out of line (a 'neurology death cult' charged with 'continental scientism', 'reductionism', and more besides). We must refuse to march under a banner that has been co-opted as a means to suppress rather than to stimulate thinking; and we must admit: Speculative Realism was dead on arrival. But the time for mourning is over, and it is now time to rally the troops under other banners, in order to return to the vital task at hand.

---

508. There is a certain decadence to the way Harman draws his historical narratives which is indicative of this. We are treated to an analysis of philosophical trends as *fashions*, whose principle virtues are *aesthetic values* such as originality, weirdness, and style. Although such commentaries are not devoid of interest in themselves, the way Harman deploys them often illicitly blurs the line between aesthetic evaluation and philosophical justification.

POSTSCRIPT: SPECULATIVE AUTOPSY

RAY BRASSIER

Any discussion of Speculative Realism needs to begin by avoiding the intermittent and pointless debate over whether Speculative Realism really exists. This question comes five years too late to be meaningful, and generally takes the form of a put-down rather than a bona fide question. Speculative Realism is now the topic of a thriving book series at a major university press, and the subject of at least one forthcoming monograph. It is embedded in the editorial policy of several philosophy journals. It has become a *terme d'art* in architecture, archaeology, geography, the visual arts, and even history. It has crossed national boundaries with ease, and is surely the central theme of discussion in the growing continental philosophy blogosphere. Speculative Realism is the topic of several postdoctoral fellowships offered in the United States this year. It has been the subject of semester-long classes at universities as well as graduate theses in Paris. Though there are still tough tests ahead concerning the breadth and durability of Speculative Realism, it has long since passed the 'existence' test to a far greater degree than most of its critics.

Graham Harman, 'The Current State of Speculative Realism' in *Speculations: A Journal of Speculative Realism* IV (2013), 22.

Has Speculative Realism passed the existence test? Graham Harman has certainly served as its indefatigable midwife. No doubt modesty forbade him from mentioning that he is commissioning editor of the 'thriving book series' he cites, and the self-volunteered editor of the new Speculative Realism section of the popular *PhilPapers* website.[1] His claim about postdoctoral fellowships and semester-long university courses sounds an impressively academic note, flagging the

---

1.   <http://philpapers.org/browse/speculative-realism>.

institutional recognition that is generally accepted as the seal of intellectual respectability. Yet here a note of caution is in order, since Ayn Rand's Objectivism and L. Ron Hubbard's Scientology have also succeeded in securing toeholds in American university programmes. Academic recognition is not compelling by itself unless we are told the names of the fellowships and institutions in question. Moreover, a sceptic might be forgiven for querying the reliability of a witness testifying to Speculative Realism's indubitable existence from within the pages of a publication whose official subtitle is 'A Journal of Speculative Realism'. And if existence is to be measured in terms of blogs, books, and Google hits, then Speculative Realism lags woefully far behind Bigfoot, Yeti, and the Loch Ness Monster, all of whom have passed Harman's 'existence test' with flying colours.

Of course, no one has ever denied the existence of *talk* about Speculative Realism. To ask whether Speculative Realism *deserves* to be treated as a cohesive philosophical movement is not to deny the existence of books, articles, and university courses that do just that. The real question is: Is this talk, and the currency of Harman's Speculative Realism brand,[2] sufficient

---

2.   Harman makes no bones about his desire to turn Speculative Realism into a brand:

The brand is not merely a degenerate practice of brainwashing consumerism, but a universally recognized method of conveying information while cutting through information clutter. Coining specific names for philosophical positions helps orient the intellectual public on the various available options while also encouraging untested permutations. If the decision were mine alone, not only would the name "speculative realism" be retained, but a logo would be designed for projection on PowerPoint screens, accompanied by a few signature bars of smoky dubstep music. It is true that such practices would invite snide commentary about "philosophy reduced to marketing gimmicks". But it would hardly matter, since attention would

to justify the claim that it qualifies as a philosophically significant movement? In order to answer this question, it is necessary to disentangle Harman's claims on behalf of Speculative Realism from the philosophical claims of the various thinkers who are now, for better or worse, associated with this supposed movement. The disparate philosophical tendencies that have been grouped together as Speculative Realism all emerged from the subdiscipline known as 'Continental philosophy'. It is primarily those interested in the Continental tradition—whose numbers are certainly not negligible, since they comprise scholars working in such fields as comparative literature, art theory, media and cultural studies, architecture, and other humanities disciplines—whose interest has been piqued by Speculative Realism. The novelty attributed to the latter is taken to reside in the way it supposedly challenges the core tenets of Continental orthodoxy. These tenets are encapsulated in the term 'correlationism', originally coined by Quentin Meillassoux in his book *After Finitude*.[3] The rejection of correlationism is supposed to be the common denominator binding 'Speculative Realists' together, despite their many evident differences.

---

thereby be drawn to the works of speculative realism, and its reputation would stand or fall based on the inherent quality of these works, of which I am confident'. ('On the Undermining of Objects: Grant, Bruno, and Radical Philosophy' in L. Bryant, G. Harman, and N. Srnicek [eds], *The Speculative Turn: Continental Realism and Materialism* [Melbourne: re-press, 2011], 21.)

While I have the highest regard for the work of Quentin Meillassoux and Iain Hamilton Grant, two of the supposed 'founders' of Speculative Realism, I do not share Harman's confidence about the quality of other works currently being marketed under this banner, or about his abilities as a judge of quality. As for 'orienting the intellectual public', this is a task best left to PR agents and journalists, not philosophers. By taking it upon himself to carry out this task, Harman can be credited with inventing a new genre: *philosophy-marketing*.

3.   Q. Meillassoux, *After Finitude: An Essay on the Necessity of Contingency*, tr. R. Brassier (London and New York: Continuum, 2008).

The question then arising is whether anti-correlationism is indeed a sufficient condition for Speculative Realism. I do not think it can be. This is not to dismiss the salience of Meillassoux's diagnosis of correlationism. A favourite ploy among those who wish to rubbish Meillassoux and Speculative Realism more generally is to deny that there is any such thing as correlationism, or that it has ever been prevalent in Continental philosophy. This is plainly false. It is true that the term has been much abused by those who, following Harman, see anti-correlationism as the defining feature of Speculative Realism. At its most extreme, this allows the accusation of 'correlationism' to become a way of caricaturing rival philosophical positions and short-circuiting debate. I do not believe that correlationism is the unmitigated 'bad thing' which it seems to be for Harman (and to a lesser extent Meillassoux), and I have learned the importance of defending the 'good', epistemic formulation of correlationism from its 'bad', sceptical version.[4] Nevertheless, I still think it patently false to deny that correlationism names a characteristic tenet of Continental philosophy. Correlationism in the 'strong' version targeted by Meillassoux is simply the denial that it makes sense to postulate things-in-themselves and it is easy to find passages by numerous Continental luminaries (not to mention analytic anti-realists) unequivocally proclaiming the nonsensicality of the Kantian *an sich*.[5]

---

4. My failure to make this distinction vitiated my discussion of Meillassoux in *Nihil Unbound* (Basingstoke: Palgrave, 2007), where I too indulged in indiscriminate anti-correlationist rhetoric which I now regret.

5. In 2006, while helping me prepare the final manuscript for *Nihil Unbound*, Damian Veal compiled a list of such passages in a document entitled 'Correlationism: The Evidence'. It featured quotations from Fichte, Schelling, Hegel, Schopenhauer, Nietzsche, Husserl, Heidegger, as well as from Carnap, Quine,

Does this mean then that anyone willing to countenance things-in-themselves counts as a Speculative Realist? Clearly not. If this were the case, Speculative Realism would count among its proponents analytic thinkers such as David Lewis, Michael Devitt, David Armstrong, Timothy Williamson, Theodore Sider, and others too numerous to mention. Anti-correlationism is simply too tenuous a criterion to be counted a sufficient condition for inclusion under the banner of Speculative Realism. Might there be a more positive criterion of inclusion? It is highly doubtful. Consider the philosophical differences between Harman's Object-Oriented Ontology, Grant's neo-idealist Naturephilosophy, Meillassoux's speculative materialism, and my own Sellarsian transcendental naturalism. The first insists that only objects exist. The second defends a dynamic ontology of powers. The third proposes that the Absolute is not what is but what could be. The last claims that thinking is embedded in a nature to which it is logically (though not causally) irreducible. What is their common feature? The fact that each stakes out a position with regard to the in-itself? But so do the analytic philosophers mentioned above. And the differences that prevent these analytic thinkers from being grouped together as proponents of a single school are surely as significant as those that divide the alleged proponents of Speculative Realism. Harman says there are things-in-themselves but they can only be alluded to, not known. Grant and Meillassoux deny that the in-itself consists of things, but affirm thought's purchase upon the Absolute. I claim that we can know things-in-themselves, but not

Goodman, Putnam, McDowell, and Brandom. Those who like to insist that correlationism does not and has never existed would do well to check the historical record.

through contact with the Absolute, since knowing takes time. What then unites us other than the sociological fact that our work tends to be classified as part of the Continental tradition, while that of Lewis, Williamson, Sider et al. is classified as analytic?

It is true that the philosophers taken to represent Speculative Realism share an antipathy to a certain philosophical sensibility characteristic of post-Heideggerian Continental philosophy: the fetishizing of finitude, voiced with a mannered portentousness that is the unfortunate consequence of anglophone writers self-consciously aping transliterated Franco-German. But impatience with the rhetoric of finitude and distaste for excessively mannered prose hardly amounts to a common philosophical agenda. Deleuze and Badiou can be credited with rejecting the pathos of finitude long before the advent of Speculative Realism. Their numerous followers share at least this much with Speculative Realists. In fact, the only unequivocally positive commonality uniting Speculative Realism's founding members is their participation in the 2007 workshop of the same name. Yet when Alberto Toscano and I coorganized this small workshop, founding a new movement was the furthest thing from our minds.[6] Whatever affinities connected the participants, they were too inchoate to be turned into a doctrinal bond, let alone a movement. Perhaps they would have burgeoned in philosophically fruitful ways had they not been prematurely petrified by branding. Be that as it may, it is not insignificant that even if they have not yet disavowed it publicly, none of the other workshop participants

---

6.   Indeed, Toscano's subsequent conscription into the ranks of Speculative Realism, much against his will, has been a source of periodic annoyance to him.

has invested in the label in anything like the way that Harman has.[7]

This is unsurprising when one considers the extent to which the label itself propagates philosophical ambiguity. For even if we grant that Speculative Realists share some sort of commitment to realism—despite being realists about very different things—in what sense is this realism supposed to be 'speculative'? Of the four alleged 'founders' of Speculative Realism, only Quentin Meillassoux espouses the term 'speculative'. He does so to distinguish his materialism from metaphysical or scientific doctrines of the same name. As used by Meillassoux, the term 'speculative' is to be understood in the Hegelian sense to mean the kind of thinking that is not content with determining its subject-matter extrinsically by appending fixed predicates to it, but instead allows subject and predicate to switch roles so that the predicate can become subject and the subject become predicate. This reversibility is of course the hallmark of dialectical thinking, of which Meillassoux is a brilliant practitioner. His 'speculative' materialism renders him far closer to Badiou and Žižek than to the Speculative Realists with whom he continues to be associated. Indeed, nothing could be less 'speculative' in Meillassoux's sense than Harman's Object-Oriented Philosophy. And while we may be more sympathetic to materialism than Harman is, neither Grant nor I endorse 'speculation' in Meillassoux's sense. Stripped of the specific philosophical meaning that it has in Meillassoux's work,

---

7.   Iain Hamilton Grant did write a short introduction to Speculative Realism for *The Philosopher's Magazine* in 2010: see I. H. Grant, 'Speculative Realism', *The Philosopher's Magazine* 50 (2010), 58–9. However, with typical self-effacement, Grant did not include his own work in this brief two-page survey. I think it fair to say he no longer has much use for the term; he has certainly not used it to characterize his own work since. Nor for that matter has Meillassoux.

the term 'speculative' is reduced to its ordinary adjectival sense, meaning 'conjectural, fanciful, unsubstantiated by evidence or fact'. Prefixed to an ill-defined 'realism', it becomes the alibi for a doctrine that wishes to spare itself the trouble of justification.

Ultimately, neither commonalities nor shared aversions suffice to clearly demarcate Speculative Realists from other philosophers. Considered as a philosophical movement, Speculative Realism is vitiated by its fatal lack of cohesiveness. Whether we try to define it negatively by what it is against or positively by what it is for, we exclude too little and include too much. Harman justifies his branding of Speculative Realism as a 'universally recognized method of conveying information while cutting through informational clutter'.[8] The problem is that those he has enlisted as the brand's representatives diverge on so many fundamentals that the noise generated by bundling them together far exceeds any possible informational content this grouping might have hoped to provide. In the absence of even a minimal positive criterion of doctrinal cohesiveness, all that is left is chatter about something called 'Speculative Realism'—placing it on an ontological par with chatter about the 'Montauk Project'. It is not difficult to see how Speculative Realism passes Harman's existence test, since this test is predicated on a principle as simple as it is dubious: *to be is to be talked about*.

But there is another more important question underlying the dispute over Speculative Realism's existence. It is the following: Is there anything of real philosophical import at stake in the controversy over what Meillassoux calls 'correlationism'? I think that there is indeed, but unfortunately this is precisely what has been obscured by the concerted attempt to brand

8.   See footnote 2 above.

Speculative Realism. The impetus for the original, eponymous workshop was to revive questions about realism, materialism, science, representation, and objectivity, that were dismissed as otiose by each of the main pillars of Continental orthodoxy: phenomenology, critical theory, and deconstruction. The synopsis for that workshop, which I composed with Alberto Toscano, is worth citing because it illustrates the shortfall between the concerns that animated the original 'Speculative Realism' event, and those of the current Speculative Realism brand:

> Contemporary 'continental' philosophy often prides itself on having overcome the age-old metaphysical battles between realism and idealism. Subject-object dualism, whose repudiation has turned into a conditioned reflex of contemporary theory, has supposedly been destroyed by the critique of representation and supplanted by various ways of thinking the fundamental correlation between thought and world.
>
> But perhaps this anti-representational (or 'correlationist') consensus—which exceeds philosophy proper and thrives in many domains of the humanities and the social sciences—hides a deeper and more insidious idealism. Is realism really so 'naive'? And is the widespread dismissal of representation and objectivity the radical, critical stance it so often claims to be?

The interest in rehabilitating representation and objectivity remains my own personal preoccupation and was certainly not shared by any of the other participants then or now. But the issue of the link between representation and objectivity generates questions about the status of scientific representation, which in turn lead to the more fundamental issue of philosophy's relation to the natural sciences.

This issue is central to Meillassoux's work, whether in the form of his attempt to provide a speculative proof of the contingency of the laws of nature or in his account of the positive 'meaninglessness' of mathematical signs.[9] But it is equally fundamental for Grant, whose reactivation of Schellingian *Naturphilosophie* requires reasserting 'the eternal and necessary bond between philosophy and physics'[10]—an interest emphatically reaffirmed by Grant's ongoing research into the philosophical implications of the 'deep-field problem' in cosmology. It is precisely this concern with renegotiating philosophy's relation to the natural sciences that is conspicuously absent from the Harman-sanctioned branding of Speculative Realism. For Harman, such concern smacks of 'scientism'. Indeed, Harman's vocal disdain for 'scientism' (not to mention 'epistemism') confirms the extent to which, notwithstanding the eccentricity of his reading of Heidegger, he remains an orthodox Heideggerian. For Harman, metaphorical allusion trumps scientific investigation and fascination with objects trumps any concern for objectivity. Indeed, the irony—as Pete Wolfendale's withering dissection of Object-Oriented Ontology demonstrates—is that in Harman's hands, Speculative Realism merely exacerbates the disdain for rationality, whether philosophical *or* scientific, which is among correlationism's more objectionable consequences. It is this *misology* which Meillassoux's *After Finitude* sought to challenge. Far from challenging it, Harman's Object-Oriented Philosophy

9.   Q. Meillassoux, 'Iteration, Reiteration, Repetition: A Speculative Analysis of the Meaningless Sign', in A. Avenessian and S. Malik (eds) *Genealogies of Speculation: Materialism and Subjectivity Since Structuralism* (London: Bloomsbury, forthcoming).

10.   See I.H. Grant, 'The "Eternal and Necessary Bond Between Philosophy and Physics"' in D. Veal (ed.), *Angelaki* 10:1 (2005), 43–59.

pushes this misology towards even more reckless extremes, such that it ends up being, as Wolfendale puts it, 'correlationism's eccentric uncle'.

The denigration of rationality often serves as an alibi for those seeking to evade the obligation to justify their philosophical claims. But this is precisely the obligation that no philosopher can shirk, and the demand for justification will not go away, no matter how stubbornly one tries to ignore it. For how are we supposed to *know* whether or not there are things in themselves, let alone how they are structured? While Meillassoux and Grant adduce different kinds of a priori proof to the effect that we can know that the in-itself exists, even though it does not consist of objects (since both Meillassoux's *surchaos* and Grant's Naturing nature are unobjectifiable), Harman remains content with asserting that the world is crammed full of objects in-themselves, whose sensual qualities veil real qualities neither we nor any other object can know. Yet as Wolfendale demonstrates, Harman fails to explain how one might ever know that there is a one-to-one correlation between, on the one hand, the sensual objects which we and other objects apprehend, and on the other, the real objects that underlie these sensual objects. This 'object-oriented' realism is dogmatic in Kant's strict sense. Unlike Meillassoux and Grant, Harman does not try to provide a rational rebuttal of Kant's edict that all metaphysical assertions about the noumenal are equally arbitrary. He simply ignores it.

More egregiously still, Harman cannot answer the simple question that would seem to be utterly fundamental for any Object-Oriented Ontology: *What is an object*? Harman's starting point is phenomenology. He generalizes intentional correlation and turns it into the basic relation through which objects interact. Yet he insists that the human-world correlate is not the indispensable condition of access to objects. But how then is it possible for us to describe the *quiddity* of objects independently of our intentional relation to them? Without intentional consciousness as source and unifier of the eidetic (object-disclosing) horizon, we have no reliable way of distinguishing between the eidetic or real features of objects and their accidental or sensual qualities. The upshot is a metaphysics in which we cannot say *what* anything really is. For if we cannot specify the essential qualities that distinguish one real object from another, how can we be sure that the discrete multiplicity of sensual objects does not mask the underlying continuity of a single, indivisible real object? Ultimately, Harman's account of 'real objects' fuses epistemic ineffability with ontological inscrutability: since real objects can never be represented, only 'alluded' to, it is impossible to say what they really are. The result, as Wolfendale shows, is a metaphysics where we can never know what we are 'really' talking about, nor explain why our allusions should succeed where our representations fail.

Graham Harman should feel honoured by what he himself recognizes as Wolfendale's 'encyclopedic diligence', even if he may be discomfited by its consequences for his own work. What Wolfendale provides us with is a compelling diagnosis of what is wrong not just with Object-Oriented Ontology, but the Speculative Realism brand to which Harman has lent his imprimatur. Wolfendale's painstaking dissection of the confusions, fallacies, and non sequiturs unleashed by this new species of speculative dogmatism is as instructive as it is devastating. And indeed, there is an appropriately dialectical paradox in the realisation that Wolfendale's autopsy for Harman's Speculative Realism brand embodies everything that the 'Speculative Realism' workshop seemed to promise: the breakout from a terminally sclerotic Continental tradition epitomized by a motley of what Lakatos called 'degenerating research programmes'.[11]

There is no little irony in the fact that this promise, briefly kindled in April 2007, was prematurely snuffed out as a result of the attempt to render Speculative Realism palatable to an audience whose sensibilities were already shaped by Continental philosophy—an audience that equates representation with repression, objectivity with oppression, and naturalism with scientism. But Wolfendale has reignited the breakout. His matchless philosophical intelligence cuts across traditions in search of the necessary resources for the construction of new conceptual possibilities, rearticulating the questions that the 'Speculative Realism' workshop had initially promised to take up. It is thus only fitting that Wolfendale's 'speculative autopsy' should also mark the birth of his own genuinely unprecedented philosophical voice.

---

11.   I. Lakatos, *The Methodology of Scientific Research Programmes: Philosophical Papers Volume 1* (Cambridge: Cambridge University Press, 1978).

INDEX OF NAMES

A

Adorno, T. 350
Althusser, L. 347
Anselm 229
ANTHEM group 380
Apel, K.O.
   'Meaning constitution and justification of validity' 345
Aristophanes 335
   The Clouds 335
Armstrong, D.M. 413
   Universals 235
Ash'arite school 98
Austrian school 212

B

Bachelard, G. 343
Badiou, A. 163, 171, 215, 222, 223, 223–224, 225, 227, 228, 229, 246, 249, 259–265, 270, 271–272, 273, 275, 315, 317, 319, 323, 341, 353–357, 359, 360, 361, 374, 414, 415
and ontological liberalism 259–265
'Being and Appearance' 224
Being and Event 215, 223, 224, 261, 262, 264
Deleuze: The Clamor of Being 353
'Kant's Subtractive Ontology' 262
'Language, Thought, Poetry' 271
Logics of Worlds 224, 259

'The Question of Being Today' 223
Barad, K. 380
   Meeting the Universe Halfway 380
Barwise, J.
   and J. Etchemendy, *Language Proof and Logic* 237
Bataille, G. 228
Baumgarten, A.
   Metaphysics 216
Bay, M. 390
Bennett, J. 210, 380
   Vibrant Matter 380, 381–382
Bergson, H. 162, 228
   Russell on 162
Bhaskar, R. 211, 283
Blackburn, S.
   Spreading the Word 309
Black, M. 128–9
   Models and Metaphors 129
Bogost, I. 4, 211, 212, 259, 266, 283, 334, 388
   Alien Phenomenology 266, 283, 334
   Unit Operations 259
Bourriaud, N. 385
   Relational Aesthetics 385
Brandom, R. 30, 92, 115–116, 119, 124, 156, 158, 231, 237, 256, 258, 274, 306, 310, 329, 330, 331, 365, 366, 405, 413
   Articulating Reasons 331
   Between Saying and Doing 156, 158, 306, 365

Making It Explicit 92, 115–116, 124, 231, 237, 256, 258, 274, 366
Reason in Philosophy 30
Tales of the Mighty Dead 30, 48, 158, 310, 330
theory of anaphoric chains 124
Brassier, R. xvi, 5, 259, 359, 402
'Concepts and Objects' 187–188, 280, 380
Nihil Unbound 412
Brentano, F. 209
Brooks, C. 368
Bryant, L. x, 4, 211, 388
The Democracy of Objects 271

C

Canguilhem, G. 343
Cantor, G.
set-theoretical
paradoxes 246–247, 267
Caputo, J.D.
The Prayers and Tears of Jacques Derrida 342
Carnap, R. 232, 232–235, 243, 244, 250, 251, 252, 308, 314, 341, 412
'Empiricism, Semantics, and Ontology' 232
'The Elimination of Metaphysics' 250
Caygill, H.
A Kant Dictionary 216, 217
Ceusters, W.
'Biomedical Ontologies' 233
Chihara, C.
Ontology and the Vicious Circle Principle 239, 246
Churchland, Paul 377
Churchland, Patricia 377
Cohen, J. 210
and I. Stewart, *The Collapse of Chaos* 210, 277, 382
Creswell, M.J. 331
Cybernetic Culture Research Unit (CCRU) 356

D

Danto, A.
The Abuse of Beauty 386
Darwin, C. 65
Davidson, D. 127, 128, 129, 310–312, 333
'On the Very Idea of a Conceptual Scheme' 311
'The Individuation of Events' 311
'The Method of Truth in Metaphysics' 311
DeLanda, M. 163, 170, 171–176, 178–180, 181, 210, 211, 281, 282, 283, 319, 323
A New Philosophy of Society 175–176, 282
Intensive Science and Virtual Philosophy 282
Deleuze, G. 30, 36, 163, 170, 171–176, 178–180, 181, 193, 210, 228–229, 236, 276, 281–283, 296, 319, 323, 353–356, 359, 360, 361, 374, 401, 403, 405, 414
and F. Guattari, *A Thousand Plateaus* 210, 282
What is Philosophy? 282, 353
Difference and Repetition 178, 229, 283
Empiricism and Subjecitivity 175–176
'I Feel I am a Pure Metaphysician' 283
plane of immanence 282
Dennett, D. 377
Derrida, J. 222–223, 227, 315, 317, 329, 333, 347, 349, 351
Acts of Religion 342
Limited Inc 351
'Ousia and Gramme' 222
Descartes, R. 98, 99, 229, 304, 330, 367
Devitt, M. 413
Duchamp, M. 386, 393

Dummett, M.
  *The Logical Basis
    of Metaphysics* 302
Dunham, J
  and Grant, I.H., *Idealism* 322

E

Eklund, M.
  'Carnap and Ontological
    Pluralism' 233
Erickson, G.W.
  and Fossa, J.A., *Dictionary of
    Paradoxes* 246
Etchemendy, J.
  and J. Barwise, *Language Proof
    and Logic* 237
Evans, G. 92, 119

F

Fichte, J.G. 321–2, 360, 412
  The Science of Knowledge 322
Fine, K.
  'Relatively Unrestricted
    Quantification' 247
  'The Question of
    Ontology' 313, 235
Fossa, J.A.
  and Erickson, G.W., *Dictionary of
    Paradoxes* 246
Foucault, M 347–8
  'Michel Foucault' 348
  'What is Enlightenment?' 348
Frege, G. 89, 115, 116–117, 118, 119,
    125, 230, 231, 234, 236, 239,
    240–242, 329, 331, 342, 343
  Foundations of Arithmetic 242

G

Gabriel, M. 212, 249, 259, 267, 270
  on fields of sense 273
  'The Meaning of "Existence" and
    the Contingency of Sense' 249

  Transcendental Ontology
    213, 267
Garcia, T. 212–214, 259, 270
  'Crossing Ways of Thinking'
    214, 270
  Form and Object 213
  on OOO 269–270
Gasset, Ortega y . 89, 122, 128,
    142, 161
  Harman on 143
  on qualities 143
Geach, P.
  'Identity' 257
Gentzen 329, 331
Girard, J.-Y.
  'Locus Solum' 240
Goodman, N. 413
Grant, I.H. 5, 359, 360, 402, 413, 415,
    418, 419
  and J. Dunham, *Idealism* 322
  'Does Nature Say What-It-Is?' 202
  'Speculative Realism' 415
  'The "Eternal and Necessary
    Bond"' 418
Greenberg, C. 368
Guattari, F. 353, 356
  and G. Deleuze, *A Thousand
    Plateaus* 210, 282
  What is Philosophy? 282, 353

H

Habermas, J. 227
Harman, G. *passim*
  'A Fresh Look at
    Zuhandenheit' 66
  'Art Without Relations' 385
  *Bruno Latour: Reassembling the
    Political* 380
  Circus Philosophicus 176, 177, 372
  Guerrilla Metaphysics 7, 29, 73, 83,
    87, 88–90, 92, 97, 100, 102–103,
    122, 127, 129, 136, 138, 139, 141,
    142–143, 147, 148–149, 150, 151,
    152, 167–168, 195–196, 211, 290,
    330, 333, 335, 369, 374, 384, 402

'I am also of the opinion that materialism must be destroyed' 74, 104–106, 184–186, 286–288

'On the Undermining of Objects' 411

'On Vicarious Causation' 87, 97, 98, 103

Quentin Meillassoux: Philosophy in the Making 6, 39, 66–67, 68, 73, 201, 225, 391, 402

'Physical Nature and the Paradox of Qualities' 124

Prince of Networks 30, 73, 88, 98, 171, 173, 177, 187, 335, 362–364, 370–371

'Response to Garcia' 211

'Space, Time, and Essence: An Object-Oriented Approach' 197–199

The Quadruple Object 72, 73, 82, 83, 84, 87, 88, 90, 91, 125, 135, 139, 140, 147, 149, 151, 158, 189, 191, 211–212, 286, 287, 288, 290

'The Revenge of the Surface' 368

'The Revival of Metaphysics in Continental Philosophy' 66, 70

'The Road to Objects' 126, 165

Tool-Being 14, 29, 33, 39, 41, 43, 45, 48, 49, 52, 53, 56, 57, 59, 62–64, 66, 70, 73, 78, 82, 83, 87, 88, 91, 103, 142, 153, 170, 199, 288–289, 290, 335, 361

Towards Speculative Realism 39, 66, 70, 124, 154, 174, 175, 193, 198, 211, 283

'Tristan Garcia and the Thing-in-itself' 270

Weird Realism 137, 206, 368, 369

Hegel, G.W.F. 30, 65, 158, 218, 228, 229, 296, 302, 307, 310, 314, 329, 330, 331, 342, 343–344, 345, 352, 405, 412, 415

Phenomenology of Spirit 158, 296, 330, 343

Science of Logic 302, 343

Heidegger, M. ix, 30, 32, 39, 40–49, 50–52, 56, 57–58, 60, 65, 66, 79–83, 87, 95, 110, 111, 143, 147, 157, 163–164, 168, 170, 175, 193, 198, 210, 216, 217, 218, 219, 220–222, 223, 225, 227, 228, 229, 233, 236, 249, 250, 251, 252, 255, 262, 264–265, 269, 284, 289, 303, 305, 314, 315, 316, 317, 319, 320, 321–322, 336, 341, 342, 344, 345, 349, 368, 375, 392, 405, 412, 418

and Nazism 344–345

Badiou on 264

Basic Problems of Phenomenology 41, 81, 221, 316

Being and Time 80, 81, 221, 268, 349

Being and Truth 345

Contributions to Philosophy 81, 219, 222

Fundamental Concepts of Metaphysics 43, 44, 217, 217–219, 219, 219–221, 221–223

Harman on 31, 40

Introduction to Metaphysics 33, 41, 219, 220, 221, 250, 252

Metaphysical Foundations of Logic 41, 221

'Only a God Can Save Us' 342

'On the Essence of Truth' 222, 345

'On the Origin of the Work of Art' 81

Poetry, Language, Thought 255

pragmatics in 321–322

'The End of Philosophy and the Task of Thinking' 221

'The Onto-Theo-Logical Constitution of Metaphysics' 219

'The Thing' 81

'What is Metaphysics?' 250

Hirsch, E. 235

Hubbard, L. Ron 410

Hume, D. 98–99, 104, 155, 157,
    160–161, 175, 305–307, 308, 315
    *An Enquiry Concerning Human
    Understanding* 305
Husserl, E. 18, 79, 84, 85, 86, 87, 88,
    89, 92, 105, 118, 120, 136–137,
    145, 147, 191, 209, 211, 218–219,
    220, 221, 222, 224, 225, 226,
    227, 228, 232, 233, 235, 259,
    262, 273, 275, 279, 284, 289,
    299, 314, 315, 316, 341, 342,
    343, 344, 347, 377, 405, 412
    Ideas 86, 343
    Logical Investigations 145, 343

I

Ireland, A.
    'Ontology for Ontology's Sake' 397

J

Jackson, F.
    'Epiphenomenal Qualia' 141
Jacquette, D.
    Ontology 236
Johnston, A. 246

K

Kant, I. 6, 65, 98, 155, 189–190,
    203, 204, 216–218, 226, , 227,
    229–230, 249, 252, 262, 284,
    306–307, 308, 320, 343, 344,
    346, 347, 348, 361, 368, 371,
    378, 403, 412, 419
    Critique of Pure Reason 217, 229,
    306, 324, 368
    fideism in 341–342
    Harman on 164–165
    *Metaphysical Foundations of
    Natural Science* 306
    objects in 260–261
    on metaphysics 306–307
    Opus Posthumum 306

reception in Continental and
    analytic traditions 342–343
    thing-in-itself 314
Kiesel, T.
    *The Genesis of Heidegger's Being
    and Time* 80
Klossowski, P. 347
K. Meehan
    and Shaw, I.G.R., 'Force-Full' 379
Kneale, W.
    Development of Logic 239, 246
Kripke, S. 79, 88–94, 119–121, 123,
    278, 311, 331
    causal theory of reference 278
    Harman on 90, 123
    Naming and Necessity 89, 92

L

Lacan, J. 262, 341, 347, 353
Ladyman, J. 104, 163, 170, 171,
    180–184, 186, 188, 194, 235,
    273, 314, 378
    and D. Ross, *Every Thing Must Go*
    73, 181–184, 194, 273, 314, 378
Lakatos, I. 421
    *Methodology of Scientific Re-
    search Programmes* 421
    Proofs and Refutations 366
Lambert, K.
    'The Philosophical Foundations of
    Free Logic' 237
Lance, M.
    'Quantification, Substitution, and
    Conceptual Content' 237
Laruelle, F. 228, 317, 341
    From Decision to Heresy 228
    *Principles of
    Non-Philosophy* 228
Latour, B. 169, 186–187, 259,
    276–280, 335, 357, 361, 380
    and G. Harman, P. Erdéyl, *The
    Prince and the Wolf* 380
    Brassier on 280
    on circulating reference 277–278

Pandora's Hope 278
The Pasteurization of France 210
*We Have Never
    Been Modern* 279
'Why has Critique Run out of
    Steam?' 357
Leibniz, G.W. 36, 65, 76, 79, 88, 91,
    98, 99, 150, 191, 192–194, 223,
    224, 229, 304, 305, 371, 392
    debate with Clark 191, 193–194
    Harman on 91
Levinas, E. 148
Lewis, D. 109, 235, 311–314, 331,
    413, 414
    Counterfactuals 312
    *On the Plurality
        of Worlds* 235, 312
Linebo, Ø.
    'Plurals, Predicates,
        and Paradox' 240
Lingis, A. 211
Lovecraft, H.P. 368
    Harman's interpretation of 137
Lowe, E.J. 235
Lyotard, J.-F. 349

M

Mackie, J.L. 309
    *Ethics: Inventing Right
        and Wrong* 309
Malebranche, N. 98
Mallarmé, S. 271
Mao Tse-Tung 353
Marcuse, H. 347
Marx, K. 347, 350
McDowell, J. 92, 119, 309, 413
    Mind, Value, and Reality 309
McLuhan, M. 368
Meillassoux, Q. 5, 36, 39, 67, 141, 199,
    200–201, 203, 222, 224–226,
    227, 228, 236, 246, 302, 315,
    317, 341–342, 359–360, 363,
    401, 402, 405, 411–412, 413,
    415–416, 418, 419

After Finitude 6, 141, 199, 200,
    203, 225, 227, 302, 342, 359,
    411, 418
and hyperchaos, *surchaos* 314, 341
'Iteration, Reiteration,
    Repetition' 418
speculation in 317
Meinong, A. 115–119, 120–121, 126,
    209, 211, 289, 295
    The Theory of Objects 209
Merleau-Ponty, M. 377
Metzinger, T. 377
Millikan, R. 377
Montague, R. 311, 331
Moore, G.E. 308, 314
Morton, T. 4, 211, 378–379, 388, 395
    Realist Magic 378–379, 395
Murphy, S.
    The Art Kettle 386
Mussell, S.
    'Object-Oriented Marxism?' 379

N

Negarestani, R. 351
Newton, I. 341
Nietzsche, F. 36, 228, 321, 345, 347,
    350, 412

O

Olive Oyl 295–296

P

Parmenides 301–302
Plato 65, 302
Pope, A. 341
Popeye 126–127, 268, 294, 295
Price, H. 233, 235
    'Metaphysics After Carnap' 233
Putnam, H. 413

Q

Quine, W.V.O. 215, 216, 233–237, 234, 235, 236, 240–245, 248, 253, 254, 263–264, 265, 283, 294, 295, 296, 308–309, 311, 312, 319, 320, 323, 329, 405, 412
  critique of Carnap 233–234
  'On the Very Idea of a Third Dogma' 311
  'On What There Is' 215, 234, 241
  The Roots of Reference 235, 243

R

Rand, A. 410
Restall, G.
  Introduction to Substructural Logics 331
Rorty, R. 377
Rosenberg, J. 377
Ross, D. 104, 163, 170, 171, 180–184, 186, 188, 194, 235, 273, 314, 378
  and J. Ladyman, *Every Thing Must Go* 73, 181–184, 194, 273, 314, 378
Russell, B. 119, 120, 162, 230–231, 234, 236, 239, 240, 241, 242, 246, 247, 253, 267, 308, 314, 329, 331, 342, 343
  Our Knowledge of the External World 162
  theory of descriptions 253
  'On Propositions' 231
  Russell's paradox 240, 246

S

Sacilotto, D. 94
Sartre, J.-P. 353
Saussure, F. de 329, 343, 350
Schelling F.W.J. 202, 307, 327, 360, 412
  and I.H. Grant 418

Schlick, M.
  'Meaning and Verification' 232
Schopenhauer, A. 412
Sellars, W. 300–301, 307, 413
  Empiricism and the Philosophy of Mind 377
  myth of the given 377
  'Philosophy and the Scientific Image of Man' 300–301
Serres, M. 210
Shakespeare, S.
  Derrida and Theology 342
Shaviro, S. 170
  'The Actual Volcano' 163, 170
  'The Universe of Things' 170
Shaw, I.G.R.
  and K. Meehan, 'Force-Full' 379
Sider, T. 413, 414
Simmons, P.
  'Meaning and Language' 118
Simondon, G. 172
Singleton, B.
  mother of 268
Socrates 300–303, 335–336
Spinoza, B. 36, 65, 224, 229, 282, 304, 305, 367
Stewart, I. 210
  Does God Play Dice? 174
  and J. Cohen, *The Collapse of Chaos* 210, 277, 382

T

Tarski, A. 311, 329
Tomberlin, J.
  'Objectual or Substitutional' 237
Toscano, A. 172, 414

V

Van Fraassen, B. 314
  The Scientific Image 314
Veal, D. 412
Vienna Circle 231, 232

W

Wallace, D. F.
  'E Unibus Pluram' 369
Warhol, A. 386
Whitehead, A.N. 36, 98, 147, 153, 163,
      169–170, 175, 193, 199, 239, 363,
      364, 366–368, 374, 392
  Process and Reality 366–368
Wiggins, D. 235
William of Occam 209
Williamson, T. 413, 414
Wilson, M.
  Wandering Significance 133
Wittgenstein, L. 132, 227, 231–232,
      308, 341, 405
  Tractatus Logico-
      Philosophicus 227, 231
Wolfe, J.
  Heidegger and Theology 342
Wolfendale, P.
  'Ariadne's Thread', 179, 282
  'Essay on Transcendental
      Realism' 308, 322
  'The Ends of Beauty' 386
  'The Greatest Mistake' 343
  'The Necessity
      of Contingency' 225
  The Question of Being 315

X

Xenophon
  *Memorable Thoughts
      of Socrates* 336

Z

Zalamea, F.
  *Synthetic Philosophy of Contem-
      porary Mathematics* 323, 365
Žižek, S. 246, 327, 341, 362, 364, 415
Zubiri, X. 18, 79, 83, 88, 91, 142

INDEX OF SUBJECTS

A

abstract concreteness 389
abstraction
  and concreteness, in critical
    discourse 350–352
accidents 16, 18, 20, 24, 138–139
  accidental vs essential features
    85–87, 92–93, 136–137, 142
  and eidos, in Harman 87, 420
  acquaintance (Russell) 124
Actor Network Theory (ANT) 169,
  210, 276, 381, 383
actual
  and virtual 171–180, 281–282
actuality 64, 72, 135, 153, 225, 312
  and possibility 44, 46, 54–55, 64,
    153, 225
  vacuous 153–154, 159, 293
adumbration (Husserl) 84–85, 138,
  146, 191
aesthetics 25, 35–36, 299, 270, 384
  Harman's 102
allure (category) 20, 24–25, 88,
  100–102, 189–191, 206–207, 384
allusion 86, 88, 206, 259, 266, 267,
  269, 271, 287, 291, 292, 293,
  317, 318, 319, 418, 420
allusiveness and elusiveness 291
allusive ontology 271
  and insincerity 286–287
ancestrality 199–201, 205–206
anthropocentrism 43, 201, 279,
  374–375
and anthropomorphism,
  in Latour 279
Apeiron 95, 176, 205, 286
arche-fossil (Meillassoux) 199–201,
  396, 402
arche-writing (Derrida) 223
argument 29, 362–368
  metaphysical 30–34
Aristotle 65, 93, 133, 177, 217, 219,
  220, 223, 300, 302, 303, 304,
  319, 328, 331, 391, 396
art
  object-oriented 383–389, 393
as-structure 40, 45, 46, 49, 60,
  63, 147
awareness 51, 59
axiomatics 263

B

Being 42, 81, 83, 265, 295, 316, 319,
  321, 324, 354–355
  and beings, in Heidegger 41
  and mathematics,
    in Badiou 261–262
  and Nothing 252–253
  and ontological liberalism 258
  and predicates, in ontological
    liberalism 256
  and substance (Heidegger) 220
  and thought 302, 324
  and thought,
    in German Idealism 307
  and thought (Parmenides) 301

as inconsistent multiplicity (Badiou) 223–224
forgetting of (Heidegger) 110, 220, 305, 345
implicitness of 263
in Heidegger 81, 218–219
is Nothing (Heidegger) 251
question of (Heidegger) ix, 32, 220–221, 303
transcendent knowledge of, in Kant 217–218
blogs ix, x, xi, 409
branding xiv, 401

C

catastrophe theory 180
category theory 224, 227, 323
in Badiou's phenomenology 260, 273
causation 13–14, 20–24, 60, 63, 67–72, 71, 100–105, 159–160, 168, 176, 180, 190, 198, 205–206, 294, 325
and representation, conflation of 100
category of 20–21, 190
causal capacities 14–16, 20, 49, 52–55, 59, 64, 68–71, 104, 153, 159–161
causal capacities vs normative functions 46–47, 56, 66
causal interaction 14, 43–45, 60–63, 68–71, 100, 167–170
Hume vs Kant on 155–157, 305–307
indirect 101
metaphysical problem of 103, 324
vicarious 21, 23, 97, 101–102, 199
circulating reference (Latour) 277–278, 279
circumspection (Heidegger) 51
coherence 366–368, 370–371, 373–376
Collapse (journal) 6, 36, 87, 225, 283, 359

confrontation (category) 20, 24, 189–190, 293–294
construction (as opposed to critique) 355–357, 367–370, 376
contiguity (category) 25, 168
Continental philosophy, Continental tradition xv, 220–221, 226, 227, 236, 317, 339–340, 343, 348–349, 349, 352–353, 356, 359, 375–376, 389, 404–405, 411, 412, 414, 417, 421–422
Cantor's paradox in 246
continuity
and discreteness 178–179
contraction (category) 25
contradiction 60–64, 76, 207, 292, 334, 363–366
correlationism 6, 35, 200–201, 202, 207, 310, 331–332, 339–341, 344, 361, 403, 405, 412, 413, 416–417
Heidegger's 317
metaphysical 315, 315–317
orthodox 349–350
retreat from, in Badiou 262
strong vs weak 203–204, 226–227, 262, 346
counterfactual 93
counting 242–243, 256–258, 272–274
count-as-one (Badiou) 260
criticism 361–362, 368–370, 384
art 350, 370, 384
cultural 368–369, 370
literary 348, 350, 368
philosophical 370
science 379
critique 335, 347–349, 392
and criticism 349–352
critical reflexes 351
critical shibboleths 352
degeneration of 350–352, 362, 376
rejection of, in Harman 361–362
of metaphysics 317–326
vs construction 355–357
Cynicism, Cynics 29, 351, 362, 368

D

Dasein 33, 40, 42, 43, 44, 48, 82, 164, 219, 221, 223, 252
deconstruction 222, 227, 314, 317, 417
dependence 50–53, 54, 55–58, 60–63, 168–170
diagram 19, 291, 293–294, 299
Die Hard 390
différance 223, 227, 314, 315, 341
differential relations 171–174, 178–180
discreteness
    and continuity 178
domination 346
    and universalism 346
duplicity (category) 25, 144, 287, 292–293
dynamic systems theory 173–175, 180, 325
dynamism
    and stasis 54

E

eidetic variation (Husserl) 85, 86, 87, 88, 137, 138, 139, 191
eidos (category) 18, 79, 84, 85, 86, 87, 88, 92, 95, 137, 147, 189, 190, 287, 293
    and accident, in Harman 87
    argument from 79, 84–88, 92, 137
Elements (Harman) 148–149, 167, 290
emanation (category) 21
emergentism 277–278, 281
Empiricism 157–158, 306
empty set 224, 227, 240, 252, 253, 262, 268
epistemic relativism 329
epistemology 65, 75, 78, 90, 184–186, 320, 321, 361
    implicit, in Harman 117
    transcendental 344
equipment (Heidegger) 52–55
    Harman on 45

Ereignis (Heidegger) 43, 223, 227, 314, 315, 316, 321, 341
error
    possibility of 76
essence 18, 54, 61, 70, 71, 78, 86–88
    and excess, in Harman 71
    and meaning, in Kripke 94, 120, 189–190
    argument from 88–95
    category of 18–21
    general, in Husserl 86
    individual, of real objects 92
Event (Badiou) 259, 356
excess 14, 69, 70, 149, 150
    argument from 39, 66–73, 74, 152
epistemic 24
    qualitative vs quantitative 70, 72
execution 41, 49, 53, 55, 58, 61, 64, 66, 153, 180
    and causation 13
    argument from 39, 49–66, 72
    as function, in Harman 64
existence 111, 119, 209–210, 215, 228, 235–236, 245, 252, 255, 294–296, 313
    in Badiou 224, 262
    in Carnap 232–233, 308–309
    in Frege 230–231
    in Frege and Russell 236–238
    in Kant 230
    in Husserl 218–219, 226–227
    in Russell 230–231
    in Quine 240–242, 245, 308–309
    of Speculative Realism 416
explanation 263–264, 272, 276–283
    in OOP 109–111, 289–290
explicitness 291, 334–335, 336, 365, 371
    and implicitness 33, 288
    Harman on 363

F

factiality (Meillassoux) 225
feeling 90, 122

and metaphor, in Harman 129
  in art 387
fictions, fictional objects 126, 212,
    242–243, 281, 294–296, 394
finitude 70, 414
  in Kant 346
first philosophy 219–220, 303
  aesthetics as 299
  metaphysics as 109, 326
fissions (Harman) 18, 293
flat ontology 211, 282
formal ontology (Husserl) 218–219
fourfold 12, 17–21, 79, 80, 81, 82, 84,
    88, 149, 150, 189, 205, 287, 288,
    289, 291, 292, 293, 373, 391
freedom 344
function 14, 46–47, 59–66, 101, 152,
    170, 180, 199
  causal capacities vs normative
    functions 46–47, 56, 66
  in Heidegger 164, 168
  functional dependence 57–59, 63,
    170
  functional relations 13, 57–59, 89,
    164, 170
  functional role 49, 56, 64, 157
  mathematical 166, 237, 239, 240,
    246–247
fusions (Harman) 24–25, 293

G

gastronomic mysticism 162, 299, 391
Gelassenheit (Heidegger) 222,
    227, 316
generality 44, 87, 147–152, 188–189,
    281, 301–302
and tool-analysis 46–49

H

haecceity, haecceitism 122–127, 135,
    147–152, 161, 292–293, 329, 332
historical narrative 30–31, 40, 97–99,
    372

historicism 345, 349, 353
holism 58, 60–63, 95, 170, 176,
    179–180, 193, 198–199, 205, 267
humility
  epistemic 165, 342, 344, 354, 375,
    376
  ontological 14, 165, 354, 357, 374,
    375, 376
  radical 401
hyperbolic reading 3, 339–340,
    391–397
Hyperchaos, surchaos (Meillassoux)
    314, 341

I

idealism 361, 417
  absolute 307, 310
  German 307, 314, 344, 360
  in Husserl 84
  transcendental 307, 308, 310
identity 116–117, 123, 170–171, 178, 182,
    185, 189–190, 224, 312, 324
  argument from 73–78, 86, 117, 329
  criterion of 224, 231, 257
  necessity of 76
identity of indiscernibles
  principle of (Leibniz) 76–78
idle talk 349
  academic 349–350
imagination 139
immediacy 89–90, 123–124, 136–141,
    145, 149, 157, 161
implicitness 46–47, 51, 61, 317, 335
  and explicitness 288
  in definition 262–263
  in quantification 244–245,
    250–251, 258
  of Being 254–255, 263–264
independence 14–15, 23–24, 71,
    163–164,
  argument from 99–102, 186
individuality 35, 36, 56, 57, 62, 64, 147,
    149–150, 152, 171–177, 180–182,
    187–188, 239, 242, 281, 324

individualism 58–60, 63–64, 95
individuation 59, 87, 88, 91, 95, 150,
    152, 171–173, 205
ineffability 55, 420
inexhaustibility 67
in-itself 204, 347
insincerity 272, 286, 335, 336
intellectual dandyism 406
intellectual intuition 346
intentionality 31, 51, 164–167, 210, 218
interdisciplinarity 377
introspective metaphysics 104–105,
    205–206, 378
invisibility 49, 52, 53, 54, 55, 57, 58,
    59, 60, 61, 66
    and totality, in Harman 58
irony 294, 334, 336, 369
isolation 15, 71, 180

J

junctions (categories) 21, 189, 293

K

knowledge 74, 100–101, 138, 183,
    203–204, 227, 262, 315–316,
    320, 329–330, 341–344,
    346–347, 361, 403
    in Harman 24, 67–72, 73, 166–167,
    374–375
    metaphysical, definition of
    217–218, 322
    metaphysical, in Harman 204–207,
    290,

L

Latour litanies 3, 212, 267–268
logic 302, 325, 331–332, 343
    constrains metaphysics 324
    free 295
logical empiricism (Carnap) 232–233
logical expressivism (Brandom) 331
logical positivism 232
logical pragmatism 322

M

Marxism 343, 381
    kitsch 351
materialism 286, 351, 381, 402, 415,
    417
    speculative 203, 401–402, 415
mathematics 225, 228, 263, 272,
    323, 360, 363–365
    in Deleuze and Badiou 223, 261,
    353–354
meaning 127–134, 200–201, 241, 280,
    311, 331–332, 361, 364–365
    as verifiability (Vienna Circle) 232
    of names 90–94
    vs experience of meaning 329
mereology 15, 56–58, 72–73, 74, 83,
    151–152, 282, 325
meta-ontology 223, 261, 272, 317,
    355
metaphor 29, 127–134, 269–270,
    274–275, 333, 335, 368, 390
    and analogy 134, 334
    and representation 273–274
    Harman on 127–129, 130
    in ontological liberalism
    267–271, 286
    in Gabriel 267
metaphysica generalis 216,
    218–219, 226, 229, 236
metaphysical teleology 65
metaphysica specialis 216, 218,
    218–219, 225, 226, 229, 236,
    273, 275
metaphysics 35, 65, 300–303,
    303–305, 318–321, 325–6,
    356, 389–390
    and metaphorics 269–270
    and ontology
    in Continental tradition 228–229
    and ontology, in Heidegger
    220–222
    and phenomenology,
    in Harman 65, 69, 86
    and science 325, 326
    and semantics 231–232

as first philosophy 109, 326
Badiou on 223
critique of 308, 315, 317, 323, 326
end of 222, 228
implicit vs explicit 323
impossiblity of (Hume) 305–306
in analytic tradition 231–236
in Derrida 222–223
in Meillassoux 224–226, 360
Kant on 306–307
problem of (Heidegger) 32
vs ontology, in Husserl 218–219
methodology 66, 100, 104, 110, 111,
        204–205, 276–277, 321–322,
        355, 361, 362, 380, 390
misology 418
modality 54–55, 65, 93, 135, 235,
        305, 306, 308
    modal mysterianism 65–66,
        152–162
model theory 237, 263–264, 311, 313
multiplicity
    and singularity, in Harman 150,
        150–151
    and unity 161
    in Badiou 223–224, 261, 262–263
    inconsistent (Badiou) 223, 341
mysticism 347, 396

N

naiveté 361
    and sincerity 335
names, naming 88–94, 115–127
    Kripke's theory of 88–94, 123
    descriptivist approaches to 119,
        230, 242
naturalism 306, 311–313, 413, 421
    Harman on 103
    Quine's 243, 265, 296, 312
nature 323, 419
Nazism
    Heidegger's 344
negative animism 396
negative theology 342

networks 169, 187–188, 281
New Materialism 380, 381, 383
noetic challenge 209, 215, 218, 224,
        245, 248, 259, 270, 271, 273,
        275, 276
nominal acts (Husserl) 89, 124
nominalism 304, 309
noncontradiction 225, 226–228
normativity 47, 56, 65, 124, 306, 354,
        366, 375
the Nothing (Heidegger) 250–252,
        261–262, 265
noumenon, noumena xvi, 6, 202,
        204, 314–315, 341, 346–347,
        361, 396, 402–403
    and phenomena 199–207,
        218–219, 226–227

O

objects xiv, 3, 4, 11, 12, 14–16, 68, 115,
        156–159, 163–164, 188, 201, 215,
        218, 226, 239, 242, 248–249,
        258, 267–269, 284–297, 297,
        379, 384, 419, 420,
    and beings 254–256, 320, 324
    and qualities 17, 150, 156–162
    in Badiou 223–224, 259–262, 273
    real 13, 17–21, 23–24, 118, 120–122,
        189, 192, 202, 205, 314, 341, 420
    sensual 15, 17–21, 23–24, 118,
        120–123, 126–127, 148–149, 189,
        202, 205
Occam's Razor 243
Occasionalism 98–99
ontography 25, 291
ontological argument 229–230
ontological commitment 110, 209,
        214–215, 215, 243, 272–273, 380
    in Quine 236–245
ontological conservatism 209, 210,
        254
    and anti-reductionism 283–284
    Badiou and 259
    in Quine 243, 245, 254–255

ontological difference 254–255, 265–266, 282

ontological egalitarianism 14, 215, 256, 270, 281, 381
    in Deleuze and Badiou 354

ontological liberalism 211–214, 245, 247, 254–255, 258, 266–267, 268–269, 271, 283–284, 284–297, 285, 319
    Badiou's role in emergence of 259–265

ontology 42
    allusive 271, 272
    and metaphysics
    in Continental tradition 228–229
    in Heidegger 220–222
    and phenomenology,
        in Husserl 219
    defined by Kant 218
    flat (DeLanda) 282–283
    formal vs regional (Husserl) 218–219, 226
    fundamental vs. regional (Heidegger) 219–220, 221–222, 299
    history of the term
        in Continental tradition 216, 216–231
        in analytic tradition 229–235
    in Badiou 223–224
    in Harman 42
    in Kant 217–218
    in Meillassoux 224–226
    in natural and informational sciences 272–273
    poetic 264, 265
    subtractive (Badiou) 261–263, 271

onto-theology 83, 111, 220, 225–227, 319

ordinary language philosophy 343

P

panpsychism 35–36, 377, 383

parsimony 263, 283,

part/whole (*see* mereology)

patriarchy 352

persistence 14, 51, 54, 56, 198

perspective 84, 138, 139, 146

phenomena (*see* noumena)

phenomenological description 30–31, 51, 55, 104

phenomenology 51, 52, 55, 61, 65, 69, 84, 105, 136, 261, 284, 321, 342, 343, 352, 377, 378, 419
    and metaphysics 125
    and metaphysics, in Harman 65, 69, 86, 266
    and ontology, in Husserl 219
    Husserlian method 88
    in Badiou 224
    phenomenological reduction (Husserl) 226–227

philosophy 397
    and science, Harman on 102

philosophy-marketing 411

physics 418

placebo affect 387

platonism 309
    Frege's 231

pluralism 345–349, 352, 357
    ontological (Carnap) 232–234

Polemic
    Harman on 7

politics
    and philosophy, in twentieth century 344–348
    OOP and 379–383

possibility 82, 225, 230
    and actuality (see actuality)
    and modality (see modality)
    possible worlds 166, 263, 312–313

postmodernism 227, 349, 353, 357, 403

poststructuralism 349, 353, 357

potentiality 159
    Harman on 154–155

pragmatics 316, 320–322, 351
    in Heidegger 321–322

pragmatism, American 342

438

INDEX OF SUBJECTS

predicates, predication 84, 114,
    119, 166, 237–239, 238–239,
    256–257,
  higher-order 230, 236, 239–241,
    243
  hypostasization of 292
  sortal 131, 256–257, 272–273, 258,
    262, 274, 284
  quasi-sortal 273–274
  non-sortal 131
  pseudo-sortal 258, 284
  systems of 272–273, 278
presence 46, 61, 62, 163
  Heidegger's critique of 40
presence-at-hand 40, 41, 45, 46, 47,
    62, 68, 80, 153, 289
pre-theoretical (Heidegger)
    80, 219–220
psychoanalysis 343, 347
psychologism 117, 125
  anti-psychologism 377
purport
  representational 113–114
  referential vs predicative 114, 117,
    120–122, 145

Q

qualia 140–141, 143, 145–146, 158, 161
qualities 12, 17, 24–25, 80–83, 88–95,
    120–121, 127, 147–152, 152–162,
    166, 188, 225, 287–288,
    292–293, 419
  accidental and eidetic 85–87
  and objects (see objects)
  bundles of 121, 183, 286, 364
  essential and inessential 88,
    138, 420
  in Harman 287
  primary and secondary
    141–142, 360
  sensual 17–21, 88–95, 136, 138–139,
    142–147, 189, 191–192, 420
  sensible 135–147, 157–158, 160
  real 17–21, 88–95, 137–139, 160–161
quantification 237–238, 240–242, 295

objectual interpretation 237, 244
restricted and unrestricted
    244–245, 250–251
  unrestricted 246–250, 256–257
  Badiou and 260–261

R

radiations (categories) 21, 150
radical alterity 347
rationalism 209, 304–305
rationality 418, 419
readiness-to-hand 40, 41, 45, 46,
    47, 289
reality, real 294–297, 308–310, 313,
    316, 318, 320, 322–324
  and appearance 219, 222–224,
    227, 275, 315, 316, 318, 321
  and the sciences 104, 324–326
  objects (see objects)
  qualities (see qualities)
realism 35, 36, 415, 419
  deflationary 308–313
  in Husserl 84
  ontic structural 180–184
  transcendental 322
reason
  in philosophy, Harman on 30
reductionism 210, 275–276, 284, 406
reference 49, 59, 89, 90, 110, 287, 288
  and predication 292
  causal theory of (Kripke) 278
  de dicto vs de re 118, 119, 121
  Frege's theory of 116
  indirect, in Harman 92
  in Heidegger (Verweis), Harman's
    reading of 56
in Russell 119
  Meinong vs Frege on 116
  Meinong's theory of 115
  sense and (Frege) 89, 116
relations 13–15, 21, 24, 56–58, 62–64,
    69, 99, 101, 153–155, 163–199,
    235, 293–294, 324
  as predicates 166–167
  Harman on 164–165

intentional 15, 24, 125–127, 164,
169, 186, 192, 209, 218
relation and non-relation 191–194
and substance 63, 100
representation 75, 77, 144–146, 278,
292, 297, 417
and causation, conflation of 100
anti-representationalism 114–115
Harman's implicit theory of 117,
120, 122, 144–145, 294
predicative and referential
dimensions of 113–114, 118,
121–122, 145, 292–293
rhetoric 267, 267–268, 328, 350, 362,
369, 371
in ontological liberalism 267
Harman on 363–364
rhetorical string theory 395
rigid designators (Kripke) 88, 90, 92,
93, 119, 124
romanticism 334
German 344
semantic 332, 368

S

scepticism 160, 316, 331, 334, 360
epistemological 207, 339, 368
metaphysical 299, 315
semantic, in Harman 329
transcendental 344
sceptico-critical hegemony 352, 356,
359, 361, 375
scholasticism 216, 229, 303–304,
391, 395–396
science 46, 137, 146, 183–185,
199–202, 206, 233, 234, 243,
245, 254, 259, 272, 277, 278,
283, 306, 308, 311–312, 323,
325, 363–365, 370, 382,
394–395, 402
and metaphysics 325–326
and philosophy, in Speculative
Realism 360–361, 418
and philosophy, Harman on
100–104,

cognitive 360, 377
empirical research and philosophy
377–378
Harman on 103, 183–184,
377–379
philosophy of, French 343
physics, Morton on 378–379
scientism 406, 418, 420
semantic grafting 133, 274–275
semantics 320, 321, 330, 331, 343
and axiomatics 263
and metaphysics 231–232
inferentialism 132
model-theoretic 311
possible world 166, 312
semantic speculation 311
sense
and reference (Frege) 89, 115–116
reflexivity of 289–290
Sense-Certainty (Hegel) 296, 329,
330, 352
sensible (see qualities)
sensuality, sensual 11–12, 13, 20, 23–
24, 60, 71, 80, 86, 94, 113–134,
138, 141, 145, 152, 154, 189, 192,
199, 202, 205, 206, 290, 292,
318, 320, 330, 332. 396
and intellectual, in Husserl 85, 137
and real 11–12, 88, 152, 285,
287, 292
qualities (see qualities)
objects (see objects)
set theory 227, 248–250, 261,
263, 355
sincerity 21, 23, 100, 121, 286,
287–288, 294, 364, 369
and naiveté 335
metaphysics of 369–370
singularity 161
and multiplicity,
in Harman 150–151
in Deleuze/DeLanda
(attractors) 174
sophism 335
sortals (see predicates)

Sosein (Meinong) 115, 118, 119, 120, 121, 230
space 18, 20, 188–199, 202, 249, 252, 287, 293, 324, 325, 346, 378
Speculations (journal) xi, xiii, 249, 409, 410
Speculative Realism ix, x, 3, 5, 6, 359–360, 401, 401–406, 402, 405, 409–421
    as brand xiv, 410, 416, 418, 420
    workshop 359, 414, 417, 421
stasis 170
    and dynamism 54
structuralism 343, 347, 349, 351, 352
stuff 388
style 30, 332, 350, 357, 368–373, 390
subsistence (Meinong) 115–120, 126, 194, 209, 253
substance 4, 41, 48, 61, 64, 71, 98, 153, 163, 234, 269–270, 289
    and Being (Heidegger) 220
    and ground 224
    and relation (see relations)
    and style 369–373
    and unity 222–224, 260–261
    as presence (Heidegger) 163, 222–223
    execution as, in Harman 64
    Spinozan 282
Supplementation
    argument from 102–105
symbolism 350, 354

T

theory facades (Wilson) 133
theory (category) 20, 88, 190
theory of types, type theory (Russell) 239–240, 248, 258, 260–261, 272
thisness (*see* haecceity)
time 18–20, 45, 55, 88, 111, 180, 188–199, 201–206, 249, 252, 262–271, 291, 293, 324, 346,
tool-analysis 39, 40, 45, 47, 48, 49, 57, 61, 62, 66, 73, 78, 79, 288–289

totality 43, 82–83, 182, 246, 248–249, 320
    and equality, in ontological liberalism 255–56
    and invisibility, in Harman 56–61
Transformers:
    Dark of the Moon 390

U

undermining
    and overmining, in Harman 286
understanding
    in Heidegger 43–46,
unity 17, 64, 80–81, 83, 122, 129–132, 152
    and substance (see substance)
universalism 344–349, 361
    and domination 346
universals 130, 152, 235, 245, 282
unrestricted quantification (see quantification)

V

vicarious causation 12, 21, 23–25, 97, 100, 102–103, 199, 376
vitalism 382–383
vividness 371–373, 390

W

the Whole 246, 262, 267, 282–283, 295
withdrawal 12, 14, 21, 39, 60, 67, 69, 71–74, 78–79, 83, 122, 161, 190,
    in Derrida 223
withdrawn numbers 395
world 43, 44, 57, 59
    and earth, in Heidegger 82
    in Heidegger 42
worlds (Badiou and Meillassoux) 224, 225–226, 260–261, 265, 273, 275